Previously published...

- Maths and Calculator skills for Science Students
  http://amzn.to/2xgED3Q
- Maths (The Chemistry bits) for GCSE Science   May 2016
  http://amzn.to/2jJxyWc
- Science revision Guide   April 2017
  http://amzn.to/2fS0pD2
- Maths Revision Guide   April 2017
- Summer Start for A-Level Chemistry   May 2017
  http://amzn.to/2suR1e5
- Atoms, Electrons, Structure and Bonding Workbook   June 2017
  http://amzn.to/2tn8Rji
- GCSE Maths Grade 7, 8 and 9 Revision Questions   September 2017
  http://amzn.to/2fGQrrz

Coming soon...

- Complete Maths workbook
- Organic Chemistry Workbook
- Maths for A-Level Chemistry
- Maths (The Physics bits) for GCSE Combined Science
- Maths (The Physics bits) for GCSE Triple Science
- Summer Start for A-Level Physics

Chances are if you want a maths/science book I've written it or I am writing it.

For full book listings visit www.PrimroseKitten.com and follow @primrose_kitten

First published 2017   Copyright; Primrose Kitten ©

Image credits, Images by Lemberg Vector studio, by Macrovector, used under license from Shutterstock.com. Pixabay. https://www.teacherspayteachers.com/Store/The-Cher-Room

Acknowledgements
Thank you to my husband for putting up with my spending every night writing this and for correcting all of my SPG mistakes. To my sons for being the inspiration behind Primrose Kitten.

Hello Lovely Kittens

Thank you so much for purchasing this revision booklet. Many items covered in here is also covered in a corresponding set of videos which I have made neat and accessible on my terrific partner platform: TuitionKit.

On TuitionKit you'll be able to schedule many of my revision videos and partner content to help you organise your revision better, breaking it down into easy to handle bitesize chunks. You'll also find many of my other playlists and great resources from other Science and Maths teachers, as well as super English teachers too.

My videos are free when you sign up at www.tuitionkit.com/primrosekitten Using the discount code "kitten" will also give you a 20% discount on all the other material on the site for all your core GCSE subject revision.

To get a flavour for how TuitionKit's great features will help you revise, go to www.tuitionkit.com and sign up for your free 48-hour trial.

Wishing you all the best with your revision!

Primrose Kitten

xoxo

Table of Content

Revision Techniques

https://www.youtube.com/playlist?list=PL7O6CcKg0HaEAmHG0SbleDHfdJOQvUcnM

- Why do you need to revise effectively? Revision techniques #1
- When should I start revising? Revision Techniques #2
- How to find your motivation and stay motivated. Revision Techniques #3
- 5 easy and effective ways to revise and study. Revision Techniques #4
- Flashcards. Revision Techniques #5
- Using past exam papers to study. Revision Techniques #6
- Colour - The easiest way to make study interesting. Revision Techniques #7
- How to revise for the new specification maths exams. Revision Techniques #8
- How to fill MASSIVE gaps in your knowledge. Revision Techniques #9
- How to best use your revision guide. Revision Techniques #10
- How best to use your revision guide, part 2. Revision techniques #11
- The easiest way to improve your grades, which you're going to hate!! Revision Techniques #12
- Study timetable. Revision techniques #13
- Study Timetable - Plan with Me. Revision Techniques #13
- Another easy way to improve your grades, which you're going to hate!! Revision Techniques #14
- Study Space. Revision Techniques #15

Don't believe me? – here are some more links to help you.

The science of revision: nine ways pupils can revise for exams more effectively.

The Guardian. Bradley Busch Psychologist @Inner_drive Tuesday 19 April 2016

Ditch the highlighter and teach a friend. Psychology shows us a lot about how to improve our memory and avoid distractions – here are some dos and don'ts

https://www.theguardian.com/teacher-network/2016/apr/19/students-revise-exams-revision-science?CMP=share_btn_tw

Revision Timetable

Planning Tips

1. Write your timetable in pencil (or make a version on the computer) so you can change things around if necessary.
2. Start by thinking about what activities you can't miss (dinner, clubs or TV programs) and put these into your timetable.
3. Plan in when you need to do your homework to get it in on time
4. On top of your homework time, aim for a minimum of 2 extra hours on a weekday and 4 hours each day over the weekend.
5. Plan to revise for 1 hour per subject each week (this is in addition to homework) fill in the table below to help you work out how much time you need to spend on revision
6. Fill in the timetable spreading out the subjects (e.g., don't do a whole day of Maths, do a bit each day) put contrasting subjects next to each other, to give your brain a break (e.g. English and Physics)
7. Stick to the timetable, it will help ensure you cover each subject and spread out your revision.

Subject	Group	Priority	Number of hours each week
Maths	Core	High (+2 hours)	
English Language	Core	High (+2 hours)	
English Literature	Core	High (+2 hours)	
	A-level choice	High (+2 hours)	
	A-level choice	High (+2 hours)	
	A-level choice	High (+2 hours)	
	A-level choice	High (+2 hours)	
	Subject I struggle with	Medium (+1 hour)	
	Subject I struggle with	Medium (+1 hour)	
	Subject I struggle with	Medium (+1 hour)	
	Subject I struggle with	Medium (+1 hour)	

Weekday

Time	Monday	Tuesday	Wednesday	Thursday	Friday
4.00 - 4.25					
5-minute break					
4.30 - 4.55					
5-minute break					
5.00 - 5.25					
5-minute break					
5.30 - 5.55					
5-minute break					
6.00 - 6.25					
5-minute break					
6.30 - 6.55					
5-minute break					
7.00 - 7.25					
5-minute break					
7.30 - 7.55					
5-minute break					
8.00 - 8.25					
5-minute break					
8.30 - 9.00					

Weekend

Time	Saturday	Time	Sunday
5-minute break			
5-minute break			
5-minute break			
5-minute break			
5-minute break			
5-minute break			

Exam command words

Command words are words in exam questions that give you clues on what the examiners are looking for.

Depending on the command word, your answer to a question will be very different.

There are four main ones you'll come across; give, describe, explain and evaluate.

Give what is in the picture.

For this answer, you simply need to state using one or two words what is in the picture

A dress

Describe what is in the picture.

For this answer, you need to tell the examiners what it looks like, or recall an event or process

An orange halter neck dress with a pale band around the waist.

Explain what is in the picture.

For this answer, you need to give reasons why something is the way it is

The dress is a summer dress so it has a halter neck, it is from the 1950s and shows the style at the time.

Evaluate what is in the picture.

Here you need to give good points, bad points, your opinion and justify your opinion

- This dress is good because it is made from a light fabric so will be cool in summer
- This dress is bad because the colour is too bright
- Overall, I think this is a good dress…
- … because it is well suited to the purpose of being a summer dress.

Calculate/ Determine use maths to work out the answer

Choose circle the answer from the selection

Compare what are the similarities and differences

Complete fill in the gaps - pay attention to any given words, some may be used more than once some not at all

Define what does the word mean?

Describe what it looks like, or recall an event or process

Design/ Plan plan something

Draw draw a scientific diagram, not an arty sketch

Estimate give a sensible guess

Evaluate give good points, bad points your option and justify your opinion

Explain give reasons why something is the way it is

Give/Name a short answer

Identify/Label name a part

Justify give and answer and support it with a reason

Measure you might need to get your ruler out for this one

Plan write a method, don't forget your variables, controls and risk assessment

Plot mark points on a graph using an x

Predict/suggest what do you think is going to happen, you may need to use information from the question and knowledge from class

Show give evidence and come to a conclusion

Sketch a rough drawing, a graph doesn't always need number labels on the axis, but it must be an accurate representation

How to answer 6-mark questions

1. Identify the command word, this tells you what the examiners are looking for. This is generally describe, explain or evaluate.
2. Go back over the question and use different colour high-lighter pens to pick out key bits of information.
3. Plan the structure of your question. Table, paragraphs, diagram.
4. Write your answer
5. Check your answer fully answers the question, make sure is it balanced and cover all the points asked for in the question.
6. Check your spelling, punctuation and grammar.

For over 100 examples of 6 mark questions, with example answers, get my book Science 6 mark answers, from my website or Amazon.

Exam dates

Dates might be changed by AQA

Exam	Units covered	2018 exam dates
For separate science and combined science 'Trilogy'		
B1	Topics 1-4	15th May 2018 –pm
B2	Topics 5-7	11th June 2018 - pm
C1	Topic 1-5	17th May 2018 – am
C2	Topics 6-10	13th June 2018 - am
P1	Topics 1-4	23rd May 2018 - pm
P2	Topics 5-8	15th June 2018 - am
For combined science 'Synergy'		
Paper 1: Life and environmental sciences		15th May 2018 – pm
Paper 2: Life and environmental sciences		23rd May 2018 - pm
Paper 3: Physical sciences		11th June 2018 - am
Paper 4: Physical sciences		13th June 2018 - am

All papers

- Contains multiple choice questions, structured questions, closed short answers questions and open long response questions
- 15% based on required practical's
- Maths requirement vary by subject - 10% of the marks in biology, 20% of the marks in chemistry and 30% of the marks in physics.

Separate Science

- 6 papers (2 biology, 2 chemistry and 2 physics, leading to 3 separate GCSEs)
- Each 1 hour 45 minutes
- Each paper is worth 50% of the GCSE
- 100 marks on each paper

Combined Science – Trilogy

- 6 papers (2 biology, 2 chemistry and 2 physics)
- Each 1 hour 15 minutes
- Each paper is worth 16.7% of the GCSE
- 70 marks on each paper

Combined Science – Synergy

- 4 papers – 2 on life and environmental science and 2 on physical science
- Each 1 hour 45 minutes
- Each paper is worth 25% of the GCSE
- 100 marks on each paper

Maths pops up in every exam; roughly 10% of the marks in biology, 20% of the marks in chemistry and 30% of the marks in physics will be based on maths skills

A workbook containing some of the mathsy skills you'll need is available from my website or from here https://youtu.be/LKPK6fZS1lQ

Specification statement	Self-assessment			Bits to help if you don't understand	
These are the bits the exam board wants you to know, make sure you can do all of these...	First review 4-7 months before exam	Second review 1-2 months before exam	Final review Week before exam	Primrose Kitten	Other places
I can rearrange equations	☺ ☺ ☹	☺ ☺ ☹	☺ ☺ ☹	https://youtu.be/mcnBaroQi_Q	TuitionKit http://bit.ly/2hJhtPP
I can solve algebraic expressions	☺ ☺ ☹	☺ ☺ ☹	☺ ☺ ☹		TuitionKit http://bit.ly/2fGCW7I
I can give numbers to a set number of significant figures	☺ ☺ ☹	☺ ☺ ☹	☺ ☺ ☹	https://youtu.be/LKPK6fZS1lQ	TuitionKit http://bit.ly/2wpK2nY
I can write numbers in standard form	☺ ☺ ☹	☺ ☺ ☹	☺ ☺ ☹	https://youtu.be/LKPK6fZS1lQ	TuitionKit http://bit.ly/2xEQdbK
I can use ratios, fractions and percentage	☺ ☺ ☹	☺ ☺ ☹	☺ ☺ ☹		TuitionKit http://bit.ly/2wp2vkl TuitionKit http://bit.ly/2fYsJnD
I can calculate a mean and understand what to do with anomalous results	☺ ☺ ☹	☺ ☺ ☹	☺ ☺ ☹	https://youtu.be/LKPK6fZS1lQ	TuitionKit http://bit.ly/2xWkbaB

I can use the symbols <, <<, >>, >, ∝, ~	☺ ☺ ☹	☺ ☺ ☹	☺ ☺ ☹		
I can find the y intercept from y=mx+c	☺ ☺ ☹	☺ ☺ ☹	☺ ☺ ☹		TuitionKit http://bit.ly/ 2yTCdsj
I can determine the gradient of a graph from the graph or from y=mx+c	☺ ☺ ☹	☺ ☺ ☹	☺ ☺ ☹		TuitionKit http://bit.ly/ 2xObyQ4
I can draw a tangent on a graph and determine the gradient	☺ ☺ ☹	☺ ☺ ☹	☺ ☺ ☹		
I can measure angles	☺ ☺ ☹	☺ ☺ ☹	☺ ☺ ☹		TuitionKit http://bit.ly/ 2yUUNQD
I can calculate the area of a triangle	☺ ☺ ☹	☺ ☺ ☹	☺ ☺ ☹		TuitionKit http://bit.ly/ 2ykFZOL
I can calculate the area of a rectangle	☺ ☺ ☹	☺ ☺ ☹	☺ ☺ ☹		
I can calculate surface area of a cuboid	☺ ☺ ☹	☺ ☺ ☹	☺ ☺ ☹		TuitionKit http://bit.ly/ 2hHVvwG
I can calculate volume of a cuboid	☺ ☺ ☹	☺ ☺ ☹	☺ ☺ ☹		TuitionKit http://bit.ly/ 2xUNMki
I can calculate probability	☺ ☺ ☹	☺ ☺ ☹	☺ ☺ ☹		TuitionKit http://bit.ly/ 2hK8wpz
I can draw and interpret frequency plots, and histograms	☺ ☺ ☹	☺ ☺ ☹	☺ ☺ ☹		TuitionKit http://bit.ly/ 2g79sAF

Maths and Calculator Skill for Science Students

Who or what is BIDMAS? And why do I have to care?

This is the way your calculator thinks, and it may not be thinking the way you want it to, this can lead to you and your calculator doing different sums and you writing down the wrong answer in the exam losing you valuable marks.

Your calculator will do things in this order...

1. Brackets
2. Indices
3. Division
4. Multiplication
5. Addition
6. Subtraction

Now I'm not going to go into much detail about this, I'll leave that to your maths teacher, but I will tell you the bits you need to know to succeed in science.

Mean average

Key Knowledge

In science we focus on the mean average (from now on I'll just say average), I'll leave median and mode to the maths department.

You need to take the results you have, add them together, and then divide by the number of results. But this is where the problem comes in...

Take this set of results 17,19,18,21

If you type 17 + 19 + 18 +21 / 4 =   you'll get the wrong answer because the calculator wants to do the division first

You need to do 17 + 19 + 18 +21 = ans/ 4 =   or (17 + 19 + 18 +21) / 4 =

Now Try These...

Result 1	Result 2	Result 3	Result 4	Average
21	25	22	26	
167	160	156	162	
15.6	15.9			
57	61	59		
99	101	103	100	
12	10			
97.56	95.76	98.99	95.97	
47	49	41		
1298	1340	1314	1327	
69	71	75	72	

Key knowledge

In science we're mean, if something looks odd we point at it and then ignore it.

An anomalous result is a result that looks out of place, one that doesn't fit the pattern (examiners love that word – pattern). I want you to be mean to those result, circle and label them then ignore them as you work out the average.

Now Try These...

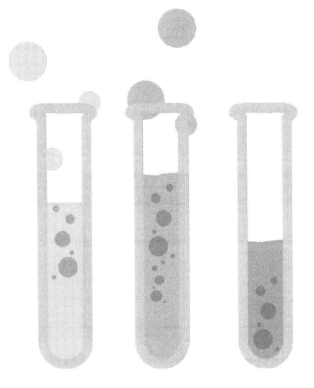

Result 1	Result 2	Result 3	Result 4	Average
75	77	51	76	
62	59	69	61	
724	720	719	736	
79	69	67	65	
0.5	0.05	0.51	0.49	
1793	1788	1893	1790	
67.5	67.9	67.8	67.4	
278	299	281	277	
45.6	47.2	47.6	47.9	
4893	4814	4905	4899	

Key Knowledge

Interval is the gap between

Range is the highest to lowest

UNITS, UNITS, UNITS – you're not getting any marks unless you write the units   down

Now Try These…

For each of the following experiments give the interval and range.

Experiment 1

Distance travelled (cm)	Time taken (s)
10	4
20	6
30	9
40	14
50	19
60	23
70	28

Interval….

Range………. To ………..

Experiment 2

Concentration of hydrochloric acid (M)	Time for reaction to take place (s)
0.25	47
0.50	49
0.75	51
1.00	53
1.25	56

Interval….

Range………. To ………..

Experiment 3

Force (N)	Extension (m)
3	0.2

5	0.3
7	0.5
9	0.6
11	0.8
13	0.9
15	1.2

Interval....

Range.......... To ....

Experiment 4

Number of marble chips	Bubbles produced
6	12
7	17
8	21
9	26

Interval....

Range.......... To ....

Experiment 5

Number of start jumps	Heart rate (bpm)
5	69
10	73
15	74
20	80
25	85
30	90
35	99

Interval....

Range.......... To ....

Key Knowledge

If you are rounding to 3 significant figures, you need to look at the fourth. If it is below 5 you round down and if it is above 5 you round up. If the number is above 0 the significant figures start with the first number, if it is below 0 the significant figures start with the first number that isn't 0.

45893 will become 46000 to 2 significant figures and 0.00734 will be 0.0073 to 2 significant figures.

Now try these...

1. Give 389540 to 4 significant figures
2. Give 85947395925 to 3 significant figures
3. Give 465906375 to 3 significant figures
4. Give 0.05678 to 3 significant figures
5. Give 0.0097495793 to 3 significant figures
6. Give 389540 to 3 significant figures
7. Give 85947395925 to 5 significant figures
8. Give 465906375 to 6 significant figures
9. Give 0.056788947585 to 7 significant figures
10. Give 0.0097495793 to 8 significant figures

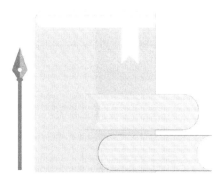

Key Knowledge

Instead of writing lots of numbers down we have a short hand way of doing it, instead of writing 3400, we put a . after the first number and then just count the numbers after it and put those above the 10. 3400 in this case becomes 3.4×10^3

Now try these…

Write each of these in standard form, give your answers to 3 significant figures

1. 893000000
2. 70900000
3. 38940000000
4. 72010000000000000
5. 642310000
6. 0.025
7. 0.000789
8. 0.000183
9. 0.00000956
10. 0.001002

Write each of these in long form

1. 6.38×10^5
2. 7.29×10^9
3. 6.09×10^3
4. 9.078×10^7
5. 8.112×10^6
6. 8.92×10^{-3}
7. 7.25×10^{-6}
8. 2.965×10^{-11}
9. 9.385×10^{-5}
10. 8.42×10^{-14}

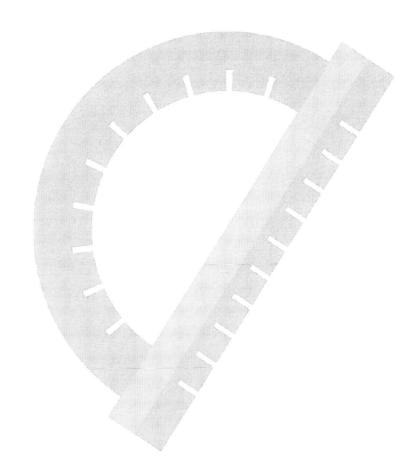

Key Knowledge

When doing sums, your calculator may give them to you as a fraction, you need to convert it into a decimal, write it down to an appropriate number of significant figures and round it.

For example 9/10 will become 0.9.

We DO NOT use a reoccurring symbol in science, leave that in maths.

Now try these...

1. 2/3
2. 6/10
3. 7/11
4. 9/12
5. 19/36
6. 1/3
7. 18/25
8. 956/1094
9. 74/97
10. 47/97

The exam questions are unlikely to be as simple as some of the examples I've used here, they will be very wordy. These questions may seem hard, but if you just break down the information into small chunks you should be fine.

1. A student runs a number of experiments to determine how many bubbles are produced when different concentrations of hydrochloric acid are added to marble chips. She tests 1M, 0.5M, 2M and then 1.5M acid.

   What is the range and interval of the concentration of acid?

2. Over a week I measured the different times it takes me to get to school, on Monday it takes 23 minutes, on Tuesday it takes 25 minutes, on Wednesday it takes 97 minutes due to traffic, on Thursday it takes 21 minutes and then on Friday it takes me 26 minutes to drive to school.

   What is the average time that it takes for me to get to work?

3. Primrose is obsessed with bringing worms into the house, on Monday she spends 5 minutes hunting for a worm and brings in 2. On Tuesday, she spends ten minutes hunting for worms and brings in 2. On Wednesday she spends 15 minutes hunting for worms and brings in 3, on Thursday she spends 20 minutes hunting and brings in 6, and then she rests on Friday?

   What is the range and interval of the hunting time?

   What is the average number of worms she brings in?

4. When stacking cups, it takes my class 210s the first time, 189s the second time 5s the third time and 192s the last time.

   Find the average and give your answer in standard form.

5. While studying for exams a student does lots of practice papers the results he gets are 89.4%, 72.8%, 10.1%, 75.9%, and 82.3%.

   What is the average?

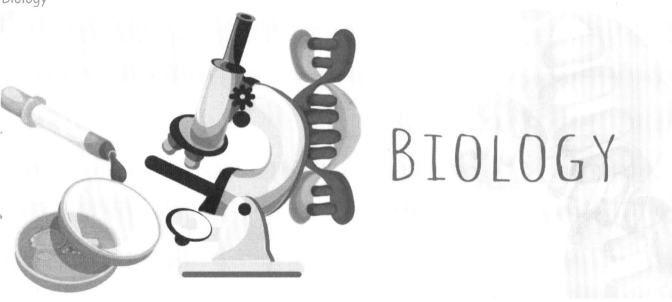

BIOLOGY

5 most common mistakes in a biology exam

1. Not referring to the graphs - if the exam question asks about a graph, make sure you refer to it in your answer. Most marks can be picked up by clearly talking about the graph
2. Ignoring the patterns and relationships – if there is a link between two things then tell the examiner about it, this is probably what they are looking for
3. Describe or explain – getting these two words confused is a common mistake in all exams but it happens more in biology than any other subject. Make sure you know what the difference is
4. Skipping levels – don't just focus on what is at the top and the bottom, remember all those important bits in-between
5. Forgetting the practical work – loads of marks can be picked up by talking about the practical's you have done in class. Just clearly state all the details and risks

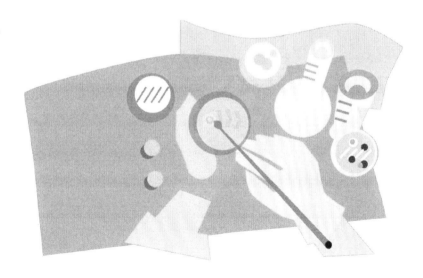

Topic Guide

Topic	First review	Second review	Third review
1 – Cell biology			
2 – Organisation			
3 – Infection and response			
4 – Bioenergetics			
5 – Homeostasis and response			
6 – Inheritance, variation and evolution			
7 – Ecology			

Topic	Quick fire questions	Whole topic summary
1 – Cell biology	https://youtu.be/E9ZiTAaRC-E	https://youtu.be/sdpmVQooYS4
2 – Organisation	https://youtu.be/QnsRz0Xhup8	https://youtu.be/DJ0IZGkDx6A
3 – Infection and response	https://youtu.be/pq3B_sozPCo	https://youtu.be/m7pxdTJ9NPI
4 – Bioenergetics	https://youtu.be/1nuYpKaQ3jA	https://youtu.be/1KIAWiHQ4sM
5 – Homeostasis and response	https://youtu.be/EMf0FbJI9BU	https://youtu.be/xOfqw7MbU8k
6 – Inheritance, variation and evolution	https://youtu.be/IL-dUnKmksY	https://youtu.be/npl10a6p8jQ
7 – Ecology	https://youtu.be/NorHSgd7Yyc	https://youtu.be/SKDn90HK98Q

Required practical's

1. Microscopy
2. Microbiology (Biology only)   https://youtu.be/SSnH7Vz0KF8
3. Osmosis
4. Enzymes
5. Food Tests
6. Photosynthesis
7. Reaction Time
8. Plant Responses
9. Field Investigations
10. Decay (Biology only)

Key Words

These are easy marks but only if you know them!

Abiotic	Non-living factors that affect organism
Active transport	Movement of ions or gasses from against the concentration gradient
Adaptation	Change in a species to suit the environment
Adrenal gland	Large gland near the kidneys that releases hormone
Aerobic	Respiration with oxygen
Allele	Different version of gene
Amino acids	Building block of proteins
Amylase	Enzyme that breaks carbohydrates into sugars
Anaerobic	Respiration without oxygen
Antibiotics	Drugs that kill bacteria
Aorta	Major blood vessel that carries oxygenated blood away from the heart
Artery	Thick wall blood vessel that carries oxygenated blood around the body
Asexual reproduction	Reproduction with only one parent, resulting in identical offspring
Aspirin	Painkiller developed from willow bark
Bacteria	Tiny organism that causes illness by releasing toxins
Benign tumour	Lump of cells that are not invading the body
Bile	Produced by the liver, neutralizes stomach acid and emulsifies fats
Biodiversity	The range of different organism that live in an environment
Biotic	Living factors that an organism
Bronchi	Braches of the trachea
Cancer	Uncontrolled cell division within the body
Capillary	Thinned walled blood vessels that allow diffusion of gases and nutrients
Carbon cycle	The movement of carbon through the environment
Carbon dioxide	Gas that has one atom of carbon and two atoms of oxygen
Cardiovascular disease	Narrowing of the blood vessels that can lead to dearth
Carnivore	Only eat animals
Cell	Small structural unit that contains a nucleus and cytoplasm
Cell membrane	Partially permeable membrane that surround the cell and control what goes in and out
Cell wall	Surrounds a cell and help maintain cell shape
Chlorophyll	Green part of a plant
Chloroplast	Where photosynthesis takes place
Chromosome	Long stretch of DNA
Community	The organism that live in a particular environment
Contraception	Mechanism to prevent pregnancy
Cystic fibrosis	Inherited disorder that cause damage to lungs

Cytoplasm	Jelly like substance within a cell
Deoxyribose nucleic acid	Long strand of bases that contain genes
Diabetes	Inability of the bod to control blood glucose levels
Diffusion	Movement of ions or gasses from a high concentration to a low concentration
Digestive system	Organ system that absorbs nutrients from food
Digitalis	Heart drug that comes from foxglove plants
Diploid	Two copies of each chromosome
Dominant	Only one copy of the gene is needed to be expressed
Ecology	The study of organism within and environment
Ecosystem	The organism and the habitat they live in
Egg	Female sex cell
Endocrine system	System that controls hormones and responses
Enzyme	Biological catalyst
Evolution	Gradual change in a species over time
Extinction	No breading pair of a species exist
Extremophile	Organism that has adapted to live at extreme conditions
Fatty acids	Can be combined with glycerol to make lipids
Follicle stimulating hormone	Hormone that causes an egg to develop
Fossils	Hard parts of long dead organism
Fungi	Group that includes mushrooms and moulds, they live of decomposing material
Gametes	Sex cells
Gene	Section of DNA, that controls a characteristic
Genome	All of the genes in an organism
Genotype	What genes are present
Glycerol	Can be combined with fatty acid to make lipids
Gonorrhoea	Bacteria that cause a sexual transmitted disease causing smelly discharge from the penis or vagina
Haploid	One copy of each chromosome
Health	State of mental and physical wellbeing
Herbivore	Only eats plant
Heterozygous	Different copies of gene
HIV	Virus that interfere with your body's ability to fight disease
Homoeostasis	Maintaining of a constant internal environment
Homozygous	Identical copies of gene
Hormones	Chemical that causes cells or tissue to respond
Immune system	Organs in the body that work together to defend against disease
In vitro fertilization	Medical treatment to aid getting pregnant
Lipase	Enzyme that breaks fats into fatty acids and glycerol
Lipids	Stores of energy that can be broken down to form fatty acids and glycerol

Luteinizing hormone	Hormone that causes and egg to be released
Malaria	Parasite transmitted by mosquitoes
Malignant tumour	Lump of cells that have developed that ability to travel to other part of the body
Measles	Viral infection causing fever and rash, most common in children
Meiosis	Type of cell division that ends in four different haploid daughter cells
Menstrual cycle	Monthly build up and breakdown of blood in the uterus
Meristem	Plant tissue found at growing tips
Metabolism	Chemical process that occur to maintain life
Mitochondria	Where respiration takes place
Mitosis	Type of cell division that ends in two identical daughter cells
Nucleus	Control centre of the cell, that holds the DNA
Oestrogen	Hormone that acts of the pituitary gland
Omnivore	Eat plants and animals
Organ system	A number of different organs working together towards one function
Osmosis	Transport of water across a partially permeable membrane
Ovaries	In women, these store the eggs
Ovulation	Releases of an egg from the ovaries
Oxygen debt	Arises after anaerobic respiration, needs oxygen to repay
Palisade mesophyll	Upper layer of cell in a leaf
Pancreas	Large gland behind the stomach which produces digestive enzymes
Pathogen	Causes illness
Penicillin	Antibiotic that comes from mould
Phenotypes	What characteristic are present
Phloem	Carries ions around a plant
Photosynthesis	Process that turns carbon dioxide and water into sugars
Pituitary gland	Located at the base of the brain, produces a large number of hormones
Plasma	Fluid part of the blood
Platelets	Small fragments of blood cells that help clotting
Pollution	Harmful substance in an environment
Polydactyly	An extra finger or toe
Predator	Eats prey
Prey	Something that gets eaten
Primary consumer	Herbivore
Protease	Enzyme that breaks proteins into amino acids
Proteins	Long chains of amino acids, that carry out the majority of functions within the body
Protist	Tiny single celled organism that can cause illness
Pulmonary artery	Blood vessel that carries deoxygenated blood from the heart to the lungs
Pulmonary vein	Blood vessel that carries oxygenated blood from the lungs to the heart
Recessive	Two identical copies of the gene are needed to be expressed

Red blood cell	Carries oxygen around the body, has no nucleus
Reflex arc	Nerve pathway including a sensory nerve a synapse and a motor nerve
Respiration	The process of turning sugars into energy, takes place in mitochondria
Respiratory system	Organ system that moves oxygen around the body
Ribosomes	Part of the cell that is responsible for producing proteins
Rose black spot	Fungal disease cause black spot on leave of plants
Salmonella	Bacteria that cause food poisoning
Selective breading	Breading of animals or plants for a particular characteristic
Sexual reproduction	Fusing of male and female gametes
Speciation	New species arising due to environmental change
Sperm	Male sex cell
Spongy mesophyll	Interior layer of cells in a lean
Stem cell	a type of cell that can differentiate into any other type of cell
Testis	In men, these are responsible for the production of sperm
Testosterone	Hormone found predominantly in men
Thyroid	Large gland in the neck which releases hormone
TMV	Virus affecting plants causing a mosaic pattern on leaves
Trachea	Long tube taking air down into the lungs
Transpiration	Process where plant absorb and lose water
Vaccines	Medication that contain inactive or dead virus to help develop immunity
Vein	Blood vessels that have values and carries deoxygenated blood back to the heart
Vena cava	Major blood vessel that carries deoxygenated blood back to the heart
Virus	DNA within a protein coat that divides by invading cells, the resulting cell death causes illness in the host
Water cycle	The movement of water through eh environment
White blood cell	Part of the immune system, produces antibodies and fights pathogens
Xylem	Carries water around a plant

The whole of biology paper 1 in only 63 minutes
https://youtu.be/mKYQ-K23Mr4

The whole of biology paper 2 in only 72 minutes
https://youtu.be/Uqti-xPnT-8

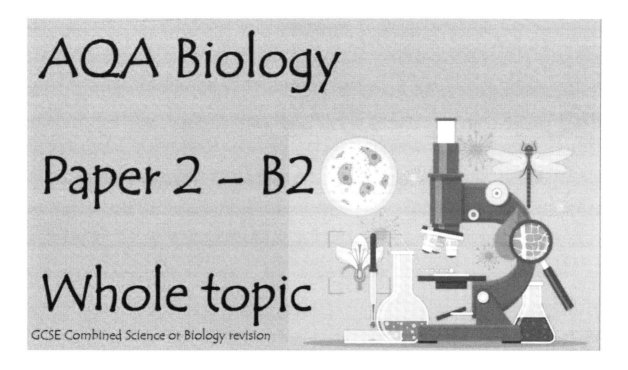

1 - Cell structure

Knowledge Checklist

Whole topic summary video https://youtu.be/sdpmVQooYS4 in only 12 minutes!!

Specification statement These are the bits the exam board wants you to know, make sure you can do all of these…	Self-assessment			Bits to help if you don't understand	
	First review 4-7 months before exam	Second review 1-2 months before exam	Final review Week before exam	Primrose Kitten	Other places
I can describe the structure of a plant cell and explain the function of all the main parts	☺ 😐 ☹	☺ 😐 ☹	☺ 😐 ☹	https://youtu.be/aM3ZfC1K6W8	TuitionKit http://bit.ly/2x6rlqz
I can describe the structure of an animal cell and explain the function of all the main parts	☺ 😐 ☹	☺ 😐 ☹	☺ 😐 ☹	https://youtu.be/FjF_PO7QVGg	
I can describe the structure of a bacterial cell	☺ 😐 ☹	☺ 😐 ☹	☺ 😐 ☹	https://youtu.be/404tQ7kLDg0	
I can describe the size of different cells	☺ 😐 ☹	☺ 😐 ☹	☺ 😐 ☹		
I can describe and explain a range of specialised cells	☺ 😐 ☹	☺ 😐 ☹	☺ 😐 ☹		TuitionKit http://bit.ly/2fpghpZ
I can explain cell differentiation	☺ 😐 ☹	☺ 😐 ☹	☺ 😐 ☹		TuitionKit http://bit.ly/2x6l1iI
I can describe how microscopy techniques have changed over time	☺ 😐 ☹	☺ 😐 ☹	☺ 😐 ☹		TuitionKit http://bit.ly/2fr7uuF
I can calculate magnification	☺ 😐 ☹	☺ 😐 ☹	☺ 😐 ☹	https://youtu.be/v-KrUP3bu24	
I can describe how bacteria divide **Biology only**	☺ 😐 ☹	☺ 😐 ☹	☺ 😐 ☹		

I can describe how to prepare an uncontained culture of bacteria using aseptic technique **Biology only**	☺ 😐 ☹	☺ 😐 ☹	☺ 😐 ☹	https://youtu.be/ 3tzrGe6EpYA	
I can describe the use of bacterial cultures grown on agar plates **Biology only**	☺ 😐 ☹	☺ 😐 ☹	☺ 😐 ☹	RP2; https://youtu.be/ SSnH7Vz0KF8	TuitionKit http://bit.ly/ 2x79KyI
I can describe the location and function of chromosomes	☺ 😐 ☹	☺ 😐 ☹	☺ 😐 ☹		TuitionKit http://bit.ly/ 2w0hS2y
I can describe each stage in mitosis	☺ 😐 ☹	☺ 😐 ☹	☺ 😐 ☹	https://youtu.be/ -POimnbaHG0	TuitionKit http://bit.ly/ 2wwUclK
I can define the term stem cell	☺ 😐 ☹	☺ 😐 ☹	☺ 😐 ☹		TuitionKit http://bit.ly/ 2f0EJE8
I can describe the function of stem cells in embryos, in adult cells and in plants	☺ 😐 ☹	☺ 😐 ☹	☺ 😐 ☹		
I can describe stem cell therapy	☺ 😐 ☹	☺ 😐 ☹	☺ 😐 ☹		
I can discuss the advantages and disadvantages that arise relating to the use of stem cells in medical treatment and ecology	☺ 😐 ☹	☺ 😐 ☹	☺ 😐 ☹		
I can define the term diffusion	☺ 😐 ☹	☺ 😐 ☹	☺ 😐 ☹		TuitionKit http://bit.ly/ 2h9Z5z9
I can recall which substances are moved by diffusion	☺ 😐 ☹	☺ 😐 ☹	☺ 😐 ☹		
I can describe the process of diffusion	☺ 😐 ☹	☺ 😐 ☹	☺ 😐 ☹		Total Learn http://bit.ly/ 2wGqSJE
I can explain how different factors affect diffusion	☺ 😐 ☹	☺ 😐 ☹	☺ 😐 ☹		
I can describe the advantage of having a large surface area to volume ratio and give examples	☺ 😐 ☹	☺ 😐 ☹	☺ 😐 ☹		
I can define the term osmosis	☺ 😐 ☹	☺ 😐 ☹	☺ 😐 ☹		
I can describe the process of osmosis	☺ 😐 ☹	☺ 😐 ☹	☺ 😐 ☹		TuitionKit http://bit.ly/ 2wj2C4Y
I can define the term active transport	☺ 😐 ☹	☺ 😐 ☹	☺ 😐 ☹		TuitionKit http://bit.ly/ 2wwUs4c
I can describe the process of active transport	☺ 😐 ☹	☺ 😐 ☹	☺ 😐 ☹		
I can give examples of active transport in action	☺ 😐 ☹	☺ 😐 ☹	☺ 😐 ☹		

This worksheet is fully supported by a video tutorial; https://youtu.be/E9ZiTAaRC-E

1. Label a plant cell.

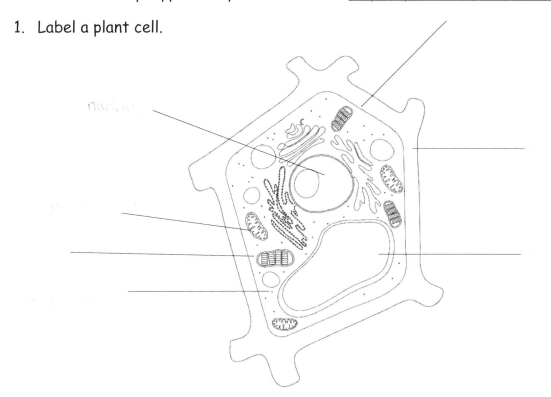

nucleus

2. Label an animal cell.

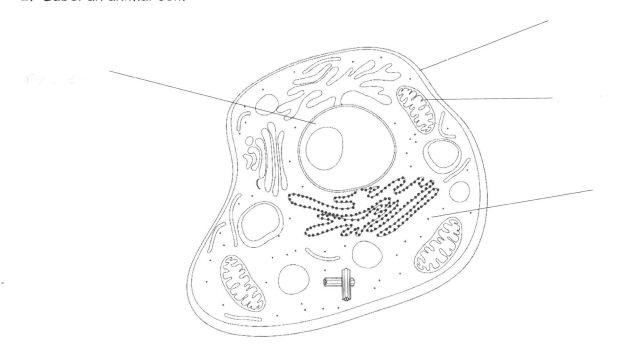

nucleus

3. Label a bacteria cell.

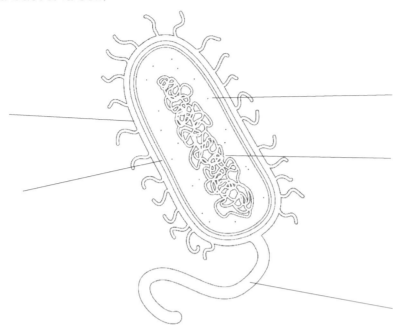

4. Give two different specialist cells.
5. What is differentiation?
6. How do you calculate magnification?
7. Where are chromosomes?
8. What do chromosomes do?
9. What is mitosis?
10. What is a stem cell?
11. What is diffusion?
12. What is osmosis?
13. What is active transport?

Whole topic summary video https://youtu.be/DJ0lZGkDx6A in only 19 minutes!!

Specification statement These are the bits the exam board wants you to know, make sure you can do all of these...	Self-assessment			Bits to help if you don't understand	
	First review 4-7 months before exam	Second review 1-2 months before exam	Final review Week before exam	Primrose Kitten	Other places
I can define the term organ system	☺ ☺ ☹	☺ ☺ ☹	☺ ☺ ☹		TuitionKit http://bit.ly/2h7mcdP
I can describe how the digestive system works	☺ ☺ ☹	☺ ☺ ☹	☺ ☺ ☹		TuitionKit http://bit.ly/2fqFxTF
I can describe how an enzyme works	☺ ☺ ☹	☺ ☺ ☹	☺ ☺ ☹		
I can explain how an enzyme is affected at different temperature and pH	☺ ☺ ☹	☺ ☺ ☹	☺ ☺ ☹		
I can describe the 'lock and key' mechanism	☺ ☺ ☹	☺ ☺ ☹	☺ ☺ ☹		
I can recall for named type of enzyme (amylase, lipase and protease) the location of production and the action	☺ ☺ ☹	☺ ☺ ☹	☺ ☺ ☹		
I can describe the function of enzymes in relation to the digestive system	☺ ☺ ☹	☺ ☺ ☹	☺ ☺ ☹		
I can recall the site of production and uses of bile	☺ ☺ ☹	☺ ☺ ☹	☺ ☺ ☹		
I can recall the organs that make up the respiratory system	☺ ☺ ☹	☺ ☺ ☹	☺ ☺ ☹		

I can describe the structure and function of the heart	☺ 😐 ☹	☺ 😐 ☹	☺ 😐 ☹	https://youtu.be/09WhIK0ueh8	TuitionKit http://bit.ly/2ha0k1h Total Learn http://bit.ly/2yJOakB
I can describe the structure and function of the lungs	☺ 😐 ☹	☺ 😐 ☹	☺ 😐 ☹		TuitionKit http://bit.ly/2f1zOmG Total Learn http://bit.ly/2yKslmA
I can describe the structure and function of the different types of blood vessel. Aorta, vena cava, pulmonary artery, pulmonary vein, coronary arteries and capillaries.	☺ 😐 ☹	☺ 😐 ☹	☺ 😐 ☹	https://youtu.be/fjrKlYKtfP4	TuitionKit http://bit.ly/2xao8rC Total Learn http://bit.ly/2iwBEkv
I can define the natural resting heart rate	☺ 😐 ☹	☺ 😐 ☹	☺ 😐 ☹		
I can explain the need for artificial pacemakers	☺ 😐 ☹	☺ 😐 ☹	☺ 😐 ☹		
I can describe the parts that make up blood, and the function of each of these parts	☺ 😐 ☹	☺ 😐 ☹	☺ 😐 ☹		TuitionKit http://bit.ly/2y5lktf Total Learn http://bit.ly/2lcUJsO http://bit.ly/2ivqdt4
I can recognise a diagram of the different blood calls	☺ 😐 ☹	☺ 😐 ☹	☺ 😐 ☹		

I can explain how different blood cells are adapted to suit a particular function	☺ ☺ ☹	☺ ☺ ☹	☺ ☺ ☹		TuitionKit http://bit.ly/ 2y5lktf Total Learn http://bit.ly/ 2yJD6E1
I can describe the impact cardiovascular disease can have on a person life	☺ ☺ ☹	☺ ☺ ☹	☺ ☺ ☹		TuitionKit http://bit.ly/ 2h9Auam
I can describe the different ways cardiovascular disease can be treated.	☺ ☺ ☹	☺ ☺ ☹	☺ ☺ ☹		
I can describe the causes of cardiovascular disease	☺ ☺ ☹	☺ ☺ ☹	☺ ☺ ☹		
I can define the term health	☺ ☺ ☹	☺ ☺ ☹	☺ ☺ ☹		
I can describe the impact disease can have on health	☺ ☺ ☹	☺ ☺ ☹	☺ ☺ ☹		
I can describe other factors (diet, stress, life) that can affect health	☺ ☺ ☹	☺ ☺ ☹	☺ ☺ ☹		
I can explain how different types of disease may interact and be triggers	☺ ☺ ☹	☺ ☺ ☹	☺ ☺ ☹		
I can interpret graphic data on diseases and disease trends	☺ ☺ ☹	☺ ☺ ☹	☺ ☺ ☹		
I can describe how to sample epidemiological data	☺ ☺ ☹	☺ ☺ ☹	☺ ☺ ☹		
I can discuss the financial cost of diseases	☺ ☺ ☹	☺ ☺ ☹	☺ ☺ ☹		
I can define the term cancer	☺ ☺ ☹	☺ ☺ ☹	☺ ☺ ☹		
I can differentiate between benign and malignant tumours	☺ ☺ ☹	☺ ☺ ☹	☺ ☺ ☹		
I can recall the different types and location of plant tissues. Epidermal tissue, palisade mesophyll, spongy mesophyll, xylem, phloem and meristem	☺ ☺ ☹	☺ ☺ ☹	☺ ☺ ☹		
I can relate the structure of plant cells to their function, including adaptations.	☺ ☺ ☹	☺ ☺ ☹	☺ ☺ ☹		
I can define the term transpiration	☺ ☺ ☹	☺ ☺ ☹	☺ ☺ ☹		

I can describe how to measure transpiration	☺ ☺ ☹	☺ ☺ ☹	☺ ☺ ☹		
I can explain the effect that temperature/humidity/air movement/light has on transpiration	☺ ☺ ☹	☺ ☺ ☹	☺ ☺ ☹		
I can define an organ system within a plant	☺ ☺ ☹	☺ ☺ ☹	☺ ☺ ☹		

This worksheet is fully supported by a video tutorial; ; https://youtu.be/QnsRzOXhup8

1. What is an organ system?
2. Name the parts of the digestive system? *mouth, oesophagus, ... in liver, pancreas, Gall bladder, Small ...... large*
3. What happens to enzymes at low temperatures? *Denature*
4. What happens to enzymes at high temperatures? *Denature*
5. What happens enzymes are there outside their optimal pH? *don't produce hydrochloric acid*
6. What is the lock and key mechanism? *Enzymes ...... together*
7. Where is amylase produced? *pancreas, small intestine*
8. What does amylase do?
9. Where is lipase produced? *pancreas, small intestine*
10. What does lipase do?
11. Where is protease produced? *stomach, pancreas, small intestine*
12. What does protease do?
13. Where is bile produced? *liver*
14. What does bile do? *helps to break down food*
15. Label the respiratory system

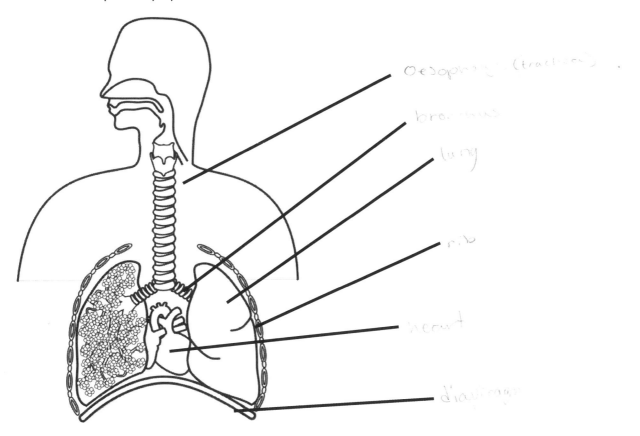

Oesophagus (trachea)
bronchus
lung
rib
heart
diaphragm

16. What does the heart do? *pumps blood around your body*

17. What do the lungs do? *help you breath*

18. Label the heart

left

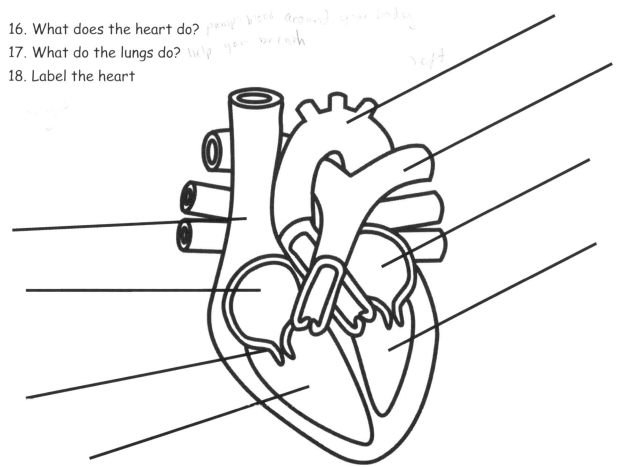

19. Draw the path the blood takes through the heart

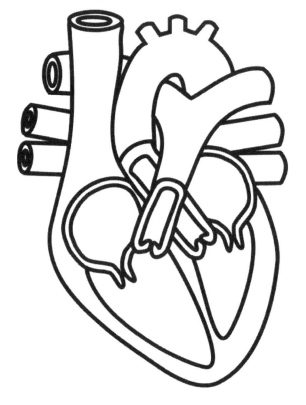

20. What does the aorta do?

21. What does the vena cava do?

22. What does the pulmonary artery do?

23. What does pulmonary vein do?

24. What is natural resting heart rate?

25. Why might you need artificial pacemaker?

26. What do red blood cells do?

27. What do white blood cells do?

28. What do platelets do?

29. What does plasma do?

30. What is cardiovascular disease?

31. What lifestyle factors can affect health?

32. What is cancer?

33. What is a benign tumour?

34. What is a malignant tumour?

35. What is epidermal tissue?

36. What is palisade mesophyll?

37. What is spongy mesophyll?

38. What is the xylem?

39. What is the phloem?

40. What is transpiration?

41. How can we measure transpiration?

Whole topic summary video https://youtu.be/m7pxdTJ9NPI in only 22 minutes!!

Specification statement These are the bits the exam board wants you to know, make sure you can do all of these...	Self-assessment			Bits to help if you don't understand	
	First review 4-7 months before exam	Second review 1-2 months before exam	Final review Week before exam	Primrose Kitten	Other places
I can describe the range of different ways diseases are caused. Viruses, bacteria, protist or fungi.	☺ 😐 ☹	☺ 😐 ☹	☺ 😐 ☹		TuitionKit http://bit.ly/2f1sjfr http://bit.ly/2h8mD41 http://bit.ly/2fc0uEW
I can describe how diseases are spread in plants and animals	☺ 😐 ☹	☺ 😐 ☹	☺ 😐 ☹		
I can define the term pathogen	☺ 😐 ☹	☺ 😐 ☹	☺ 😐 ☹		
I can describe how bacteria reproduce inside the body	☺ 😐 ☹	☺ 😐 ☹	☺ 😐 ☹		TuitionKit http://bit.ly/2f1sjfr
I can describe how viruses reproduce inside the body	☺ 😐 ☹	☺ 😐 ☹	☺ 😐 ☹		
I can explain how bacteria can make a person feel ill	☺ 😐 ☹	☺ 😐 ☹	☺ 😐 ☹		
I can explain how viruses can make a person feel ill	☺ 😐 ☹	☺ 😐 ☹	☺ 😐 ☹		
I can describe the spread and implication of measles	☺ 😐 ☹	☺ 😐 ☹	☺ 😐 ☹		
I can describe the spread and implication of HIV	☺ 😐 ☹	☺ 😐 ☹	☺ 😐 ☹		

I can describe the spread and implication of TMV	☺ ☺ ☹	☺ ☺ ☹	☺ ☺ ☹		
I can describe the spread and implication of *Salmonella*	☺ ☺ ☹	☺ ☺ ☹	☺ ☺ ☹		TuitionKit http://bit.ly/ 2f1sjfr
I can describe the spread and implication of gonorrhoea	☺ ☺ ☹	☺ ☺ ☹	☺ ☺ ☹		
I can describe the spread and implication of Rose Black Spot	☺ ☺ ☹	☺ ☺ ☹	☺ ☺ ☹		TuitionKit http://bit.ly/ 2h8mD41
I can describe the spread and implication of malaria	☺ ☺ ☹	☺ ☺ ☹	☺ ☺ ☹		TuitionKit http://bit.ly/ 2fc0uEW
I can describe how the body protects itself from disease, including skin, nose, trachea, bronchi and stomach	☺ ☺ ☹	☺ ☺ ☹	☺ ☺ ☹		TuitionKit http://bit.ly/ 2w1fY1u
I can explain the role of the immune system	☺ ☺ ☹	☺ ☺ ☹	☺ ☺ ☹		
I can describe the different roles white blood cells play in the immune system	☺ ☺ ☹	☺ ☺ ☹	☺ ☺ ☹		
I can describe how vaccination can prevent illness	☺ ☺ ☹	☺ ☺ ☹	☺ ☺ ☹		
I can explain how vaccines work	☺ ☺ ☹	☺ ☺ ☹	☺ ☺ ☹		
I can explain the need for antibiotics	☺ ☺ ☹	☺ ☺ ☹	☺ ☺ ☹		
I can explain how antibiotics work	☺ ☺ ☹	☺ ☺ ☹	☺ ☺ ☹		TuitionKit http://bit.ly/ 2fg3uue
I can describe the problem of emerging antibiotic resistance	☺ ☺ ☹	☺ ☺ ☹	☺ ☺ ☹		
I can describe the use of painkillers	☺ ☺ ☹	☺ ☺ ☹	☺ ☺ ☹		
I can describe the process involved in developing a new drug and bringing it to market	☺ ☺ ☹	☺ ☺ ☹	☺ ☺ ☹		TuitionKit http://bit.ly/ 2y5oIV1
I can describe how digitalis, aspirin and penicillin were discovered	☺ ☺ ☹	☺ ☺ ☹	☺ ☺ ☹		
I can recall that new drugs are tested for toxicity, efficacy and dose	☺ ☺ ☹	☺ ☺ ☹	☺ ☺ ☹		

I can describe how monoclonal antibodies are produced **Biology only** **Higher tier only**	☺ ☺ ☹	☺ ☺ ☹	☺ ☺ ☹		TuitionKit http://bit.ly/2fq3uue
I can describe how monoclonal antibodies can be used **Biology only** **Higher tier only**	☺ ☺ ☹	☺ ☺ ☹	☺ ☺ ☹		
I can evaluate the advantages and disadvantages of monoclonal antibodies **Biology only** **Higher tier only**	☺ ☺ ☹	☺ ☺ ☹	☺ ☺ ☹		
I can describe how a disease can affect a plant **Biology only** **Higher tier only**	☺ ☺ ☹	☺ ☺ ☹	☺ ☺ ☹		TuitionKit http://bit.ly/2jzh3Me
I can recall how plant disease can be identified **Biology only** **Higher tier only**	☺ ☺ ☹	☺ ☺ ☹	☺ ☺ ☹		
I can describe the range of pathogens that can infect a plant **Biology only**	☺ ☺ ☹	☺ ☺ ☹	☺ ☺ ☹		
I can recall the spread of and damage done by tobacco mosaic virus **Biology only**	☺ ☺ ☹	☺ ☺ ☹	☺ ☺ ☹		
I can recall the spread of and damage done by black spot disease **Biology only**	☺ ☺ ☹	☺ ☺ ☹	☺ ☺ ☹		
I can recall the spread of and damage done by aphids **Biology only**	☺ ☺ ☹	☺ ☺ ☹	☺ ☺ ☹		
I can explain how plants can be damaged by ion deficiency **Biology only**	☺ ☺ ☹	☺ ☺ ☹	☺ ☺ ☹		
I can describe the range of plant defences, including physical, chemical and mechanical **Biology only**	☺ ☺ ☹	☺ ☺ ☹	☺ ☺ ☹		TuitionKit http://bit.ly/2y5kpJp

Quick Fire Questions

This worksheet is fully supported by a video tutorial; https://youtu.be/pq3B_sozPCo

1. Define pathogen. cause illness
2. What is a virus? infects all cells
3. What is bacteria? single type of DNA
4. What is a protist?
5. What is fungi? (mushrooms)
6. How can diseases be spread in plants?
7. How can diseases be spread in animals?
8. How do bacteria reproduce inside the body?
9. How do viruses reproduce inside body?
10. How can bacteria make a person feel ill?
11. How can a virus make a person feel ill?
12. What is measles?
13. What is HIV?
14. What is TMV?
15. What is salmonella? food poisoning
16. What is gonorrhoea?
17. What is Rose Black Spot?
18. What is malaria?
19. How does the skin help protect the body?
20. How does the nose help protect the body?
21. How does the trachea help protect the body?
22. How does the bronchi help protect the body?
23. How does the stomach help protect the body?
24. What is the role of the immune system?
25. What do white blood cells do?
26. How do vaccinations work? inject dead cell for your body to fight off
27. What are antibiotics? medicine which helps infection go
28. What is antibiotic resistance?
29. What are painkillers for? relieving pain
30. Where it is digitalis come from?

31. Where does aspirin come from?

32. Where does penicillin come from?

33. What are the three things that new drugs need to be tested for?

4 – Bioenergetics

Knowledge Checklist

Whole topic summary video https://youtu.be/1KIAWiHQ4sM in only 11 minutes!!

Specification statement These are the bits the exam board wants you to know, make sure you can do all of these...	Self-assessment			Bits to help if you don't understand	
	First review 4-7 months before exam	Second review 1-2 months before exam	Final review Week before exam	Primrose Kitten	Other places
I can recall the word and symbol equation for photosynthesis	☺ ☺ ☹	☺ ☺ ☹	☺ ☺ ☹		TuitionKit http://bit.ly/2xaLKwl
I can describe the transfer of energy in photosynthesis	☺ ☺ ☹	☺ ☺ ☹	☺ ☺ ☹		
I can explain how different factors affect the rate of photosynthesis. Including temperature, light intensity, carbon dioxide concentration and the amount of chlorophyll	☺ ☺ ☹	☺ ☺ ☹	☺ ☺ ☹		TuitionKit http://bit.ly/2jyc7r2
I can explain that more than one factor may be limiting the rate of photosynthesis **Higher tier only**	☺ ☺ ☹	☺ ☺ ☹	☺ ☺ ☹		
I can explain the graphs showing how a limiting factor will affect the rate of photosynthesis **Higher tier only**	☺ ☺ ☹	☺ ☺ ☹	☺ ☺ ☹		
I can describe what the glucose produced in photosynthesis can be used for	☺ ☺ ☹	☺ ☺ ☹	☺ ☺ ☹		TuitionKit http://bit.ly/2fcwetD
I can recall the respiration is an exothermic reaction	☺ ☺ ☹	☺ ☺ ☹	☺ ☺ ☹		
I can recall the word and symbol equation for respiration	☺ ☺ ☹	☺ ☺ ☹	☺ ☺ ☹		Total Learn http://bit.ly/2yFT8kI

I can describe the process of aerobic respiration; in regard to oxygen, the products and the amount of energy	☺ ☻ ☹	☺ ☻ ☹	☺ ☻ ☹		
I can describe the process of anaerobic respiration; in regard to oxygen, the products and the amount of energy	☺ ☻ ☹	☺ ☻ ☹	☺ ☻ ☹		TuitionKit http://bit.ly/ 2xGYYSV
I can describe what an organism needs energy for	☺ ☻ ☹	☺ ☻ ☹	☺ ☻ ☹		
I can recall the equation for anaerobic respiration	☺ ☻ ☹	☺ ☻ ☹	☺ ☻ ☹		
I can recall the equation for anaerobic respiration in plants and yeast cells	☺ ☻ ☹	☺ ☻ ☹	☺ ☻ ☹		
I can explain the importance of anaerobic respiration in plants and yeast cells for the food industry	☺ ☻ ☹	☺ ☻ ☹	☺ ☻ ☹		
I can recall the need for energy during exercise	☺ ☻ ☹	☺ ☻ ☹	☺ ☻ ☹		TuitionKit http://bit.ly/ 2wwYhXj
I can describe the effect of exercise on the body	☺ ☻ ☹	☺ ☻ ☹	☺ ☻ ☹		
I can define the term oxygen debt	☺ ☻ ☹	☺ ☻ ☹	☺ ☻ ☹		http://bit.ly/ 2fr4CO8
I can explain how an oxygen debt can be repaid **Higher tier only**	☺ ☻ ☹	☺ ☻ ☹	☺ ☻ ☹		
I can define the term metabolism	☺ ☻ ☹	☺ ☻ ☹	☺ ☻ ☹		TuitionKit http://bit.ly/ 2h8HcRi
I can explain the role of sugars; amino acids; fatty acids; glycerol; carbohydrates; proteins and lipids	☺ ☻ ☹	☺ ☻ ☹	☺ ☻ ☹		
I can describe the use of energy in the synthesis of new molecules	☺ ☻ ☹	☺ ☻ ☹	☺ ☻ ☹		
I can describe the conversion of glucose to starch, glycogen and cellulose	☺ ☻ ☹	☺ ☻ ☹	☺ ☻ ☹		
I can describe the formation of lipids from glycerol and fatty acids	☺ ☻ ☹	☺ ☻ ☹	☺ ☻ ☹		
I can describe the synthesis of proteins from amino acids	☺ ☻ ☹	☺ ☻ ☹	☺ ☻ ☹		

I can describe the synthesis of amino acids from glucose and nitrate ions	☺ ☺ ☹	☺ ☺ ☹	☺ ☺ ☹		
I can describe the breakdown of proteins, forming urea	☺ ☺ ☹	☺ ☺ ☹	☺ ☺ ☹		

This worksheet is fully supported by a video tutorial; https://youtu.be/1nuYpKaQ3jA

1.   What is the word equation for photosynthesis?
2.   What is the chemical symbol for carbon dioxide?
3.   What is the chemical symbol for water?
4.   What is the chemical symbol for oxygen gas?
5.   What is the chemical symbol for glucose?
6.   What is the symbol equation for photosynthesis?
7.   How is energy transferred in photosynthesis?
8.   What factors might affect photosynthesis?
9.   How does temperature affect photosynthesis?
10. How does light intensity affect photosynthesis?
11. How does carbon dioxide concentration affect photosynthesis?
12. Sketch the graph to show how light intensity affect photosynthesis (Higher tier only)
13. Sketch the graph to show how temperature affects photosynthesis (Higher tier only)
14. Sketch the graph to show how carbon dioxide concentration affects photosynthesis (Higher tier only)
15. Is respiration exothermic or endothermic?
16. What is the word equation for respiration?
17. What is the symbol equation for respiration?
18. What is anaerobic respiration?
19. What is equation for anaerobic respiration?
20. What is anaerobic respiration in yeast cells?
21. How are the products of anaerobic respiration useful in the food industry?
22. What is oxygen debt?
23. Define metabolism.
24. What do sugars do?
25. What do amino acids do?
26. What do fatty acids do?
27. What does glycerol do?
28. What do carbohydrates do?
29. What do proteins do?
30. What do lipids do?
31. What can glucose be converted to?
32. What are lipids formed from?
33. What are proteins formed from?
34. What are amino acid formed from?
35. What do proteins are broken down into?

Biology Paper 1 Checklist – What to do before the exam!

Watched the whole topic video   https://youtu.be/mKYQ-K23Mr4   ☐

Answered the quick-fire questions   ☐

Looked at the practical videos   ☐

Learnt the keywords   ☐

Filled in the crosswords   ☐

5 – Homeostasis and Response

Knowledge Checklist

Whole topic summary video https://youtu.be/xOfqw7MbU8k in only 20 minutes!!

Specification statement These are the bits the exam board wants you to know, make sure you can do all of these…	Self-assessment			Bits to help if you don't understand	
	First review 4-7 months before exam	Second review 1-2 months before exam	Final review Week before exam	Primrose Kitten	Other places
I can define the term homoeostasis	☺ ☺ ☹	☺ ☺ ☹	☺ ☺ ☹		TuitionKit http://bit.ly/2x43Tg3
I can explain the need for homoeostasis within the context of the human body, including; blood glucose, temperature and water	☺ ☺ ☹	☺ ☺ ☹	☺ ☺ ☹		Total Learn http://bit.ly/2gzchKy
I can describe the role of receptors; the brain; the CNS; the pancreas; effectors, muscles; glands in homeostasis	☺ ☺ ☹	☺ ☺ ☹	☺ ☺ ☹		
I can describe the structure of the nervous system	☺ ☺ ☹	☺ ☺ ☹	☺ ☺ ☹		TuitionKit http://bit.ly/2fc8hTp
I can describe how the nervous system works in reacting to surroundings and coordinating behaviour	☺ ☺ ☹	☺ ☺ ☹	☺ ☺ ☹		
I can describe the path a signal takes along the receptor via the CNS	☺ ☺ ☹	☺ ☺ ☹	☺ ☺ ☹		
I can explain a reflex arc	☺ ☺ ☹	☺ ☺ ☹	☺ ☺ ☹		
I can describe the function of the brain **Biology only**	☺ ☺ ☹	☺ ☺ ☹	☺ ☺ ☹		TuitionKit http://bit.ly/2f2c95n

I can identify the different parts of the brain **Biology only**	☺ ☺ ☹	☺ ☺ ☹	☺ ☺ ☹		
I can explain the problems with investigating brain function **Biology only** **Higher tier only**	☺ ☺ ☹	☺ ☺ ☹	☺ ☺ ☹		
I can describe how doctors can map regions of the brain **Biology only** **Higher tier only**	☺ ☺ ☹	☺ ☺ ☹	☺ ☺ ☹		
I can describe the structure of the eye **Biology only**	☺ ☺ ☹	☺ ☺ ☹	☺ ☺ ☹	https://youtu.be/wr3RWxV1JX8	TuitionKit http://bit.ly/2f1zkNn
I can explain the function of the different parts of the eye **Biology only**	☺ ☺ ☹	☺ ☺ ☹	☺ ☺ ☹		
I can describe what happens to the eye when it focuses on near or far objects **Biology only**	☺ ☺ ☹	☺ ☺ ☹	☺ ☺ ☹		
I can describe short sightedness and long sightedness **Biology only**	☺ ☺ ☹	☺ ☺ ☹	☺ ☺ ☹	https://youtu.be/aRDt8PUhv4c	
I can explain how short sightedness and long sightedness can be corrected **Biology only**	☺ ☺ ☹	☺ ☺ ☹	☺ ☺ ☹		
I can interpret ray diagrams **Biology only**	☺ ☺ ☹	☺ ☺ ☹	☺ ☺ ☹		
I can describe how the body controls internal temperature **Biology only**	☺ ☺ ☹	☺ ☺ ☹	☺ ☺ ☹		TuitionKit http://bit.ly/2x4kW1p
I can explain how the body controls internal temperature **Biology only** **Higher tier only**	☺ ☺ ☹	☺ ☺ ☹	☺ ☺ ☹		
I can describe the parts of the endocrine system and how they work together	☺ ☺ ☹	☺ ☺ ☹	☺ ☺ ☹		TuitionKit http://bit.ly/2fbCdis
I can describe the importance of the pituitary gland	☺ ☺ ☹	☺ ☺ ☹	☺ ☺ ☹		

I can identify the locations of the pituitary gland; pancreas; thyroid; adrenal gland; ovary and testes	☺ 😐 ☹	☺ 😐 ☹	☺ 😐 ☹		
I can describe how blood glucose concentration is monitored	☺ 😐 ☹	☺ 😐 ☹	☺ 😐 ☹		TuitionKit http://bit.ly/ 2xH7e5k
I can explain what happens when blood glucose is too high	☺ 😐 ☹	☺ 😐 ☹	☺ 😐 ☹		
I can describe how insulin controls blood glucose levels	☺ 😐 ☹	☺ 😐 ☹	☺ 😐 ☹		
I can describe the cause, symptoms and treatment for type 1 diabetes	☺ 😐 ☹	☺ 😐 ☹	☺ 😐 ☹		
I can describe the cause, symptoms and treatment for type 2 diabetes	☺ 😐 ☹	☺ 😐 ☹	☺ 😐 ☹		Total Learn http://bit.ly/ 2y3fgBh
I can explain what happens when blood glucose is too low **Higher tier only**	☺ 😐 ☹	☺ 😐 ☹	☺ 😐 ☹		
I can explain the negative feedback loop that controls blood glucose levels **Higher tier only**	☺ 😐 ☹	☺ 😐 ☹	☺ 😐 ☹		Total Learn http://bit.ly/ 2yNEHuz
I can describe the effect osmosis has on cells **Biology only**	☺ 😐 ☹	☺ 😐 ☹	☺ 😐 ☹		
I can describe how water leaves and enters the body **Biology only**	☺ 😐 ☹	☺ 😐 ☹	☺ 😐 ☹		TuitionKit http://bit.ly/ 2h6ZS3T
I can describe what happens to cells if they lose or gain too much water **Biology only**	☺ 😐 ☹	☺ 😐 ☹	☺ 😐 ☹		
I can explain the need for amino acids to be excreted **Biology only** **Higher tier only**	☺ 😐 ☹	☺ 😐 ☹	☺ 😐 ☹		
I can describe the function of the kidneys **Biology only**	☺ 😐 ☹	☺ 😐 ☹	☺ 😐 ☹		

I can explain the effect that ADH has on the kidneys and blood water concentration **Biology only** **Higher tier only**	☺ ☺ ☹	☺ ☺ ☹	☺ ☺ ☹		TuitionKit http://bit.ly/ 2x7DEmm
I can describe the treatment for kidney failure **Biology only**	☺ ☺ ☹	☺ ☺ ☹	☺ ☺ ☹		TuitionKit http://bit.ly/ 2h9ZVfD
I can describe the roles of the different hormones in the menstrual cycle	☺ ☺ ☹	☺ ☺ ☹	☺ ☺ ☹		TuitionKit http://bit.ly/ 2frojpb
I can describe the roles of the different hormones in puberty	☺ ☺ ☹	☺ ☺ ☹	☺ ☺ ☹		
I can describe ovulation	☺ ☺ ☹	☺ ☺ ☹	☺ ☺ ☹		
I can describe the role of testosterone	☺ ☺ ☹	☺ ☺ ☹	☺ ☺ ☹		
I can describe the interaction between FSH, LH and oestrogen in the menstrual cycle **Higher tier only**	☺ ☺ ☹	☺ ☺ ☹	☺ ☺ ☹		
I can describe different method of contraception, including hormonal and non-hormonal methods	☺ ☺ ☹	☺ ☺ ☹	☺ ☺ ☹		TuitionKit http://bit.ly/ 2y5Zl5u
I can explain different method of contraception, including hormonal and non-hormonal methods	☺ ☺ ☹	☺ ☺ ☹	☺ ☺ ☹		
I can describe the need for treatment for infertility **Higher tier only**	☺ ☺ ☹	☺ ☺ ☹	☺ ☺ ☹	https://youtu.be/ LrwgFZaGpvY	TuitionKit http://bit.ly/ 2fr34nw
I can explain the process of IVF **Higher tier only**	☺ ☺ ☹	☺ ☺ ☹	☺ ☺ ☹		
I can evaluate the positive and negative effects of IVF **Higher tier only**	☺ ☺ ☹	☺ ☺ ☹	☺ ☺ ☹		
I can explain the role and regulation of thyroxine in the body **Higher tier only**	☺ ☺ ☹	☺ ☺ ☹	☺ ☺ ☹		
I can explain the role and regulation of adrenaline in the body **Higher tier only**	☺ ☺ ☹	☺ ☺ ☹	☺ ☺ ☹		

I can explain what happens in phototropism **Biology only**	☺ ☺ ☹	☺ ☺ ☹	☺ ☺ ☹		TuitionKit http://bit.ly/ 2jxILt1
I can explain what happens in gravitropism or geotropism **Biology only**	☺ ☺ ☹	☺ ☺ ☹	☺ ☺ ☹	https://youtu.be/ 57IXUG0CHSQ	
I can explain the role and mechanism of gibberellins **Biology only**	☺ ☺ ☹	☺ ☺ ☹	☺ ☺ ☹		TuitionKit http://bit.ly/ 2x4pp4d
I can explain the role and mechanism of ethene **Biology only**	☺ ☺ ☹	☺ ☺ ☹	☺ ☺ ☹		
I can explain the role and mechanism of auxins **Biology only** **Higher tier only**	☺ ☺ ☹	☺ ☺ ☹	☺ ☺ ☹		

This video is fully supported by a video tutorial; https://youtu.be/EMf0FbJI9BU

1. Define homoeostasis.
2. What does the brain do in homeostasis?
3. What does central nervous system do in homeostasis?
4. What is the endocrine system?
5. Where is the pituitary gland?
6. Where is the pancreas?
7. Where is the thyroid?
8. Where is the adrenal gland?
9. Where are the ovaries?
10. Where are the testis?
11. How is blood glucose monitored?
12. What happens when blood glucose is too high?
13. What is the menstrual cycle?
14. What is ovulation?
15. What is testosterone?
16. What is contraception?

Higher tier only

17. What happens when blood glucose is too low?
18. What is a negative feedback loop?
19. What is FSH?
20. What is LH?
21. What is oestrogen?
22. Where is FSH produced?
23. Where does FSH act?
24. Where is LH produced?
25. Where does LH act?
26. Where is oestrogen produced?
27. Where does oestrogen act?
28. What is IVF?
29. Give two positives about IVF?
30. Give two negatives about IVF?
31. What is thyroxine?
32. Where is thyroxine produced?
33. Where does thyroxine act?
34. What is adrenaline?

35. Where is adrenaline produced?

36. Where does adrenaline act?

Biology Only

37. Label these different parts of the brain.

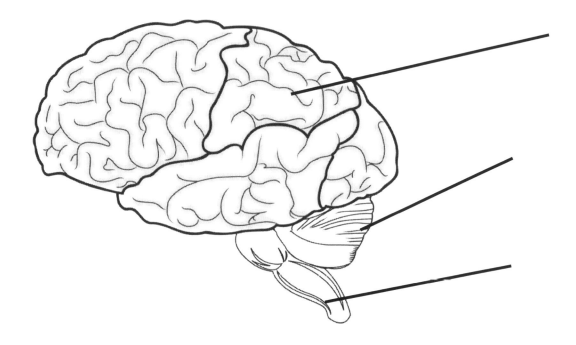

38. Label these different parts of the eye.

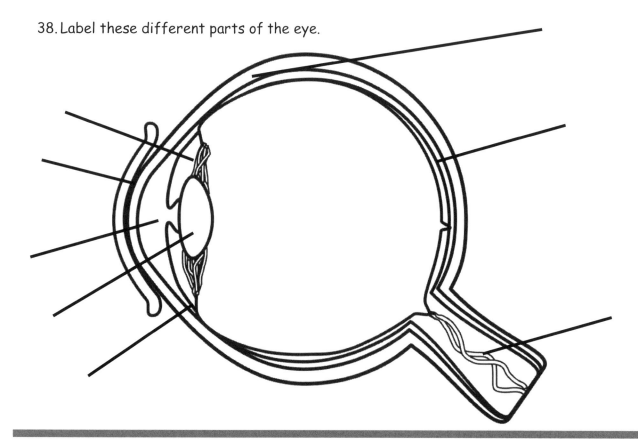

39. What is short-sightedness?
40. What is long-sightedness?
41. How can short-sightedness be corrected?
42. How can long-sightedness be corrected?
43. What is osmosis?
44. How does water leave the body?
45. How does water get into the body?
46. What happens to cells if they lose too much water?
47. What happens to cells if there is too much water?
48. What do the kidneys do?
49. What is the treatment for kidney failure?
50. What is phototropism?
51. What is geotropism?
52. What is the role of gibberellins?
53. What does ADH stand for?
54. What does ADHD do?

6 – Inheritance, variation and evolution

Knowledge Checklist

Whole topic summary video https://youtu.be/npl10a6p8jQ in only 33 minutes!!

Specification statement These are the bits the exam board wants you to know, make sure you can do all of these…	Self-assessment			Bits to help if you don't understand	
	First review 4-7 months before exam	Second review 1-2 months before exam	Final review Week before exam	Primrose Kitten	Other places
I can describe the differences in the end result of mitosis and meiosis	☺ ☐ ☹	☺ ☐ ☹	☺ ☐ ☹	https://youtu.be/ pi6sbTc4wBo	TuitionKit http://bit.ly/ 2f2e2PA
I can recall the names of the male and female gametes in plants and animals	☺ ☐ ☹	☺ ☐ ☹	☺ ☐ ☹		
I can describe the process of meiosis	☺ ☐ ☹	☺ ☐ ☹	☺ ☐ ☹	https://youtu.be/ pi6sbTc4wBo	TuitionKit http://bit.ly/ 2f2e2PA
I can describe the process of asexual reproduction	☺ ☐ ☹	☺ ☐ ☹	☺ ☐ ☹		
I can describe the advantages and disadvantages of sexual and asexual reproduction **Biology only**	☺ ☐ ☹	☺ ☐ ☹	☺ ☐ ☹		TuitionKit http://bit.ly/ 2f21ojx
I can describe the structure of DNA	☺ ☐ ☹	☺ ☐ ☹	☺ ☐ ☹	https://youtu.be/ erZB_EhuKbA	
I can describe the structure of a chromosome	☺ ☐ ☹	☺ ☐ ☹	☺ ☐ ☹		
I can define the term gene	☺ ☐ ☹	☺ ☐ ☹	☺ ☐ ☹		
I can define the term genome	☺ ☐ ☹	☺ ☐ ☹	☺ ☐ ☹		
I can describe the structure of DNA including the nucleotide, sugar and phosphate groups **Biology only**	☺ ☐ ☹	☺ ☐ ☹	☺ ☐ ☹	https://youtu.be/ erZB_EhuKbA	

I can recall the different bases in DNA **Biology only**	☺ ☺ ☹	☺ ☺ ☹	☺ ☺ ☹		
I can describe how different sequences of DNA code for amino acids **Biology only**	☺ ☺ ☹	☺ ☺ ☹	☺ ☺ ☹		
I can describe the process of protein synthesis **Biology only** **Higher tier only**	☺ ☺ ☹	☺ ☺ ☹	☺ ☺ ☹		
I can describe how variations in DNA can affect the protein being made **Biology only** **Higher tier only**	☺ ☺ ☹	☺ ☺ ☹	☺ ☺ ☹		
I can recall that the bases C and G match up and the bases A and T match up **Biology only** **Higher tier only**	☺ ☺ ☹	☺ ☺ ☹	☺ ☺ ☹		
I can describe the process of protein synthesis **Biology only** **Higher tier only**	☺ ☺ ☹	☺ ☺ ☹	☺ ☺ ☹		
I can describe the process of protein folding **Biology only** **Higher tier only**	☺ ☺ ☹	☺ ☺ ☹	☺ ☺ ☹		
I can describe the effect a mutation can have on a protein **Biology only** **Higher tier only**	☺ ☺ ☹	☺ ☺ ☹	☺ ☺ ☹		
I can describe the effect a mutation can have on an enzyme **Biology only** **Higher tier only**	☺ ☺ ☹	☺ ☺ ☹	☺ ☺ ☹		
I can explain non-coding DNA **Biology only** **Higher tier only**	☺ ☺ ☹	☺ ☺ ☹	☺ ☺ ☹		
I can define the term gamete	☺ ☺ ☹	☺ ☺ ☹	☺ ☺ ☹		
I can define the term chromosome	☺ ☺ ☹	☺ ☺ ☹	☺ ☺ ☹		

I can define the term gene	☺ ☺ ☹	☺ ☺ ☹	☺ ☺ ☹		
I can define the term allele	☺ ☺ ☹	☺ ☺ ☹	☺ ☺ ☹		
I can define the term dominant	☺ ☺ ☹	☺ ☺ ☹	☺ ☺ ☹		
I can define the term recessive	☺ ☺ ☹	☺ ☺ ☹	☺ ☺ ☹		
I can define the term homozygous	☺ ☺ ☹	☺ ☺ ☹	☺ ☺ ☹		
I can define the term heterozygous	☺ ☺ ☹	☺ ☺ ☹	☺ ☺ ☹		
I can define the term genotype	☺ ☺ ☹	☺ ☺ ☹	☺ ☺ ☹		
I can define the term phenotype	☺ ☺ ☹	☺ ☺ ☹	☺ ☺ ☹		
I can explain how characteristic can be controlled by genes	☺ ☺ ☹	☺ ☺ ☹	☺ ☺ ☹		
I can predict the results of a genetic cross by completing a Punnett square diagram	☺ ☺ ☹	☺ ☺ ☹	☺ ☺ ☹	https://youtu.be/ gWaNm1eOIH0	
I can describe the phenotype and genotype of a person with polydactyly	☺ ☺ ☹	☺ ☺ ☹	☺ ☺ ☹		
I can describe the phenotype and genotype of a person with cystic fibrosis	☺ ☺ ☹	☺ ☺ ☹	☺ ☺ ☹		
I can make an informed judgement about embryo screening	☺ ☺ ☹	☺ ☺ ☹	☺ ☺ ☹		
I can recall the number of pairs of chromosomes in a human body cell	☺ ☺ ☹	☺ ☺ ☹	☺ ☺ ☹		
I can recall that sex is determine by the X and Y chromosomes	☺ ☺ ☹	☺ ☺ ☹	☺ ☺ ☹		
I can describe how phenotype can be influenced by genes and the environment	☺ ☺ ☹	☺ ☺ ☹	☺ ☺ ☹		
I can recall that difference in a population in variation	☺ ☺ ☹	☺ ☺ ☹	☺ ☺ ☹		
I can describe the factors that affect variation within a population	☺ ☺ ☹	☺ ☺ ☹	☺ ☺ ☹		
I can recall that mutations continuously occur	☺ ☺ ☹	☺ ☺ ☹	☺ ☺ ☹		
I can define evolution	☺ ☺ ☹	☺ ☺ ☹	☺ ☺ ☹		TuitionKit http://bit.ly/ 2h90Clx

I can describe the theory of evolution	☺ ☺ ☹	☺ ☺ ☹	☺ ☺ ☹		
I can explain natural selection	☺ ☺ ☹	☺ ☺ ☹	☺ ☺ ☹		
I can explain speciation	☺ ☺ ☹	☺ ☺ ☹	☺ ☺ ☹		
I can describe the impact of selective breading	☺ ☺ ☹	☺ ☺ ☹	☺ ☺ ☹		
I can define the term genetic engineering	☺ ☺ ☹	☺ ☺ ☹	☺ ☺ ☹		
I can describe the use of genetic engineering in plants	☺ ☺ ☹	☺ ☺ ☹	☺ ☺ ☹		
I can describe the use of genetically engineered bacteria to produce insulin.	☺ ☺ ☹	☺ ☺ ☹	☺ ☺ ☹		
I can evaluate the advantages and disadvantages of genetic engineering in agriculture	☺ ☺ ☹	☺ ☺ ☹	☺ ☺ ☹		
I can describe the process of producing a genetically modified crop	☺ ☺ ☹	☺ ☺ ☹	☺ ☺ ☹		
I can explain the potential for genetic modification to treat inherited disorders	☺ ☺ ☹	☺ ☺ ☹	☺ ☺ ☹		
I can explain the process of producing a genetically modified crop **Higher tier only**	☺ ☺ ☹	☺ ☺ ☹	☺ ☺ ☹		
I can describe the process of cloning via cuttings **Biology only**	☺ ☺ ☹	☺ ☺ ☹	☺ ☺ ☹		
I can describe the process of cloning via tissue culture **Biology only**	☺ ☺ ☹	☺ ☺ ☹	☺ ☺ ☹		
I can describe the process of cloning via embryo transplant **Biology only**	☺ ☺ ☹	☺ ☺ ☹	☺ ☺ ☹		
I can describe the process of cloning via adult cell cloning **Biology only**	☺ ☺ ☹	☺ ☺ ☹	☺ ☺ ☹		
I can explain how Darwin came to propose the theory of evolution **Biology only**	☺ ☺ ☹	☺ ☺ ☹	☺ ☺ ☹		

I can explain the theory of evolution **Biology only**	☺ ☺ ☹	☺ ☺ ☹	☺ ☺ ☹		TuitionKit http://bit.ly/2h90Clx
I can discuss the controversy around Darwin's ideas when they were published **Biology only**	☺ ☺ ☹	☺ ☺ ☹	☺ ☺ ☹		
I can discuss other theories of evolution, such as Lamarck's ideas **Biology only**	☺ ☺ ☹	☺ ☺ ☹	☺ ☺ ☹		
I can define the term speciation **Biology only**	☺ ☺ ☹	☺ ☺ ☹	☺ ☺ ☹		
I can describe Wallace's theory of evolution **Biology only**	☺ ☺ ☹	☺ ☺ ☹	☺ ☺ ☹		
I can describe the steps that lead to a new species **Biology only**	☺ ☺ ☹	☺ ☺ ☹	☺ ☺ ☹		
I can describe the work that Mendel did **Biology only**	☺ ☺ ☹	☺ ☺ ☹	☺ ☺ ☹		
I can explain the evidence for evolution	☺ ☺ ☹	☺ ☺ ☹	☺ ☺ ☹		
I can describe how fossils arise	☺ ☺ ☹	☺ ☺ ☹	☺ ☺ ☹		TuitionKit http://bit.ly/2xb1tLU
I can explain why not all organism leave fossils	☺ ☺ ☹	☺ ☺ ☹	☺ ☺ ☹		
I can describe what fossils teach us	☺ ☺ ☹	☺ ☺ ☹	☺ ☺ ☹		
I can use an evolutionary tree	☺ ☺ ☹	☺ ☺ ☹	☺ ☺ ☹	https://youtu.be/rTHVPh1kO5o	https://phet.colorado.edu/en/simulation/natural-selection
I can define the term extinction	☺ ☺ ☹	☺ ☺ ☹	☺ ☺ ☹		
I can describe the factors that lead to an extinction	☺ ☺ ☹	☺ ☺ ☹	☺ ☺ ☹		
I can explain why bacteria can evolve quickly	☺ ☺ ☹	☺ ☺ ☹	☺ ☺ ☹		

I can describe why antibiotic resistance could arise	☺ ☺ ☹	☺ ☺ ☹	☺ ☺ ☹		
I can describe the effect of MRSA (and other antibiotic resistance strains of bacteria) have on humans	☺ ☺ ☹	☺ ☺ ☹	☺ ☺ ☹		
I can describe why the development of new antibiotics is slow	☺ ☺ ☹	☺ ☺ ☹	☺ ☺ ☹		
I can describe the system of classification that Linnaeus developed	☺ ☺ ☹	☺ ☺ ☹	☺ ☺ ☹		Total Learn http://bit.ly/ 2zJwh5D
I can determine an organism's genus and species from a tree	☺ ☺ ☹	☺ ☺ ☹	☺ ☺ ☹		
I can describe how developments in biology can impact on classification	☺ ☺ ☹	☺ ☺ ☹	☺ ☺ ☹		
I can describe the 'three domain system' of archaea, bacteria and eukaryote	☺ ☺ ☹	☺ ☺ ☹	☺ ☺ ☹		

This worksheet is fully supported by a video tutorial; https://youtu.be/IL-dUnKmksY

1. How many cells are produced at the end of mitosis?
2. How many cells are produced at the end of meiosis?
3. What are the male gametes in plants?
4. What the female gametes in plants?
5. What are the male gametes in animals?
6. What are the female gametes in animals?
7. What is the basic structure of DNA?
8. Define gene.
9. Define genome.
10. Define gamete.
11. Define chromosome.
12. Define allele.
13. Define dominant.
14. Define recessive.
15. Define homozygous.
16. Define heterozygous.
17. Defined genotype.
18. Define phenotype.
19. What is polydactyly?
20. Is polydactyly dominant or recessive?
21. What is cystic fibrosis?
22. Is cystic fibrosis dominant or recessive?
23. How many pairs of chromosomes in human body cell?
24. What sex is XX?
25. What sex is XY?
26. Define evolution.
27. Define natural selection.
28. Despite the speciation.
29. What evidence is there for evolution?
30. How do fossils arise?
31. Define extinction.
32. What things lead to extinction?
33. Why can bacteria evolve quickly?
34. What is MRSA?
35. Why is the development of antibiotics so slow?

Biology only

36. What are the advantages of sexual reproduction?
37. With the disadvantages of sexual production?
38. What are the advantages of asexual reproduction?
39. What are the disadvantages of asexual reproduction?
40. What is the basic structure of DNA?
41. What are the bases in DNA?
42. How does DNA code for amino acids?
43. How do amino acids produce proteins?
44. How do variations in DNA affect the protein being made?
45. What affect might a mutation have on an enzyme?
46. What was Darwin's theory?
47. What was the controversy behind Darwin's theory?
48. What was the Lamarck's theory?

7 – Ecology

Knowledge Checklist

Whole topic summary video https://youtu.be/SKDn90HK98Q

Specification statement These are the bits the exam board wants you to know, make sure you can do all of these…	Self-assessment			Bits to help if you don't understand	
	First review 4-7 months before exam	Second review 1-2 months before exam	Final review Week before exam	Primrose Kitten	Other places
I can describe the levels of organisation in an ecosystem	☺ ☺ ☹	☺ ☺ ☹	☺ ☺ ☹		
I can define the term community	☺ ☺ ☹	☺ ☺ ☹	☺ ☺ ☹		
I can describe interdependence in a community	☺ ☺ ☹	☺ ☺ ☹	☺ ☺ ☹		
I can describe competition in a community	☺ ☺ ☹	☺ ☺ ☹	☺ ☺ ☹		
I can define the term ecosystem	☺ ☺ ☹	☺ ☺ ☹	☺ ☺ ☹		
I can describe what an organism needs to survive and reproduce	☺ ☺ ☹	☺ ☺ ☹	☺ ☺ ☹		
I can describe what different organisms compete for	☺ ☺ ☹	☺ ☺ ☹	☺ ☺ ☹		
I can define the term abiotic factor	☺ ☺ ☹	☺ ☺ ☹	☺ ☺ ☹		
I can recall a list of abiotic factors including; light intensity, temperature, water levels, pH, ion content, wind, carbon dioxide and oxygen levels	☺ ☺ ☹	☺ ☺ ☹	☺ ☺ ☹		
I can describe how a change in abiotic factors could affect a community	☺ ☺ ☹	☺ ☺ ☹	☺ ☺ ☹		
I can define the term biotic factor	☺ ☺ ☹	☺ ☺ ☹	☺ ☺ ☹		

I can describe how a change in biotic factors could affect a community	☺ 😐 ☹	☺ 😐 ☹	☺ 😐 ☹		
I can recall a list of biotic factors including; food, predators and pathogens.	☺ 😐 ☹	☺ 😐 ☹	☺ 😐 ☹		
I can define the term adaptation	☺ 😐 ☹	☺ 😐 ☹	☺ 😐 ☹		
I can describe why animals and plants need adaptations	☺ 😐 ☹	☺ 😐 ☹	☺ 😐 ☹		
I can define the term extremophile	☺ 😐 ☹	☺ 😐 ☹	☺ 😐 ☹		
I can give examples of plant and animal adaptations	☺ 😐 ☹	☺ 😐 ☹	☺ 😐 ☹		
I can describe where the biomass on Earth comes from	☺ 😐 ☹	☺ 😐 ☹	☺ 😐 ☹		
I can draw a food chain	☺ 😐 ☹	☺ 😐 ☹	☺ 😐 ☹		
I can explain where the energy is a food chain comes from	☺ 😐 ☹	☺ 😐 ☹	☺ 😐 ☹		
I can describe how to use a quadrate	☺ 😐 ☹	☺ 😐 ☹	☺ 😐 ☹		
I can describe how to use a transect	☺ 😐 ☹	☺ 😐 ☹	☺ 😐 ☹		
I can describe how to determine the abundance and distribution of species in an ecosystem	☺ 😐 ☹	☺ 😐 ☹	☺ 😐 ☹		
I can define the term producer	☺ 😐 ☹	☺ 😐 ☹	☺ 😐 ☹		
I can define the term primary consumer	☺ 😐 ☹	☺ 😐 ☹	☺ 😐 ☹		
I can define the term secondary consumer	☺ 😐 ☹	☺ 😐 ☹	☺ 😐 ☹		
I can define the term tertiary consumer	☺ 😐 ☹	☺ 😐 ☹	☺ 😐 ☹		
I can define the term prey	☺ 😐 ☹	☺ 😐 ☹	☺ 😐 ☹		
I can describe the carbon cycle	☺ 😐 ☹	☺ 😐 ☹	☺ 😐 ☹	https://youtu.be/ Uoqp7QjWW-M	
I can describe the water cycle	☺ 😐 ☹	☺ 😐 ☹	☺ 😐 ☹	https://youtu.be/ Dt25c1VODSE	
I can recall that materials are recycled through biotic and abiotic part of an ecosystem and provide building blocks for the future.	☺ 😐 ☹	☺ 😐 ☹	☺ 😐 ☹		

I can describe the role of microorganisms in cycling materials	☺ ☺ ☹	☺ ☺ ☹	☺ ☺ ☹	
I can define the terms decay and decomposition **Biology only**	☺ ☺ ☹	☺ ☺ ☹	☺ ☺ ☹	
I can describe how differences in temperature can affect the rate of decomposition **Biology only**	☺ ☺ ☹	☺ ☺ ☹	☺ ☺ ☹	
I can describe how differences in oxygen can affect the rate of decomposition **Biology only**	☺ ☺ ☹	☺ ☺ ☹	☺ ☺ ☹	
I can describe how differences in water can affect the rate of decomposition **Biology only**	☺ ☺ ☹	☺ ☺ ☹	☺ ☺ ☹	
I can explain why gardeners compost **Biology only**	☺ ☺ ☹	☺ ☺ ☹	☺ ☺ ☹	
I can describe how decay can lead to the production of biogas **Biology only**	☺ ☺ ☹	☺ ☺ ☹	☺ ☺ ☹	
I can evaluate the impact of environmental changes (including temperature, water and the atmosphere) on the distribution of a species **Biology only**	☺ ☺ ☹	☺ ☺ ☹	☺ ☺ ☹		TuitionKit http://bit.ly/2yfsyvO
I can define the term biodiversity	☺ ☺ ☹	☺ ☺ ☹	☺ ☺ ☹		TuitionKit http://bit.ly/2xpTFpN
I can explain the needs for biodiversity	☺ ☺ ☹	☺ ☺ ☹	☺ ☺ ☹	
I can describe the impact that humans have on biodiversity	☺ ☺ ☹	☺ ☺ ☹	☺ ☺ ☹	
I can explain the rise in pollution	☺ ☺ ☹	☺ ☺ ☹	☺ ☺ ☹	
I can describe the range of different sources of pollution, including; in water, in air and in land	☺ ☺ ☹	☺ ☺ ☹	☺ ☺ ☹		TuitionKit http://bit.ly/2f2cbdE
I can describe the effect that pollution has of plants and animals	☺ ☺ ☹	☺ ☺ ☹	☺ ☺ ☹	

I can describe the impact that humans have on land use and the effect this has on plant and animal life	☺ ☺ ☹	☺ ☺ ☹	☺ ☺ ☹		TuitionKit http://bit.ly/ 2h6qsdE
I can describe the impact of the destruction of peat bogs	☺ ☺ ☹	☺ ☺ ☹	☺ ☺ ☹	https://youtu.be/u pdz4Xbiia4	
I can describe the impact of deforestation	☺ ☺ ☹	☺ ☺ ☹	☺ ☺ ☹		TuitionKit http://bit.ly/ 2h71jzj
I can recall the reasons for deforestation	☺ ☺ ☹	☺ ☺ ☹	☺ ☺ ☹		
I can describe the biological consequences of global warming	☺ ☺ ☹	☺ ☺ ☹	☺ ☺ ☹		TuitionKit http://bit.ly/ 2xaBX9x
I can recall the gases that contribute to global warming	☺ ☺ ☹	☺ ☺ ☹	☺ ☺ ☹	https://youtu.be/ y5PZ1RN5mt0	
I can describe how humans can have a positive and a negative impact on biodiversity	☺ ☺ ☹	☺ ☺ ☹	☺ ☺ ☹		
I can discuss the range of programmes that aim to reduce the negative effect of humans on biodiversity	☺ ☺ ☹	☺ ☺ ☹	☺ ☺ ☹		
I can define the term trophic level **Biology only**	☺ ☺ ☹	☺ ☺ ☹	☺ ☺ ☹		
I can use number to represent trophic levels **Biology only**	☺ ☺ ☹	☺ ☺ ☹	☺ ☺ ☹		
I can describe the differences between the trophic levels **Biology only**	☺ ☺ ☹	☺ ☺ ☹	☺ ☺ ☹		
I can describe the role of decomposers **Biology only**	☺ ☺ ☹	☺ ☺ ☹	☺ ☺ ☹		
I can construct a pyramid of biomass **Biology only**	☺ ☺ ☹	☺ ☺ ☹	☺ ☺ ☹		
I can interpret a pyramid of biomass **Biology only**	☺ ☺ ☹	☺ ☺ ☹	☺ ☺ ☹		
I can explain how energy is lost between trophic levels **Biology only**	☺ ☺ ☹	☺ ☺ ☹	☺ ☺ ☹		

I can recall that roughly 10% of the energy is transferred to the next trophic level **Biology only**	☺ ☻ ☹	☺ ☻ ☹	☺ ☻ ☹		
I can define the term food security **Biology only**	☺ ☻ ☹	☺ ☻ ☹	☺ ☻ ☹		TuitionKit http://bit.ly/ 2y5FraQ
I can explain the factors affecting food security **Biology only**	☺ ☻ ☹	☺ ☻ ☹	☺ ☻ ☹		
I can describe the need to find sustainable methods for food production **Biology only**	☺ ☻ ☹	☺ ☻ ☹	☺ ☻ ☹		
I can describe ways to improve the efficiency of food production **Biology only**	☺ ☻ ☹	☺ ☻ ☹	☺ ☻ ☹		
I can describe why some farmers use high protein foods **Biology only**	☺ ☻ ☹	☺ ☻ ☹	☺ ☻ ☹		TuitionKit http://bit.ly/ 2x4Yq8I
I can describe the need for sustainable fisheries **Biology only**	☺ ☻ ☹	☺ ☻ ☹	☺ ☻ ☹		TuitionKit http://bit.ly/ 2yf2l0f
I can explain the methods used to keep fish stocks at a sustainable level **Biology only**	☺ ☻ ☹	☺ ☻ ☹	☺ ☻ ☹		
I can describe the advances in biotechnology as they apply to agriculture **Biology only**	☺ ☻ ☹	☺ ☻ ☹	☺ ☻ ☹		TuitionKit http://bit.ly/ 2xHnALf
I can describe that microorganism can be cultured for food **Biology only**	☺ ☻ ☹	☺ ☻ ☹	☺ ☻ ☹		

This worksheet is fully supported by a video tutorial; https://youtu.be/NorHSgd7Yyc

1. Define ecosystem.
2. Define community.
3. Define interdependence.
4. Define competition.
5. What does an organism need to survive and reproduce?
6. What do different organisms compete for?
7. Define abiotic factor.
8. List eight abiotic factors.
9. How can a change in abiotic factors affect the community?
10. Define biotic factors.
11. How can a change in biotic factors affect the community?
12. List three biotic factors.
13. Define adaptation.
14. Why do animals need to adapt?
15. Define extremophile.
16. Give an example of a plant adaptation.
17. Give an example of an animal adaptation.
18. Where does energy in a food chain come from?
19. Define the term producer.
20. Define the term primary consumer.
21. Define the term secondary consumer.
22. Define the term tertiary consumer.
23. Define the term prey.
24. Define the term biodiversity.
25. Why do we need biodiversity?
26. What is pollution?
27. What impact can pollution have on plants?
28. What impact can pollution have on animals?
29. What impact can humans have on land usage?
30. What is the impact of deforestation?
31. What are the reasons for deforestation?
32. What the consequences of global warming?
33. What gases contribute to global warming?

Biology only

34. Define the term decay.
35. Define the term decomposition.
36. How can temperature affect the rate of decomposition?
37. How can oxygen affect the rate of decomposition?
38. How can water affect the rate of decomposition?
39. How can decay lead to the production of biogas?
40. Define the term biodiversity.
41. What is the differences between trophic levels?
42. What is the role of a decomposer?
43. How is energy lost between trophic levels?
44. What is food security?
45. How can we increase efficiency of the production?
46. How can microorganisms be cultured for food?

Biology Paper 2 Checklist – What to do before the exam!

Watched the whole topic video   https://youtu.be/Uqti-xPnT-8   ☐

Answered the quick-fire questions   ☐

Looked at the practical videos   ☐

Learnt the keywords   ☐

Filled in the crosswords   ☐

Crosswords

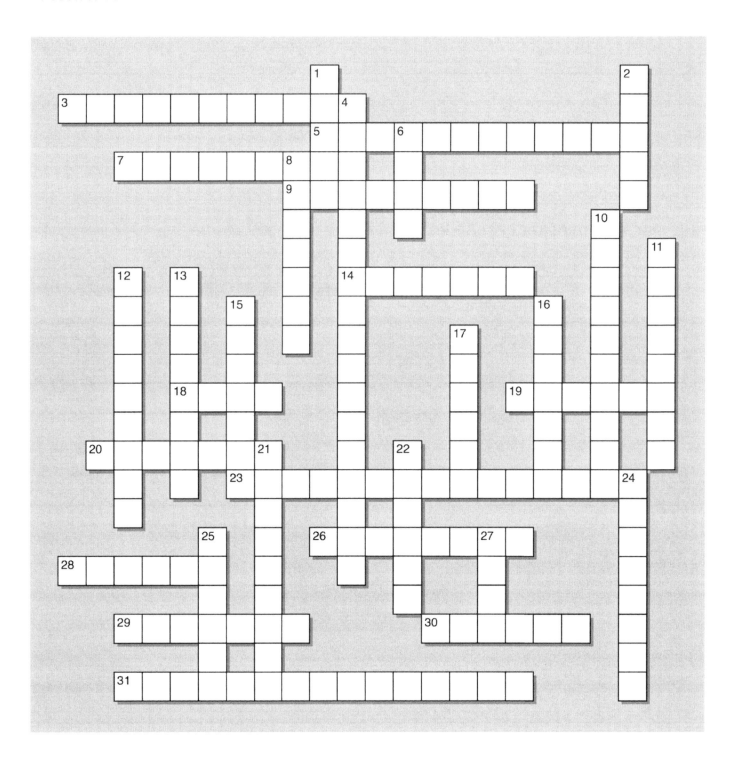

Across

3) lump of cells that are not invading the body

5) carries oxygen around the body, has no nucleus

7) small fragments of blood cells that help clotting

9) Thinned walled blood vessels that allow diffusion of gases and nutrients

14) Enzyme that breaks carbohydrates into sugars

18) Small structural unit that contains a nucleus and cytoplasm

19) fluid part of the blood

20) one copy of each chromosome

23) organ system that absorbs nutrients from food

26) Major blood vessel that carries deoxygenated blood back to the heart

28) state of mental and physical wellbeing

29) Type of cell division that ends in two identical daughter cells

30) uncontrolled cell division within the body

31) Blood vessel that carries deoxygenated blood from the heart to the lungs

Down

1) Major blood vessel that carries oxygenated blood away from the heart

2) carries water around a plant

4) organ system that moves oxygen around the body

6) Produced by the liver, neutralizes stomach acid and emulsifies fats

8) the study of organism within and environment

10) long stretch of DNA

11) Enzyme that breaks proteins into amino acids

12) jelly like substance within a cell

13) a type of cell that can differentiate into any other type of cell

15) two copies of each chromosome

16) control centre of the cell, that holds the DNA

17) Biological catalyst

21) movement of ions or gasses from a high concentration to a low concentration

22) Enzyme that breaks fats into fatty acids and glycerol

24) plant tissue found at growing tips

25) carries ions around a plant

27) Blood vessels that have values and carries deoxygenated blood back to the heart

Biology Crossword 2

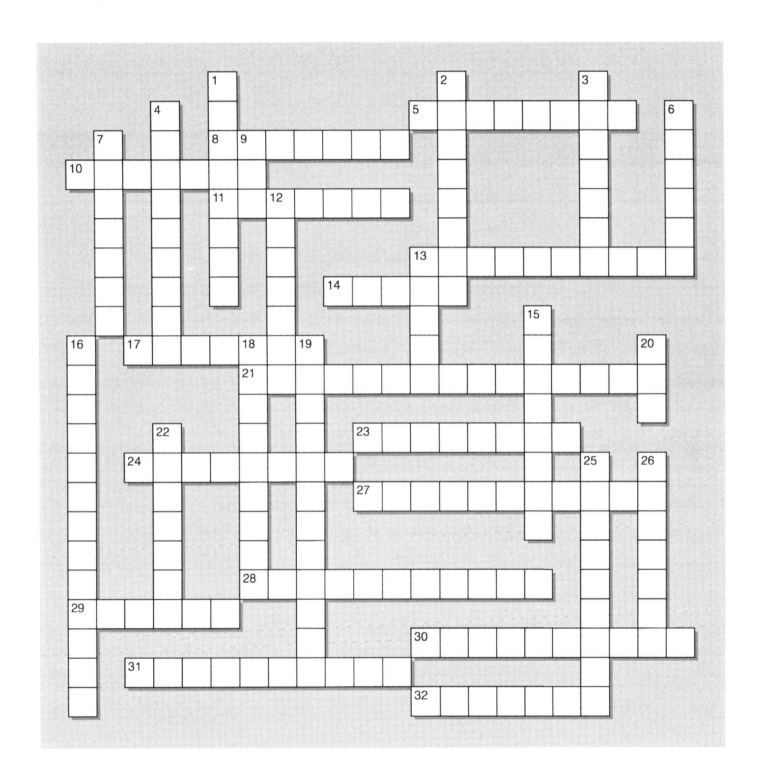

Across

5) medication that contain inactive or dead virus to help develop immunity

8) large gland in the neck which releases hormone

10) braches of the trachea

11) in women, these store the eggs

13) can be combined with glycerol to make lipids

14) DNA within a protein coat that divides by invading cells, the resulting cell death causes illness in the host

17) parasite transmitted by mosquitoes

21) system that controls hormones and responses

23) inability of the bod to control blood glucose levels

24) long chains of amino acids, that carry out the majority of functions within the body

27) drugs that kill bacteria

28) green part of a plant

29) in men, these are responsible for the production of sperm

30) chemical process that occur to maintain life

31) arises after anaerobic respiration, needs oxygen to repay

32) viral infection causing fever and rash, most common in children

Down

1) causes illness

2) large gland behind the stomach which produces digestive enzymes

3) respiration with oxygen

4) bacteria that cause a sexual transmitted disease causing smelly discharge from the penis or vagina

6) stores of energy that can be broken down to form fatty acids and glycerol

7) long tube taking air down into the lungs

9) virus that interfere with your body's ability to fight disease

12) painkiller developed from willow bark

13) group that includes mushrooms and moulds, they live of decomposing material

15) can be combined with fatty acid to make lipids

16) process where plant absorb and lose water

18) nerve pathway including a sensory nerve a synapse and a motor nerve

19) large gland near the kidneys that releases hormone

20) virus affecting plants causing a mosaic pattern on leaves

22) tiny single celled organism that can cause illness

25) heart drug that comes from Foxglove plants

26) transport of water across a partially permeable membrane

Biology Crossword 3

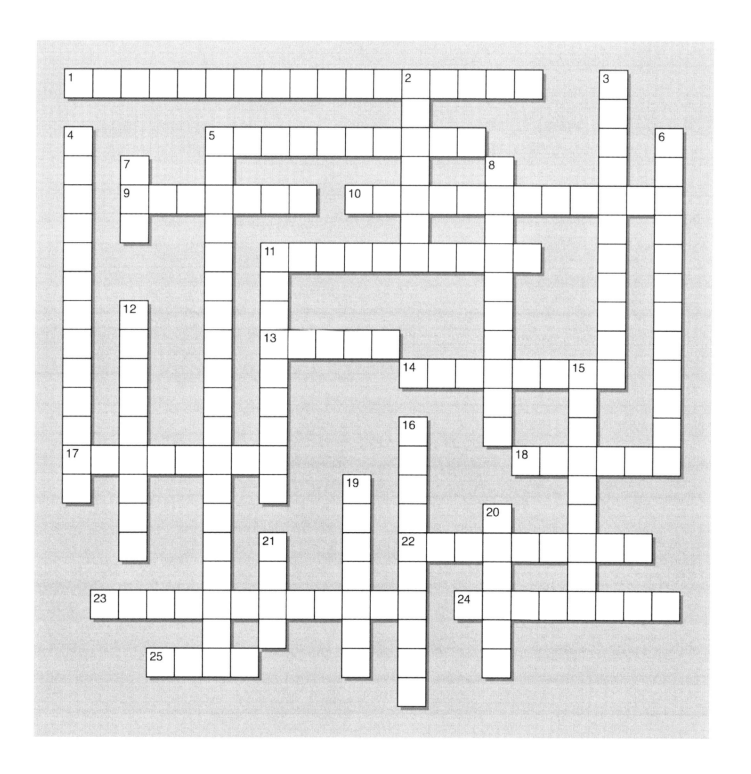

Across

1) breading of animals or plants for a particular characteristic

5) change in a species to suit the environment

9) sex cells

10) different copies of gene

11) no breading pair of a species exist

13) male sex cell

14) what genes are present

17) eat plants and animals

18) different version of gene

22) two identical copies of the gene are needed to be expressed

23) the range of different organism that live in an environment

24) only one copy of the gene is needed to be expressed

25) section of DNA, that controls a characteristic

Down

2) non-living factors that affect organism

3) the movement of carbon through the environment

4) mechanism to prevent pregnancy

5) reproduction with only one parent, resulting in identical offspring

6) hormone found predominantly in men

7) female sex cell

8) identical copies of gene

11) the organism and the habitat they live in

12) the organism that live in a particular environment

15) harmful substance in an environment

16) the movement of water through eh environment

19) hard parts of long dead organism

20) all of the genes in an organism

21) something that gets eaten

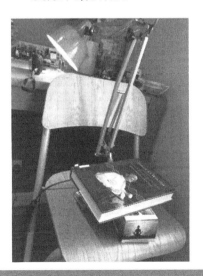

PATREON

Join my lovely, friendly community over at
https://www.patreon.com/PrimroseKitten

- Find out what happens behind the scenes
- Get a first look at new videos
- Get advanced copies of sheets and books
- Spread out your revision and get sent flash cards and predicted papers each month

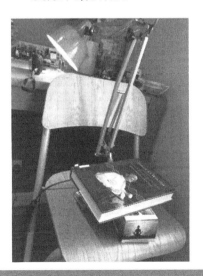

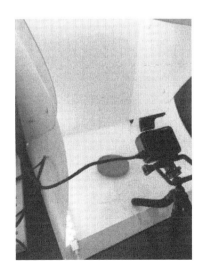

Chemistry

5 most common mistakes in a chemistry exam

1. Drawing the wrong number of bonds in organic chemistry
2. Being too wishy washy in colour changes
3. Putting numbers in the wrong place
4. Missing out (or adding in too many) capital letters
5. Keep numbers in your calculator memory to avoid rounding errors

Important tips

- When balancing equations, if you really, really can't work it out. Write 2 as the answer
- If you've forgotten the reaction conditions, write 'hot and a catalyst'

Topic Guide

Topic	First review	Second review	Third review
1 – Atomic Structure and the Periodic Table			
2 – Bonding, Structure and the Properties of Matter			
3 – Quantitative Chemistry			
4 – Chemical Changes			
5 – Energy Changes			
6 – The Rate and Extent of Chemical Change			
7 – Organic Chemistry			
8 – Chemical Analysis			
9 – Chemistry of the Atmosphere			
10 – Using Resources			

Topic	Quick fire questions	Whole topic video
C1 – Paper 1. Topic 1-5		https://youtu.be/esov5nKDJCk
C2 – Paper 2. Topics 6-10		
1 – Atomic Structure and the Periodic Table	https://youtu.be/mjlIPJ_cO18	https://youtu.be/bgyuXU97jaI
2 – Bonding, Structure and the Properties of Matter	https://youtu.be/9bbCFUyluWg	https://youtu.be/YpEQ-NWxKBc
3 – Quantitative Chemistry	https://youtu.be/8uqWdmIKd7c	https://youtu.be/eAibVvhmsK0
4 – Chemical Changes	https://youtu.be/7Nrma6vOA8I	https://youtu.be/KTmXEIiU_Go
5 – Energy Changes	https://youtu.be/PQtjfRolMAE	https://youtu.be/L7829UGifpM
6 – The Rate and Extent of Chemical Change	https://youtu.be/C-tHYZwisNs	https://youtu.be/7i90fiz9SmY
7 – Organic Chemistry	https://youtu.be/sE2DPOx48kE	https://youtu.be/ZeUNWY7YDAo
8 – Chemical Analysis	https://youtu.be/vMKAHdoc-g0	https://youtu.be/YyUQiUddBA4
9 – Chemistry of the Atmosphere	https://youtu.be/DznhhA2QHUg	https://youtu.be/gxCRsqXZzeU
10 – Using Resources	https://youtu.be/xBUXqfa2gHo	https://youtu.be/KyVf2bVLl08

Equation Sheet

Percentage yield = $\dfrac{\text{Actual yield}}{\text{Theoretical yield}}$

Atom Economy = $\dfrac{M_r \text{ of atoms in the required products}}{M_r \text{ of reactants}}$

Moles = $\dfrac{\text{mass}}{M_r}$

Concentration (mol/dm^3) = $\dfrac{\text{amount (mol)}}{\text{volume (dm}^3\text{)}}$

Formula of common acids and compounds

Hydrochloric acid	HCl
Sulphuric acid	H_2SO_4
Nitric acid	HNO_3
Water	H_2O
Carbon dioxide	CO_2
Oxygen gas	O_2
Hydrogen gas	H_2
Nitrogen gas	N_2

Reference table of common formulae

They won't give you these in the exam - so learn them!!!

Available as flashcards on my website

As a general rule, elements in group one form +1 ions, group 2 form +2 ions, group 6 form -2 ions and group 7 form -1 ions.

Positive		Negative	
Hydrogen	H^+	Fluoride	F^-
Lithium	Li^+	Chloride	Cl^-
Sodium	Na^+	Bromide	Br^-
Potassium	K^+	Iodide	I^-
Copper (I)	Cu^+	Hydroxide	OH^-
Silver	Ag^+	Nitrate	NO_3^-
Ammonium	NH_4^+	Nitrite	NO_2^-
		Hydrogencarbonate	HCO_3^-
Magnesium	Mg^{2+}	Hydrogensulfate	HSO_4^-
Barium	Ba^{2+}		
Strontium	Sr^{2+}	Sulfate	SO_4^{2-}
Calcium	Ca^{2+}	Carbonate	CO_3^{2-}
Iron (II)	Fe^{2+}	Sulfide	S^{2-}
Copper (II)	Cu^{2+}	Oxide	O^{2-}
Nickel (II)	Ni^{2+}		
Zinc	Zn^{2+}	Nitride	N^{3-}
Tin (II)	Sn^{2+}	Phosphate	PO_4^{3-}
Lead (II)	Pb^{2+}		
Chromium	Cr^{3+}		
Iron (III)	Fe^{3+}		
Aluminium	Al^{3+}		

The Reactivity Series

You need to learn the order and how to use it!

Element	Chemical symbol	Metal or non-metal	How it is found on the earth?	Method of extraction?
Potassium				
Lithium				
Calcium				
Magnesium				
Aluminium				
Carbon				
Zinc				
Iron				
Hydrogen				
Copper				
Silver				
Gold				
Platinum				

Required practical's

1. Making Salts
   -Copper Sulfate Crystals - Separating solids from a solution by filtering and crystallisation   https://youtu.be/ttsAmaNu4ao
   -Practical questions in an exam   https://youtu.be/BmaXoGTAmeA
2. Neutralisation (Chemistry only)
   -How to carry out a titration   https://youtu.be/MDWVrTW0nq8
   -How to read a burette   https://youtu.be/yVF6Gn7HmWk
   -Indicators for titrations - Methyl orange and phenolphthalein
                                    https://youtu.be/XPTnZnbXgDs
   -Titration Method.   https://youtu.be/2hv2hS6zdh0
3. Electrolysis
   -The electrolysis of sodium sulfate.   https://youtu.be/hcQHxKMpr60
   -The electrolysis of sodium chloride solution (brine).
                                    https://youtu.be/r0kbEj2PDEg
   -The electrolysis of copper (II) sulfate.   https://youtu.be/L_BjGKdM2Bk
   -The electrolysis of copper (II) chloride.   https://youtu.be/E6npZEyaASk
4. Temperature Changes
   -Temperature change of neutralization.   https://youtu.be/Bz0C9mmF2tw
5. Rates of Reaction
   -Measuring the rate of a reaction by collecting gas - Marble chips and hydrochloric acid   https://youtu.be/SXUWo-V-WgQ
   -Measuring the rate of a reaction by loss of mass
                                    https://youtu.be/0RUYNpdnALg
   -Measuring the rate of reaction by disappearing cross - Sodium thiosulfate and hydrochloric acid.   https://youtu.be/CwK4-_Xq2yI
6. Chromatography
   -Chromatography.   https://youtu.be/kxrjvLvbY28
   -Chromatography-Why do you need to use a pencil to draw the start line?
                                    https://youtu.be/4n9LzquhqdQ
7. Ion Identification (Chemistry only)
   -Flame tests for positive ions.   https://youtu.be/i3fEVB9VN0Y
   -Test for Positive Ions.   https://youtu.be/ESQYWh02Ykg
   -Test for Halide Ions.   https://youtu.be/XtQ4hHZzX2k
   -Test for Sulfate Ions.   https://youtu.be/k5qMGgmQDwo
   -Test for Carbonate Ions.   https://youtu.be/7AGBLbl7AHE
   - Anion and Cation Ion Identification Summary (Negative and Positive Ions) and Practice   https://youtu.be/LC4Nxd5dwEM
8. Water purification

Key Words

These are easy marks, but only if you know them!!

Acid	A solution that has a low pH due to the hydrogen ions
Activation energy	The energy needed to start reaction
Alkali	A solution that has a high pH due to hydroxide ions
Alkali metal	Highly reactive metals found on the left-hand side of the periodic table
Alkanes	Hydrocarbon containing only single bonds
Alkenes	Hydrocarbon containing double bonds
Alloy	Mixture of atoms that lead to distorted layers that cannot slide
Atom	Small part of matter, made up from a mixture of protons, neutrons and electrons
Atom economy	A way of determining how many of the reactant atoms made it into the desired product
Atomic number	The number of protons in an atom
Bioleaching	Mining low yield ores using bacteria
Boiling point	Point at which a liquid turns into a gas
Bromine water	Orange liquid that can be used to test for double bonds
Carbon footprint	The atom of carbon that is released into the atmosphere based on your daily activities
Catalyst	Something that speeds up a react of reaction without being use dup
Chromatography	Method of separating out mixtures
Combustion	Burning of a compound in oxygen
Compound	Two or more elements chemically bonded together
Covalent bonding	Sharing of electron between two non-metals
Cracking	Breaking a long hydrocarbon chain to short hydrocarbon chains
Crude oil	A mixture of different length hydrocarbon chains made from decomposing dead plant and animals
Desalination	Removal of salt from water
Diamond	Giant covalent compound where each carbon atom makes four bonds
Displacement	A type of reaction where one element replaces another in a compound
Electrolysis	Separating compounds using electricity
Electron	Found in the shells around the nucleus, has a charge of minus one and no mass
Element	Group of (or single) atoms that all have the same chemical characteristics, can be found on the periodic table
Endothermic	A reaction that takes in energy
Exothermic	A reaction that releases energy
Flammability	The tendency for a substance to catch fire
Formulation	Mixture of compounds

Fractional distillation	Separating out a mixture of different length hydrocarbon chains based upon boiling point
Gas	A state of matter where the atoms move atom in a fast and random matter, can be compressed and flow
Graphite	Giant covalent compound where each carbon atom makes three bonds
Greenhouse gas	Gas that traps infra-red radiation
Halogen	Highly reactive non-metals found on the right-hand side of the periodic table
Hydrocarbon	A compound that only has carbon and hydrogen in it
Ion	Atoms that has lost or gained electrons
Ionic bonding	Transfer of electrons between a metal and a non-metal
Liquid	A state of matter, where the atoms can move and flow but they cannot be compressed
Mass number	the number of protons and neutrons in an atom
Melting point	Point at which a solid turns into a liquid
Metal	On the left-hand side of the periodic table, form positive ions
Mixture	Lots of different elements that may or may not be chemically bonded together
Mole	The molecular mass in grams
Neutralization	Mixing of an acid and an alkali to give a pH of 7
Neutron	Found in the nucleus of atoms, has no charge and a mass of one
Nobel gas	Unreactive gases found on the right of the periodic table
Non-metal	On the right-hand side of the periodic table, form negative ions
Nucleus	In the centre of atoms, contains the protons and the neutrons
Oxidation	Loss of electrons
Percentage yield	A way of determining how much yield you get from a reaction
Periodic table	A way of sorting out the elements
pH	How acid or alkali a solution is
Phytomining	Mining low yield ores using plants
Portable water	Water that is safe to drink
Proton	Found in the nucleus of atoms, has a charge of plus one and a mass of one
Reactivity series	List of metals in order of reactivity
Reduction	Gain of electrons
Reversible reaction	A reaction that can go in either direction
Solid	A state of matter, where the atoms vibrate around a fixed position
Titration	Method for determining concentration of solution
Transition metal	Group of metal that are in the middle of the periodic table, form colour compounds and can be used as catalysts
Viscosity	How easily pourable something is

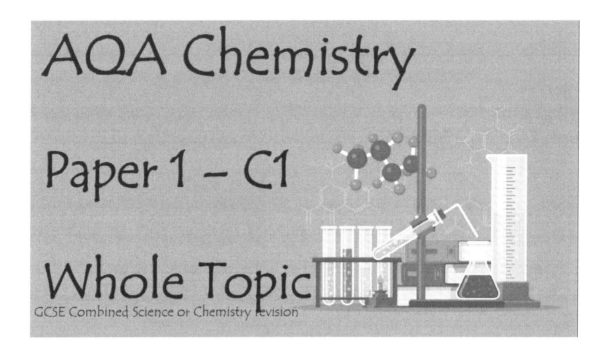

The whole of chemistry paper 1 in only 72 minutes

https://youtu.be/MpQ-3YAwNhI

The whole of chemistry paper 2 in only 49 minutes

https://youtu.be/_HJu8WTtZJU

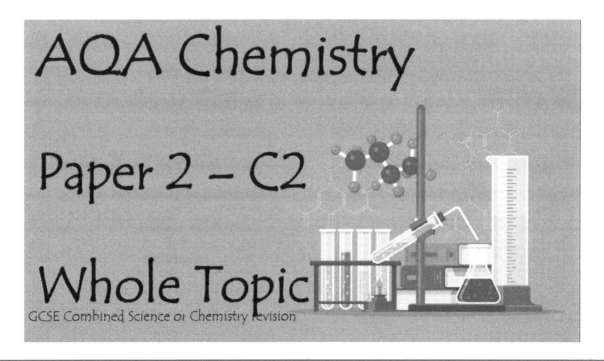

1 – Atomic Structure and the Periodic Table

Knowledge Checklist

Whole topic summary https://youtu.be/bgyuXU97jaI in only 21 minutes!!

Specification statement These are the bits the exam board wants you to know, make sure you can do all of these…	Self-assessment			Bits to help if you don't understand	
	First review 4-7 months before exam	Second review 1-2 months before exam	Final review Week before exam	Primrose Kitten	Other places
I can recall that all substances are made from atoms	☺ ☺ ☹	☺ ☺ ☹	☺ ☺ ☹		TuitionKit http://bit.ly/ 2h7Gx2F
I can recall the that periodic table shows the range of elements that are known to exist	☺ ☺ ☹	☺ ☺ ☹	☺ ☺ ☹	https://youtu.be/ GhOkzDuHIDc	
I can interpret the symbols on the periodic table and use them to identify elements	☺ ☺ ☹	☺ ☺ ☹	☺ ☺ ☹	https://youtu.be/ PdujMRxEbn4	
I can define the term compound	☺ ☺ ☹	☺ ☺ ☹	☺ ☺ ☹	https://youtu.be/ tguhuiq9tVs	TuitionKit http://bit.ly/ 2h7Gx2F
I can describe the structure of an atom	☺ ☺ ☹	☺ ☺ ☹	☺ ☺ ☹		TuitionKit http://bit.ly/ 2h7Gx2F
I can recall the relative size of an atom and a nucleus	☺ ☺ ☹	☺ ☺ ☹	☺ ☺ ☹		
I can recall the relative masses of the three subatomic particles	☺ ☺ ☹	☺ ☺ ☹	☺ ☺ ☹		Total Learn http://bit.ly/ 2lesH0e
I can use the periodic table to state the number of protons, electrons and neutrons in an element	☺ ☺ ☹	☺ ☺ ☹	☺ ☺ ☹	https://youtu.be/ ljyzVt8bJSA https://youtu.be/ Hq6YMQnR0P0	TuitionKit http://bit.ly/ 2yhbgP4
I can define the terms mass number and atomic number	☺ ☺ ☹	☺ ☺ ☹	☺ ☺ ☹		

I can represent a reaction using a word equation	☺ ☺ ☹	☺ ☺ ☹	☺ ☺ ☹	https://youtu.be/ X8jivOqwVok	https://phet. colorado.edu/ en/simulation /balancing- chemical- equations
I can represent a reaction using a balanced symbol equation	☺ ☺ ☹	☺ ☺ ☹	☺ ☺ ☹	https://youtu.be/ TOwb4z-_kmY https://youtu.be/ 5GmsOx_DcOM	
I can define the term mixture	☺ ☺ ☹	☺ ☺ ☹	☺ ☺ ☹	https://youtu.be/ tguhuiq9tVs	TuitionKit http://bit.ly/ 2x6vLxn
I can describe different way to separate mixtures using physical processes	☺ ☺ ☹	☺ ☺ ☹	☺ ☺ ☹	https://youtu.be/ NJYnoXUWa2o https://youtu.be/ bAgLzQ_a1jQ	
I can describe how a scientific model can be developed	☺ ☺ ☹	☺ ☺ ☹	☺ ☺ ☹		
I can describe the plum pudding model of the atom	☺ ☺ ☹	☺ ☺ ☹	☺ ☺ ☹	https://youtu.be/ nbwcngWsXAU	
I can describe how Rutherford and Marsden's experiments lead to the nuclear model of the atom, and the ideas the Bohr contributed to the model	☺ ☺ ☹	☺ ☺ ☹	☺ ☺ ☹		TuitionKit http://bit.ly/ 2hdYZqT
I can state the Chadwick showed the existence of the neutrons	☺ ☺ ☹	☺ ☺ ☹	☺ ☺ ☹		
I can draw the electronic structure of the first 20 elements on the periodic table	☺ ☺ ☹	☺ ☺ ☹	☺ ☺ ☹	https://youtu.be/ bgWKesHbLnE	TuitionKit http://bit.ly/ 2w16S54
I can use numbers to represent the electronic structure of the first 20 elements on the periodic table	☺ ☺ ☹	☺ ☺ ☹	☺ ☺ ☹		
I can recall the relative charges of the three subatomic particles	☺ ☺ ☹	☺ ☺ ☹	☺ ☺ ☹		
I can explain why atoms have no overall charge	☺ ☺ ☹	☺ ☺ ☹	☺ ☺ ☹	https://youtu.be/ M5qfMT-ePrQ	
I can describe the formation of ions	☺ ☺ ☹	☺ ☺ ☹	☺ ☺ ☹		
I can recall that metals will go on to form positive ions	☺ ☺ ☹	☺ ☺ ☹	☺ ☺ ☹		

I can recall the non-metals will go on to form negative ions	☺ ☺ ☹	☺ ☺ ☹	☺ ☺ ☹		
I can describe the location of metals and non-metals on the periodic table	☺ ☺ ☹	☺ ☺ ☹	☺ ☺ ☹		
I can describe the use of periods and groups to classify parts of the periodic table	☺ ☺ ☹	☺ ☺ ☹	☺ ☺ ☹	https://youtu.be/ GhOkzDuHIDc https://youtu.be/ 8GYMLQt18zQ	Total Learn http://bit.ly/ 2i2fEtG http://bit.ly/ 2z36acS
I can describe the development of the early periodic table	☺ ☺ ☹	☺ ☺ ☹	☺ ☺ ☹	https://youtu.be/ WXnD0UWlYyk	TuitionKit http://bit.ly/ 2w0tEtX Total Learn http://bit.ly/ 2yJEcj7
I can describe how Mendeleev developed the periodic table	☺ ☺ ☹	☺ ☺ ☹	☺ ☺ ☹		
I can describe the properties of the noble gasses (in group -0)	☺ ☺ ☹	☺ ☺ ☹	☺ ☺ ☹	https://youtu.be/ GhOkzDuHIDc	TuitionKit http://bit.ly/ 2xIH4PM
I can recall that the boiling points of noble gases increase as you go down the periodic table	☺ ☺ ☹	☺ ☺ ☹	☺ ☺ ☹		
I can describe the properties of group 1 metals	☺ ☺ ☹	☺ ☺ ☹	☺ ☺ ☹	https://youtu.be/ UNewX9i1Nh4 With water; https://youtu.be/ t1Kpyyvgncw	TuitionKit http://bit.ly/ 2h99hEo Total Learn http://bit.ly/ 2y1OjTv
I can describe the reactions of group 1 metals	☺ ☺ ☹	☺ ☺ ☹	☺ ☺ ☹		
I can recall that the reactivity of group 1 metals increases as you go down the group.	☺ ☺ ☹	☺ ☺ ☹	☺ ☺ ☹	https://youtu.be/ 5rXKPc-Jy_Y	
I can recall that group 7 element are non-metals and are found as diatomic molecules	☺ ☺ ☹	☺ ☺ ☹	☺ ☺ ☹	https://youtu.be/ vK5yc2RR0XQ	TuitionKit http://bit.ly/ 2fcbxOj
I can describe the reactions of group 7 non-metals	☺ ☺ ☹	☺ ☺ ☹	☺ ☺ ☹		
I can describe the patterns in melting point, boiling point and reactivity in group 7	☺ ☺ ☹	☺ ☺ ☹	☺ ☺ ☹		
I can describe displacement reaction in relation to group 7 elements	☺ ☺ ☹	☺ ☺ ☹	☺ ☺ ☹		

I can describe the properties of transition metals **Chemistry only**	☺ ☺ ☹	☺ ☺ ☹	☺ ☺ ☹	https://youtu.be/ Tw3NJ_it3tc	TuitionKit http://bit.ly/ 2h7pk9G
I can describe the uses of transition metals **Chemistry only**	☺ ☺ ☹	☺ ☺ ☹	☺ ☺ ☹		
I can recall that transition metals form different coloured compounds **Chemistry only**	☺ ☺ ☹	☺ ☺ ☹	☺ ☺ ☹		

Quick fire questions;

This worksheet is fully supported by a video tutorial; https://youtu.be/mjIIPJ_cO18

1. What element is represented by W?
2. What element is represented by Na?
3. What element is represented by Si?
4. What element is represented by Co?
5. What element is represented by Fe?
6. What group is oxygen in?
7. What group is argon in?
8. What group is potassium in?
9. What group is sulfur in?
10. What group is chlorine in?
11. What period is phosphorous in?
12. What period is nitrogen in?
13. What period is calcium in?
14. What period is gallium in?
15. What period is carbon in?
16. What is a compound?
17. What is a mixture?
18. Give three ways of separating out mixtures.
19. What is the name for CO_2?
20. What is the name for H_2O?
21. What did Chadwick discover?
22. What experiment did Rutherford do?
23. What type of foil did Rutherford use?
24. What did Rutherford fire at the foil?
25. What model of the atom was Rutherford testing?
26. What did Rutherford discover?
27. What was the new model of the atom called?
28. Where are electrons?
29. Where are protons?
30. Where are neutrons?
31. What charge do protons have?
32. What charge do neutrons have?
33. What charge do electrons have?
34. What mass do protons have?

35. What mass do electrons have?

36. What mass do neutrons have?

37. What does the atomic number tell us?

38. What does the mass number tell us?

39. How do you find the number of protons in an atom?

40. How do you find the number of electrons in an atom?

41. How do you find the number of neutrons in an atom?

42. How do you find the number of protons in an ion?

43. How do you find the number of electrons in an ion?

44. How do you find the number of neutrons in an ion?

45. How many electrons fit on the first shell?

46. How many electrons fit on the second shell?

47. How many electrons fit on the third shell?

48. What element has the electronic structure 2,8,1?

49. What element has the electronic structure 2,3?

50. What element has the electronic structure 2,8,5?

51. What element has the electronic structure 2?

52. What element has the electronic structure 2,8,8,1?

53. What type of ions do metals form (positive/negative)?

54. What type of ions do non-metals form (positive/negative)?

55. What bonding occurs between two non-metals?

56. What bonding occurs between a metal and a non-metal?

57. What happens to the electrons in covalent bonding?

58. What happens to the electrons in ionic bonding?

59. How did Mendeleev organise his periodic table?

60. Why did Mendeleev leave gaps in his periodic table?

61. On which side (left/right) of the periodic table are metals found?

62. On which side (left/right) of the periodic table are non-metals found?

63. What is another name for group 1?

64. How reactive are group 1 elements?

65. How does reactivity change as you go down group 1?

66. How does sodium react with water?

67. How does sodium react with oxygen?

68. How does sodium react with chlorine?

69. What is another name for group 0/8?

70. How reactive are group 0 elements?

71. How does boiling point change as you go down group 0?

72. What is another name for group 7?

73. How reactive are group 7 elements?
74. How does boiling point change as you go down group 7?
75. How does reactivity change as you go down group 7?

GCSE Chemistry Separate Science Only

76. What are the properties of transition metals?
77. Give a use for transition metals
78. What colour does iron (II) go?
79. What colour does iron (III) go?
80. What colour does copper (II) go?

Whole topic summary https://youtu.be/YpEQ-NWxKBc in only 15 minutes!

Specification statement These are the bits the exam board wants you to know, make sure you can do all of these...	Self-assessment			Bits to help if you don't understand	
	First review 4-7 months before exam	Second review 1-2 months before exam	Final review Week before exam	Primrose Kitten	Other places
I can represent a solid, a liquid and a gas by drawing the arrangement of atoms	☺ ☺ ☹	☺ ☺ ☹	☺ ☺ ☹	https://youtu.be/hs9DIOqzgRg	TuitionKit http://bit.ly/2h9Yfma
I can recall that energy is needed to change state	☺ ☺ ☹	☺ ☺ ☹	☺ ☺ ☹		Total Learn http://bit.ly/2z33uMm
I can predict the state of a substance at a given temperature	☺ ☺ ☹	☺ ☺ ☹	☺ ☺ ☹		
I can use appropriate state symbol in an equation	☺ ☺ ☹	☺ ☺ ☹	☺ ☺ ☹		
I can recall that ionic bonding occurs between a metal and a non-metal	☺ ☺ ☹	☺ ☺ ☹	☺ ☺ ☹	https://youtu.be/TI6xRyWDtok	TuitionKit http://bit.ly/2xqBlNt
I can describe the formation of ions	☺ ☺ ☹	☺ ☺ ☹	☺ ☺ ☹	https://youtu.be/M5qfMT-ePrQ	http://bit.ly/2x5Jo2A
I can recall that metals will go on to form positive ions	☺ ☺ ☹	☺ ☺ ☹	☺ ☺ ☹	https://youtu.be/746sTyJqrJo	
I can recall the non-metals will go on to form negative ions	☺ ☺ ☹	☺ ☺ ☹	☺ ☺ ☹	https://youtu.be/9K3RvTg-LwU	
I can describe the location of metals and non-metals on the periodic table	☺ ☺ ☹	☺ ☺ ☹	☺ ☺ ☹		
I can describe ionic bonding as the strong electrostatic attraction between oppositely charged ions	☺ ☺ ☹	☺ ☺ ☹	☺ ☺ ☹	https://youtu.be/2-LeqYeejcE	

I can draw dot and cross diagrams to show ionic bonding between group 1 and group 2 metals and group 6 and group 7 non-metals.	☺ ☺ ☹	☺ ☺ ☹	☺ ☺ ☹	https://youtu.be/gbx1pcFn4ws	
I can recall that covalent bonding occurs between 2 non-metals	☺ ☺ ☹	☺ ☺ ☹	☺ ☺ ☹	https://youtu.be/4I4IqZ2qcfU	TuitionKit http://bit.ly/2h8thL0 http://bit.ly/2xID3e0
I can represent the bonding in covalent compounds as a dot and cross diagram (hydrogen, chlorine, oxygen, nitrogen, hydrogen chloride, ammonia and methane)	☺ ☺ ☹	☺ ☺ ☹	☺ ☺ ☹		
I can draw covalent compounds using lines to represent electron pairs	☺ ☺ ☹	☺ ☺ ☹	☺ ☺ ☹		
I can recall the names and formula of common covalent compounds	☺ ☺ ☹	☺ ☺ ☹	☺ ☺ ☹		
I can recall that covalent compounds can be small and simple or giant.	☺ ☺ ☹	☺ ☺ ☹	☺ ☺ ☹		
I can work out the formula of a compound from a picture	☺ ☺ ☹	☺ ☺ ☹	☺ ☺ ☹		
I can explain how strong metallic bonds arise	☺ ☺ ☹	☺ ☺ ☹	☺ ☺ ☹		TuitionKit http://bit.ly/2x7YzG2
I can explain why most metal have high melting and boiling points	☺ ☺ ☹	☺ ☺ ☹	☺ ☺ ☹		
I can describe the pattern of atoms in a pure metal	☺ ☺ ☹	☺ ☺ ☹	☺ ☺ ☹		
I can explain why pure metals are not used often	☺ ☺ ☹	☺ ☺ ☹	☺ ☺ ☹		
I can describe and explain the arrangement of atoms in an alloy	☺ ☺ ☹	☺ ☺ ☹	☺ ☺ ☹		
I can describe the advantages of an alloy over pure metals	☺ ☺ ☹	☺ ☺ ☹	☺ ☺ ☹	https://youtu.be/Lgfskmrx3Aw	TuitionKit http://bit.ly/2xcaxQJ
I can explain how metals conduct electricity	☺ ☺ ☹	☺ ☺ ☹	☺ ☺ ☹		
I can describe the structure of an ionic compounds	☺ ☺ ☹	☺ ☺ ☹	☺ ☺ ☹	https://youtu.be/TI6xRyWDtok	Total Learn http://bit.ly/2yK5zJK
I can describe the properties of an ionic compounds	☺ ☺ ☹	☺ ☺ ☹	☺ ☺ ☹	https://youtu.be/2-LeqYeejcE	
I can describe the structure of a simple covalent compounds	☺ ☺ ☹	☺ ☺ ☹	☺ ☺ ☹		Total Learn http://bit.ly/2lcY7nw
I can describe the properties of a simple covalent compounds	☺ ☺ ☹	☺ ☺ ☹	☺ ☺ ☹		

I can describe the structure of a giant covalent compounds	☺ ☺ ☹	☺ ☺ ☹	☺ ☺ ☹		
I can describe the properties of a giant covalent compounds	☺ ☺ ☹	☺ ☺ ☹	☺ ☺ ☹		
I can use experimental data to determine if a compound is ionic, simple covalent or giant covalent.	☺ ☺ ☹	☺ ☺ ☹	☺ ☺ ☹		
I can describe the structure of a polymer	☺ ☺ ☹	☺ ☺ ☹	☺ ☺ ☹		TuitionKit http://bit.ly/ 2xIoIyo
I can describe the properties of a polymer	☺ ☺ ☹	☺ ☺ ☹	☺ ☺ ☹		
I can describe how the bonding in diamond affects the properties	☺ ☺ ☹	☺ ☺ ☹	☺ ☺ ☹	https://youtu.be /uN_nzg0wits	
I can explain the difference in bonding between diamond and graphite	☺ ☺ ☹	☺ ☺ ☹	☺ ☺ ☹	https://youtu.be /NoCCdXFRi3g	
I can describe how the bonding in graphite affects the properties	☺ ☺ ☹	☺ ☺ ☹	☺ ☺ ☹		
I can describe how the structure of graphene give it properties that can be useful in the modern world	☺ ☺ ☹	☺ ☺ ☹	☺ ☺ ☹		TuitionKit http://bit.ly/ 2frJuHO
I can describe how the structure of fullerenes give them properties that can be useful in the modern world	☺ ☺ ☹	☺ ☺ ☹	☺ ☺ ☹	https://youtu.be /lYXoEzHtPGo	
I can describe how the structure of carbon nanotubes give them properties that can be useful in the modern world	☺ ☺ ☹	☺ ☺ ☹	☺ ☺ ☹		
I can recall the size of nanoparticles **Chemistry only**	☺ ☺ ☹	☺ ☺ ☹	☺ ☺ ☹		TuitionKit http://bit.ly/ 2fdhk6c
I can recall why nanoparticle have different properties **Chemistry only**	☺ ☺ ☹	☺ ☺ ☹	☺ ☺ ☹		The strange new world of Nanoscience, narrated by Stephen Fry http://bit.ly/ 2wseIVH
I can describe the uses of nanoparticles **Chemistry only**	☺ ☺ ☹	☺ ☺ ☹	☺ ☺ ☹		
I can discuss the advantages and disadvantage of using nanoparticles **Chemistry only**	☺ ☺ ☹	☺ ☺ ☹	☺ ☺ ☹		

Quick fire questions;

This worksheet is fully supported by a video tutorial; https://youtu.be/9bbCFUyluWg

1. Draw the arrangement of particles in a solid.
2. Draw the arrangement of particles in a liquid.
3. Draw the arrangement of particles in a gas.
4. What is it called when a solid turns into liquid?
5. What is it called when a liquid turns into a gas?
6. What is it called when a gas turns into liquid?
7. What is it called when a liquid turns into a solid?
8. What is the boiling point?
9. What is the condensing point?
10. What does this state symbol mean (s)? solid
11. What does this state symbol mean (l)? liquid
12. What does this state symbol mean (g)? gas
13. What does this state symbol mean (aq)?
14. What is ionic bonding?
15. How are ions formed?
16. What type of ions with a metal form?
17. What type of ions will a non-metal form?
18. Where are metals on the periodic table
19. Where are non-metals on the periodic table?
20. What is an ionic bond?
21. Draw a dot and cross diagram to show the bonding in sodium chloride.
22. Draw a dot and cross diagram to show the bonding in magnesium chloride.
23. Draw a dot and cross diagram to show the bonding in magnesium oxide.
24. What is covalent bonding?
25. List six simple covalent compounds.
26. Give the formula of oxygen gas.
27. Give the formula of nitrogen gas.
28. Give the formula of hydrogen chloride.
29. Give the formula of ammonia.
30. Give the formula of methane.
31. Give the formula of hydrogen gas.
32. Give the formula of water. H_2O
33. Give the formula of carbon dioxide.
34. Draw the bonding in water.

35. Draw the bonding in carbon dioxide.

36. Draw the bonding in chlorine gas.

37. Draw the bonding in nitrogen gas.

38. Draw the bonding in oxygen gas.

39. Draw the bonding in hydrochloric acid.

40. Draw the bonding in ammonia.

41. Draw the bonding in methane.

42. In a covalent bonding diagram what does each line represent?

43. Give two examples of giant covalent compounds.

44. How does metallic bonding arise?

45. Why do metals have high boiling and melting points?

46. How are atoms in a pure metal arranged?

47. How are atoms in an alloy arranged?

48. Why do people use alloys and not pure metals?

49. How do metals conduct electricity?

50. Describe the structure of an ionic compound.

51. Describe the properties of an ionic compound.

52. Describe the structure of a simple covalent compound.

53. Describe the properties of a simple covalent compound.

54. Describe the structure of giant covalent compound.

55. Describe the properties of a giant covalent compound.

56. What is a monomer?

57. What is a polymer?

58. Describe the structure of a polymer.

59. **Which element is both diamond and graphite made from?**

60. Describe the bonding in diamond.

61. Describe the difference between the bonding in diamonds and the bonding in graphite?

62. What are the properties of graphite?

63. What are the uses of graphene?

64. What are the uses of fullerenes?

65. Describe the structure of fullerenes.

66. Describe the structure of carbon nanotubes.

Chemistry only

67. What is the size of a nanoparticle?

68. Why do nanoparticles have different properties?

69. What can nanoparticle be used for?

70. What are the advantages and disadvantages of nanoparticles?

Whole topic summary https://youtu.be/eAibVvhmsK0 in only 12 minutes!!

Specification statement These are the bits the exam board wants you to know, make sure you can do all of these…	Self-assessment			Bits to help if you don't understand	
	First review 4-7 months before exam	Second review 1-2 months before exam	Final review Week before exam	Primrose Kitten	Other places
I can describe different ways of measuring the mass or volume of a product of a reactant	☺ 😐 ☹	☺ 😐 ☹	☺ 😐 ☹		
I can explain why the mass of a reaction appears to change	☺ 😐 ☹	☺ 😐 ☹	☺ 😐 ☹	https://youtu.be/WqhZBnR743I	
I can explain that in any measurement there is a degree of uncertainty	☺ 😐 ☹	☺ 😐 ☹	☺ 😐 ☹		
I can calculate the concentration of a solution from the masses used	☺ 😐 ☹	☺ 😐 ☹	☺ 😐 ☹		Total Learn http://bit.ly/2i0YCfL
I can represent a reaction using a word equation	☺ 😐 ☹	☺ 😐 ☹	☺ 😐 ☹	https://youtu.be/X8jiv0qwVok	
I can represent a reaction using a balanced symbol equation	☺ 😐 ☹	☺ 😐 ☹	☺ 😐 ☹	https://youtu.be/T0wb4z-_kmY https://youtu.be/5GmsOx_DcOM	TuitionKit http://bit.ly/2ymP1Hf Total Learn http://bit.ly/2yZs9jZ

I can calculate the relative formula mass (M_r) of a compound from the relative atomic (A_r) masses of the elements	☺ ☺ ☹	☺ ☺ ☹	☺ ☺ ☹	https://youtu.be/ 8W9D8fiNodQ https://youtu.be/ EPX7UKE22Gs	TuitionKit http://bit.ly/ 2jHbk7h Total Learn http://bit.ly/ 2xk1MUD
I can define the term mole **Higher tier only**	☺ ☺ ☹	☺ ☺ ☹	☺ ☺ ☹		
I can calculate the number of moles from the mass **Higher tier only**	☺ ☺ ☹	☺ ☺ ☹	☺ ☺ ☹	https://youtu.be/ JN_qmij-pkQ	TuitionKit http://bit.ly/ 2xNfoJt Total Learn http://bit.ly/ 2zVLn87
I can describe the number of particles in one mole as being equal to Avogadro's constant **Higher tier only**	☺ ☺ ☹	☺ ☺ ☹	☺ ☺ ☹		
I can calculate the mass of a reactant or a product given the equation **Higher tier only**	☺ ☺ ☹	☺ ☺ ☹	☺ ☺ ☹		TuitionKit http://bit.ly/ 2hdquAp Total Learn http://bit.ly/ 2gL00Tb
I can balance equation given information about the number of moles involved. **Higher tier only**	☺ ☺ ☹	☺ ☺ ☹	☺ ☺ ☹		
I can describe when a reactant would be used in excess **Higher tier only**	☺ ☺ ☹	☺ ☺ ☹	☺ ☺ ☹		
I can calculate the percentage yield of a reaction **Chemistry only**	☺ ☺ ☹	☺ ☺ ☹	☺ ☺ ☹		TuitionKit http://bit.ly/ 2w5C17y
I can calculate the atom economy of a reaction **Chemistry only**	☺ ☺ ☹	☺ ☺ ☹	☺ ☺ ☹		TuitionKit http://bit.ly/ 2hfcVgn
I can explain why a reaction may not give the expected yield **Chemistry only**	☺ ☺ ☹	☺ ☺ ☹	☺ ☺ ☹		TuitionKit http://bit.ly/ 2fi3xLG

I can carry out a titration	☺ ☺ ☹	☺ ☺ ☹	☺ ☺ ☹	https://youtu.be/MDWVrTWOnq8 https://youtu.be/yVF6Gn7HmWk https://youtu.be/XPTnZnbXgDs https://youtu.be/2hv2hS6zdh0	
I can calculate the concentration of a solution in mol/dm³ **Chemistry only** **Higher tier only**	☺ ☺ ☹	☺ ☺ ☹	☺ ☺ ☹	https://youtu.be/hhkt3ZZ-pvQ	TuitionKit http://bit.ly/2hctzk5
I can carry out titration calculations **Chemistry only** **Higher tier only**	☺ ☺ ☹	☺ ☺ ☹	☺ ☺ ☹		
I can recall that a gas takes up 24dm³ under standard condition **Chemistry only** **Higher tier only**	☺ ☺ ☹	☺ ☺ ☹	☺ ☺ ☹		Total Learn http://bit.ly/2loDvsw
I can calculate the volume of a gas **Chemistry only** **Higher tier only**	☺ ☺ ☹	☺ ☺ ☹	☺ ☺ ☹		TuitionKit http://bit.ly/2yoA3ka Total Learn http://bit.ly/2loDvsw

Quick fire questions;

This worksheet is fully supported by a video tutorial; https://youtu.be/8uqWdmIKd7c

1. Give three ways of measuring the mass or volume of a product or a reactant.
2. How do you calculate the concentration of a solution?
3. Give the formula of oxygen gas.
4. Give the formula of nitrogen gas.
5. Give the formula of hydrogen chloride.
6. Give the formula of ammonia.
7. Give the formula of methane.
8. Give the formula of hydrogen gas.
9. Give the formula of water.
10. Give the formula of carbon dioxide.
11. Balance this $N_2 + \ldots\ldots H_2 \rightarrow \ldots\ldots NH_3$
12. Balance this $CaCl_2 + KOH \rightarrow Ca(OH)_2 + KCl$
13. Ammonia reacts with oxygen gas; write this as a balanced symbol equation.
14. Magnesium reacts with carbon dioxide; write this is a balanced symbol equation.
15. Define relative formula mass (M_r).
16. Define relative atomic mass (A_r).
17. What is the mass of argon?
18. What is the mass of calcium?
19. What is the mass of H_2SO_4?
20. What is the mass of MgO?

Higher tier only

21. What does the term mole mean?
22. What is equation for calculating moles?
23. What is Avogadro's constant?

Chemistry only

24. How do you calculate percentage yield of reaction?
25. How do you calculate the atom economy of a reaction?
26. Why might a reaction not give the expected yield?
27. What is the colour change in phenolphthalein?
28. What is the colour change in the methyl orange?

Higher tier

29. How do you calculate the concentration of the solution?
30. How much volume does 1 moles of gas take up at standard conditions?

4 – Chemical Changes

Knowledge Checklist

Whole topic summary https://youtu.be/KTmXEIiU_Go in only 16 minutes!!

Specification statement These are the bits the exam board wants you to know, make sure you can do all of these…	Self-assessment			Bits to help if you don't understand	
	First review 4-7 months before exam	Second review 1-2 months before exam	Final review Week before exam	Primrose Kitten	Other places
I can describe the reaction between metal and oxygen	☺ ☺ ☹	☺ ☺ ☹	☺ ☺ ☹		
I can recall the order of the reactivity series	☺ ☺ ☹	☺ ☺ ☹	☺ ☺ ☹		TuitionKit http://bit.ly /2xv1LNZ Total Learn http://bit.ly /2i0QOKN
I can describe when a displacement reaction might take place	☺ ☺ ☹	☺ ☺ ☹	☺ ☺ ☹	https://youtu.be/ 7Pm5-ox6YGM	
I can use experimental data to work out the order of reactivity	☺ ☺ ☹	☺ ☺ ☹	☺ ☺ ☹		
I can describe how unreactive metals are found in the Earth	☺ ☺ ☹	☺ ☺ ☹	☺ ☺ ☹		
I can describe reduction	☺ ☺ ☹	☺ ☺ ☹	☺ ☺ ☹		
I can describe the process of extracting aluminium by electrolysis	☺ ☺ ☹	☺ ☺ ☹	☺ ☺ ☹	https://youtu.be/ h0G0ebmztUQ	TuitionKit http://bit.ly /2heSYpD
I can describe oxidation as the loss of electrons **Higher tier only**	☺ ☺ ☹	☺ ☺ ☹	☺ ☺ ☹	"OILRIG" https://youtu.be/ -5fL5IOPSfs	
I can describe reduction as a gain of electrons **Higher tier only**	☺ ☺ ☹	☺ ☺ ☹	☺ ☺ ☹		

I can write balanced ionic half equations **Higher tier only**	☺ ☺ ☹	☺ ☺ ☹	☺ ☺ ☹	https://youtu.be/vbic3491cE8	
I can determine which element in a reaction is oxidised or reduced from the equation **Higher tier only**	☺ ☺ ☹	☺ ☺ ☹	☺ ☺ ☹		
I can use the general equation to give the products from a reaction	☺ ☺ ☹	☺ ☺ ☹	☺ ☺ ☹	https://youtu.be/Sh3tOH95-AQ https://youtu.be/Gstk2bhzBVQ https://youtu.be/-kwhGkvUjoQ	TuitionKit http://bit.ly/2hdd7QE Total Learn http://bit.ly/2w4JYJZ http://bit.ly/2ze5vFB
I can determine the formula of a salt from common ions	☺ ☺ ☹	☺ ☺ ☹	☺ ☺ ☹		Common ions flash cards on www.primrosekitten.com
I can describe how to make a pure salt	☺ ☺ ☹	☺ ☺ ☹	☺ ☺ ☹	RP1; https://youtu.be/ttsAmaNu4ao https://youtu.be/BmaXoGTAmeA	TuitionKit http://bit.ly/2yoMoF8
I can describe the ions that lead to acidic and alkaline conditions	☺ ☺ ☹	☺ ☺ ☹	☺ ☺ ☹	https://youtu.be/CvmhbNYroeo	
I can use the pH scale to describe how acidic or alkaline a solution is	☺ ☺ ☹	☺ ☺ ☹	☺ ☺ ☹		TuitionKit http://bit.ly/2xkyZzj
I can use an equation to show neutralisation	☺ ☺ ☹	☺ ☺ ☹	☺ ☺ ☹		Total learn http://bit.ly/2fg1gAL

I can carry out a titration	☺ 😐 ☹	☺ 😐 ☹	☺ 😐 ☹	https://youtu.be/ MDWVrTWOnq8 https://youtu.be/ yVF6Gn7HmWk https://youtu.be/ XPTnZnbXgDs https://youtu.be/ 2hv2hS6zdh0	TuitionKit http://bit.ly /2xOvRqx
I can calculate a concentration from titration data **Chemistry only**	☺ 😐 ☹	☺ 😐 ☹	☺ 😐 ☹	https://youtu.be/ hhkt3ZZ-pvQ	
I can give examples of strong and weak acids **Higher tier only**	☺ 😐 ☹	☺ 😐 ☹	☺ 😐 ☹	https://youtu.be/ bdUas8qRUew	TuitionKit http://bit.ly /2f7RL2N
I can describe how concentration relates to pH **Higher tier only**	☺ 😐 ☹	☺ 😐 ☹	☺ 😐 ☹		Total Learn http://bit.ly /2fg1gAL
I can use the terms strong, weak, concentrated and dilute in term of acids **Higher tier only**	☺ 😐 ☹	☺ 😐 ☹	☺ 😐 ☹		
I can explain why compounds need to be molten or dissolved to conduct	☺ 😐 ☹	☺ 😐 ☹	☺ 😐 ☹	https://youtu.be/ m1NURA22XTk RP5;	
I can describe the movement of ions during electrolysis	☺ 😐 ☹	☺ 😐 ☹	☺ 😐 ☹	https://youtu.be/ hcQHxKMpr60	
I can predict the products of electrolysis	☺ 😐 ☹	☺ 😐 ☹	☺ 😐 ☹	https://youtu.be/ xCSa3YQbGRc https://youtu.be/ r0kbEj2PDEg https://youtu.be/ L_BjGKdM2Bk https://youtu.be/ E6npZEyaASk	TuitionKit http://bit.ly /2xudbBI Total Learn http://bit.ly /2y2Gmsk

I can write balanced half equations to describe what happens at each electrode	☺ ☺ ☹	☺ ☺ ☹	☺ ☺ ☹	https://youtu.be/vbic3491cE8	TuitionKit http://bit.ly/2xbbnOe
I can describe how to test for the production of chlorine gas	☺ ☺ ☹	☺ ☺ ☹	☺ ☺ ☹		
I can describe how to test for the production of hydrogen gas	☺ ☺ ☹	☺ ☺ ☹	☺ ☺ ☹	https://youtu.be/wuNB1n5z9QM	
I can describe how to test for the production of oxygen gas	☺ ☺ ☹	☺ ☺ ☹	☺ ☺ ☹		
I can describe what happens to aqueous solutions that are electrolysed	☺ ☺ ☹	☺ ☺ ☹	☺ ☺ ☹		

This worksheet is fully supported by a video tutorial; https://youtu.be/7Nrma6v0A8I

1. Describe what happens when a metal reacts with oxygen.
2. List the order of the reactivity series.
3. How are unreactive metals found?
4. What is the formula of magnesium oxide?
5. What is the formula of calcium hydroxide?
6. What ion is responsible for acidity?
7. What ion is responsible for alkalinity?
8. Is pH1 acid, alkali or neutral?
9. Is pH7 acid, alkali or neutral?
10. Is pH14 acid, alkali or neutral?
11. Write down the neutralisation equation.
12. When do ionic compounds conduct electricity?
13. Why do ionic compounds need to molten or dissolved to conduct?
14. What happens to positive ions during electrolysis?
15. What happens negative ions during electrolysis?
16. If a metal chloride is being electrolysed what gas will be produced?
17. If metal sulfate is being electrolysed what gas will be produced?
18. How do you test for chlorine gas?
19. How do you test for hydrogen gas?
20. How do you test for oxygen gas?

Higher tier only

21. What is reduction?
22. What is oxidation?
23. Balance this ....Cl^- .... $\rightarrow Cl_2$
24. Balance this Mg^{2+} .... $\rightarrow$ Mg
25. Give an example of a strong acid.
26. Give an example of a weak acid.
27. What is a concentrated acid?
28. What is a dilute acid?

Whole topic summary https://youtu.be/L7829UGifpM in only 9 minutes

Specification statement These are the bits the exam board wants you to know, make sure you can do all of these...	Self-assessment			Bits to help if you don't understand	
	First review 4-7 months before exam	Second review 1-2 months before exam	Final review Week before exam	Primrose Kitten	Other places
I can describe the energy changes in an exothermic or and endothermic reaction	☺ ☺ ☹	☺ ☺ ☹	☺ ☺ ☹	RP4; https://youtu.be/BzOC9mmF2tw	TuitionKit http://bit.ly/2xe67a7
I can give uses for endothermic and exothermic reactions	☺ ☺ ☹	☺ ☺ ☹	☺ ☺ ☹		
I can draw the reaction profiles for endothermic and exothermic reactions	☺ ☺ ☹	☺ ☺ ☹	☺ ☺ ☹	https://youtu.be/bMndHV8m-w8	TuitionKit http://bit.ly/2ybyoxk
I can determine the energy change in a reaction	☺ ☺ ☹	☺ ☺ ☹	☺ ☺ ☹	https://youtu.be/kvxTE-U-oZY	TuitionKit http://bit.ly/2xjL8ob
I can recall that energy is needed to break bonds **Higher tier only**	☺ ☺ ☹	☺ ☺ ☹	☺ ☺ ☹	https://youtu.be/OHxSWa_36_s	
I can recall that energy is released when bonds are made **Higher tier only**	☺ ☺ ☹	☺ ☺ ☹	☺ ☺ ☹		
I can calculate the energy change in a reaction **Higher tier only**	☺ ☺ ☹	☺ ☺ ☹	☺ ☺ ☹	https://youtu.be/B3hs4GEgJQc	
I can describe how a simple cell works **Chemistry only**	☺ ☺ ☹	☺ ☺ ☹	☺ ☺ ☹		TuitionKit http://bit.ly/2f81p5A

I can recall that a battery is two or more cells **Chemistry only**	☺ ☺ ☹	☺ ☺ ☹	☺ ☺ ☹		
I can describe the difference between rechargeable and non-rechargeable batteries **Chemistry only**	☺ ☺ ☹	☺ ☺ ☹	☺ ☺ ☹		
I can describe the reaction in a hydrogen fuel cell **Chemistry only**	☺ ☺ ☹	☺ ☺ ☹	☺ ☺ ☹	https://youtu.be/ sO4uUdKpDEo	TuitionKit http://bit.ly /2w51Gx2
I can evaluate the use of hydrogen fuel cells **Chemistry only**	☺ ☺ ☹	☺ ☺ ☹	☺ ☺ ☹		
I can write half equations for the reactions that take place **Chemistry only**	☺ ☺ ☹	☺ ☺ ☹	☺ ☺ ☹		

This worksheet is fully supported by a video tutorial; https://youtu.be/PQtjfRolMAE

1. Define exothermic.
2. Define endothermic.
3. Draw the reaction profile for an endothermic reaction.
4. Draw the reaction profile for an exothermic reaction.
5. If energy is needed what is happening to the bonds?
6. If energy is released what is happening to the bonds?
7. How do you calculate the energy change in a reaction?

Chemistry only

8. How does simple cell work?
9. What is the difference between a battery and cell?
10. What is the difference between rechargeable non-rechargeable batteries?

Chemistry Paper 1 Checklist – What to do before the exam!

Watched the whole topic video   https://youtu.be/MpQ-3YAwNhI ☐

Learnt all the ions ☐

Practiced the equations ☐

Answered the quick-fire questions ☐

Looked at the practical videos ☐

Learnt the keywords ☐

Filled in the crosswords ☐

Whole topic summary https://youtu.be/7i90fiz9SmY in only 13 minutes!!

Specification statement These are the bits the exam board wants you to know, make sure you can do all of these…	Self-assessment			Bits to help if you don't understand	
	First review 4-7 months before exam	Second review 1-2 months before exam	Final review Week before exam	Primrose Kitten	Other places
I can calculate the mean rate of a reaction	☺ ☺ ☹	☺ ☺ ☹	☺ ☺ ☹		TuitionKit http://bit.ly/2xO6go6
I can recall ways to measure the quantity of a reactant of product	☺ ☺ ☹	☺ ☺ ☹	☺ ☺ ☹		
I can recall the units for measuring rate of reaction	☺ ☺ ☹	☺ ☺ ☹	☺ ☺ ☹		
I can give the quantity of a reactant in moles	☺ ☺ ☹	☺ ☺ ☹	☺ ☺ ☹		
I can draw a graph to show the progress of a reaction by showing the reactant being used up or a product being formed	☺ ☺ ☹	☺ ☺ ☹	☺ ☺ ☹		
I can draw tangents to curves and interpret the slope of these	☺ ☺ ☹	☺ ☺ ☹	☺ ☺ ☹		
I can calculate the gradient of a curve from the tangent	☺ ☺ ☹	☺ ☺ ☹	☺ ☺ ☹		
I can describe how to investigate the rate of a reaction	☺ ☺ ☹	☺ ☺ ☹	☺ ☺ ☹	RP; https://youtu.be/SXUWo-V-WgQ https://youtu.be/0RUYNpdnALg https://youtu.be/CwK4-_Xg2yI	

I can describe and explain how a change in temperature will affect a rate of a reaction	☺ 😐 ☹	☺ 😐 ☹	☺ 😐 ☹		TuitionKit http://bit.ly /2xP6lrA
I can describe and explain how a change in pressure will affect a rate of a reaction	☺ 😐 ☹	☺ 😐 ☹	☺ 😐 ☹		
I can describe and explain how a change in concentration will affect a rate of a reaction	☺ 😐 ☹	☺ 😐 ☹	☺ 😐 ☹		
I can describe and explain how a change in surface area will affect a rate of a reaction	☺ 😐 ☹	☺ 😐 ☹	☺ 😐 ☹	https://youtu.be/ IdVJpLQEFKw https://youtu.be/ IdVJpLQEFKw	
I can describe and explain how catalyst will affect a rate of a reaction	☺ 😐 ☹	☺ 😐 ☹	☺ 😐 ☹		
I can use collision theory to explain how different factors (temperature/ pressure/ concentration/ surface area) will affect the rate of a reaction	☺ 😐 ☹	☺ 😐 ☹	☺ 😐 ☹		
I can describe how a catalyst lowers activation energy	☺ 😐 ☹	☺ 😐 ☹	☺ 😐 ☹		
I can draw an energy profile diagram for a catalysed and an uncatalysed reaction	☺ 😐 ☹	☺ 😐 ☹	☺ 😐 ☹		
I can use symbols to represent a reversible reaction	☺ 😐 ☹	☺ 😐 ☹	☺ 😐 ☹		TuitionKit http://bit.ly /2hcggjQ
I can describe what happens to ammonium chloride upon heating and cooling	☺ 😐 ☹	☺ 😐 ☹	☺ 😐 ☹		
I can describe what happens to copper sulfate upon addition and removal of water	☺ 😐 ☹	☺ 😐 ☹	☺ 😐 ☹	https://youtu.be/ Ie2P68YfYWIv	
I can describe what happens to the energy in a reversible reaction, where one direction is exothermic and the other is endothermic **Higher tier only**	☺ 😐 ☹	☺ 😐 ☹	☺ 😐 ☹		TuitionKit http://bit.ly /2f6YNEY

I can describe what is happening to the rate of reactions when they have reached equilibrium **Higher tier only**	☺ 😐 ☹	☺ 😐 ☹	☺ 😐 ☹		TuitionKit http://bit.ly /2yaWloC
I can determine the effects that a change in temperature will have on the system, according to Le Chatelier's Principle **Higher tier only**	☺ 😐 ☹	☺ 😐 ☹	☺ 😐 ☹		TuitionKit http://bit.ly /2ynjLb5
I can determine the effects that a change in concentration will have on the system, according to Le Chatelier's Principle **Higher tier only**	☺ 😐 ☹	☺ 😐 ☹	☺ 😐 ☹		
I can determine the effects that a change in pressure will have on the system, according to Le Chatelier's Principle **Higher tier only**	☺ 😐 ☹	☺ 😐 ☹	☺ 😐 ☹		TuitionKit http://bit.ly /2fiboJb

This worksheet is fully supported by a video tutorial; https://youtu.be/C-tHYZwisNs

1. How do you measure the rate of reaction?
2. Give two ways to measure the quantity of reactant or product.
3. What are the units for measuring rate of reaction?
4. How do you calculate the gradient for a tangent?
5. Give three ways to measure the rate of reaction.
6. How can a change in temperature affect the rate of reaction?
7. How a change in pressure affect the rate of reaction?
8. How can a change in concentration affect the rate of reaction?
9. How can a change in surface area affect the rate of reaction?
10. What is a catalyst?
11. How can a catalyst affect the rate of reaction?
12. Sketch an energy profile for catalysed and an uncatalysed reaction.
13. What symbol represents a reversible reaction?
14. What happens to ammonium chloride upon heating and cooling?
15. What happens to copper sulfate on the addition and removal of water?

Higher tier only

16. What is Le Chatelier's Principle

7 – Organic Chemistry

Knowledge Checklist

Whole topic summary https://youtu.be/ZeUNWY7YDAo in only 15 minutes!!

Specification statement These are the bits the exam board wants you to know, make sure you can do all of these...	Self-assessment			Bits to help if you don't understand	
	First review 4-7 months before exam	Second review 1-2 months before exam	Final review Week before exam	Primrose Kitten	Other places
I can define the term hydrocarbon	☺☺☹	☺☺☹	☺☺☹	https://youtu.be/ VdstfH3CbvU https://youtu.be/ FE_wFJDXm8E	TuitionKit http://bit.ly /2hgdYww
I can describe the makeup of crude oil	☺☺☹	☺☺☹	☺☺☹	https://youtu.be/ XXncE3cZ4H8	
I can give and use the general formula for alkanes	☺☺☹	☺☺☹	☺☺☹	https://youtu.be/ 5kpo5W0UaX8	
I can name and draw the first 4 alkanes	☺☺☹	☺☺☹	☺☺☹		
I can recall why we need to distil oil into fractions	☺☺☹	☺☺☹	☺☺☹	https://youtu.be/ XXncE3cZ4H8 https://youtu.be/ eUmRR7y5HGc	
I can state some uses for the fractions of crude oil	☺☺☹	☺☺☹	☺☺☹		
I can describe the process of fractional distillation	☺☺☹	☺☺☹	☺☺☹		TuitionKit http://bit.ly /2jGyD13
I can recall how boiling point changes with chain length	☺☺☹	☺☺☹	☺☺☹		
I can recall how viscosity changes with chain length	☺☺☹	☺☺☹	☺☺☹		
I can recall how flammability changes with chain length	☺☺☹	☺☺☹	☺☺☹		
I can recall the equation for complete combustion	☺☺☹	☺☺☹	☺☺☹	https://youtu.be/ Garj40Fyfuk	

I can describe the reasons why we need to crack long hydrocarbon chains	☺ ☻ ☹	☺ ☻ ☹	☺ ☻ ☹		TuitionKit http://bit.ly /2xew6ym
I can describe the process of cracking by steam and via a catalyst	☺ ☻ ☹	☺ ☻ ☹	☺ ☻ ☹		
I can describe the results of testing for alkenes with bromine water	☺ ☻ ☹	☺ ☻ ☹	☺ ☻ ☹	https://youtu.be/ UQhyzisHawI	
I can recall and use the general formula for alkenes **Chemistry only**	☺ ☻ ☹	☺ ☻ ☹	☺ ☻ ☹	https://youtu.be/ jFIWdxfQGMs	TuitionKit http://bit.ly /2wvPb20
I can describe alkenes as unsaturated **Chemistry only**	☺ ☻ ☹	☺ ☻ ☹	☺ ☻ ☹		
I can name and draw the first four alkenes **Chemistry only**	☺ ☻ ☹	☺ ☻ ☹	☺ ☻ ☹	https://youtu.be/ YNHKmgMKVI0	
I can recall the equation for incomplete combustion **Chemistry only**	☺ ☻ ☹	☺ ☻ ☹	☺ ☻ ☹	https://youtu.be/ Garj40Fyfuk	
I can compare complete and incomplete combustions **Chemistry only**	☺ ☻ ☹	☺ ☻ ☹	☺ ☻ ☹		
I can describe the reaction of alkenes with hydrogen **Chemistry only**	☺ ☻ ☹	☺ ☻ ☹	☺ ☻ ☹		
I can describe the reaction of alkenes with water **Chemistry only**	☺ ☻ ☹	☺ ☻ ☹	☺ ☻ ☹		
I can describe the reaction of alkenes with the halogens **Chemistry only**	☺ ☻ ☹	☺ ☻ ☹	☺ ☻ ☹		
I can recall the functional group for alcohols **Chemistry only**	☺ ☻ ☹	☺ ☻ ☹	☺ ☻ ☹	https://youtu.be/ DVY3YCpfNo4	TuitionKit http://bit.ly /2xOeCfk
I can name and draw the first four alcohols **Chemistry only**	☺ ☻ ☹	☺ ☻ ☹	☺ ☻ ☹		
I can recall the main uses for alcohols **Chemistry only**	☺ ☻ ☹	☺ ☻ ☹	☺ ☻ ☹		

I can describe what happens when alcohols react with sodium **Chemistry only**	☺ ☺ ☹	☺ ☺ ☹	☺ ☺ ☹		
I can describe what happens when alcohols react with oxygen **Chemistry only**	☺ ☺ ☹	☺ ☺ ☹	☺ ☺ ☹		
I can describe what happens when alcohols react with water **Chemistry only**	☺ ☺ ☹	☺ ☺ ☹	☺ ☺ ☹		
I can describe what happens when alcohols react with an oxidising agent **Chemistry only**	☺ ☺ ☹	☺ ☺ ☹	☺ ☺ ☹		
I can describe the conditions needed for fermentation **Chemistry only**	☺ ☺ ☹	☺ ☺ ☹	☺ ☺ ☹		
I can recall the functional group for carboxylic acids **Chemistry only**	☺ ☺ ☹	☺ ☺ ☹	☺ ☺ ☹	https://youtu.be/uIHoLv4_Zlg https://youtu.be/LG1PzsuDuck	TuitionKit http://bit.ly/2xedXAE
I can name and draw the first four carboxylic acids **Chemistry only**	☺ ☺ ☹	☺ ☺ ☹	☺ ☺ ☹		
I can recall the main uses for carboxylic acids **Chemistry only**					
I can describe what happens when carboxylic acids react with carbonates **Chemistry only**	☺ ☺ ☹	☺ ☺ ☹	☺ ☺ ☹		
I can describe what happens when carboxylic acids react with water **Chemistry only**	☺ ☺ ☹	☺ ☺ ☹	☺ ☺ ☹		
I can describe what happens when carboxylic acids react with alcohols **Chemistry only**	☺ ☺ ☹	☺ ☺ ☹	☺ ☺ ☹		
I can name and draw ethyl ethanoate **Chemistry only**	☺ ☺ ☹	☺ ☺ ☹	☺ ☺ ☹		

I can define the terms monomer and polymer **Chemistry only**	☺ ☺ ☹	☺ ☺ ☹	☺ ☺ ☹		
I can explain the process of polymerisation **Chemistry only**	☺ ☺ ☹	☺ ☺ ☹	☺ ☺ ☹		
I can draw a polymer from a given monomer **Chemistry only**	☺ ☺ ☹	☺ ☺ ☹	☺ ☺ ☹		
I can draw the monomer from a given polymer **Chemistry only**	☺ ☺ ☹	☺ ☺ ☹	☺ ☺ ☹		
I can recall that condensation polymerisation involved monomers with different functional groups **Chemistry only** **Higher tier only**	☺ ☺ ☹	☺ ☺ ☹	☺ ☺ ☹		TuitionKit http://bit.ly /2xjMTlb
I can recall that condensation polymerisation involves the loss of a small molecules **Chemistry only** **Higher tier only**	☺ ☺ ☹	☺ ☺ ☹	☺ ☺ ☹		
I can explain the basic principles of condensation polymerisation **Chemistry only** **Higher tier only**	☺ ☺ ☹	☺ ☺ ☹	☺ ☺ ☹		
I can draw a polymer from a given monomer **Chemistry only** **Higher tier only**	☺ ☺ ☹	☺ ☺ ☹	☺ ☺ ☹		
I can draw the monomer from a given polymer **Chemistry only** **Higher tier only**	☺ ☺ ☹	☺ ☺ ☹	☺ ☺ ☹		
I can recall what DNA is **Chemistry only**	☺ ☺ ☹	☺ ☺ ☹	☺ ☺ ☹	https://youtu.be/ erZB_EhuKbA	TuitionKit http://bit.ly /2xjLcEd
I can recall the structure of DNA **Chemistry only**	☺ ☺ ☹	☺ ☺ ☹	☺ ☺ ☹		
I can recall how DNA relates to amino acids **Chemistry only**	☺ ☺ ☹	☺ ☺ ☹	☺ ☺ ☹		TuitionKit http://bit.ly /2fxiw1k

I can identify the two different functional groups in amino acid **Chemistry only**	☺ ☺ ☹	☺ ☺ ☹	☺ ☺ ☹		
I can describe how an amino acid polymerises **Chemistry only**	☺ ☺ ☹	☺ ☺ ☹	☺ ☺ ☹		
I can describe the process of amino acids joining together to form a polymer **Chemistry only**	☺ ☺ ☹	☺ ☺ ☹	☺ ☺ ☹		

This worksheet is fully supported by a video tutorial; https://youtu.be/sE2DP0x48kE

1. Define hydrocarbon.
2. What is crude oil made up from?
3. What is the general formula for alkanes?
4. Draw methane.
5. Draw ethane.
6. Draw propane.
7. Draw butane.
8. Why do we need to separate crude oil into fractions?
9. How does boiling point change with chain length?
10. How does viscosity change with chain length?
11. How does flammability change with chain length?
12. Write the word equation for complete combustion.
13. Why do we need to crack long hydrocarbons?
14. How do we test for alkenes?

Chemistry Only

15. What is the general formula for alkenes?
16. What does unsaturated mean?
17. Draw ethene.
18. Draw propene.
19. Draw butene.
20. Draw pentene.
21. What is the word equation for incomplete combustion?
22. What is the difference between complete and incomplete combustion?
23. Describe the reaction of an alkene with a halogen.
24. Describe the reaction of an alkene with water.
25. Describe the reaction of an alkene with hydrogen.
26. What is the functional group for alcohol?
27. Draw methanol.
28. Draw ethanol.
29. Draw propanol.
30. Draw butanol.
31. What is the main use of alcohol?
32. What happens when alcohol reacted oxygen?
33. What are the conditions needed for fermentation?

34. Draw the functional group for a carboxylic acid.
35. Draw methanoic acid.
36. Draw ethanoic acid.
37. Draw propanoic acid.
38. Draw butanoic acid.
39. What are the uses for carboxylic acids?
40. What happens when a carboxylic acid reacts with a carbonate?
41. What happens when a carboxylic acid reacts with water?
42. What happens when a carboxylic acid reacts with alcohol?
43. Draw ethyl ethanoate.
44. Define monomer.
45. Define polymer.
46. Describe polymerisation.
47. What is condensation polymerisation?
48. What is the structure of DNA?
49. How does DNA relate to amino acids?
50. Draw the basic structure of an amino acid.

8 – Chemical Analysis

Knowledge Checklist

Whole topic summary https://youtu.be/YyUQiUddBA4 in only 6 minutes!!

Specification statement These are the bits the exam board wants you to know, make sure you can do all of these...	Self-assessment			Bits to help if you don't understand	
	First review 4-7 months before exam	Second review 1-2 months before exam	Final review Week before exam	Primrose Kitten	Other places
I can recall the difference between a pure substance and a mixture	☺ ☺ ☹	☺ ☺ ☹	☺ ☺ ☹		TuitionKit http://bit.ly /2wuWTsX
I can define the term formulation	☺ ☺ ☹	☺ ☺ ☹	☺ ☺ ☹		
I can use the melting point of a substance to determine if it is pure or a mixture	☺ ☺ ☹	☺ ☺ ☹	☺ ☺ ☹		
I can give everyday example of formulations	☺ ☺ ☹	☺ ☺ ☹	☺ ☺ ☹		
I can describe how chromatography can be used to identify if a compound is pure or a mixture	☺ ☺ ☹	☺ ☺ ☹	☺ ☺ ☹		TuitionKit http://bit.ly /2ww3J1C
I can calculate R_f values	☺ ☺ ☹	☺ ☺ ☹	☺ ☺ ☹		
I can recall the test for hydrogen	☺ ☺ ☹	☺ ☺ ☹	☺ ☺ ☹	https://youtu.be /wuNB1n5z9QM	TuitionKit http://bit.ly /2ynX32F
I can recall the test for oxygen	☺ ☺ ☹	☺ ☺ ☹	☺ ☺ ☹		
I can recall the test for carbon dioxide	☺ ☺ ☹	☺ ☺ ☹	☺ ☺ ☹	https://youtu.be /QR6GsydYUSI	
I can recall the test for chlorine	☺ ☺ ☹	☺ ☺ ☹	☺ ☺ ☹		
I can recall the colours of the flame test (lithium, sodium, potassium, calcium, copper) **Chemistry only**	☺ ☺ ☹	☺ ☺ ☹	☺ ☺ ☹	https://youtu.be /i3fEVB9VNOY https://youtu.be /LC4Nxd5dwEM	TuitionKit http://bit.ly /2he5l9f

I can recall the result for testing with sodium hydroxide (aluminium, calcium, magnesium, copper (II), iron (II), iron (III)) **Chemistry only**	☺ ☺ ☹	☺ ☺ ☹	☺ ☺ ☹	https://youtu.be /ESQYWh02Ykg	TuitionKit http://bit.ly /2xv04QR
I can write balanced equation for reactions with sodium hydroxide (aluminium, calcium, magnesium, copper (II), iron (II), iron (III)) **Chemistry only**	☺ ☺ ☹	☺ ☺ ☹	☺ ☺ ☹		
I can recall the test for carbonate ions **Chemistry only**	☺ ☺ ☹	☺ ☺ ☹	☺ ☺ ☹	https://youtu.be /7AGBLbl7AHE	TuitionKit http://bit.ly /2xcyLeo
I can recall the test for halide ions **Chemistry only**	☺ ☺ ☹	☺ ☺ ☹	☺ ☺ ☹	https://youtu.be /XtQ4hHZzX2k	
I can recall the test for sulfate ions **Chemistry only**	☺ ☺ ☹	☺ ☺ ☹	☺ ☺ ☹	https://youtu.be /k5gMGgmQDwo	
I can give the advantages and disadvantages of using instrumental method to identify ions rather than the ones used in class **Chemistry only**	☺ ☺ ☹	☺ ☺ ☹	☺ ☺ ☹		
I can describe the use of flame emission spectroscopy **Chemistry only**	☺ ☺ ☹	☺ ☺ ☹	☺ ☺ ☹		TuitionKit http://bit.ly /2yc7Fkg
I can interpret results of flame test emission spectroscopy **Chemistry only**	☺ ☺ ☹	☺ ☺ ☹	☺ ☺ ☹		

Quick Fire Questions.

This worksheet is fully supported by a video tutorial; https://youtu.be/vMKAHdoc-g0

1. Define mixture.
2. Defiant formulation.
3. Define melting point.
4. How can melting point be used to determine if a compound is pure or not?
5. How can chromatography be used to determine if a compound is pure or not?
6. How do you calculate R_f values?
7. What is the test for hydrogen gas?
8. What is the test oxygen gas?
9. What is the test for carbon dioxide?
10. What is the test for chlorine gas?

Chemistry only

11. What colour flame test for lithium go?
12. What colour flame test for sodium go?
13. What colour flame test for potassium go?
14. What colour flame test for calcium go?
15. What colour flame test for copper go?
16. What happens when you react aluminium with sodium hydroxide?
17. What happens when you react calcium with sodium hydroxide?
18. What happens when you react magnesium with sodium hydroxide?
19. What happens when you react copper (II) with sodium hydroxide?
20. What happens when you react iron (II) with sodium hydroxide?
21. What happens when you react iron (III) with sodium hydroxide?
22. What is the test carbonate ions?
23. What is the test for halide ions?
24. What is the test for sulfate ions?

Whole topic revision summary https://youtu.be/gxCRsqXZzeU in only 6 minutes!!

Specification statement These are the bits the exam board wants you to know, make sure you can do all of these...	Self-assessment			Bits to help if you don't understand	
	First review 4-7 months before exam	Second review 1-2 months before exam	Final review Week before exam	Primrose Kitten	Other places
I can state the different proportions of the gases in the current atmosphere	☺ ☺ ☹	☺ ☺ ☹	☺ ☺ ☹	https://youtu.be/7IIF4Ydb5J0	TuitionKit http://bit.ly/2xOaI5Z
I can state that the Earth's atmosphere has changed over time	☺ ☺ ☹	☺ ☺ ☹	☺ ☺ ☹	https://youtu.be/EYeh1FhEmmU	TuitionKit http://bit.ly/2hg9VA9
I can describe that changes that have led to the evolution of today's atmosphere	☺ ☺ ☹	☺ ☺ ☹	☺ ☺ ☹	https://youtu.be/KMK8Bo6XdSc	
I can explain how the levels of oxygen increased	☺ ☺ ☹	☺ ☺ ☹	☺ ☺ ☹		TuitionKit http://bit.ly/2jI4tdX
I can explain how the levels of carbon dioxide decreased	☺ ☺ ☹	☺ ☺ ☹	☺ ☺ ☹		
I can state the greenhouse gases	☺ ☺ ☹	☺ ☺ ☹	☺ ☺ ☹	https://youtu.be/y5PZ1RN5mt0	TuitionKit http://bit.ly/2jJXD7R
I can describe how these gases interact with radiation	☺ ☺ ☹	☺ ☺ ☹	☺ ☺ ☹	https://youtu.be/9IvHkJxVukw	
I can describe the effect an increased level of these gases in the atmosphere has on the climate	☺ ☺ ☹	☺ ☺ ☹	☺ ☺ ☹	https://youtu.be/PK8aljEFRKA	
I can recall which activities contribute to increased levels of greenhouse gases in the atmosphere	☺ ☺ ☹	☺ ☺ ☹	☺ ☺ ☹	https://youtu.be/y5PZ1RN5mt0	TuitionKit http://bit.ly/2xvnWUr

I can recall what the predictions are for the effect of greenhouse gases of future temperature levels	☺ 😐 ☹	☺ 😐 ☹	☺ 😐 ☹		TuitionKit http://bit.ly /2f7QtF7
I can discuss the limitations of scientific models	☺ 😐 ☹	☺ 😐 ☹	☺ 😐 ☹		
I can define the term carbon footprint	☺ 😐 ☹	☺ 😐 ☹	☺ 😐 ☹		TuitionKit http://bit.ly /2f8AYg7
I can list the major sources of atmospheric pollution	☺ 😐 ☹	☺ 😐 ☹	☺ 😐 ☹		TuitionKit http://bit.ly /2xcvZFG
I can describe the effects that carbon dioxide has on the atmosphere	☺ 😐 ☹	☺ 😐 ☹	☺ 😐 ☹	https://youtu.be /PK8aljEFRKA	
I can describe the effects that sulfur dioxide has on the atmosphere	☺ 😐 ☹	☺ 😐 ☹	☺ 😐 ☹	https://youtu.be /nitv5kjgTKQ	
I can describe the effects that water vapour has on the atmosphere	☺ 😐 ☹	☺ 😐 ☹	☺ 😐 ☹		
I can describe the effects that carbon monoxide has on the atmosphere	☺ 😐 ☹	☺ 😐 ☹	☺ 😐 ☹		
I can describe the effects that nitrogen oxides have on the atmosphere	☺ 😐 ☹	☺ 😐 ☹	☺ 😐 ☹		
I can describe the effects that carbon particles have on the atmosphere	☺ 😐 ☹	☺ 😐 ☹	☺ 😐 ☹	https://youtu.be /Ut4xCQnSldM	
I can describe the effects that pollution has on humans, animals and plants	☺ 😐 ☹	☺ 😐 ☹	☺ 😐 ☹		

This worksheet is fully supported by a video tutorial; https://youtu.be/DznhhA2QHUg

1. How much oxygen is there in the atmosphere?
2. How much carbon dioxide is there in the atmosphere?
3. How much nitrogen is there in the atmosphere?
4. How was the early atmosphere different to todays?
5. What led to an increase in oxygen in the atmosphere?
6. What led to the increase in nitrogen in the atmosphere?
7. Give two things that led to a decrease in carbon dioxide in the atmosphere.
8. What are three greenhouse gases?
9. How do greenhouse gases interact with radiation?
10. What impact does increased level of these gases in the atmosphere have on the climate?
11. Give two activities that lead to an increased level of greenhouse gases in the atmosphere.
12. What are the predictions of the effects of greenhouse gases on future temperature levels?
13. Define the term carbon footprint.
14. What are the major sources of atmospheric pollution?
15. What affect does carbon dioxide have on the atmosphere?
16. What affect does sulfur dioxide have on the atmosphere?
17. What affect does water vapour have on the atmosphere?
18. What affect does carbon monoxide have on the atmosphere?
19. What affect does nitrogen oxides have on the atmosphere?
20. What affect do carbon particles have on the atmosphere?
21. What affect does pollution have on humans?
22. What affects does pollution have on plants?
23. What affect does pollution have on animals?

10 – Using Resources

Knowledge Checklist

Whole topic summary https://youtu.be/KyVf2bVLl08 in only 10 minutes!!

Specification statement These are the bits the exam board wants you to know, make sure you can do all of these…	Self-assessment			Bits to help if you don't understand	
	First review 4-7 months before exam	Second review 1-2 months before exam	Final review Week before exam	Primrose Kitten	Other places
I can describe the different ways humans use the Earth's resources, including warmth, shelter, food and transport	☺ ☺ ☹	☺ ☺ ☹	☺ ☺ ☹		
I can state the resources we get from the Earth come from a range of sources including the land, oceans and atmosphere	☺ ☺ ☹	☺ ☺ ☹	☺ ☺ ☹		
I can differentiate between finite and renewable resources	☺ ☺ ☹	☺ ☺ ☹	☺ ☺ ☹		
I can state the importance of water to human life	☺ ☺ ☹	☺ ☺ ☹	☺ ☺ ☹		
I can recall the methods used to produce portable water	☺ ☺ ☹	☺ ☺ ☹	☺ ☺ ☹	https://youtu.be /YdfVe8AIRgc	TuitionKit http://bit.ly /2xPWWQg
I can describe the ways of sterilising water	☺ ☺ ☹	☺ ☺ ☹	☺ ☺ ☹		
I can describe the process of desalination	☺ ☺ ☹	☺ ☺ ☹	☺ ☺ ☹		
I can recall the difference between pure and portable water	☺ ☺ ☹	☺ ☺ ☹	☺ ☺ ☹		
I can describe the process of waste water treatment	☺ ☺ ☹	☺ ☺ ☹	☺ ☺ ☹	https://youtu.be /xJkKCzApbhM	TuitionKit http://bit.ly /2heNcnW
I can describe different method for purifying water	☺ ☺ ☹	☺ ☺ ☹	☺ ☺ ☹		

I can explain the reasons for developing new method to extract metals from the Earth	☺ ☺ ☹	☺ ☺ ☹	☺ ☺ ☹		TuitionKit http://bit.ly /2fxzrkk
I can describe the process of bioleaching	☺ ☺ ☹	☺ ☺ ☹	☺ ☺ ☹		
I can describe the process of phytomining	☺ ☺ ☹	☺ ☺ ☹	☺ ☺ ☹		
I can assess the impact of raw materials, manufacturing, packaging, uses and disposal of an object	☺ ☺ ☹	☺ ☺ ☹	☺ ☺ ☹		
I can analyse Life Cycle Assessments	☺ ☺ ☹	☺ ☺ ☹	☺ ☺ ☹		
I can describe ways of reducing the amount of resources used.	☺ ☺ ☹	☺ ☺ ☹	☺ ☺ ☹		TuitionKit http://bit.ly /2yby6Xr
I can describe the process of rusting **Chemistry only**	☺ ☺ ☹	☺ ☺ ☹	☺ ☺ ☹	https://youtu.be /LQ-prcAHM_U	
I can describe ways to prevent corrosion **Chemistry only**	☺ ☺ ☹	☺ ☺ ☹	☺ ☺ ☹		TuitionKit http://bit.ly /2ycbHt4
I can interpret result that show which factors affect rusting **Chemistry only**	☺ ☺ ☹	☺ ☺ ☹	☺ ☺ ☹	https://youtu.be /LQ-prcAHM_U	
I can describe the structure of an alloy **Chemistry only**	☺ ☺ ☹	☺ ☺ ☹	☺ ☺ ☹		TuitionKit http://bit.ly /2w4OI2c
I can describe how the structure of an alloy relates to its properties **Chemistry only**	☺ ☺ ☹	☺ ☺ ☹	☺ ☺ ☹		
I can state the composition of most of the glass we use **Chemistry only**	☺ ☺ ☹	☺ ☺ ☹	☺ ☺ ☹		
I can describe the makeup of clay ceramics **Chemistry only**	☺ ☺ ☹	☺ ☺ ☹	☺ ☺ ☹		TuitionKit http://bit.ly /2xcGuZF
I can link the properties of polymers to their structure **Chemistry only**	☺ ☺ ☹	☺ ☺ ☹	☺ ☺ ☹	https://youtu.be /bPFn7Lehr6s	TuitionKit http://bit.ly /2xfeKRG

I can define the term composite and describe some uses **Chemistry only**	☺ ☻ ☹	☺ ☻ ☹	☺ ☻ ☹		
I can recall what the Haber process is used for **Chemistry only**	☺ ☻ ☹	☺ ☻ ☹	☺ ☻ ☹	https://youtu.be/0Yz1EgqfxAk	TuitionKit http://bit.ly/2ybTlYX
I can state the source of nitrogen and hydrogen **Chemistry only**	☺ ☻ ☹	☺ ☻ ☹	☺ ☻ ☹	https://youtu.be/sqq8iSFH4KU	
I can state the conditions needed for the Haber process **Chemistry only**	☺ ☻ ☹	☺ ☻ ☹	☺ ☻ ☹		
I can apply the principles of dynamic equilibrium to the Haber process **Chemistry only**	☺ ☻ ☹	☺ ☻ ☹	☺ ☻ ☹		
I can describe the production and uses of NPK fertilisers **Chemistry only**	☺ ☻ ☹	☺ ☻ ☹	☺ ☻ ☹		TuitionKit http://bit.ly/2wFjb6E

This worksheet is fully supported by a video tutorial; https://youtu.be/xBUXqfa2gHo

1. What different ways can humans use the Earth's resources?
2. Give 3 resources we get from the Earth.
3. Define finite resource.
4. Define renewable resource.
5. How do you produce portable water?
6. How do you sterilise water?
7. How do you desalinate water?
8. Why do we need to develop new methods to extract materials from the Earth?
9. What is bioleaching?
10. What is phytomining?
11. How do we assess the impact of an object?
12. How do we analyse a life-cycle assessment?
13. How can you reduce amount of resources used?

Chemistry Only

14. What is rusting?
15. How can we prevent corrosion?
16. What is the structure of an alloy?
17. How does the structure of an ally relate to its properties?
18. What is the composition of most of the glass we use?
19. What are clay ceramics?
20. How do the structure of polymers link to their properties?
21. What is the Haber process used for?
22. In the Haber process, where does the nitrogen and hydrogen come from?
23. In the Haber process, what are the conditions needed?

Chemistry Paper 2 Checklist – What to do before the exam!

Watched the whole topic video   https://youtu.be/_HJu8WTtZJU ☐

Learnt all the ions ☐

Practiced the equations ☐

Answered the quick-fire questions ☐

Looked at the practical videos ☐

Learnt the keywords ☐

Filled in the crosswords ☐

Crosswords

Chemistry Crossword 1

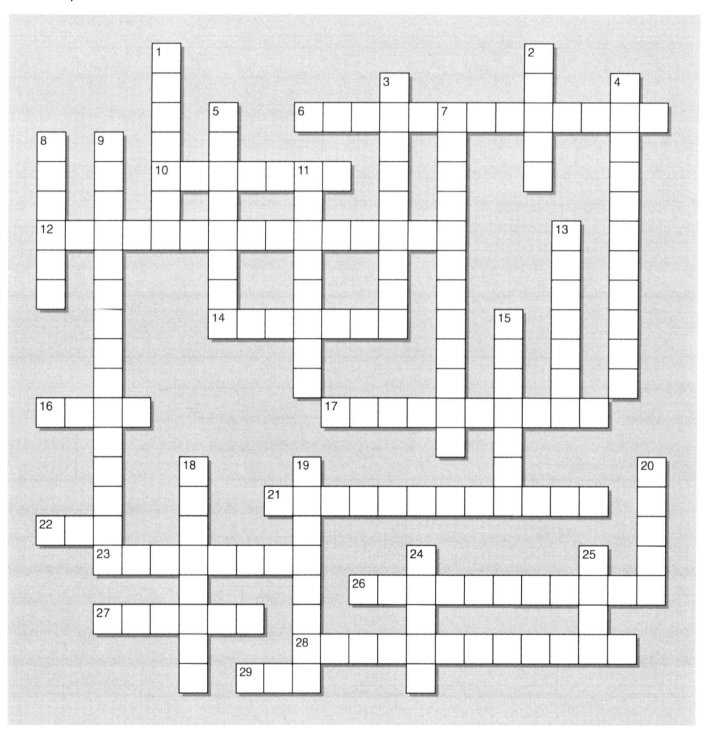

Across

6) a way of sorting out the elements

10) group of (or single) atoms that all have the same chemical characteristics, can be found on the periodic table

12) group of metal that are in the middle of the periodic table, form colour compounds and can be used as catalysts

14) found in the nucleus of atoms, has no charge and a mass of one

16) small part of matter, made up from a mixture of protons, neutrons and electrons

17) the number of protons and neutrons in an atom

21) transfer of electrons between a metal and a non-metal

22) atoms that has lost or gained electrons

23) giant covalent compound where each carbon atom makes three bonds

26) a way of determining how many of the reactant atoms made it into the desired product

27) a state of matter, where the atoms can move and flow but they cannot be compressed

28) the number of protons in an atom

29) a state of matter where the atoms move atom in a fast and random matter, can be compressed and flow

Down

1) in the centre of atoms, contains the protons and the neutrons   nucleus

2) on the left-hand side of the periodic table, form positive ions   metals

3) method for determining concentration of solution

4) highly reactive metals found on the left-hand side of the periodic table

5) found in the shells around the nucleus, has a charge of minus one and no mass   electrons

7) a type of reaction where one element replaces another in a compound

8) found in the nucleus of atoms, has a charge of plus one and a mass of one   proton

9) sharing of electron between two non-metals

11) on the right-hand side of the periodic table, form negative ions

13) lots of different elements that may or may not be chemically bonded together

15) giant covalent compound where each carbon atom makes four bonds

18) two or more elements chemically bonded together

19) unreactive gases found on the right of the periodic table

20) mixture of atoms that lead to distorted layers that cannot slide

24) a state of matter, where the atoms vibrate around a fixed position   solid

25) the molecular mass in grams

Chemistry Crossword 2

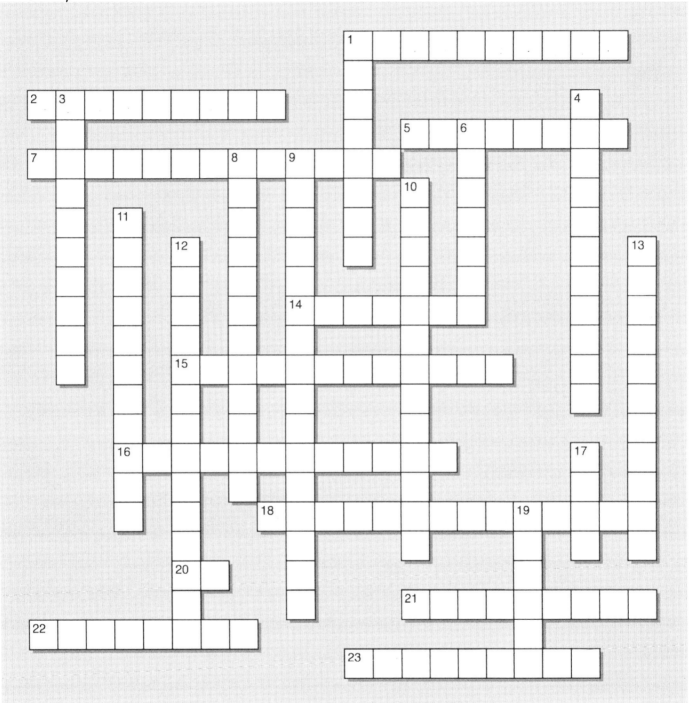

Across

1) burning of a compound in oxygen

2) gain of electrons

5) breaking a long hydrocarbon chain to short hydrocarbon chains

7) water that is safe to drink

14) hydrocarbon containing double bonds

15) point at which a solid turns into a liquid

16) orange liquid that can be used to test for double bonds

18) mixing of an acid and an alkali to give a pH of 7

20) how acid or alkali a solution is

21) loss of electrons

22) something that speeds up a react of reaction without being use dup

23) how easily pourable something is

Down

1) a mixture of different length hydrocarbon chains made from decomposing dead plant and animals

3) a reaction that releases energy

4) a reaction that takes in energy

6) hydrocarbon containing only single bonds

8) separating compounds using electricity

9) the energy needed to start reaction

10) gas that traps i-redadiation

11) a compound that only has carbon and hydrogen in it

12) method of separating out mixtures

13) mining low yield ores using plants

17) a solution that has a low pH due to the hydrogen ions

19) a solution that has a high pH due to hydroxide ions

Maths (The Chemistry bits) for Science Students

Periodic Table

Due to copyright restrictions this periodic table is a bit different to the one you'll see in the exam, if you want to use the one for your exam board, you can down load it and ignore this one.

Periods → go across

The period tells you the number of electron shells

Groups – go down

The group tells you the number of electrons on the out shell

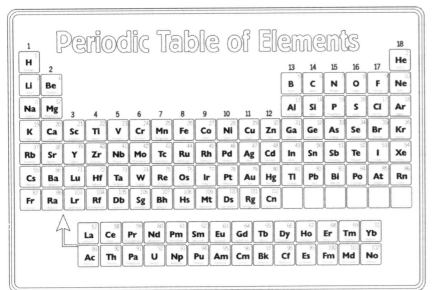

The periodic table tells us so much about the structure of atoms!

It can remind you how many electrons go in each shell, notice in the first period there are two elements, and in the first electron shell there are two electron, in the second period there are 8 electrons, and in the second shell there are 8 electrons.

Element	Period	Group
Calcium		
Beryllium		
Nitrogen		
Aluminium		
Sulfur		

The mass number is the larger of the two numbers, in the box, it doesn't matter where its positioned and when I say larger I don't mean the size of the writing.

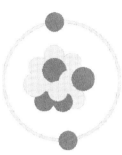

For each of the following give the mass number and the atomic number.

Element	Mass number	Atomic number
5 B Boron 11		
12 Mg Magnesium 24		
24 Cr Chromium 52		
11 Na Sodium 23		
14 Si Silicon 28		
Oxygen		
Helium		
	45	
	31	
		29

The number of protons is the atomic number

In an atom the number of electrons is also the atomic number

The number of neutrons is the mass number minus the atomic number

Element	Number of protons	Number of electrons	Number of neutrons
17 Cl Chlorine 35.5			
35 Br Bromine 80			
28 Ni Nickel 59			
8 O Oxygen 16			
53 I Iodine 127			
Argon			
Boron			
	56		
		27	
			16

An isotope is an element that the same number of protons and electrons but a different number of neutrons.

We write these with the name first then the mass number, for example carbon-12 is carbon with a mass of 12 and carbon -13 is carbon with a mass of 13.

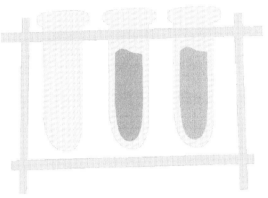

Element	Number of protons	Number of electrons	Number of neutrons
Carbon-13			
Oxygen-18			
Nitrogen -16			
Iron-55			
Magnesium-26			
Argon-41			
Sulfur-34			
Fluorine-17			
Hydrogen-3			
Calcium-38			

Ions

When an atom gains or losses and electrons it becomes an ion.

Element	Atom		Ion		Charge
	Number of protons	Number of electrons	Number of protons	Number of electrons	
Sodium					Na^+
Magnesium					Mg^{2+}
Oxygen					O^{2-}
Fluorine					F^-
Chlorine					Cl^-
Lithium					Li^+
Calcium					Ca^{2+}
Potassium					K^+
	3				Li^-
	53			54	

Remember elements are found on the periodic table, the small number after each element tells you how many of that elements there is in a compound.

Compound	Number of elements	Number of atoms
H_2O		
O_2		
$CaCO_3$		
NH_3		
CH_4		
H_2SO_4		
HCl		
HNO_3		
CuO		
SO_2		

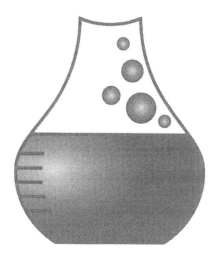

The brackets mean that everything inside the brackets get multiplied by the small number outside the brackets.

Compound	Number of elements	Number of atoms
$Ca(OH)_2$		
$Cu(NO_3)_2$		
$Cr_2(SO_4)_3$		
$Fe_2(SO_4)_3$		

When a reaction takes place we don't lose any mass and we don't gain any mass, in other words the left hand side must weigh the same as the right hand side.

Fill in the missing bits below

Magnesium	+	Oxygen	→	Magnesium oxide		
5g	+	0.1g	→	……………		

Sodium	+	Water	→	Sodium hydroxide	+	Hydrogen
2.1g	+	0.5g	→	2.3g	+	……………

Silver sulfate	+	Magnesium	→	Magnesium sulfate	+	Silver
14.65g	+	7.56g	→	13.98g	+	…………

Calcium	+	Hydrochloric acid	→	Calcium chloride	+	Hydrogen
17.0g	+	……….	→	19.2g	+	0.9g

Iron oxide	+	Carbon	→	Iron	+	Carbon dioxide
45.8g	+	…………	→	52.3g	+	1.2g

Easy – grade 5

1. ....H_2 + O_2 → ....H_2O
2. H_2 + Cl_2 → ....HCl
3. ....Mg + O_2 → ....MgO
4. N_2 + ...H_2 → ....NH_3
5. ....Zn + O_2 → ....ZnO
6. N_2 + O_2 → ....NO
7. ....K + S → K_2S
8. Mg + ...HCl → $MgCl_2$ + H_2
9. ....Na + ...H_2O → ....NaOH + H_2
10. ....Ca + O_2 → ....CaO
11. Ca + ...HCl → $CaCl_2$ + H_2
12. ....Na + Cl_2 → ....NaCl
13. ....SO_2 + O_2 → ....SO_3
14. ....KOH + $MgSO_4$ → $Mg(OH)_2$ + K_2SO_4
15. K_2O_2 + ...H_2O → H_2O_2 + ...KOH
16. .....Na + ...H_2O → .....NaOH + H_2
17. ....NaOH + H_3PO_4 → Na_3PO_4 + ...H_2O
18. ....K + ...H_2O → ....KOH + H_2
19. Ag_2SO_4 + Mg → $MgSO_4$ + ...Ag
20. ....Al + ...O_2 → ....Al_2O_3

1. $Fe_2O_3 + Al \rightarrow Fe + Al_2O_3$
2. $N_2 + Cl_2 \rightarrow NCl_3$
3. $C + Cl_2 \rightarrow CCl_4$
4. $CaCl_2 + KOH \rightarrow Ca(OH)_2 + KCl$
5. $P_4 + Cl_2 \rightarrow PCl_3$
6. $C_2H_4 + O_2 \rightarrow CO_2 + H_2O$
7. $Mg + CO_2 \rightarrow MgO + C$
8. $H_2O_2 \rightarrow H_2O + O_2$
9. $C_2H_6 + O_2 \rightarrow CO_2 + H_2O$
10. $Fe_2O_3 + C \rightarrow Fe + CO$
11. $TiCl_4 + Mg \rightarrow MgCl_2 + Ti$
12. $PH_3 + O_2 \rightarrow P_2O_3 + H_2O$
13. $PH_5 + O_2 \rightarrow P_2O_5 + H_2O$
14. $CuCl_2 + NaOH \rightarrow Cu(OH)_2 + NaCl$
15. $KI + Pb(NO_3)_2 \rightarrow KNO_3 + PbI_2$
16. $PCl_3 + H_2O \rightarrow P(OH)_3 + HCl$
17. $C_3H_8 + O_2 \rightarrow CO_2 + H_2O$
18. $Pb(NO_3)_2 \rightarrow PbO + NO_2 + O_2$
19. $C_6H_{12}O_6 + O_2 \rightarrow H_2O + CO_2$
20. $NH_3 + O_2 \rightarrow NO + H_2O$

1. $Mg + HIO_3 \rightarrow MgIO_3 + H_2$
2. $BaCl_2 + Na_2SO_4 \rightarrow NaCl + BaSO_4$
3. $NaI + HOCl \rightarrow NaIO_3 + HCl$
4. $Al + MnO_2 \rightarrow Al_2O_3 + Mn$
5. $Ba(OH)_2 + H_2SO_4 \rightarrow BaSO_4 + H_2O$
6. $K_2CO_3 + AgNO_3 \rightarrow KNO_3 + Ag_2CO_3$
7. $Sr(ClO_4)_2 + K_2SO_4 \rightarrow SrSO_4 + KClO_4$
8. $Al + H_2SO_4 \rightarrow Al_2(SO_4)_3 + H_2$
9. $HNO_3 + H_2S \rightarrow NO + S + H_2O$
10. $Pb(NO_3)_2 + KCl \rightarrow PbCl_2 + KNO_3$
11. $MgCO_3 + HNO_3 \rightarrow Mg(NO_3)_2 + H_2O + CO_2$
12. $H_2SO_4 + NaOH \rightarrow Na_2SO_4 + H_2O$
13. $SO_2 + HNO_2 \rightarrow H_2SO_4 + NO$
14. $HI + H_2SO_4 \rightarrow H_2O + H_2S + I_2$
15. $HCl + Al(OH)_3 \rightarrow H_2O + AlCl_3$
16. $NaOH + CuSO_4 \rightarrow Na_2SO_4 + Cu(OH)_2$
17. $HF + Ba(NO_3)_2 \rightarrow HNO_3 + BaF_2$
18. $NO_2 + H_2 \rightarrow NH_3 + H_2O$
19. $NH_3 + O_2 \rightarrow NO + H_2O$
20. $HCl + FeCl_2 + H_2O_2 \rightarrow FeCl_3 + H_2O$

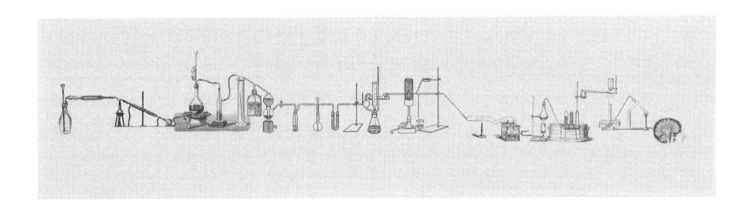

To find the mass of the compound, add the mass numbers of the elements together.

Compound	Relative mass
H_2O	
O_2	
$CaCO_3$	
NH_3	
CH_4	
H_2SO_4	
HCl	
HNO_3	
CuO	
$Ca(OH)_2$	
$Cu(NO_3)_2$	
$Cr_2(SO_4)_3$	
$Fe_2(SO_4)_3$	

If you've ever wondered why Cl has a mass of 35.5 then this section is for you. The mass shown on the periodic table is an average mass of all the isotopes found on Earth. Give all answers to 4 significant figures.

1. Chlorine is found as 2 naturally occurring isotopes ^{35}Cl and ^{37}Cl, 75% of the chlorine is ^{35}Cl and 25% is ^{37}Cl, calculate the relative atomic mass of chlorine from its isotopes.
2. Bromine is found as 50% ^{79}Br and 50% ^{81}Br, what is the average relative atomic mass?
3. Iron can be found as 4 different naturally occurring isotopes, the most common (91.6%) is ^{56}Fe, followed by (5.9%) ^{54}Fe, (2.2%) ^{57}Fe and (0.2%) ^{58}Fe, what is the relative isotopic mass of iron?
4. Calcium can be found as a wide range of different isotopes, the one with the highest percentage is ^{40}Ca (96.9%), followed by ^{44}Ca (2.0%) ^{42}Ca (0.8%) ^{48}Ca (0.2%) and ^{43}Ca (0.1%) what is the relative atomic mass of calcium?
5. Iridium is listed on the periodic table as having a mass of 192.2, it has 2 naturally occurring isotopes ^{191}Ir and ^{193}Ir. What are the relative percentages of each isotope?

Moles = mass in grams / relative mass

Compound	Relative mass	Mass in grams	Moles
N_2		28	
CO_2		22	
CaO		112	
Fe_2O_3		40	
PCl_3		27.5	
$Mg(OH)_2$			2
$KHSO_4$			0.75
Na_2SO_4			2.3
H_3AsO_4			0.67
$Cu(NO_3)_2$			1.56

1. 1.8g of water is used in a reaction, how many moles are being used?
2. If 3 moles of magnesium hydroxide are required for a practical, how much should the students weigh out?
3. When decomposing calcium carbonate 1.75 moles of calcium hydroxide is produced, how much does it weigh?
4. After a reaction had finished it was found that a solid has lost 0.5 moles of nitrogen gas. How much did the weight of the solid reduce by?
5. 5.2g of hydrogen peroxide (H_2O_2) decomposed to make water and oxygen gas, how many moles of oxygen were released?

When I'm baking cakes I follow a recipe, and always expect to end up with 24 lovely yummy cupcakes!

This never actually works, I always end up with less cupcakes then I want!

This is the difference between theoretical yield (how many you expect to get) and actual yield (how many you actually get).

To calculate the percentage yield we divide the actual mass by the theoretical mass and turn it into a percentage.

1. In a reaction a student expected to produce 56g of calcium oxide, they only produced 42g. What is the percentage yield?
2. An industrial reaction was expected to give a total of 1.53 tonnes, in the end it was found that 0.95 tonnes was produced, find the percentage yield.
3. When a reaction is performed on an industrial scale it is found that only 95Kg is produced, it was expected that 145kg would be produced. What is the percentage yield?
4. While in the lab a student was expecting to make 65g of magnesium oxide, she only produced 54g, what is the percentage yield?
5. When producing ammonia from nitrogen and hydrogen, the theoretical yield was 1.75kg, in reality 0.35kg less then this was produced. Calculate the percentage yield and give reason that the actual yield was less than the theoretical yield.

These questions combine reacting masses and percentage yield, if you haven't covered reacting masses yet do that first and come back here.

6. In the following reaction $Fe_3O_2 + 3CO \rightarrow 2Fe + 3CO_2$, 0.95Kg of iron ore yields 0.46kg of iron, calculate the percentage yield.
7. 1000 tonnes of Cyclohexane (M_r=98) reacts to produce 834 tonnes of methylene cyclohexane (M_r=96) what is the percentage yield.
8. Ethanoic acid (CH_3COOH) is reacted with ethanol (C_2H_5OH) to produce ethyl ethanoate ($CH_3COOC_2H_5$), if we start with 21g of ethanol and produce 36g of ethyl ethanoate, calculate the percentage yield.

Atom economy is a lot like percentage yield but we need to look at the M_r not the mass.

% atom economy = $\underline{M_r \text{ useful product}}$
M_r total reactants

This is one example where producing ethanol from crude oil is advantageous to producing it from fermentation as there is no waste product.

1. Calculate the atom economy for the production of iron from its ore. $Fe_3O_2 + 3CO \rightarrow 2Fe + 3CO_2$.
2. Photosynthesis produces glucose from carbon dioxide and water, what is the atom economy of this reaction?
   $6CO_2 + 6H_2O \rightarrow C_6H_{12}O_6 + 6O_2$
3. The reaction for producing copper hydroxide is $CuCl_2 + NaOH \rightarrow Cu(OH)_2 + NaCl$, calculate the atom economy of this reaction.
4. Calculate the atom economy when producing calcium oxide from calcium carbonate
5. Compare the atom economy when producing ethanol by hydration and by fermentation.

We use half equations to describe what goes on at each electrode during electrolysis, you can only add or take away electrons and make sure that the elements and charges are balanced.

Label each reaction as oxidation or reduction and give the location where it happens

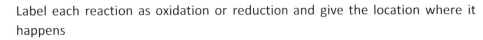

Reaction	Oxidation or Reduction	Anode or Cathode
$Cu^{2+} \ldots\ldots\ldots \rightarrow Cu$		
$F^- \ldots\ldots\ldots \rightarrow F_2$		
$Na^+ \ldots\ldots\ldots \rightarrow Na$		
$O^{2-} \rightarrow O_2 \ldots\ldots\ldots$		
$Al^{3+} \ldots\ldots\ldots \rightarrow Al$		
$Li^+ \ldots\ldots\ldots \rightarrow Li$		
$Cl^- \rightarrow Cl_2 \ldots\ldots\ldots$		
$H^+ \ldots\ldots\ldots \rightarrow H_2$		
$S^{2-} \ldots\ldots\ldots \rightarrow S$		
$Mg^{2+} \ldots\ldots\ldots \rightarrow Mg$		

Oxidation   Positive

Is   Anode

Loss   (of electrons)   Negative

Reduction   Is

Is   Cathode

Gain   (of electrons)

We can use equations to predict how much of a substance can be formed when a reaction takes place. There are two ways to do this, by using mole calculations or approaching it as a simple ratios question.

1. Water can be split into hydrogen and oxygen ($2H_2O \rightarrow 2H_2 + O_2$) how much oxygen would be produced from 56g of water?
2. Hydrogen peroxide can be broken down to water and oxygen gas ($2H_2O_2 \rightarrow 2H_2O + O_2$) how much hydrogen peroxide will be needed to make 17g of oxygen?
3. Magnesium chloride can be produced by the reaction of sodium metal with chlorine gas, ($Mg + Cl_2 \rightarrow MgCl_2$) how much magnesium is needed to produce 193.5g of magnesium chloride?
4. The reaction between limewater (calcium hydroxide) and carbon dioxide produces a white precipitate (the cloudy bits) how much calcium carbonate is produced from 196g of limewater? ($Ca(OH)_2 + CO_2 \rightarrow CaCO_3 + H_2O$)
5. Aluminium reacts with oxygen to produce aluminium oxide ($Al + O_2 \rightarrow Al_2O_3$) how much aluminium oxide will be produced from 36g of aluminium metal?

For each of these you are expected to first write and balance the equation.

6. Copper oxide (CuO) is reacted with hydrogen gas (H_2) to produce copper and water, how much copper oxide is needed to give 21g of copper?
7. Propane gas burns completely in oxygen, how much carbon dioxide will be produced if 19g of propane is burnt?
8. In respiration glucose is converted to carbon dioxide and water, if 36g of glucose is reacted how much carbon dioxide will be produced?
9. Calcium carbonate reacts with hydrochloric acid how much carbon dioxide is produced from 21g of hydrochloric acid?
10. Iron metal is reacted with hydrochloric acid and 17.9g iron chloride is produced, how much iron is needed?

Avogadro's constant and gas volume

A mole has a fixed number of particles in it, 6.02×10^{23} and one moles of gas takes up 24dm^3 of space.

You can think of it like a shoe collection, each collection is going to take the same amount of space. Just some collections are going to be full of flip flops, some full of fabulous, colourful high heels and some are going to be full of walking boots, but it not a complete collection until there are 6.02×10^{23} shoes in it.......I wish ☺

Compound	M_r	Mass in grams	Number of moles	Number of particles	Gas volume (dm^3)
KOH			1		
CO_2			0.5		
NaOH			2		
$CaCO_3$		50			
PCl_3		34.375			
SF_6		14.6			
MgO				6.02×10^{23}	
C_2H_6					24
NH_3					6
$P(OH)_3$					2

Each bond has a certain amount of energy associated with it, this energy is released when a bonds are made (an exothermic process) and energy is needed to break bonds (an endothermic process) to find the total energy given off or taken in during a reaction you needed to find the difference.

Bond energy rules

a) Write the balanced equation for the reaction
b) Draw the structural formula for each compound
c) List the types of bonds
d) List the number of each type of bond
e) Use the table to work out the energy associated with each bond
f) Multiply the number of bonds by the energy for that bond
g) Work out the total amount for bond breaking and bond making
h) Work out the difference

Bond	Bond energy in kJ per mole
H – H	436
O = O	498
O – H	464
C – H	435
C – Cl	327
C = O	805
Cl–Cl	242
H–Cl	431
H-Br	366
Br-Br	193

Bond energy questions

1. Burning hydrogen (H-H) in oxygen (O=O) will give off water (H-O-H), calculate the energy change for this reaction.
2. Hydrogen bromide breaks down to form hydrogen gas and bromine gas, what is the energy change?
3. Hydrogen and chlorine can be reacted together to make hydrochloric acid, calculate the energy change for this reaction.
4. The combustion of methane in oxygen give off water and carbon dioxide (C=O=C) calculate the energy change for this reaction.
5. Methane reacts with chlorine gas to give chloromethane and hydrochloric acid, calculate the energy change for this reaction.

This is potentially the hardest maths you'll come across, I'm going to break it down bit by bit.

In a titration we're looking for the end point where $H^+ = OH^-$

dm^3 = 1 litre

A mole is the M_r in grams

mol/dm^3 is saying 1 mole dissolved in 1 litre

You don't get given these equations in the exam, you need to remember them

$$n = c \times v$$

n = number of moles (mol)

c = concentration (mol/dm^3)

v = volume (dm^3)

1. Calculate the number of moles in $4dm^3$ of 1.2 mol/dm^3 HCl.
2. Calculate the number of moles in $2dm^3$ of 0.3 mol/dm^3 NaOH
3. Calculate the number of moles of KOH in $25cm^3$ of 0.2 mol/dm^3
4. Find the concentration of 3mol HBr in a $2dm^3$ solution
5. Calculate the concentration in 1mol of NaOH in $30cm^3$ of solution
6. Calculate the volume of 2.3 mol/dm^3 solution that contains 0.5mol HCl

$$m = n \times M_r$$

m = mass (g)

n = number of moles (mol)

M_r = relative formula mass

1. What mass of NaOH is there in $2dm^3$ of 0.3 mol/dm^3 solution?
2. What mass of H_2SO_4 is there in $3dm^3$ of 2 mol/dm^3 solution?
3. What is the mass of NaOH in $25cm^3$ of 0.3 mol/dm^3 solution?
4. What is the mass of HNO_3 that would dissolve in $500cm^3$ of water to produce a 2 mol/dm^3 solution?

Assuming acid is known and alkali is unknown, if opposite is true just reverse.

a) Calculate the number of moles of acid used
b) Using this find the number of H^+ ions involved in the reaction
c) This is equal to the number of OH^- ions involved in the reaction
d) Calculate the number of moles of alkali used
e) Calculate the concentration of the alkali

Titration calculations

1. $25cm^3$ of NaOH was neutralised by $15cm^3$ of 0.2 mol/dm^3 HCl, calculate the concentration of the alkali.
2. A solution of sodium hydroxide at 0.25 mol/dm^3, was used in a titration using a phenolphthalein indicator it was found that $25cm^3$ of this solution was titrated with $22.5cm^3$ of hydrochloric acid. What was the concentration of the acid?
3. $20.0cm^3$ of sulfuric acid was titrated against 0.05 mol/dm^3 potassium hydroxide. If the acid required $36.0cm^3$ of the alkali to be neutralised, what is the concentration of the acid?
4. $20cm^3$ of a solution made from pure barium hydroxide (containing 2.74g in $100cm^3$) is titrated, using phenolphthalein indicator, against $18.7cm^3$ of hydrochloric acid. What was the concentration of the HCl?
5. $25.0cm^3$ of sodium hydroxide (0.100 mol/dm^3) was titrated with $30.0cm^3$ of sulfuric acid. Find the concentration of the acid in g/dm^3.
6. $25.0cm^3$ of a solution of sodium hydroxide was pipetted into a conical flask and titrated with 0.200 mol/dm^3 (0.2M) HCl. Using a methyl orange indicator it was found that 15.0cm3 of the acid was required to neutralise the alkali. Calculate the molarity of the sodium hydroxide and the concentration in g/dm^3.
7. 4.90g of pure sulfuric acid was dissolved in water, the total resulting volume was $200cm^3$, $20.7cm^3$ of this solution was found after titration to need $10.0cm^3$ of sodium hydroxide to be neutralised. What is the concentration of sodium hydroxide?

Physics

5 most common mistakes in a physics exam

1. Not knowing your units - this comes up a lot as separate marks and your formula sheet will be useless if don't know these
2. Not being able to rearrange equations - if you want to get the top grades you'll need to use sophisticated maths skills
3. We don't use reoccurring in science - you need to round to the nearest whole number
4. Store numbers in your calculator's memory - so you don't make an error due to rounding
5. Missing out the keywords – easy, easy makes here but you need to learn them!!

Topic Guide

Topic	First review	Second review	Third review
1 – Energy			
2 – Electricity			
3 – Particle Model of Matter			
4 – Atomic Structure			
5 – Forces			
6 – Waves			
7 – Magnetism and Electromagnets			
8 – Space Physics			

Topic	Quick fire questions	Whole topic summary
1 – Energy	https://youtu.be/q5CwATii6OA	https://youtu.be/tDkBhy-Y1Z8
2 – Electricity	https://youtu.be/62RyyfKZoYg	https://youtu.be/jSA4WaLSVEA
3 – Particle Model of Matter	https://youtu.be/z9L6zfMVk3U	https://youtu.be/cZz9oGgJOL0
4 – Atomic Structure	https://youtu.be/bRzRjfvoU-E	https://youtu.be/YFVYUSvUBoo
5 – Forces	https://youtu.be/jfjb1pnH8zw	https://youtu.be/Rz4XBSKNGXg
6 – Waves	https://youtu.be/AEFwEDC6DkQ	https://youtu.be/9JPNVJ_LC3E
7 – Magnetism and Electromagnets	https://youtu.be/LyflUYL4FvM	https://youtu.be/mnigg3MGslY
8 – Space Physics	https://youtu.be/f3Rf1aVStIk	https://youtu.be/Mdi0i24tNT0

Required practical's

1. Specific Heat Capacity
2. Thermal Insulation (Physics only)
3. Resistance
4. I-V characteristics
5. Density
6. Force and extension   https://youtu.be/-Qk9WBOQW4w
7. Acceleration
8. Waves
9. Reflection (Physics only)
10. Surfaces   https://youtu.be/kDLx36gDz80

Units and equations available as readymade flashcards from my website

Topic 1 – Energy

Equation	Symbol	Unit
$E_k = \frac{1}{2} mv^2$	E_k = kinetic energy m = mass v = speed	E_k = J (joules) m = kg (kilograms) v = m/s (meters per second)
$E_e = \frac{1}{2} ke^2$ Given in the exam	E_e = elastic potential energy k = spring constant e = extension	E_e = J (joules) k = N/m (newtons per meter) e = m (meters)
$E_p = mgh$	E_p = gravitational potential energy m = mass g = gravitational field strength h = height	E_p = J (joules) m = kg (kilograms) g = N/kg (newtons per kilogram) h = m (meters)
$\Delta E = mc\Delta\theta$ Given in the exam	ΔE = change in thermal energy m = mass c = specific heat capacity $\Delta\theta$ = temperature change	ΔE = J (joules) m = kg (kilograms) c = J/kg°C (joules per kilogram degree Celsius) $\Delta\theta$ = °C (degree Celsius)
$P = \dfrac{E}{T}$	P = power E = energy transferred t = time	P = W (watts) E = J (joules) t = s (seconds)
$P = \dfrac{W}{T}$	P = power W = work done t = time	P = W (watts) E = J (joules) t = s (seconds)
Efficiency = $\dfrac{\text{useful energy out}}{\text{total energy in}}$		
Efficiency = $\dfrac{\text{useful power out}}{\text{total power in}}$		

Topic 2 – Electricity

Equation	Symbols	Units
$Q = It$	Q = Charge I = Current t = Time	Q = C (coulombs) I = A (amps) t = s (seconds)
$V = IR$	V = Potential difference I = Current R = Resistance	V = V (volts) I = A (amps) R = Ω (ohms)
$P = VI$	P = Power V = Potential difference I = Current	P = W (watts) V = V (volts) I = A (amps)
$P = I^2R$	P = Power I = Current R = Resistance	P = W (watts) I = A (amps) R = Ω (ohms)
$E = Pt$	E = Energy P = Power t = Time	E = J (joules) P = W (watts) t = s (seconds)
$E = QV$	E = Energy Q = Charge V = Potential difference	E = J (joules) Q = C (coulombs) V = V (volts)

Topic 3 – Particle Model of Matter

Equation	Symbols	Units
$\rho = \dfrac{m}{V}$	ρ = density m = mass V = volume	ρ = kg/m³ (kilograms per meter cubed m = kg (kilograms) V = m³ (meters cubed)
$\Delta E = mc\Delta\theta$ Given in the exam	ΔE = change in thermal energy m = mass c = specific heat capacity Δθ = temperature change	ΔE = J (joules) m = kg (kilograms) c = J/kg°C (joules per kilogram degree Celsius) Δθ = °C (degree Celsius)
$E = mL$ Given in the exam	E = Energy m = mass L = specific latent heat	E = J (joules) m = kg (kilograms) L = J/kg (joules per kilogram)
$pV = constant$ Physics only Given in the exam	p = pressure V = volume	p = Pa (pascals) V = m³ (meters cubed)

Equation	Symbols	Units
$W = mg$	W = weight m = mass g = gravitational field strength	W = N (newton's) m = kg (kilograms) g = N/kg (newtons per kilogram)
$W = Fs$	W = work done F = force s = distance	W = J (joules) F = N (newtons) s = m (meters)
$F = ke$	F = force k = spring constant e = extension	F = N (newtons) k = N/m (newtons per meter) e = m (meters)
$E_e = \frac{1}{2} ke^2$ Given in the exam	E_e = elastic potential energy k = spring constant e = extension	E_e = J (joules) k = N/m (newtons per meter) e = m (meters)
$M = Fd$ Physics only	M = moment F = force d = distance	M = Nm (newton-meters) F = N (newtons) d = m (meters)
$p = \dfrac{F}{A}$ Physics only	p = pressure F = force A = area	p = Pa (pascals) F = N (newtons) A = m^2 (meters squared)
$p = h\rho g$ Physics only Higher tier only Given in the exam	p = pressure h = height ρ = density g = gravitational field strength	p = Pa (pascals) h = m (meters) ρ = kg/m^3 (kilograms per meter cubed g = N/kg (newtons per kilogram)
$s = vt$	s = distance v = speed t = time	s = m (meters) v = m/s (meters per second) t = s (seconds)
$a = \dfrac{\Delta v}{t}$	a = acceleration Δv = change in velocity t = time	a = m/s^2 (meters per second squared) Δv = m/s (meters per second) t = s (seconds)

Equation	Symbols	Units
$v^2 - u^2 = 2as$ Given in the exam	v = final velocity u = initial velocity a = acceleration s = distance	v = m/s (meters per second) u = m/s (meters per second) a = m/s² (meters per second squared) s = m (meters)
$F = ma$	F = force m = mass a = acceleration	F = N (newtons) m = kg (kilograms) a = m/s² (meters per second squared)
$p = mv$ Higher tier only	p = momentum m = mass v = velocity	p = kg m/s (kilograms metre per second) m = kg (kilograms) v = m/s (meters per second)
$F = \dfrac{m\, \Delta v}{\Delta t}$ Physics only Higher tier only Given in the exam	F = force m = mass v = velocity t = time	F = N (newtons) m = kg (kilograms) v = m/s (meters per second) t = s (seconds)

Topic 6 – Waves

Equation	Symbols	Units
Period = $\dfrac{1}{\text{Frequency}}$ Given in the exam		Period = s (seconds) Frequency = Hz (hertz)
$T = \dfrac{1}{F}$	T = Period f = frequency	T = s (seconds) f = Hz (hertz)
$v = f\lambda$	v = velocity f = frequency λ = wavelength (lambda)	v = m/s (meters per second) f = Hz (hertz) λ = m (meters)
Magnification = $\dfrac{\text{image height}}{\text{object height}}$ Physics only Given in the exam		Ratio, so has no units

Equation	Symbols	Units
$F = BIl$ Note this is a capital I and a lowercase l Higher tier only Given in the exam	F = force B = magnetic flux density I = Current l = length	F = N (newtons) B = T (tesla) I = A (Amps or Amperes) l = m (meters)
$\dfrac{V_p}{V_s} = \dfrac{n_p}{n_s}$ Physics only Higher tier only Given in the exam	V_p = potential difference across the primary coil V_s = potential difference across the secondary coil n_p = number of turns on the primary coil n_s = number of turns on the secondary coil	V_p = V (volts) V_s = V (volts) n_p and n_s have no units as they are just numbers
$V_s I_s = V_p I_p$ Physics only Higher tier only Given in the exam	V_s = potential difference across the secondary coil V_p = potential difference across the primary coil I_s = current in the secondary coil I_p = current in the primary coil $V_s I_s$ = power output $V_p I_p$ = power input	V_s = V (volts) V_p = V (volts) I_s = A (Amps or Amperes) I_p = A (Amps or Amperes)

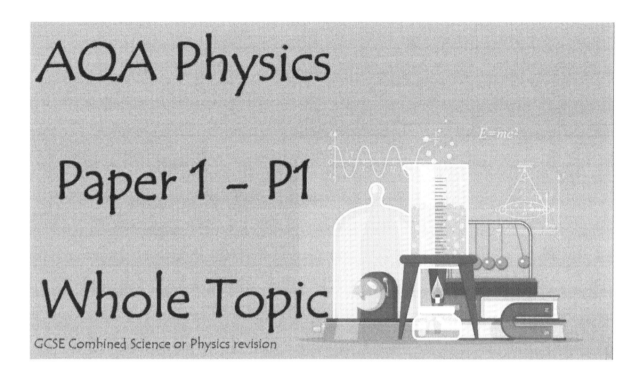

The whole of physics paper 1 in only 40 minutes

https://youtu.be/xtw-ZOnllA4

The whole of physics paper 2 in only 48 minutes

https://youtu.be/X1aMXCr75Kw

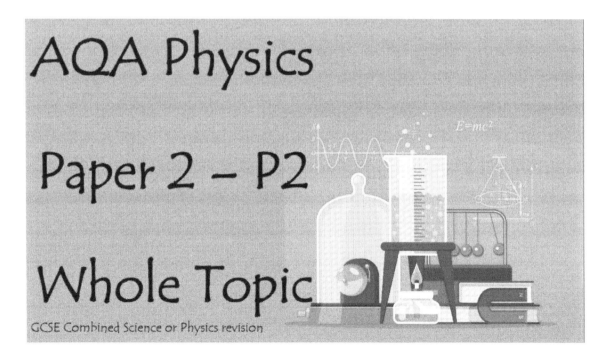

1 – Energy

Knowledge Checklist

Specification statement These are the bits the exam board wants you to know, make sure you can do all of these...	Self-assessment			Bits to help if you don't understand	
	First review 4-7 months before exam	Second review 1-2 months before exam	Final review Week before exam	Primrose Kitten	Other places
I can recall the different types of energy and give examples	☺ ☺ ☹	☺ ☺ ☹	☺ ☺ ☹	https://youtu.be/ ujdUEwMfIok	TuitionKit http://bit.ly/ 2iWfKai
I can describe the energy changes involved in a range of common situations	☺ ☺ ☹	☺ ☺ ☹	☺ ☺ ☹	https://youtu.be/ nd97wwioCX4	TuitionKit http://bit.ly/ 2xSlW69
I can define the term system	☺ ☺ ☹	☺ ☺ ☹	☺ ☺ ☹		
I can recall that energy cannot be created or destroyed	☺ ☺ ☹	☺ ☺ ☹	☺ ☺ ☹		
I can use describe how kinetic energy changes over time	☺ ☺ ☹	☺ ☺ ☹	☺ ☺ ☹		TuitionKit http://bit.ly/ 2hAvJYp
I can recall the units needed for $E_k = \frac{1}{2} mv^2$	☺ ☺ ☹	☺ ☺ ☹	☺ ☺ ☹	https://youtu.be/ RRm_8BDgH1M	Flashcards available on www.primrose kitten.com
I can rearrange $E_k = \frac{1}{2} mv^2$	☺ ☺ ☹	☺ ☺ ☹	☺ ☺ ☹		
I can use $E_k = \frac{1}{2} mv^2$	☺ ☺ ☹	☺ ☺ ☹	☺ ☺ ☹		
I can use describe how elastic potential energy changes	☺ ☺ ☹	☺ ☺ ☹	☺ ☺ ☹		TuitionKit http://bit.ly/ 2lJWnm4
I can recall the units needed for $E_e = \frac{1}{2} ke^2$	☺ ☺ ☹	☺ ☺ ☹	☺ ☺ ☹		Flashcards available on www.primrose kitten.com
I can rearrange $E_e = \frac{1}{2} ke^2$	☺ ☺ ☹	☺ ☺ ☹	☺ ☺ ☹		
I can use $E_e = \frac{1}{2} ke^2$	☺ ☺ ☹	☺ ☺ ☹	☺ ☺ ☹		

I can use describe how gravitational potential energy changes	☺ ☺ ☹	☺ ☺ ☹	☺ ☺ ☹		TuitionKit http://bit.ly/ 2zb6KVw
I can recall the units needed for $E_p = mgh$	☺ ☺ ☹	☺ ☺ ☹	☺ ☺ ☹		Flashcards available on www.primrose kitten.com
I can rearrange $E_p = mgh$	☺ ☺ ☹	☺ ☺ ☹	☺ ☺ ☹		
I can use $E_p = mgh$	☺ ☺ ☹	☺ ☺ ☹	☺ ☺ ☹		
I can use describe how objects have different specific heat capacities	☺ ☺ ☹	☺ ☺ ☹	☺ ☺ ☹	https://youtu.be/ _gooQFvVqzk	TuitionKit http://bit.ly/ 2zdTPjd
I can recall the units needed for $\Delta E = mc\Delta\theta$	☺ ☺ ☹	☺ ☺ ☹	☺ ☺ ☹		Flashcards available on www.primrose kitten.com
I can rearrange $\Delta E = mc\Delta\theta$	☺ ☺ ☹	☺ ☺ ☹	☺ ☺ ☹		
I can use $\Delta E = mc\Delta\theta$	☺ ☺ ☹	☺ ☺ ☹	☺ ☺ ☹		
I can use define power	☺ ☺ ☹	☺ ☺ ☹	☺ ☺ ☹		
I can recall the units needed for $P = \dfrac{E}{T}$	☺ ☺ ☹	☺ ☺ ☹	☺ ☺ ☹		TuitionKit http://bit.ly/ 2zeModI Flashcards available on www.primrose kitten.com
I can rearrange $P = \dfrac{E}{T}$	☺ ☺ ☹	☺ ☺ ☹	☺ ☺ ☹		
I can use $P = \dfrac{E}{T}$	☺ ☺ ☹	☺ ☺ ☹	☺ ☺ ☹		
I can recall the units needed for $P = \dfrac{W}{T}$	☺ ☺ ☹	☺ ☺ ☹	☺ ☺ ☹		Flashcards available on www.primrose kitten.com
I can rearrange $P = \dfrac{W}{T}$	☺ ☺ ☹	☺ ☺ ☹	☺ ☺ ☹		
I can use $P = \dfrac{W}{T}$	☺ ☺ ☹	☺ ☺ ☹	☺ ☺ ☹		

Statement	Self-assessment 1	Self-assessment 2	Self-assessment 3	Video	Resource
I can recall that energy cannot be created or destroyed	☺ 😐 ☹	☺ 😐 ☹	☺ 😐 ☹		
I can describe what happen to wasted energy	☺ 😐 ☹	☺ 😐 ☹	☺ 😐 ☹		TuitionKit http://bit.ly/2xQdPqD
I can recall ways to reduce wasted energy	☺ 😐 ☹	☺ 😐 ☹	☺ 😐 ☹		
I can describe how insulation can reduce energy loss	☺ 😐 ☹	☺ 😐 ☹	☺ 😐 ☹		TuitionKit http://bit.ly/2yviwKN
I can describe why a system might not be 100% efficient	☺ 😐 ☹	☺ 😐 ☹	☺ 😐 ☹		
I can describe whys to increase the efficiency of a system	☺ 😐 ☹	☺ 😐 ☹	☺ 😐 ☹		
I can recall the units needed for $\text{Efficiency} = \dfrac{\text{useful energy out}}{\text{total energy in}}$	☺ 😐 ☹	☺ 😐 ☹	☺ 😐 ☹	https://youtu.be/GVSiL39bnrc	TuitionKit http://bit.ly/2zg8xrZ
I can rearrange $\text{Efficiency} = \dfrac{\text{useful energy out}}{\text{total energy in}}$	☺ 😐 ☹	☺ 😐 ☹	☺ 😐 ☹		
I can use $\text{Efficiency} = \dfrac{\text{useful energy out}}{\text{total energy in}}$	☺ 😐 ☹	☺ 😐 ☹	☺ 😐 ☹		
I can recall the units needed for $\text{Efficiency} = \dfrac{\text{useful power out}}{\text{total power in}}$	☺ 😐 ☹	☺ 😐 ☹	☺ 😐 ☹		
I can rearrange $\text{Efficiency} = \dfrac{\text{useful power out}}{\text{total power in}}$	☺ 😐 ☹	☺ 😐 ☹	☺ 😐 ☹		
I can use $\text{Efficiency} = \dfrac{\text{useful power out}}{\text{total power in}}$	☺ 😐 ☹	☺ 😐 ☹	☺ 😐 ☹		
I can state the different sources that can be used to get energy	☺ 😐 ☹	☺ 😐 ☹	☺ 😐 ☹		
I can determine if a resource is renewable or finite	☺ 😐 ☹	☺ 😐 ☹	☺ 😐 ☹		
I can consider the impact that using these resources has on the environment	☺ 😐 ☹	☺ 😐 ☹	☺ 😐 ☹		
I can discuss the advantages and disadvantages of each source of energy	☺ 😐 ☹	☺ 😐 ☹	☺ 😐 ☹		TuitionKit http://bit.ly/2A8S4CU

Quick fire questions;

This worksheet is fully supported by a video tutorial; https://youtu.be/q5CwATii6OA

1. What are the different types of energy?
2. What energy changes happen in a lightbulb?
3. What energy changes happen in TV?
4. What does the word system mean?
5. What is the law of conservation of energy?
6. What is the equation linking kinetic energy, mass and velocity?
7. What are the units for velocity?
8. What are the units for mass?
9. What are the units for kinetic energy?
10. What is elastic potential energy?
11. What is equation linking elastic potential energy, the spring constant and extension?
12. What are units for elastic potential energy?
13. What are the units for the spring constant?
14. What are the units for extension?
15. What is gravitational potential energy?
16. What is the equation linking gravitational potential energy, mass, gravity and height?
17. What are the units for gravitational potential energy?
18. What is the value and the units for gravity?
19. What are the units for height?
20. What does this symbol mean Δ?
21. What is specific heat capacity?
22. What is the equation linking changing energy, mass, specific heat capacity and change in temperature?
23. What are the units for energy?
24. What are the units for specific heat capacity?
25. What are the units for change in temperature?
26. What is the equation linking power, energy and time?
27. What are the units of power?
28. What are the units for time?
29. What is the equation linking power, work done and time?
30. What are the units for work done?
31. What happens to waste energy?

32. How can we reduce wasting energy?

33. Give three examples of insulation that can be used in the house.

34. Why is a system not 100% efficient?

35. What is the equation for working out efficiency?

36. What are the units for efficiency?

37. What different ways we can get energy?

38. What is a renewable resource?

39. What is finite resource?

Whole topic summary https://youtu.be/jSA4WaLSVEA in only 10 minutes!!

Specification statement These are the bits the exam board wants you to know, make sure you can do all of these…	Self-assessment			Bits to help if you don't understand	
	First review 4-7 months before exam	Second review 1-2 months before exam	Final review Week before exam	Primrose Kitten	Other places
I can draw and use the common circuit symbols	☺ ☹ ☹	☺ ☹ ☹	☺ ☹ ☹	https://youtu.be/ HiVcnpDQOcI	Circuit symbol flashcard on www.primrose kitten.com TuitionKit http://bit.ly/ 2zydUDJ
I can draw series and parallel circuits	☺ ☹ ☹	☺ ☹ ☹	☺ ☹ ☹	https://youtu.be/ 2QBTaq63mYk https://youtu.be/ rbLqufYEVN8 https://youtu.be/ xZXKaQW2jBc https://youtu.be/ oBuewt6m_KM	
I can define the terms charge and current	☺ ☹ ☹	☺ ☹ ☹	☺ ☹ ☹	https://youtu.be/ k3vCg3lGpys	TuitionKit http://bit.ly/ 2A8qx4H

I can recall the units needed for Q = It	☺ ☺ ☹	☺ ☺ ☹	☺ ☺ ☹		Flashcards available on www.primrose kitten.com
I can rearrange Q = It	☺ ☺ ☹	☺ ☺ ☹	☺ ☺ ☹		
I can use Q = It	☺ ☺ ☹	☺ ☺ ☹	☺ ☺ ☹		
I can define the terms potential difference and resistance	☺ ☺ ☹	☺ ☺ ☹	☺ ☺ ☹	https://youtu.be/ k3vCg3lGpys	
I can recall the units needed for V = IR	☺ ☺ ☹	☺ ☺ ☹	☺ ☺ ☹		Flashcards available on www.primrose kitten.com
I can rearrange V = IR	☺ ☺ ☹	☺ ☺ ☹	☺ ☺ ☹		
I can use V = IR	☺ ☺ ☹	☺ ☺ ☹	☺ ☺ ☹		
I can draw and explain current-potential difference graphs for ohmic conductors, filament lamps and diodes	☺ ☺ ☹	☺ ☺ ☹	☺ ☺ ☹	https://youtu.be/ fxDNqQ3hH2A https://youtu.be/ ylHsTMAGV1I	
I can explain the change in resistance of a thermistor as the temperature changes	☺ ☺ ☹	☺ ☺ ☹	☺ ☺ ☹	https://youtu.be/ 2PdHk4wa5Bg https://youtu.be/ Ra7sqF8oZxg	
I can explain the change in resistance of an LDR as the light intensity changes	☺ ☺ ☹	☺ ☺ ☹	☺ ☺ ☹	https://youtu.be/ Ra7sqF8oZxg https://youtu.be/ iUnMBMmkxnY	
I can describe the way current behaves in a series circuit	☺ ☺ ☹	☺ ☺ ☹	☺ ☺ ☹	https://youtu.be/ g2kUj3xfM90	https://phet. colorado.edu/ en/simulation /legacy/circu it- construction- kit-ac- virtual-lab
I can describe the way potential difference behaves in a series circuit	☺ ☺ ☹	☺ ☺ ☹	☺ ☺ ☹	https://youtu.be/ E70eNm2lITI https://youtu.be/ OdmmKxa0Nhs	
I can describe the way resistance behaves in a series circuit	☺ ☺ ☹	☺ ☺ ☹	☺ ☺ ☹		TuitionKit

I can describe the way current behaves in a parallel circuit	☺ ☻ ☹	☺ ☻ ☹	☺ ☻ ☹	https://youtu.be/g2kUj3xfM90	http://bit.ly/2A7SZUn
I can describe the way potential difference behaves in a parallel circuit	☺ ☻ ☹	☺ ☻ ☹	☺ ☻ ☹		http://bit.ly/2zfGSoZ
I can describe the way resistance behaves in a parallel circuit	☺ ☻ ☹	☺ ☻ ☹	☺ ☻ ☹		
I can recall the voltage and frequency of mains electricity in the UK	☺ ☻ ☹	☺ ☻ ☹	☺ ☻ ☹		
I can explain the difference between direct current and alternating current	☺ ☻ ☹	☺ ☻ ☹	☺ ☻ ☹		TuitionKit http://bit.ly/2zyA9th
I can describe the inside of a plug	☺ ☻ ☹	☺ ☻ ☹	☺ ☻ ☹	https://youtu.be/Ke4yyUZH-hY	Warren Nash https://youtu.be/COWlYUvzgZI TuitionKit http://bit.ly/2iyfdaL
I can describe the safety features of a plug	☺ ☻ ☹	☺ ☻ ☹	☺ ☻ ☹		
I can describe how power in a circuit is related to the potential difference	☺ ☻ ☹	☺ ☻ ☹	☺ ☻ ☹		
I can recall the units needed for $P = VI$	☺ ☻ ☹	☺ ☻ ☹	☺ ☻ ☹		Flashcards available on www.primrosekitten.com
I can rearrange $P = VI$	☺ ☻ ☹	☺ ☻ ☹	☺ ☻ ☹		
I can use $P = VI$	☺ ☻ ☹	☺ ☻ ☹	☺ ☻ ☹		TuitionKit http://bit.ly/2zgEmkC
I can recall the units needed for $P = I^2R$	☺ ☻ ☹	☺ ☻ ☹	☺ ☻ ☹		Flashcards available on www.primrosekitten.com
I can rearrange $P = I^2R$	☺ ☻ ☹	☺ ☻ ☹	☺ ☻ ☹		
I can use $P = I^2R$	☺ ☻ ☹	☺ ☻ ☹	☺ ☻ ☹		
I can describe how domestic appliances transfer energy	☺ ☻ ☹	☺ ☻ ☹	☺ ☻ ☹		

I can recall the units needed for E = Pt	☺ 😐 ☹	☺ 😐 ☹	☺ 😐 ☹		Flashcards available on www.primrose kitten.com
I can rearrange E = Pt	☺ 😐 ☹	☺ 😐 ☹	☺ 😐 ☹		
I can use E = Pt	☺ 😐 ☹	☺ 😐 ☹	☺ 😐 ☹		TuitionKit http://bit.ly/ 2j3vKrn
I can recall the units needed for E = QV	☺ 😐 ☹	☺ 😐 ☹	☺ 😐 ☹		Flashcards available on www.primrose kitten.com
I can rearrange E = QV	☺ 😐 ☹	☺ 😐 ☹	☺ 😐 ☹		
I can use E = QV	☺ 😐 ☹	☺ 😐 ☹	☺ 😐 ☹		
I can describe the part of the National Grid and how they interact with each other	☺ 😐 ☹	☺ 😐 ☹	☺ 😐 ☹		TuitionKit http://bit.ly/ 2zfB4OU
I can describe how step-up and step-down transformers work	☺ 😐 ☹	☺ 😐 ☹	☺ 😐 ☹		
I can describe the circumstances in which an object might become charged **-Physics only**	☺ 😐 ☹	☺ 😐 ☹	☺ 😐 ☹		
I can describe what happens what two charged objects are bought close together **-Physics only**	☺ 😐 ☹	☺ 😐 ☹	☺ 😐 ☹		
I can state that a charged object creates an electric field around itself **-Physics only**	☺ 😐 ☹	☺ 😐 ☹	☺ 😐 ☹		
I can draw the electric field pattern for an object **-Physics only**	☺ 😐 ☹	☺ 😐 ☹	☺ 😐 ☹		

This worksheet is fully supported by a video tutorial; https://youtu.be/62RyyfKZoYg

1. Draw the symbol for a cell.
2. Draw the symbol for a battery.
3. What is the difference between a battery and a cell?
4. Draw the symbol for an ammeter.
5. How must an ammeter be placed in a circuit?
6. Draw the symbol for a voltmeter.
7. How must a voltmeter be placed in a circuit?
8. Draw the symbol for a lamp.
9. Draw the symbol for a diode.
10. Draw the symbol for a resistor.
11. Draw the symbol for a LED (light emitting diodes).
12. Draw the symbol for a variable resistor.
13. Draw the symbol for a LDR (light dependent resistor).
14. Draw the symbol for a fuse.
15. Draw the symbol for a thermistor.
16. Draw the symbol for an open switch.
17. Draw the symbol for a closed switch.
18. What is difference between series and parallel circuits?
19. Define charge.
20. Define current.
21. What is equation taking charge, current and time?
22. What are the units for charge?
23. What are the units for current?
24. What are the units for time?
25. Define potential difference.
26. Define resistance.
27. What is equation linking potential difference, current and resistance?
28. What are the units of potential difference?
29. What are the units for resistance?
30. Draw the current-potential different graphs for a conductor.
31. Draw the current-potential different graphs for lamp.
32. Draw the current-potential different graphs for a diode.
33. How does resistance of a thermistor change as temperature changes?
34. How does resistance of an LDR change as light intensity changes?
35. How does current behave in a series circuit?

36. How does potential difference behave in a series circuit?
37. How does resistance behave in a series circuit?
38. How does current behave in a parallel circuit?
39. How does potential difference behave in a parallel circuit?
40. How does resistance behave in a parallel circuit?
41. What is the voltage of mains electricity in the UK?
42. What is the frequency of mains electricity in the UK?
43. What is the difference between alternating and direct current?
44. What are the three wires inside a plug?
45. What are the safety features on a plug?
46. What is equation linking power, current and potential difference?
47. What are the units for power?
48. What is the equation linking power, current and resistance?
49. What is equation linking energy, power and time?
50. What are the units for energy?
51. What are the units for time?
52. What is equation linking energy, charge and potential difference?
53. What is the National Grid?
54. What does step up transformer do?
55. What does a step-down transformer do?

Knowledge Checklist

Whole topic summary video; https://youtu.be/cZz9oGgJOL0 only 6 minutes!

Specification statement	Self-assessment			Bits to help if you don't understand	
These are the bits the exam board wants you to know, make sure you can do all of these…	First review 4-7 months before exam	Second review 1-2 months before exam	Final review Week before exam	Primrose Kitten	Other places
I can recall the arrangement of particles in a solid, a liquid and a gas	☺ ☹ ☹	☺ ☹ ☹	☺ ☹ ☹	https://youtu.be/hs9DIOqzgRg	TuitionKit http://bit.ly/2h4Sl2j
I can describe the energy changes that happen when a substance changes state	☺ ☹ ☹	☺ ☹ ☹	☺ ☹ ☹		Total Learn http://bit.ly/2z33uMm
I can describe the energy in the atoms and molecules as internal energy	☺ ☹ ☹	☺ ☹ ☹	☺ ☹ ☹		
I can explain that a change in the internal energy will lead to a change in temperature or a change in state	☺ ☹ ☹	☺ ☹ ☹	☺ ☹ ☹		
I can define density	☺ ☹ ☹	☺ ☹ ☹	☺ ☹ ☹		TuitionKit http://bit.ly/2zfUMtH Total Learn http://bit.ly/2gF1277
I can recall the units needed for $\rho = \dfrac{m}{V}$	☺ ☹ ☹	☺ ☹ ☹	☺ ☹ ☹		Flashcards available on www.primrosekitten.com
I can rearrange $\rho = \dfrac{m}{V}$	☺ ☹ ☹	☺ ☹ ☹	☺ ☹ ☹		
I can use $\rho = \dfrac{m}{V}$	☺ ☹ ☹	☺ ☹ ☹	☺ ☹ ☹		

I can define specific heat capacity and specific latent heat	☺ ☺ ☹	☺ ☺ ☹	☺ ☺ ☹	
I can recall the units needed for ΔE = mcΔθ	☺ ☺ ☹	☺ ☺ ☹	☺ ☺ ☹	Flashcards available on www.primrose kitten.com
I can rearrange ΔE = mcΔθ	☺ ☺ ☹	☺ ☺ ☹	☺ ☺ ☹	
I can use ΔE = mcΔθ	☺ ☺ ☹	☺ ☺ ☹	☺ ☺ ☹	
I can recall the units needed for E = mL	☺ ☺ ☹	☺ ☺ ☹	☺ ☺ ☹	Flashcards available on www.primrose kitten.com
I can rearrange E = mL	☺ ☺ ☹	☺ ☺ ☹	☺ ☺ ☹	
I can use E = mL	☺ ☺ ☹	☺ ☺ ☹	☺ ☺ ☹	TuitionKit http://bit.ly/ 2j1WZmb
I can describe the movement of particles in a gas	☺ ☺ ☹	☺ ☺ ☹	☺ ☺ ☹	
I can relate the temperature of the gas to the average kinetic energy of the system	☺ ☺ ☹	☺ ☺ ☹	☺ ☺ ☹	
I can explain how the motion of a gas relates to the pressure in a system	☺ ☺ ☹	☺ ☺ ☹	☺ ☺ ☹	
I can relate the volume of a gas to the pressure **-Physics only**	☺ ☺ ☹	☺ ☺ ☹	☺ ☺ ☹	TuitionKit http://bit.ly/ 2hHthz3
I can recall the units needed for pV = constant **-Physics only**	☺ ☺ ☹	☺ ☺ ☹	☺ ☺ ☹	Flashcards available on www.primrose kitten.com
I can rearrange pV = constant **-Physics only**	☺ ☺ ☹	☺ ☺ ☹	☺ ☺ ☹	
I can use pV = constant **-Physics only**	☺ ☺ ☹	☺ ☺ ☹	☺ ☺ ☹	
I can explain how doing work on a system can increase the temperature **-Physics only**	☺ ☺ ☹	☺ ☺ ☹	☺ ☺ ☹	

This worksheet is fully supported by a video tutorial; https://youtu.be/z9L6zfMVk3U

1. Draw arrangement of particles in a solid.
2. Draw the arrangement of particles in liquid.
3. Draw the arrangement of particles in a gas.
4. Define density.
5. What is the equation linking density, mass and volume?
6. What are the units for density?
7. What are units the mass?
8. What are the units for volume?
9. What is specific heat capacity?
10. What is specific latent heat?
11. What is the equation linking energy change, mass, specific heat capacity and change in temperature?
12. What are the units for energy change?
13. What are the units for specific heat capacity?
14. What are the units for temperature change?
15. What is equation linking energy, mass and specific latent heat?
16. What are the units for specific latent heat?

Physics only

17. What is relationship between volume of gas and pressure?
18. What is the equation linking pressure, volume and the constant?
19. What are the units of pressure?

4 - Atomic Structure

Knowledge Checklist

Whole topic summary video https://youtu.be/YFVYUSvUBoo in only 15 minutes

Specification statement These are the bits the exam board wants you to know, make sure you can do all of these...	Self-assessment			Bits to help if you don't understand	
	First review 4-7 months before exam	Second review 1-2 months before exam	Final review Week before exam	Primrose Kitten	Other places
I can recall the size of an atom	☺ ☺ ☹	☺ ☺ ☹	☺ ☺ ☹		
I can recall the structure of an atom	☺ ☺ ☹	☺ ☺ ☹	☺ ☺ ☹	https://youtu.be /ljyzVt8bJSA	Total Learn http://bit.ly/ 2lesH0e
I can recall the parts of an atom	☺ ☺ ☹	☺ ☺ ☹	☺ ☺ ☹		
I can recall the mass, charge and location of the subatomic particles	☺ ☺ ☹	☺ ☺ ☹	☺ ☺ ☹		
I can recall the electrons are arranged in energy levels (shells)	☺ ☺ ☹	☺ ☺ ☹	☺ ☺ ☹	https://youtu.be /bgWKesHbLnE	
I can explain that the position of electrons may change with the absorption or emission of electromagnetic radiation	☺ ☺ ☹	☺ ☺ ☹	☺ ☺ ☹		
I can define the terms atomic number and mass number	☺ ☺ ☹	☺ ☺ ☹	☺ ☺ ☹	https://youtu.be /ljyzVt8bJSA	
I can work out the number of protons, electrons and neutrons an atom has	☺ ☺ ☹	☺ ☺ ☹	☺ ☺ ☹	https://youtu.be /CEJ8WoNFFSI	
I can explain why atoms have no overall charge	☺ ☺ ☹	☺ ☺ ☹	☺ ☺ ☹	https://youtu.be /M5qfMT-ePrQ	
I can explain why ions have a charge	☺ ☺ ☹	☺ ☺ ☹	☺ ☺ ☹	https://youtu.be /746sTyJgrJo	
I can define the term isotope	☺ ☺ ☹	☺ ☺ ☹	☺ ☺ ☹		

I can work out the number of protons, electrons and neutrons and isotope has	☺ ☺ ☹	☺ ☺ ☹	☺ ☺ ☹	https://youtu.be /fIC2B935oXQ	TuitionKit http://bit.ly/ 2zkpC3Y
I can describe how and why a scientific model changes over time	☺ ☺ ☹	☺ ☺ ☹	☺ ☺ ☹		
I can describe the plum pudding model of the atom	☺ ☺ ☹	☺ ☺ ☹	☺ ☺ ☹	https://youtu.be /nbwcngWsXAU	
I can explain why Rutherford's experiment that disproved the plum pudding model	☺ ☺ ☹	☺ ☺ ☹	☺ ☺ ☹		
I can describe how Bohr adapted the model of the atom	☺ ☺ ☹	☺ ☺ ☹	☺ ☺ ☹		
I can recall what Chadwick added to the model of the atom	☺ ☺ ☹	☺ ☺ ☹	☺ ☺ ☹		
I can describe the process of radioactive decay	☺ ☺ ☹	☺ ☺ ☹	☺ ☺ ☹		Total Learn http://bit.ly/ 2yFW80v
I can recall that activity is measured in Becquerel's (Bq)	☺ ☺ ☹	☺ ☺ ☹	☺ ☺ ☹		
I can describe what a Geiger-Muller tubes does	☺ ☺ ☹	☺ ☺ ☹	☺ ☺ ☹		
I can describe the different types of radiation	☺ ☺ ☹	☺ ☺ ☹	☺ ☺ ☹	https://youtu.be /NzGkp8ZcjZ0	TuitionKit http://bit.ly/ 2zgyW9e
I can represent radioactive decay by nuclear equations	☺ ☺ ☹	☺ ☺ ☹	☺ ☺ ☹	https://youtu.be /L99xBAZY4AE	
I can define the term half-life	☺ ☺ ☹	☺ ☺ ☹	☺ ☺ ☹	https://youtu.be /A9ej_7z03O8	TuitionKit http://bit.ly/ 2yvFukX
I can relate half-life to radioactive decay	☺ ☺ ☹	☺ ☺ ☹	☺ ☺ ☹		
I can determine half-life from graphic or mathematical information	☺ ☺ ☹	☺ ☺ ☹	☺ ☺ ☹		
I can describe what radioactive contamination is	☺ ☺ ☹	☺ ☺ ☹	☺ ☺ ☹		
I can describe the precautions that need to be taken around radioactive contamination	☺ ☺ ☹	☺ ☺ ☹	☺ ☺ ☹		
I can recall the different sources of background radiation **-Physics only**	☺ ☺ ☹	☺ ☺ ☹	☺ ☺ ☹	https://youtu.be /LlVoVvpeQ5o	

I can describe what may affect a person dose of radiation **-Physics only**	☺ ☺ ☹	☺ ☺ ☹	☺ ☺ ☹		
I can recall that different isotopes have different half lives **-Physics only**	☺ ☺ ☹	☺ ☺ ☹	☺ ☺ ☹		
I can describe the different uses of radioactivity **-Physics only**	☺ ☺ ☹	☺ ☺ ☹	☺ ☺ ☹	https://youtu.be /LeRaJN2WpV0	
I can describe nuclear **-Physics only**	☺ ☺ ☹	☺ ☺ ☹	☺ ☺ ☹	https://youtu.be /I97zD2WACzo	
I can describe the chain reaction that can occur from nuclear fission **-Physics only**	☺ ☺ ☹	☺ ☺ ☹	☺ ☺ ☹		TuitionKit http://bit.ly/ 2h6sPtE
I can describe nuclear fusion **-Physics only**	☺ ☺ ☹	☺ ☺ ☹	☺ ☺ ☹	https://youtu.be /Iek-hpiMhTs	TuitionKit http://bit.ly/ 2j25VI8

This worksheet is fully supported by a video tutorial; https://youtu.be/bRzRjfvoU-E

1. How big is an atom?
2. What is the mass of a proton?
3. What is the mass of a neutron?
4. What is the mass of an electron?
5. What is the charge on a proton?
6. What is the charge on an electron?
7. What is the charge on a neutron?
8. Where are protons found?
9. Where are neutrons found?
10. Where are electrons found?
11. What happens to electrons when they absorb or emit radiation?
12. What is the atomic number?
13. What is the mass number?
14. How do you find the number of protons an atom has?
15. How do you find the number of electrons an atom has?
16. How do you find the number of neutrons an atom has?
17. Why do atoms have no overall charge?
18. How do ions get charged?
19. What is an isotope?
20. What was the plum-pudding model?
21. What did Rutherford do?
22. What did Bohr do?
23. What did Chadwick do?
24. What is radioactive decay?
25. What are the units for radioactivity?
26. What are the three different types of radiation?
27. What is half-life?

Physics only

28. What the sources of background radiation?
29. What is nuclear fusion?
30. What is nuclear fission?

Physics Paper 1 Checklist – What to do before the exam!

Watched the whole topic video   https://youtu.be/xtw-ZOnllA4   ☐

Learnt all the equations   ☐

Recall all the units   https://youtu.be/FaXds9xjxFk   ☐

Practiced rearranging equations   ☐

Answered the quick-fire questions   ☐

Looked at the practical videos   ☐

Filled in the crosswords   ☐

https://youtu.be/Rz4XBSKNGXg in only 16 minutes!

Specification statement These are the bits the exam board wants you to know, make sure you can do all of these...	Self-assessment			Bits to help if you don't understand	
	First review 4-7 months before exam	Second review 1-2 months before exam	Final review Week before exam	Primrose Kitten	Other places
I can define the terms scalar and vector quantities	☺ ☺ ☹	☺ ☺ ☹	☺ ☺ ☹	https://youtu.be/ 5Xcie8V-UTw	TuitionKit http://bit.ly/ 2Am7pkP
I can give examples of contact and non-contact forces	☺ ☺ ☹	☺ ☺ ☹	☺ ☺ ☹		
I can represent the forces acting on an object as vectors	☺ ☺ ☹	☺ ☺ ☹	☺ ☺ ☹		
I can calculate the resultant force on an object	☺ ☺ ☹	☺ ☺ ☹	☺ ☺ ☹	https://youtu.be/ Oa9LglsNm2o	TuitionKit http://bit.ly/ 2h5es8M
I can recall the difference between weight and mass	☺ ☺ ☹	☺ ☺ ☹	☺ ☺ ☹		
I can recall how to measure weight	☺ ☺ ☹	☺ ☺ ☹	☺ ☺ ☹		
I can recall the units needed for $W = mg$	☺ ☺ ☹	☺ ☺ ☹	☺ ☺ ☹		Flashcards available on www.primrose kitten.com
I can rearrange $W = mg$	☺ ☺ ☹	☺ ☺ ☹	☺ ☺ ☹		
I can use $W = mg$	☺ ☺ ☹	☺ ☺ ☹	☺ ☺ ☹		
I can describe what happens to an object when work is done on it	☺ ☺ ☹	☺ ☺ ☹	☺ ☺ ☹		
I can recall the units needed for $W = Fs$	☺ ☺ ☹	☺ ☺ ☹	☺ ☺ ☹		Flashcards available on www.primrose kitten.com

I can rearrange W = Fs	☺ ☺ ☹	☺ ☺ ☹	☺ ☺ ☹		
I can use W = Fs	☺ ☺ ☹	☺ ☺ ☹	☺ ☺ ☹		
I can convert between joules and newton-meters	☺ ☺ ☹	☺ ☺ ☹	☺ ☺ ☹		
I can explain why an object may change shape when a force is applied	☺ ☺ ☹	☺ ☺ ☹	☺ ☺ ☹		TuitionKit http://bit.ly/ 2zf23Ya
I can explain what happens to an elastic object up to and then beyond the limit or proportionality	☺ ☺ ☹	☺ ☺ ☹	☺ ☺ ☹		
I can recall the units needed for F = ke	☺ ☺ ☹	☺ ☺ ☹	☺ ☺ ☹		Flashcards available on www.primrose kitten.com
I can rearrange F = ke	☺ ☺ ☹	☺ ☺ ☹	☺ ☺ ☹		
I can use F = ke	☺ ☺ ☹	☺ ☺ ☹	☺ ☺ ☹		
I can recall the units needed for $E_e = \frac{1}{2} ke^2$	☺ ☺ ☹	☺ ☺ ☹	☺ ☺ ☹		Flashcards available on www.primrose kitten.com
I can rearrange $E_e = \frac{1}{2} ke^2$	☺ ☺ ☹	☺ ☺ ☹	☺ ☺ ☹		
I can use $E_e = \frac{1}{2} ke^2$	☺ ☺ ☹	☺ ☺ ☹	☺ ☺ ☹		
I can describe how application of a force can cause an object to rotate **-Physics only**	☺ ☺ ☹	☺ ☺ ☹	☺ ☺ ☹	https://youtu.be/ 73t8QjZvMVI https://youtu.be/ UiqGL-DCaBI https://youtu.be/ WpT655stxUQ https://youtu.be/ 6aAljgK3kx8	
I can recall the units needed for M = Fd **-Physics only**	☺ ☺ ☹	☺ ☺ ☹	☺ ☺ ☹		Flashcards available on www.primrose kitten.com
I can rearrange M = Fd **-Physics only**	☺ ☺ ☹	☺ ☺ ☹	☺ ☺ ☹		
I can use M = Fd **-Physics only**	☺ ☺ ☹	☺ ☺ ☹	☺ ☺ ☹		TuitionKit http://bit.ly/ 2AjsvjA
I can describe what happens to an object if the clockwise and anti-clockwise forces are balanced or unbalanced **-Physics only**	☺ ☺ ☹	☺ ☺ ☹	☺ ☺ ☹		
I can explain how levers and gears work **-Physics only**	☺ ☺ ☹	☺ ☺ ☹	☺ ☺ ☹		TuitionKit http://bit.ly/ 2h77BvR

I can recall that a fluid can be either liquid or a gas	☺ ☹ ☹	☺ ☹ ☹	☺ ☹ ☹		
I can state that liquids are incompressible	☺ ☹ ☹	☺ ☹ ☹	☺ ☹ ☹		
I can recall the units needed for p = $\frac{F}{A}$	☺ ☹ ☹	☺ ☹ ☹	☺ ☹ ☹		Flashcards available on www.primrose kitten.com
I can rearrange p = $\frac{F}{A}$	☺ ☹ ☹	☺ ☹ ☹	☺ ☹ ☹		
I can use p = $\frac{F}{A}$	☺ ☹ ☹	☺ ☹ ☹	☺ ☹ ☹		TuitionKit http://bit.ly/ 2zybcOX
I can calculate pressure at different points in a liquid **Higher Tier Only**	☺ ☹ ☹	☺ ☹ ☹	☺ ☹ ☹		
I can describe the factors which cause an object to either sink or float **Higher Tier Only**	☺ ☹ ☹	☺ ☹ ☹	☺ ☹ ☹		
I can recall the units needed for p = hρg **Higher Tier Only**	☺ ☹ ☹	☺ ☹ ☹	☺ ☹ ☹		Flashcards available on www.primrose kitten.com
I can rearrange p = hρg **Higher Tier Only**	☺ ☹ ☹	☺ ☹ ☹	☺ ☹ ☹		
I can use p = hρg **Higher Tier Only**	☺ ☹ ☹	☺ ☹ ☹	☺ ☹ ☹		
I can describe how the atmosphere around the Earth changes as the distance from the Earth changes **Higher Tier Only**	☺ ☹ ☹	☺ ☹ ☹	☺ ☹ ☹		TuitionKit http://bit.ly/ 2lTCuJh
I can describe distance as a scalar quantity	☺ ☹ ☹	☺ ☹ ☹	☺ ☹ ☹	https://youtu.be/ 5Xcie8V-UTw	
I can describe displacement as a vector quantity	☺ ☹ ☹	☺ ☹ ☹	☺ ☹ ☹		
I can describe speed as a scalar quantity	☺ ☹ ☹	☺ ☹ ☹	☺ ☹ ☹	https://youtu.be/ 5Xcie8V-UTw	
I can describe velocity as a vector quantity	☺ ☹ ☹	☺ ☹ ☹	☺ ☹ ☹	https://youtu.be/ Nfm0a1Ui5pw	

I can recall the units needed for s = vt	☺ ☺ ☹	☺ ☺ ☹	☺ ☺ ☹		Flashcards available on www.primrose kitten.com
I can rearrange s = vt	☺ ☺ ☹	☺ ☺ ☹	☺ ☺ ☹		
I can use s = vt	☺ ☺ ☹	☺ ☺ ☹	☺ ☺ ☹		
I can state that the speed of an object is constantly changing	☺ ☺ ☹	☺ ☺ ☹	☺ ☺ ☹		
I can draw and interpret distance-time graphs	☺ ☺ ☹	☺ ☺ ☹	☺ ☺ ☹	https://youtu.be/7OEL6bupk8A	TuitionKit http://bit.ly/2zdYbXB
I can calculate the speed of an object from a distance time graph	☺ ☺ ☹	☺ ☺ ☹	☺ ☺ ☹		
I can describe the difference between speed and velocity	☺ ☺ ☹	☺ ☺ ☹	☺ ☺ ☹		
I can describe situations where an object has a constant speed but is accelerating	☺ ☺ ☹	☺ ☺ ☹	☺ ☺ ☹		
I can draw and interpret velocity-time graphs	☺ ☺ ☹	☺ ☺ ☹	☺ ☺ ☹	https://youtu.be/ZTwy8BYOhCs	TuitionKit http://bit.ly/2hf1kBM
I can calculate the distance travelled by an object from a velocity-time graph	☺ ☺ ☹	☺ ☺ ☹	☺ ☺ ☹		
I can define acceleration	☺ ☺ ☹	☺ ☺ ☹	☺ ☺ ☹		
I can calculate the acceleration of an object from a velocity-time graph	☺ ☺ ☹	☺ ☺ ☹	☺ ☺ ☹	https://youtu.be/ZTwy8BYOhCs	
I can recall the units needed for $a = \frac{\Delta v}{t}$	☺ ☺ ☹	☺ ☺ ☹	☺ ☺ ☹		Flashcards available on www.primrose kitten.com
I can rearrange $a = \frac{\Delta v}{t}$	☺ ☺ ☹	☺ ☺ ☹	☺ ☺ ☹		
I can use $a = \frac{\Delta v}{t}$	☺ ☺ ☹	☺ ☺ ☹	☺ ☺ ☹		
I can recall the units needed for $v^2 - u^2 = 2as$	☺ ☺ ☹	☺ ☺ ☹	☺ ☺ ☹		Flashcards available on www.primrose kitten.com
I can rearrange $v^2 - u^2 = 2as$	☺ ☺ ☹	☺ ☺ ☹	☺ ☺ ☹		

I can use $v^2 - u^2 = 2as$	☺ 😐 ☹	☺ 😐 ☹	☺ 😐 ☹	
I can recall that an object free falling due to the force of gravity has an acceleration of 9.8m/s^2	☺ 😐 ☹	☺ 😐 ☹	☺ 😐 ☹	
I can describe how an object reaches terminal velocity	☺ 😐 ☹	☺ 😐 ☹	☺ 😐 ☹	TuitionKit http://bit.ly/ 2AI59Kv
I can draw and interpret velocity-time graphs for objects that have reached terminal velocity	☺ 😐 ☹	☺ 😐 ☹	☺ 😐 ☹	
I can describe the forces on a moving object	☺ 😐 ☹	☺ 😐 ☹	☺ 😐 ☹	
I can describe how an object is moving if the resultant force on it is 0	☺ 😐 ☹	☺ 😐 ☹	☺ 😐 ☹	https://youtu.be/ Oa9LglsNm2o
I can apply Newton's First Law to explain the motion of objects	☺ 😐 ☹	☺ 😐 ☹	☺ 😐 ☹	
I can describe inertia	☺ 😐 ☹	☺ 😐 ☹	☺ 😐 ☹	
I can describe the relationship between the mass of an object and its acceleration	☺ 😐 ☹	☺ 😐 ☹	☺ 😐 ☹	
I can recall the units needed for F = ma	☺ 😐 ☹	☺ 😐 ☹	☺ 😐 ☹	Flashcards available on www.primrose kitten.com
I can rearrange F = ma	☺ 😐 ☹	☺ 😐 ☹	☺ 😐 ☹	
I can use F = ma	☺ 😐 ☹	☺ 😐 ☹	☺ 😐 ☹	TuitionKit http://bit.ly/ 2j0YW29
I can describe what happens when two objects interact	☺ 😐 ☹	☺ 😐 ☹	☺ 😐 ☹	
I can describe stopping distance as a combination of reaction time and breaking distance	☺ 😐 ☹	☺ 😐 ☹	☺ 😐 ☹	
I can describe the factors that affect reaction time	☺ 😐 ☹	☺ 😐 ☹	☺ 😐 ☹	
I can describe the factors that affect breaking distance	☺ 😐 ☹	☺ 😐 ☹	☺ 😐 ☹	TuitionKit http://bit.ly/ 2ywNdPW
I can explain features in a car that are design to make it safer	☺ 😐 ☹	☺ 😐 ☹	☺ 😐 ☹	TuitionKit http://bit.ly/ 2yxHid5

I can describe momentum as a property of moving objects **Higher Tier Only**	☺ ☺ ☹	☺ ☺ ☹	☺ ☺ ☹		
I can state the law of conservation of momentum **Higher Tier Only**	☺ ☺ ☹	☺ ☺ ☹	☺ ☺ ☹		
I can recall the units needed for p = mv **Higher Tier Only**	☺ ☺ ☹	☺ ☺ ☹	☺ ☺ ☹		Flashcards available on www.primrose kitten.com
I can rearrange p = mv **Higher Tier Only**	☺ ☺ ☹	☺ ☺ ☹	☺ ☺ ☹		
I can use p = mv **Higher Tier Only**	☺ ☺ ☹	☺ ☺ ☹	☺ ☺ ☹		TuitionKit http://bit.ly/ 2h5RChq
I can calculate momentum when two objects collide **Physics only**	☺ ☺ ☹	☺ ☺ ☹	☺ ☺ ☹		
I can recall the units needed for $F = \dfrac{m \, \Delta v}{\Delta t}$ **Physics only**	☺ ☺ ☹	☺ ☺ ☹	☺ ☺ ☹		Flashcards available on www.primrose kitten.com
I can rearrange $F = \dfrac{m \, \Delta v}{\Delta t}$ **Physics only**	☺ ☺ ☹	☺ ☺ ☹	☺ ☺ ☹		
I can use $F = \dfrac{m \, \Delta v}{\Delta t}$ **Physics only**	☺ ☺ ☹	☺ ☺ ☹	☺ ☺ ☹		

This worksheet is fully supported by a video tutorial; https://youtu.be/jfjb1pnH8zw

1. Define scaler quantity.
2. Define vector quantity.
3. Give an example of a contact force.
4. Given an example of a non-contact force.
5. How do you calculate resultant force?
6. What is the difference between mass and weight?
7. What is the equation linking weight, mass and gravity?
8. What are the units for weight?
9. What are the units for mass?
10. What are the units for gravity?
11. What is equation linking work, force and distance?
12. What are the units for work?
13. What are the units for force?
14. What are the units for distance?
15. How do you convert between Joules and Newton-metres?
16. What happens to an elastic object up to the limit of proportionality?
17. What happens to an elastic object after the limit of proportionality?
18. What is equation linking force, the spring constant and extension?
19. What are the units for force?
20. What the units for the spring constant?
21. What are the units for extension?
22. What is the equation linking elastic potential energy, the spring constant and extension?
23. What are the units for elastic potential energy?
24. What are the units for the spring constant?
25. What are the units for extension?
26. What is a fluid?
27. Can a fluid be compressed?
28. What is equation linking pressure, force and area?
29. What are the units for pressure?
30. What are the units for force?
31. What are the units for area?
32. Is distance a scalar or vector quantity?
33. Is displacement a scalar or vector quantity?
34. Is speed a scalar or vector quantity?
35. Is velocity a scalar or vector quantity?

36. What is the equation linking distance, velocity and time?
37. What are the units for distance?
38. What are the units for velocity?
39. What are the units for time?
40. How do you calculate the speed of an object from a distance-time graph?
41. When can an object have constant speed but still be accelerating?
42. How do you calculate the distance travelled from a velocity-time graph?
43. What is acceleration?
44. How do you calculate acceleration from a velocity-time graph?
45. What is the equation linking acceleration, change of in velocity and distance?
46. What are the units for acceleration?
47. What are the units for change in velocity?
48. What are the units of time?
49. What is the equation linking final velocity, initial velocity, acceleration and time?
50. If an object is falling due to gravity what acceleration does it have?
51. Define terminal velocity.
52. How is an object moving if the resultant force is zero?
53. What is Newton's first law.
54. Define inertia.
55. What is the equation linking force, mass and acceleration?
56. What are the units for force?
57. What are the units for mass?
58. What are the units for acceleration?
59. What is stopping distance?
60. Give two factors that can affect reaction time.
61. Give two factors that can affect braking distance.

Higher tier only

62. What factors can cause an object to float or sink?
63. What is equation linking pressure, height, density and gravitational field strength?
64. What are the units for pressure?
65. What are the units for height?
66. What are the units for density?
67. What are the units and value for gravitational field strength?
68. What is the law of conservation of the momentum?
69. What is equation linking the momentum, mass and velocity?
70. What are the units for momentum?
71. What are the units for mass?
72. What are the units for velocity?

Physics Only

73. What is equation linking moment, force and distance?
74. What are the units for moment?
75. What are the units for force?
76. What are the units the for distance?
77. What happens to an object if the clockwise and anticlockwise forces are balanced?
78. What happens to an object if the clockwise anticlockwise forces are unbalanced?
79. What is the equation linking force, mass, change in velocity and change the time?

6 – Waves

Knowledge Checklist

Whole topic summary video https://youtu.be/9JPNVJ_LC3E in only 15 minutes.

Specification statement These are the bits the exam board wants you to know, make sure you can do all of these…	Self-assessment			Bits to help if you don't understand	
	First review 4-7 months before exam	Second review 1-2 months before exam	Final review Week before exam	Primrose Kitten	Other places
I can draw and label transverse and longitudinal waves	☺ 😐 ☹	☺ 😐 ☹	☺ 😐 ☹		
I can describe the direction of movement and the direction of energy transfer for both transverse and longitudinal waves	☺ 😐 ☹	☺ 😐 ☹	☺ 😐 ☹		
I can define the terms, amplitude, wavelength and frequency	☺ 😐 ☹	☺ 😐 ☹	☺ 😐 ☹		
I can recall the units needed for $T = \dfrac{1}{f}$	☺ 😐 ☹	☺ 😐 ☹	☺ 😐 ☹		Flashcards available on www.primrose kitten.com
I can rearrange $T = \dfrac{1}{f}$	☺ 😐 ☹	☺ 😐 ☹	☺ 😐 ☹		
I can use $T = \dfrac{1}{F}$	☺ 😐 ☹	☺ 😐 ☹	☺ 😐 ☹		
I can describe how to measure the speed of waves	☺ 😐 ☹	☺ 😐 ☹	☺ 😐 ☹		
I can recall the units needed for $v = f\lambda$	☺ 😐 ☹	☺ 😐 ☹	☺ 😐 ☹		Flashcards available on www.primrose kitten.com
I can rearrange $v = f\lambda$	☺ 😐 ☹	☺ 😐 ☹	☺ 😐 ☹		
I can use $v = f\lambda$	☺ 😐 ☹	☺ 😐 ☹	☺ 😐 ☹		

I can construct ray diagrams to show what happens to a wave when it is reflected **Physics only**	☺ ☻ ☹	☺ ☻ ☹	☺ ☻ ☹		TuitionKit http://bit.ly/2zl5izi
I can describe what happens to a wave when it hits a boundary **Physics only**	☺ ☻ ☹	☺ ☻ ☹	☺ ☻ ☹		
I can describe how a sound wave travels **Higher tier only** **Physics only**	☺ ☻ ☹	☺ ☻ ☹	☺ ☻ ☹		TuitionKit http://bit.ly/2zlVZz5
I can describe how an ear detects sound **Higher tier only** **Physics only**	☺ ☻ ☹	☺ ☻ ☹	☺ ☻ ☹		
I can recall the range of human hearing **Higher tier only** **Physics only**	☺ ☻ ☹	☺ ☻ ☹	☺ ☻ ☹		
I can explain how echo can be used to determine distances **Higher tier only** **Physics only**	☺ ☻ ☹	☺ ☻ ☹	☺ ☻ ☹		
I can explain how changes in a wave can be used for detection and exploration **Higher tier only** **Physics only**	☺ ☻ ☹	☺ ☻ ☹	☺ ☻ ☹		
I can describe what happens to an ultrasound wave when it hits a boundary and how this property can be used for imaging **Higher tier only** **Physics only**	☺ ☻ ☹	☺ ☻ ☹	☺ ☻ ☹		TuitionKit http://bit.ly/2AmIyNM
I can describe how information from P-waves and S-waves can be used to provide evidence for the structure of the Earth **Higher tier only** **Physics only**	☺ ☻ ☹	☺ ☻ ☹	☺ ☻ ☹		TuitionKit http://bit.ly/2zhUdgG

I can recall the order of the electromagnetic waves	☺ ☺ ☹	☺ ☺ ☹	☺ ☺ ☹		TuitionKit http://bit.ly/2zyk0UR
I can recall that electromagnetic waves are transverse and form a continue spectrum	☺ ☺ ☹	☺ ☺ ☹	☺ ☺ ☹		
I can recall uses and properties of each part of the spectrum	☺ ☺ ☹	☺ ☺ ☹	☺ ☺ ☹		
I can draw a ray diagram to show what happens when a wave is diffracted **Higher tier only**	☺ ☺ ☹	☺ ☺ ☹	☺ ☺ ☹		
I can describe what happens to the path of a wave when is refracted **Higher tier only**	☺ ☺ ☹	☺ ☺ ☹	☺ ☺ ☹		
I can explain why refraction happen **Higher tier only**	☺ ☺ ☹	☺ ☺ ☹	☺ ☺ ☹	https://youtu.be/CrC1IlSy-bQ	
I can explain how an alternating current may produce radio waves **Higher tier only**	☺ ☺ ☹	☺ ☺ ☹	☺ ☺ ☹		
I can describe that a wave may be absorb, transmitted, refracted or reflected when it hits a surface **Higher tier only**	☺ ☺ ☹	☺ ☺ ☹	☺ ☺ ☹		
I can recall which surfaces absorb, emit and radiation **Higher tier only**	☺ ☺ ☹	☺ ☺ ☹	☺ ☺ ☹	https://youtu.be/kDLx36gDz80	
I can describe the circumstances in which a converging lens should be used **Physics only**	☺ ☺ ☹	☺ ☺ ☹	☺ ☺ ☹	https://youtu.be/4H9PAx90qMQ https://youtu.be/19SLrBwZYSA https://youtu.be/aRDt8PUhv4c	TuitionKit http://bit.ly/2A9ctrJ
I can construct a ray diagram for a converging lens **Physics only**	☺ ☺ ☹	☺ ☺ ☹	☺ ☺ ☹		
I can describe the image formed by a converging lens **Physics only**	☺ ☺ ☹	☺ ☺ ☹	☺ ☺ ☹		TuitionKit http://bit.ly/2hIHKLe

I can describe the circumstances in which a diverging lens should be used **Physics only**	☺ ☺ ☹	☺ ☺ ☹	☺ ☺ ☹	
I can construct a ray diagram for a diverging lens **Physics only**	☺ ☺ ☹	☺ ☺ ☹	☺ ☺ ☹	
I can describe the image formed by a diverging lens **Physics only**	☺ ☺ ☹	☺ ☺ ☹	☺ ☺ ☹	
I can rearrange Magnification = image height / object height **Physics only**	☺ ☺ ☹	☺ ☺ ☹	☺ ☺ ☹	https://youtu.be/v-KrUP3bu24
I can use Magnification = image height / object height **Physics only**	☺ ☺ ☹	☺ ☺ ☹	☺ ☺ ☹	
I can recall the order of light in the visible spectrum **Physics only**	☺ ☺ ☹	☺ ☺ ☹	☺ ☺ ☹	
I can recall the relative wavelengths and frequencies of the different parts of the visible light spectrum **Physics only**	☺ ☺ ☹	☺ ☺ ☹	☺ ☺ ☹	
I can describe that objects absorb and transmit light of different wavelengths **Physics only**	☺ ☺ ☹	☺ ☺ ☹	☺ ☺ ☹	
I can describe the difference between objects that are opaque, transparent and translucent **Physics only**	☺ ☺ ☹	☺ ☺ ☹	☺ ☺ ☹	
I can describe what happen to light when it is passed through a filter **Physics only**	☺ ☺ ☹	☺ ☺ ☹	☺ ☺ ☹	
I can recall that all objects emit infrared radiation **Physics only**	☺ ☺ ☹	☺ ☺ ☹	☺ ☺ ☹	

I can explain what a perfect black body is **Physics only**	☺ ☺ ☹	☺ ☺ ☹	☺ ☺ ☹		
I can explain that the intensity and wavelength distribution depends on the temperature of the object **Physics only**	☺ ☺ ☹	☺ ☺ ☹	☺ ☺ ☹		
I can explain anybody is constantly absorbing and emitting radiation, and the balanced between the two determines the temperature **Physics only**	☺ ☺ ☹	☺ ☺ ☹	☺ ☺ ☹		

This worksheet is fully supported by a video tutorial; https://youtu.be/AEFwEDC6DkQ

1. Sketch and label a transverse wave.
2. Sketch and label a longitudinal wave.
3. Define amplitude.
4. Define wavelength.
5. What is equation linking time period and frequency?
6. What are the units for time period?
7. What are the units for frequency?
8. What is equation linking wave speed, frequency and wavelength?
9. What are the units for wavelength?
10. What are the units for wave speed?
11. What is order of the electromagnetic waves?
12. What can radio-waves be used for?
13. What can microwaves be used for
14. What can infrared be used for?
15. What can visible light be used for?
16. What can ultraviolet be used for?
17. What can gamma rays be used for?
18. What can x-rays be used for?

Higher tier only

19. What happens when a wave is diffracted?
20. What happens when a wave is refracted?
21. Why does refraction happen?
22. Which surfaces absorb radiation?
23. Which surfaces emit radiation?

Physics only

24. What image is formed by converging lens?
25. When can converging lens be used?
26. When should a diverging lens be used?
27. What image is formed by diverging lens?
28. How do you calculate magnification?
29. What are the units for magnification?
30. What is the order of light in the visible spectrum?

31. What does opaque mean?

32. What does transparent mean?

33. What does translucent mean?

34. What happens to light when is passes through a filter?

Higher tier only

35. How to soundwaves travel?

36. What is the range of human hearing?

37. What is the P-wave?

38. What is an S-wave?

7 - Magnetism and Electromagnets

Knowledge Checklist

Whole topic summary video; https://youtu.be/mnigg3MGslY in only 8 minutes!!

Specification statement These are the bits the exam board wants you to know, make sure you can do all of these…	Self-assessment			Bits to help if you don't understand	
	First review 4-7 months before exam	Second review 1-2 months before exam	Final review Week before exam	Primrose Kitten	Other places
I can describe what happens when two like or unlike poles are placed next to each other	☺ ☺ ☹	☺ ☺ ☹	☺ ☺ ☹		
I can describe that a permanent magnet also has a magnetic field	☺ ☺ ☹	☺ ☺ ☹	☺ ☺ ☹		
I can recall that an induced magnet is a temporary magnet, when placed in a magnetic field	☺ ☺ ☹	☺ ☺ ☹	☺ ☺ ☹		
I can recall which materials are magnetic	☺ ☺ ☹	☺ ☺ ☹	☺ ☺ ☹		
I can relate the strength of the magnetic field to the proximity of the object	☺ ☺ ☹	☺ ☺ ☹	☺ ☺ ☹		
I can describe the direction of a magnetic field	☺ ☺ ☹	☺ ☺ ☹	☺ ☺ ☹	https://youtu.be/ VOOkOHKIcjQ	
I can plot a magnetic field	☺ ☺ ☹	☺ ☺ ☹	☺ ☺ ☹		
I can describe how a current can produce a magnetic field	☺ ☺ ☹	☺ ☺ ☹	☺ ☺ ☹		
I can describe how to change the strength of an electromagnet	☺ ☺ ☹	☺ ☺ ☹	☺ ☺ ☹		
I can explain how an electromagnet works	☺ ☺ ☹	☺ ☺ ☹	☺ ☺ ☹	https://youtu.be/ OBvFwTaIca8 https://youtu.be/ 6GMAK_evAz8	

I can use Flemings left hand rule to find the direction of the force **Higher tier only**	☺ 😐 ☹	☺ 😐 ☹	☺ 😐 ☹	https://youtu.be/whfpEeoHxNw	
I can recall what factors affect the size of the force **Higher tier only**	☺ 😐 ☹	☺ 😐 ☹	☺ 😐 ☹		
I can define magnetic flux density **Higher tier only**	☺ 😐 ☹	☺ 😐 ☹	☺ 😐 ☹		
I can recall the units needed for F = BIl **Higher tier only**	☺ 😐 ☹	☺ 😐 ☹	☺ 😐 ☹		Flashcards available on www.primrose kitten.com
I can rearrange F = BIl **Higher tier only**	☺ 😐 ☹	☺ 😐 ☹	☺ 😐 ☹		
I can use F = BIl **Higher tier only**	☺ 😐 ☹	☺ 😐 ☹	☺ 😐 ☹		
I can describe how an electric motor works **Higher tier only**	☺ 😐 ☹	☺ 😐 ☹	☺ 😐 ☹		
I can explain how the forces causes the rotation of the coil **Higher tier only**	☺ 😐 ☹	☺ 😐 ☹	☺ 😐 ☹		
I can explain how a moving-coil loudspeaker works **Higher tier only**	☺ 😐 ☹	☺ 😐 ☹	☺ 😐 ☹		
I can explain how a moving-coil microphone works **Higher tier only**	☺ 😐 ☹	☺ 😐 ☹	☺ 😐 ☹		
I can explain the generator effect **Higher tier only** **Physics only**	☺ 😐 ☹	☺ 😐 ☹	☺ 😐 ☹		
I can recall the factors that can affect the size of the induced potential **Higher tier only** **Physics only**	☺ 😐 ☹	☺ 😐 ☹	☺ 😐 ☹		
I can apply the generator effect **Higher tier only** **Physics only**	☺ 😐 ☹	☺ 😐 ☹	☺ 😐 ☹		

I can describe how the generator effect can produce ac and dc current **Higher tier only** **Physics only**	☺ ☺ ☹	☺ ☺ ☹	☺ ☺ ☹		
I can describe the structure of a transformer **Higher tier only** **Physics only**	☺ ☺ ☹	☺ ☺ ☹	☺ ☺ ☹	https://youtu.be/jXC2BvL-Ffk	
I can recall the units needed for $\dfrac{V_p}{V_s} = \dfrac{n_p}{n_s}$ **Higher tier only** **Physics only**	☺ ☺ ☹	☺ ☺ ☹	☺ ☺ ☹		Flashcards available on www.primrose kitten.com
I can rearrange $\dfrac{V_p}{V_s} = \dfrac{n_p}{n_s}$ **Higher tier only** **Physics only**	☺ ☺ ☹	☺ ☺ ☹	☺ ☺ ☹		
I can use $\dfrac{V_p}{V_s} = \dfrac{n_p}{n_s}$ **Higher tier only** **Physics only**	☺ ☺ ☹	☺ ☺ ☹	☺ ☺ ☹		
I can recall the units needed for $V_s I_s = V_p I_p$ **Higher tier only** **Physics only**	☺ ☺ ☹	☺ ☺ ☹	☺ ☺ ☹		Flashcards available on www.primrose kitten.com
I can rearrange $V_s I_s = V_p I_p$ **Higher tier only** **Physics only**	☺ ☺ ☹	☺ ☺ ☹	☺ ☺ ☹		
I can use $V_s I_s = V_p I_p$ **Higher tier only** **Physics only**	☺ ☺ ☹	☺ ☺ ☹	☺ ☺ ☹		

This worksheet is fully supported by a video tutorial; https://youtu.be/LyflUYL4FvM

1. What happens when you place like poles on a magnet next to each other?
2. What happens when you place unlike poles on a magnet next to each other?
3. Which materials are magnetic?
4. What is the direction of the magnetic field?
5. How do you change strength of an electromagnet?

Higher Tier Only

6. Define magnetic flux density.
7. What is the equation linking force, magnetic flux density, current and length?
8. What are the units for force?
9. What are the units for magnetic flux density?
10. What are the units for current?
11. What are the units for length?

Physics only

12. What is equation linking voltage at the primary coil, number of turns on the primary coil, voltage at the secondary coil, and number of turns on the secondary coil?
13. What are the units for voltage at the primary coil and voltage at the secondary coil?
14. What is equation linking voltage at the secondary coil, current at the secondary coil, voltage the primary coil, current at the primary coil?

Whole topic summary video; https://youtu.be/Mdi0i24tNT0 in only 8 minutes!

Specification statement These are the bits the exam board wants you to know, make sure you can do all of these...	Self-assessment			Bits to help if you don't understand	
	First review 4-7 months before exam	Second review 1-2 months before exam	Final review Week before exam	Primrose Kitten	Other places
I can describe our Solar system	☺ ☺ ☹	☺ ☺ ☹	☺ ☺ ☹		
I can describe our galaxy	☺ ☺ ☹	☺ ☺ ☹	☺ ☺ ☹		
I can describe the life cycle of a star	☺ ☺ ☹	☺ ☺ ☹	☺ ☺ ☹	https://youtu.be/RclIGz7AoIU	
I can describe the processes that go on in the centre of a star	☺ ☺ ☹	☺ ☺ ☹	☺ ☺ ☹		
I can recall the difference between natural and artificial satellites	☺ ☺ ☹	☺ ☺ ☹	☺ ☺ ☹		
I can describe how an object maintains its orbit	☺ ☺ ☹	☺ ☺ ☹	☺ ☺ ☹		
I can describe how velocity can change while speed remains constant	☺ ☺ ☹	☺ ☺ ☹	☺ ☺ ☹		
I can describe how red and blue shift occur	☺ ☺ ☹	☺ ☺ ☹	☺ ☺ ☹		
I can explain what red and blue shift show use	☺ ☺ ☹	☺ ☺ ☹	☺ ☺ ☹		
I can explain how red shift provides evidence for the Big Bang	☺ ☺ ☹	☺ ☺ ☹	☺ ☺ ☹	https://youtu.be/OlERzqXHXFw	

This worksheet is fully supported by a video tutorial; https://youtu.be/f3Rf1aVStIk

1. Give the order of objects in our solar system.
2. What is a galaxy?
3. Give the life cycle of a small star.
4. Give the life cycle of a large star.
5. What happens at the centre of a star?
6. What is a natural satellite?
7. What is an artificial satellite?
8. How does an object maintain its orbit?
9. How can an object change velocity while speed remains constant?
10. What is Redshift?
11. What is blue shift?
12. How does Redshift via evidence for the big bang?

Physics Paper 2 Checklist – What to do before the exam!

Watched the whole topic video   https://youtu.be/X1aMXCr75Kw   ☐

Learnt all the equations   ☐

Recall all the units   https://youtu.be/FaXds9xjxFk   ☐

Practiced rearranging equations   ☐

Answered the quick-fire questions   ☐

Looked at the practical videos   ☐

Filled in the crosswords   ☐

Crosswords

Physics Units

Across

7) the units for force

9) the units for charge

10) the units for mass

11) the units for current

12) the units for time period

13) the units for power

14) the units for frequency

16) the units for pressure

18) the units for initial velocity

20) the units for volume

21) the units for specific latent heat

22) the units for density

Down

1) the units for the spring constant

2) the units for potential difference

3) the units for acceleration

4) the units for work done

5) the units for gravitational field strength

6) the units for moment

8) the units for area

15) the units for resistance

17) the units for length

19) the units for magnetic flux density

Rearranging Equations.

E = m x c x θ

Make m the subject of the formula

E = m x c x θ

Make c the subject of the formula

E = m x c x θ

Make θ the subject of the formula

Efficiency = <u>useful energy out</u>   total
energy in

Make useful energy out the subject of the formula

Efficiency = <u>useful energy out</u>   total
energy in

Make total energy in the subject of the formula

Efficiency = $\dfrac{\text{useful power out}}{\text{power in}}$ total

Make useful power out the subject of the formula

Efficiency = $\dfrac{\text{useful power out}}{\text{power in}}$ total

Make total power in the subject of the formula

E = P x t

Make P the subject of the formula

E = P x t

Make t the subject of the formula

V = f x λ

Make f the subject of the formula

V = f x λ

Make λ the subject of the formula

Converting standard units

Number in question	Is this the correct unit?	Converted
5m		
Electrical energy 19J		
17˚C		
21J		
Electrical time 30 minutes		
10cm		
Electrical energy 7J		
45 minutes		
175g		
3Km		
93 ˚C		
Electrical energy 17kJ		
56 KJ		
Electrical time 3 hours		
95cm		

- Grab a coloured pen/pencil
- Draw a big circle around any numbers in the question
- Work out what each number stands for
- Use the formula sheet to find an equation with each of these in (they may give you the equation)
- Write down the equation (this will generally give you the first mark)
- Write the numbers from the question in, just below the equation (this will be the next mark)
- Do the math (third mark)
- Give the answer with correct units (final mark)
- If you miss the unit, you'll miss a mark!!!!

Physics questions tend to have a lot of words in but it's the numbers that are important. Pulling the numbers out of the jumble for words is a skill that needs to be practiced. These questions must be answered fully using the rules.

Easy

1. Blah blah blah blah blah 1200 joules of energy are supplied blah blah blah blah. The useful energy blah blah blah blah blah blah 720 joules blah blah blah blah.   (4 marks)

2. blah blah blah blah blah blah blah blah blah blah blah of 2,000 KW. blah blah blah blah blah blah blah blah blah blah blah blah blah blah blah 6 hours. Calculate the energy output in kilowatt-hours blah blah blah blah blah blah.   (4 marks)

3. blah blah blah blah 1 kg blah 15 MJ of energy in blah blah blah blah. Blah blah blah blah blah blah blah 13.5 MJ out blah blah blah blah. Calculate the efficiency of blah.   (4 marks)

4. blah blah blah blah blah blah blah blah blah blah blah blah blah blah. blah blah blah blah blah blah blah blah blah blah blah. blah blah blah blah 10 kg, blah blah blah blah 20 °C, blah blah blah blah blah blah 510 J/kg °C. Calculate the energy blah blah blah blah blah blah blah blah blah blah blah blah blah blah   (4 marks)

5. blah blah blah blah blah blah 2 kg blah blah blah blah blah blah blah blah blah blah. blah blah blah blah blah blah blah blah blah 7 °C. blah blah blah blah blah blah blah blah blah blah blah blah blah 3800 J/kg °C. blah blah blah blah blah blah blah.   (4 marks)

1. blah blah blah blah blah blah blah blah from 50°C to 58°C blah blah blah blah blah blah blah blah blah 4032 J blah blah blah blah blah. Calculate the mass blah blah blah blah blah blah blah blah. Specific heat capacity of water = 4200 J/kg°C   (4 marks)

2. blah blah blah blah blah blah blah blah blah blah blah blah blah 3.0×10^8 m/s. blah blah blah blah blah blah blah blah blah blah blah blah 25 metres. Calculate the frequency blah blah blah blah blah blah blah blah blah blah blah blah blah blah blah   (4 marks)

3. blah blah blah blah blah blah blah blah blah blah blah blah blah blah blah blah. blah blah blah blah blah blah blah blah blah blah 1.8×10^9 Hz blah blah blah blah blah blah blah blah blah blah 3.0×10^8 m/s. Calculate the wavelength blah blah blah blah blah.   (4 marks)

4. blah blah blah blah blah blah blah blah blah blah blah blah blah. blah blah blah blah blah blah blah blah blah blah 12.5 mm, blah blah blah blah blah blah blah blah blah. blah blah blah blah blah blah blah blah 300 000 000 m/s. Find the frequency   (4 marks)

Specific Heat Capacity.

$E = m \times c \times \theta$

- E= Energy (J)
- m= Mass (kg)
- c= Specific heat capacity (J/Kg °C)
- Θ= Temperature change (°C)

Easy

Fill in the missing value

Energy (J)	Mass (kg)	Specific heat capacity (J/Kg °C)	Temperature change (°C)
	2	1500	5
	4	1950	27
	7	2575	15
	19	5328	23
	26	9502	61

1. A block of mass 1.5Kg is heated until it has increased in temperature by 7°C, the specific heat capacity of the material is 750 J/Kg °C. How much energy was transferred?
2. 2Kg of water was heated up by 25°C, the specific heat capacity of water is 4181 J/Kg °C, how much energy was needed to heat up the water?
3. A material that has a specific heat capacity of 5872 J/Kg °C and has a mass of 1.2Kg is heated, and the temperature goes up by 12°C, how much energy did this take?
4. A pan of soup in heated up for lunch, to make it the right temperature to eat it has to be heated up by 39°C, the soup weighs 0.75Kg and the soup has a specific heat capacity of 932 J/Kg °C, how much energy was needed to make it nice to eat?
5. Find the energy needed to heat up a 2.5Kg stone by 17°C, the specific heat capacity of the stone is 4583 J/Kg °C.

Medium

Fill in the missing value

Energy (J)	Mass (kg)	Specific heat capacity (J/Kg °C)	Temperature change (°C)
4589		567	15
184	56		62
873956	2	205	
693		826	34
828	68		13

1. It requires 46.7J of energy to increase the temperature of a block by 15°C, the specific heat capacity of the block is 6934 J/Kg °C, find the mass of the block.

2. The sand dunes in the Rub' al Khali desert in Saudi Arabia absorbs heat energy throughout the day, a 0.5Kg sample of sand was tested to see if it was made of the same composition of rock as sand of other deserts around the world. The sample absorbed 45J of energy and this increased the temperature of the water by only 2 °C, find the specific heat capacity.

3. A block was heated (using 67J) by 17 °C, it is known that the specific heat capacity of the block is 6578 J/Kg °C, find the mass of the block.

4. A sample of liquid is taken from a region that is known to be volcanic, this sample is weighed at 0.25Kg, and it needs to be heated up with 46J of energy, if the specific heat capacity of the block is 4181 J/Kg °C, what did the temperature rise by?

5. A car is made from many different types of metal, it has to perform well when the engine has been running for a long period of time and producing a lots of heat. It then may be subjected to high temperatures when outside during the summer. Designers need to know that the car will be able to withstand these conditions, testing how the different metals react to heat is important. The first sample that was tested started at 25°C it was heated for 15 minutes and absorbed 68J of energy. The mass of the sample was 1.5Kg and the specific heat capacity was 4920 J/Kg °C, what was the final temperature of the block?

Hard

Material	Specific heat capacity (J/Kg °C)
Water	4181
Copper	3850
Iron	4500
Gold	1290

Fill in the missing value

Energy	Mass	Specific heat capacity (J/Kg °C)	Start temperature (°C)	End temperature (°C)	Temperature change (°C)
155J	123g		24	29	
1.25KJ		567	37	42	
3.9KJ	0.65Kg	5924	19		
345J		6011	78	91	
0.4KJ	12.5Kg		36	39	

1. A 750g block of iron was heated using 0.75KJ of energy, if the starting temperature was 29 °C what was the final temperature?

2. A gold sample that was being tested started at 31°C, it then absorbed 1.29KJ of energy and ended up measuring at 48°C what was the mass of the block?

3. Plumbing in old houses uses a large amount of copper pipes. In the winter the temperature plummets and if these pipes fall to a temperature of 2°C they start to encounter problems. To get the pipes to a safer temperature of 7°C, energy needs to be transferred, in this case by heat. If 0.95KJ of heat energy is put into the pipes what is the mass of the pipe that will be safe?

4. A 750g mystery sample is heated from 25°C by the absorption of 14.5KJ of energy, the final temperature of 40°C, what is the block made from?

5. Identify the material that requires 60.70KJ of energy to increase the temperature of 1500g increase by 9°C.

You may have noticed that the efficiency and energy equation is very similar to the efficiency and power equation. Here I am going to combine them both as they are handled in a similar way.

Easy

Useful Energy Out/ Useful Power Out	Total Energy In/ Total Power In	Efficiency
15J	45J	
25W	95W	
19J	178J	
79W	152W	
89J	109J	

1. The total amount of energy going into a hairdryer is 28J the useful energy coming out is only 15J, calculate the efficiency.
2. A TV on standby consumes a total of 198W of power, the tiny useful light on the front uses 19W of that power, calculate the efficiency.
3. A toaster gives out 194J of heat energy, the total energy in is 258J, calculate the efficiency.
4. A mobile phone takes in 45W of power and the useful power out is only 17W, calculate the efficiency.
5. A projector gives out light, sound and heat energy, the useful light energy given out is 59J, the electrical energy going in to the projector is 95J, calculate the efficiency.

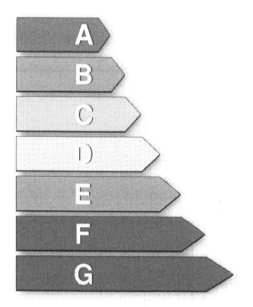

Medium

Useful Energy Out/ Useful Power Out	Total Energy In/ Total Power In	Efficiency
	159J	0.8
	74W	32%
	874J	0.47
	82W	27%
	90J	0.95

1. A mobile phones gives out 35J of light, 47J of heat and 17J of sound energy, calculate the efficiency.
2. A microwave takes in 59W and the wasted power is only 12W, calculate the efficiency.
3. A wind turbine is only 75% efficient; it takes in 35GW of power, what is the output?
4. When running tests, a student found that two different televisions took in and used different amount of energy. Both gave out 956J of heat energy but TV-A gave out 179J of light and 578J of sound energy. TV-B gave out 589J of sound energy, 19J of kinetic energy and 482J of light energy. Which one was more efficient?
5. If a mobile phone is 0.65 efficient and uses 1.2KW of energy, what is the useful energy?

Hard

Useful Energy Out/ Useful Power Out	Total Energy In/ Total Power In	Efficiency
34J		0.92
796W		61%
739J		0.71
45W		97%
90J		0.09

1. If a computer is 67% efficient, and gives out 79J of light, 42J of sound and 12J of kinetic energy. What was the total energy input?

2. After testing a range of computers the worst one was found to have an efficiency of 0.26 and the useful power rating was 1455W, the most efficient had an output of 1.25 KW and an efficiency of 45%. What was the difference in the total power consumed by each computer?

3. If a heater gives out 1.25KW of heat while working at 0.98 efficiency, what was the total power input?

4. An electric car requires recharging every 145km, it gives off 45kJ of heat energy, 1900J of sound energy, it runs at 78.3% efficiency, what is the total energy input?

5. If a desktop computer is 69% efficiency, and a laptop runs at 0.66 efficiency, both waste 93W what was the input for each?

E = P x t

- E= Energy (J)
- P= Power (W)
- t= Time (s)

Easy

Energy (J)	Power (W)	Time (s)
	46	5
	873	73
	63	3
	12	93
	9	6

1. How much energy is used if a 14W hairdryer is used for 45 seconds?
2. Calculate the amount of energy used if a phone is on for 103 seconds and uses 2W each second.
3. Find the amount of energy that is used when a TV (that uses 450W each second) is watched for 5 minutes
4. If you use your hair straighnters for 10 minutes and they use 67W each second, find the amount of energy comsumed.
5. Calcualte the amount of energy used when you play Xbox for 25 minutes, assume it uses 56W of energy each second.

Medium

Energy (J)	Power (W)	Time (s)
345	34	
67		17
1.25	12	
6783		53
90	37	

1. Find the amount of power used when a phone is on for 60 seconds, if 15J of energy are consumed.
2. A projector needs 45W and 67J to play a clip of Primrose being cute, how long is the video clip?
3. If an iPad is used for 15 minutes, and in this time 750J of energy are needed to keep it on, how much power is needed?
4. A student uses a calculator in an exam, the total time the calculator is in use is 4 minutes and 42 seconds. This means that 67J of energy was used, how much power was needed for this?
5. Give the time in minutes that it will take for a device to consume 459J of energy and 172W of power.

Hard

Energy	Power	Time
174J	1.3kW	
5.6kJ		15 minutes
90J	450W	
3.76kJ		2 hours
176J	31.5W	

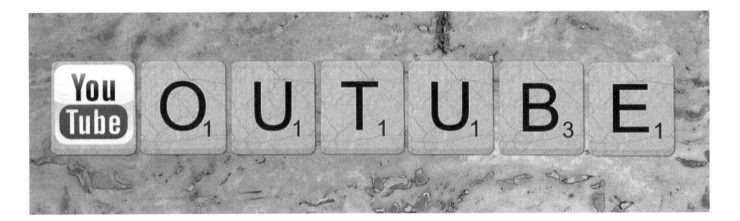

1. If wathcing YouTube clips for 90 miutes uses 1.2kJ of energy, calcaulate the power needed.
2. My coffee maker gets used on a very regular basis it needs 1.25kJ of energy and 750W of power to make my hazelnutt latte, how long does it take?
3. An iPhone needs 4.6kJ of energy to run for 2 ¼ hours, find the power needed for this.
4. Primrose likes to sit on a hot water bottle, this needs hot water from the kettle. Making her hot water bottle takes 3.56kJ and 15W how long does she have to wait?
5. How much power is needed to run a DS for 3 hours? It uses 0.34kJ of energy in this time.

The same equation comes up twice in P1, with similar but different units. AND just to really test you they use another equation that isn't on the formual sheet, they might give it to you in an exam they might not!! The tricky bit is not getting £ and p mixed up.

E = P x t

- E= Energy (kWh)
- P= Power (kW)
- t= Time (h)

Total cost of electricty = number of kilowatt-hours x cost per kilowatt-hour

Easy

Energy (kWh)	Power (kW)	Time (h)
	45	3
	67	4
	27	6
	48	2
	93	9

Cost of electricity (p)	Number of kilowatt-hours (kWh)	Cost per kilowatt-hour (p)
	17	13
	35	14
	83	9
	3	15
	75	21

1. How much energy is used if a device uses 45 kW each hour and is used for 7 hours?
2. If a computer is used for 3 hours and uses 19.5 kW each hour how much energy is used in total?
3. When a projector is used in a lesson it runs for 2 hours, if it uses 17.9 kW per hour, how much energy has been used?
4. A toy train is used for half an hour, each hour it uses 1.2kW, how much energy was needed in total?
5. The photocopier in the staffroom is very busy between 12pm and 1.30pm, if it needs 45 kW of power for each hour it is used, how much energy is needed?
6. Electricity cost 14p per kWh, if 45 kWh are used how much has been spent on electricity?
7. If plugging in your phone to charge uses 9.2 kWh and it cost 9p per kWh how much does it cost to charge your phone?
8. Boiling a kettle takes 2.1 kWh of energy, if it cost 11p per kWh how much does it cost?
9. One electricity company charges 12p kWh, if 6.5 kWh are used, how much does this cost?
10. If the cost of electricity is set at 29p per kWh and then 83 kWh are used, what is the total price?

Medium

Cost of electricity	Number of kilowatt-hours (kWh)	Cost per kilowatt-hour (p)
£3.45	54	
97p		14
£1.25	23	
£2.94		7
67p	16	

Cost of electricity (p)	Energy (kWh)	Power (kW)	Time (h)	Cost per kilowatt-hour (p)
		36	7	12
		41	3	14
		84	2	9
		35	4	8
		12	4	12.5

1. The total spent on electricity was 45p, if only 2kWh of energy was used how much is the unit price for electricity?
2. It cost £1.34 to charge your iPad, if the cost of electricity is 19p per kWh how much energy was used?
3. The amount spent to boil a kettle is 45p, if 12.5 kWh are used how much does each kWh cost?
4. The electricity charge for watching YouTube clips on your computer is only 97p, if the electricity company charges 11.75p per kWh hour much energy was used?
5. A device uses 56kWh of energy and the total cost of electricity was £1.45, how much does each unit of electricity cost?
6. GTA is played constantly for 5 hours, this needed 6.7kW for each hour. If electricity cost 12p for each unit used, calculate the total cost.
7. Your central heating is turned on for 6 hours each day and needs 1.9kW for each hour it's on. If electricity cost 11.5p calculate the cost of heating a house for a whole week.
8. My laptop needs to charge for 6 hours to fill up the battery, this needs 1.45kW each hour to charge it, and the cost for electricity is 17p per kWh.
9. An electric car needs to be connected to a power point for 4.5 hours so that it can make a long journey. The power point supplies 2.00 kW of power each hour and the cost of this is 21p per unit. What is the total cost?
10. An electricity company charges 5p per kWh and has a standing charge of 49p per day. A busy household uses electricity for 13 hours each day and each hour needs an average of 11.9 kW of power to supply all of their devices. What will the total cost be for March?

Hard

Cost of electricity	Energy	Power	Time	Cost per kilowatt-hour
	45 kWh	5000W		45p
£9.14	1.2 kWh	4.5 kW		
	49 kWh	120 W		12p
£4.53	26 kWh	20 kW		
£3.67	14 kWh	900 W		

1. A set of lights uses 39kWh of electricity each hour, if they run for 5 hours and each kWh costs 8p, what will the total cost of electricity be?

2. Running a sound check for the school production cost £15, if this takes 210kWh and uses 35 kW each hour, find the unit cost of electricity.

3. It costs £5.97 to play computer games all evening, the electricity company charges a very reasonable 6.5p per unit of electricity used with a standing charge of 29p per day. If the console uses 7.5 kW each hour, how long was the game played for?

4. Running a computer and projector for a whole day in school, cost £51.54. The computer uses 14kW each hour and the projector 9.75 kW each hour. If electricity cost 31p per unit and the school day started at 8.45am, what time does the final bell ring?

5. Charging a phone and a tablet at the same time uses 30 kW, half way through the charging time the tablet is unplugged and the power usage drops to 1/3 of the original. If the tablet is charged for 2 hours and electricity cost 9p per kWh, calculate the total cost.

This is a topic that comes up a lot, often hidden inside long wordy 6 or 4 mark questions. The maths here is lovely and easy; you just need to be familiar with it!

Divide the cost of installing by the reduction in energy bills and that will give you the payback time.

Type of energy saving	Cost to install	Reduction in energy bills each year	Payback time
Double glazing	£15,000	£120	
Loft insulation	£4,500	£800	
Draught excluders	£35	£20	
Jacket on hot water tank	£20	£60	
Carpet	£450	£75	
Curtains	£575	£45	
Solar panels	£25,000	£500	

1. Which type of insulation should a home owner consider installing first?
2. Which type of insulation is not cost effective?
3. What other things might a homeowner take into account when consider whether to install double glazing or not?
4. Why might someone not be thinking about payback time when putting in curtains or carpet?
5. What other factors does a homeowner need to think about before installing solar panels?

$V = f \times \lambda$

- V= Wave speed (m/s)
- f= Frequency (Hz)
- λ= Wavelength (m)

Easy

Wave speed (m/s)	Frequency (Hz)	Wavelength (m)
	35	1.5
	268	20
	2500	57
	836	29
	39	53

1. Find the speed of a wave, when the wave has a frequency of 500Hz and a wavelength of 2m.
2. A wave has a wavelength of 3.75m and a frequency of 78Hz, what is the speed of the wave?
3. The speed of a wave can be determined from the frequency and the wavelength, if a wave has a frequency 600Hz and a wavelength of 45m, find the speed.
4. The frequency of a wave is 750Hz and the wavelength of this wave is 90m, what speed is the wave travelling at?
5. A wave passes a fixed point 5 times each second, the distance between the peaks of each wave is 0.5m; how fast is the wave travelling?

Medium

- The speed of light is 3.0×10^8 m/s.
- Questions that are in standard form require answers in standard form.
- All waves travel at the same speed in a vacuum.

Wave speed (m/s)	Frequency (Hz)	Wavelength (m)
3890	28	
87328		3790
38	204	
39		47
4925	486	

1. If a wave is travelling at 20,000 m/s and the wavelength of this wave is 5m, what is the frequency?
2. If a wave is going at 400,000 m/s and has a frequency of 250Hz, what is the wavelength?
3. Find the frequency of a wave that is travelling at 10m/s and has wavelength of 0.6 m.
4. What is the frequency of a wave that is travelling at the speed of light and has a wavelength of 4.5×10^4 m?
5. A wave travelling through space has a frequency of 3.9×10^{-2} Hz, what is the distance between the peaks of the waves?

Hard

- The speed of light is 3.00×10^8 m/s.
- Questions that are in standard form require answers in standard form.
- All waves travel at the same speed in a vacuum.

Wave speed (m/s)	Frequency	Wavelength
373		100cm
900	450cHz	
271		2.5km
42,800	5kHz	
602,000		538cm

1. Find the speed of a wave with a frequency of 9.36×10^6 kHz and a wavelength of 10.5cm.
2. A wave travelling through space at the speed of light and has a wavelength of 1.75 km, what is the frequency of the wave?
3. Find the wavelength of a wave that is travelling at 6.80×10^6 m/s and has a frequency of 3.98×10^4 Hz.
4. A wave is travelling at 4.59km/h and it has a wavelength of 4m, find the frequency.
5. Two waves are travelling through space one has a wavelength of 3.7×10^4 m and the other has a wavelength of 8.4×10^5 m, what is the difference in the frequencies of these waves?

This is a combination of all equations, follow the rules on at the beginning of the book to answer these, the first thing you will need to do is work out which equation you will need to use.

1. Find the amount of energy used by a device, if it uses 45W in 150s.
2. How fast is a wave moving if it has a frequency of 45Hz and a wavelength of 4m?
3. If a device uses 45J of energy and it is supplied with 125J of energy, how efficient is the device?
4. Find the amount of energy needed to run an iPhone for 1 minute if it uses 12W each second.
5. Electricity cost 15p per kWh, if 250kWh are used what is the total cost of electricity?
6. A wave has a frequency of 79.5Hz, the wavelength is 45.9m, what is the speed of this wave?
7. The specific heat capacity of an object is 4398 J/kg °C, the object being heated has a mass of 2.5k kg and the temperature change is 4.8°C. How much energy was needed to heat this up?
8. A computer usefully uses only 160W of power that is supplied to it. If the total power supplied to the computer is 1904W, how efficient was the device?
9. A block that has a mass of 90 kg, is heated up by 17 °C, if the specific heat capacity of this block is 3905 J/kg °C, how much energy was needed to heat up this block?
10. A TV is on for 7 hours, each hour it uses 45kW of power, how much electrical energy was used in this time?

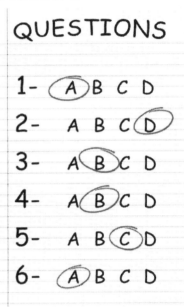

QUESTIONS

1- (A) B C D
2- A B C (D)
3- A (B) C D
4- A (B) C D
5- A B (C) D
6- (A) B C D

Medium

1. A wave is travelling at the speed of sound and has a frequency of 2.5×10^6 Hz, what is the wavelength?
2. A device is 80% efficient, if the total power supplied to the device is 450W how much is useful power?
3. To run a projector 390kWh of energy is needed, the school day runs from 8.45am to 3.15pm. If the projector is on the whole time how much power has been used?
4. 3094J of energy is needed to heat an object up by 28°C, if the mass of the object is 45kg what is the specific heat capacity?
5. 392J is consumed by when charging an iPad, if it's only plugged in for 45s, how much power is used?
6. If a wind turbine has an efficiency of 0.95 and 6704J of energy is supplied, how much is wasted
7. Find the frequency of a wave that has a wavelength of 1.46×10^6 m and a speed of 2.74×10^7 Hz.
8. If a device runs using 38J of energy and is on for 14s, how much power is used each second?
9. During the spring the nice warm weather means the central heating doesn't come on very often. On average it only turns on for 2 hours and 45 minutes each day. An electricity company charges a standing charge of 29p each day and 4.5p per unit of electricity. If the cost for a 2-week period is £4.98 how much power does it use each hour?
10. Find the mass of the block that needs 3925J of energy to increase its temperature by 34.5 °C. The specific heat capacity of this block is 2945 J/kg °C.

Hard

1. Calculate the time that was needed for a device to cost 98p to charge, assume this device uses 750W each minute and the unit price is 14p per kWh.
2. The total energy usage of a school over a week is 4.56×10^7kJ, how much power is used?
3. A 1050g block is dived into two, one half is heated until the block has changed temperature from 21 °C to 39 °C, the energy needed for this was only 1.6kJ, calculate the specific heat capacity of the block.

4. My coffee maker is only 35% efficient; it wastes 45J of energy every time I make my latte. How much energy is supplied to the coffee machine?
5. A console uses 8550kJ of energy when is being played, if it uses 0.95kW; in hours how long was it played for?
6. A wave travels at the speed of light, if the wavelength is 1.64×10^4cm, what is the speed?
7. Electricity costs 24p each day, in July the total cost for electricity was £887.84. Each day the total energy usage is 1420kWh. What is the unit cost of electricity?
8. A phone wastes 49J of as heat energy and uses 78J as light energy, if it has an efficiency of 72% how much useful sound energy is there?
9. Two blocks of mass 950g are heated up for 90 minutes. Block-A has a specific heat capacity of 1894J/kg °C, Block-B has a specific heat capacity of 2845 J/kg °C. If the total amount of energy used in this was 4.5kJ and both blocks started at 21°C, calculate the final temperature of both.
10. Light that comes from distance galaxies is red-shifted. We can use the information to determine how far away a star is. If light from star-A has a frequency of 5.23×10^4 Hz and light from star-B has a frequency of 5.43×10^5 Hz, mathematically show which star is further away?

$E_k = \frac{1}{2}mv^2$

- ½ is just a number
- E_k = kinetic energy (J)
- m = mass (kg)
- v = velocity (m/s) v^2 is just the square of the velocity not the whole thing.

Easy

Don't forget its v^2

Kinetic energy (J)	½	Mass (kg)	Velocity (m/s)
	0.5	2	0.75
	0.5	7	4
	0.5	7.8	5
	0.5	4.2	8.2
	0.5	9.75	0.5

1. Find the kinetic energy when a 1.2kg object is travelling at 2m/s.
2. What is the kinetic energy when Primrose (1.8kg) is running at 0.45m/s?
3. Calculate the amount of kinetic energy of an object moving at 1.67m/s, if the object has a mass of 2.4kg
4. How much kinetic energy does a 5kg object have when it is travelling at 9m/s?
5. Work out the value for kinetic energy when an 4kg object is moving is at 4m/s

Medium

Kinetic energy (J)	Mass (kg)	Velocity (m/s)
128	79	
594		4.9
56	8	
29		2.5
78	7.5	

1. Primrose (1.8kg) picks up a frog (45g) and runs at 0.3m/s, what is the kinetic energy?
2. If it needs 125J to move a 4kg object, how fast does it move?
3. If it requires 92J to move an object at a speed of 2.5m/s, what is the mass of the object?
4. To get an object travelling at 17m/s it requires a total of 148.7J of energy, what is the mass of the object?
5. To get a toy train moving at 0.75m/s it needs to be pushed with 19J of energy, what is the mass of the train?

Hard

Kinetic energy	Mass	Velocity
1.2kJ	5kg	
450J	95g	
0.98kJ		8.2m/s
3.78kJ		0.27km/h
58J		1.2km/h

1. It requires 25.23J to push a toy train at a speed of 5.8m/s. If each cart has a mass of 250g, how many carts make up the train?
2. An object needs 0.97kJ of energy to travel at a speed of 19.67m/s, what is the mass of the object?
3. An object that has a mass of 750g and is joined by an object twice the mass and another three times to mass to make one large object, if it needs 6.7J of energy to be moved what is the final velocity?

4. How much energy is needed to move a 1.2g object at a speed of 2.9km/h. Give your answer in standard form.
5. To move a large block, it needs 1.025kJ of energy, if the mass of the object is 1298g, what is the velocity that it's moving with?

Super Hard

1. An object has a weight of 170N, and needs 29J of energy to move. What velocity is it moving with?
2. An object of mass 15kg, starts moving with a velocity of 21m/s and over 15s accelerates at a rate of 3.9m/s^2 to its final speed. What is the kinetic energy needed to move the object at its final speed?
3. After rolling for 12 minutes a large rock lands at the bottom of a hill with a final mass of 12.6kg. The final velocity was 30m/s and during its journey the rock accelerated at 0.01m/s^2 and lost 10% of its mass. What was the kinetic energy at the beginning of the journey?
4. An object with a mass of 1.2kg falls 2.7m, what velocity does it fall with?
5. A car that was accelerating at a rate of 34m/s^2 hits an objects and stops immediately. It's hits with a force of 124N. If it was travelling with 379J just before it hit, what was the final velocity?

Speed = <u>distance</u>
          time

wave speed (meter per second, m/s)

distance (meters, m)

time (seconds, s)

Easy

Wave speed (m/s)	Distance (m)	Time (s)
	4.5	15
	0.2	73
	1.8	48
	3.2	26
	5.9	2

1. If a wave has travelled 7m in 14s what is the wave speed?
2. Find the wave speed when a wave travels 8.9m in 120s.
3. Calculate the speed of a wave when it moves 18m in 62 seconds.
4. If it takes 45 seconds for a wave to go 6.7m, what is the speed of the wave?
5. A wave takes 38s to go 7.9m, what speed is the wave travelling at?

Medium

Wave speed (m/s)	Distance (m)	Time (s)
45	5	
8		5.9
9.8	6.2	
18		6.3
42	5	

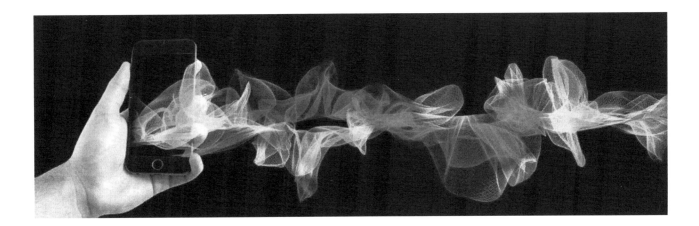

1. If a wave is travelling at 56m/s and takes 8s, how far has it travelled?
2. Find the time it takes a wave to travel 17m if it is moving at 6.2m/s.
3. Calculate the distance a wave will travel in 45s if the speed of the wave is 600m/s.
4. If it takes 2 ½ minutes for a wave to travel and it is travelling at 98m/s, how far has it travelled?
5. A boat is surveying the bottom of an ocean; in water a sound waves travels at 330m/s. It takes 4 minutes from the time the signal leaves the boat for it to return, how deep is that part of the ocean?

Hard

Wave speed	Distance	Time
450m/s	45m	
728m/s		1 hour 20 minutes
23m/s	1.5km	
4543m/s		45 minutes
3m/s	250cm	

1. An echo is heard in a cave, if the sound is travelling at 330m/s and it takes 4.7s for the sound to be reflected back, how deep is the cave?
2. Ultrasounds can be used to detect foetal abnormalities and to look at soft tissue, the wave bounces back very quickly at an approximate speed to 1540m/s. If the distance from the probe to the foetus is 5cm, how quickly will the pictures appear on the computer screen?
3. The bottom of the ocean is covered in old sunken pirate boats that are full of treasure. To find these pirate ships modern boats use sonar to see what is on the bottom of the ocean. If the speed of the sonar is 330m/s and the bottom is predicted to be 15km down, how long until the signal comes back?
4. Bats use echo location to help them move around at night. Two bats are flying apart, it takes 0.5s for a bat to hear a signal sent from the other bat. If the speed of sound is 330m/s how far apart are they?
5. A wave is travelling at 4.5km/h how far will it have travelled in 67s?

Power, current and potential difference

$P=IV$

P = Power (Watts, W)

I = Current (amps or amperes, A)

V = Potential difference (volts, V)

Easy

Power (W)	Current (A)	Potential difference (V)
	5	7
	8	3
	13	8
	9.9	15
	42	0.9

1. Find the power in a circuit where there is 5 amps of current and the potential difference is 17 volts
2. If the potential difference across a bulb is 4.3V and the current flowing is 1.8A what is the power supplied?
3. In a circuit a 7A current flows across a bulb and in this circuit there is a 6.7V potential difference, what is the power in the circuit?
4. When 9V of potential difference is found across a component and the current is known to be 4.6A, what is the power going to be?
5. Calculate the power in a circuit when the current is 56A and the potential difference is 4.9V.

Medium

Power (W)	Current (A)	Potential difference (V)
4.6	1.9	
9.8		3.1
45	5.9	
73		8
109	59	

1. If there is 76W of power in a circuit and the potential difference is 5.9V what is the current?
2. Calculate the potential difference in a circuit where the current is 8A and the power is 18W.
3. What is the potential difference across a bulb when the current is 5A and the power is 19W?
4. A parallel circuit has 4 branches, each branch has 2 bulbs and a switch. There are 3 cells that make up the battery, the potential difference across the battery is measured at 6V, if the power is 21W, what is the current is the circuit?
5. Work out the current in a circuit that has 4 1.5V cells in a battery and has 31W of power.

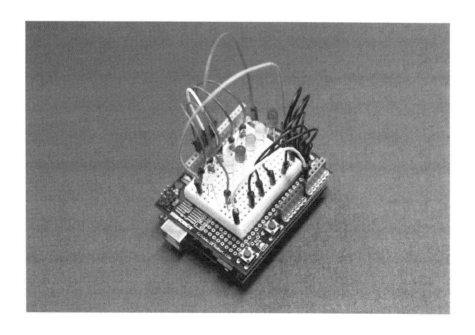

Hard

Power	Current	Potential difference
1.3kW	950mA	
0.8kW		0.2kV
56W	8A	
0.045kW		25V
1.45×10^9W	9.37×10^2A	

1. The power in a circuit is 1.2kW and the current is 45A, what is the potential difference?
2. Calculate the current in a circuit where the potential difference is 0.6kV and the power is 900W.
3. Find the potential difference across a bulb if the current flowing is 500mA and the power is 2W.
4. Work out the current when a circuit has 3 2V cells and power of 0.6kW.
5. What is the potential difference in a circuit when the flow of current is measured as 4kA and the power at 6kW?

Pressure (Pa) = <u>Force (N)</u>

   Area (m²)

Hints; the standard unit for pressure is Pascals, sometimes exam questions want the answers in N/cm², read what the question says carefully.

Easy

1. Explain why the force is normally applied to the small cylinder?
2. A boat applies a 70N force to a lake; the bottom of the boat covers an area of 1.2m². Find the pressure exerted on the lake by the boat.
3. What is the pressure if the force is 7N and the area is 25cm²? Give pressure in N/cm².
4. The force on the first piston is 80N, the area is 50cm², find the pressure. Give pressure in N/cm².
5. If the force is 50N and the area 10cm², give the pressure. Give pressure in N/cm².

Medium

6. If the area of the first piston is 23cm² calcaulte the resultant pressure that a force of 12.5 N creates. If the same piston is connected up by hydraulics to a second piston, how large does the surface area have to be to lift a car of 20,000N?
7. If a 457Pa pressure is applied to the first piston, and the second piston has a surface area of 0.6m². What is the force that will be applied?
8. The force in the first piston is 15N, the area of the first piston is 0.0005m², find the pressure and the force on the second piston, if its area is 0.0012m².
9. To lift a car a hydraulic jack requires a pressure of 20Pa, to be exerted on an area of 5.2m². What is the force needed?
10. The master piston applies a pressure of 1.5×60^6 Pa to a liquid. The area of this piston is 5.6×10^{-5} m², calculate the force.

Hard

11. Primrose the kitten has a mass of 1.8kg, each of her feet covers an area of 2cm², how much pressure does she exert on me, when she wakes me up in the morning?

$$\frac{V_p}{V_s} = \frac{n_p}{n_s}$$

$$V_p \times I_p = V_s \times I_s$$

- V_p=Potential difference across the primary coil   (V)
- V_s= Potential difference across the secondary coil   (V)
- n_p=Number of turns in primary coil
- n_s=Number of turns in secondary coil
- I_p=Current in the primary coil   (A)
- I_s= Current in the secondary coil   (A)

1. What is the difference between a step-up and a step-down transformer? Your answer should include a simple sketch of each and an example where they are useful

2. What is the potential difference leaving a power station and the potential difference entering a house? Why are they different?

3. Describe how a transform works, you should include a simple sketch including.

4. How is a switch mode transformer different?

5. If the primary coil has 450 turns and the secondary coil has 200 turns. The supply to the primary coil is 100V, find the potential difference across the secondary coil.

6. The primary coil has a potential difference of 120V across it and the secondary coil has 300V, find the number of turn in the secondary coil if the primary has 97.

7. A transformer has a potential difference of 15V across its secondary coil, find the potential difference across the primary if the primary coil has 40 turns and the secondary coil has 20 turns

8. A transformer has 10V across the primary coil and 5V across the secondary coil, if the primary coil has 20 turns how many does the secondary coil have?

9. A transformer is used to step-down a potential difference of 230V to 10V, if the secondary coil has 6 turns how many does the primary coil have?

10. A transformer has 50 turns in the secondary coil and 500 in the primary, if the potential difference in the secondary coil is 120V find the potential difference across the primary coil.

11. Find the current in the secondary coil, if the current in the primary coil is 7A, the potential difference across the primary coil is 30V and across the secondary coil is 10V.

12. Find the potential difference across the primary coil , if the potential difference across the secondary is 20V, the current in the primary coil is 22A and in the secondary y coil is 17A

13. A transformer changes 30V to 12V in a lamp, where the current is 4amps, find the current in the mains.

14. Calculate the potential difference in the secondary coil and the current in the primary coil. The number of turn in the primary coil is 575, the number of turns in the secondary coil is 50, the current in the secondary coil is 3.45A, the potential difference across the primary coil is 230V

Answers

Maths and Calculator skills

The playlist with videos working through all the answers can be found at
https://www.youtube.com/playlist?list=PL7O6CcKg0HaFRvd1xkDz6VTR3SXRqKpCz

Mean averages

Result 1	Result 2	Result 3	Result 4	Average
21	25	22	26	**23.5**
167	160	156	162	**161.25**
15.6	15.9			**15.75**
57	61	59		**59**
99	101	103	100	**100.75**
12	10			**11**
97.56	95.76	98.99	95.97	**97.07**
47	49	41		**45.7**
1298	1340	1314	1327	**1319.75**
69	71	75	72	**71.75**

Anomalies

Result 1	Result 2	Result 3	Result 4	Average
75	77	**51**	76	**76**
62	59	**69**	61	**60.7**
724	720	719	**736**	**721**
79	69	67	65	**67**
0.5	**0.05**	0.51	0.49	**0.5**
1793	1788	**1893**	1790	**1790.3**
67.5	67.9	67.8	67.4	**67.65**
278	**299**	281	277	**278.7**
45.6	47.2	47.6	47.9	**47.6**
4893	**4814**	4905	4899	**4899**

Interval and range

Experiment 1

Interval **10cm**   Range **10cm** To **70cm**

Experiment 2

Interval **0.25M**   Range **0.25M** To **1.25M**

Experiment 3

Interval **2N**   Range **3N** To **15N**

Experiment 4

Interval **1 chip**   Range **6 chips** To **9 chips**

Experiment 5

Interval **5 star jumps**   Range **5 star jumps** To **35 star jumps**

Rounding

1. Give 389540 to 4 significant figures   **389500**
2. Give 85947395925 to 3 significant figures   **85900000000**
3. Give 465906375 to 3 significant figures   **466000000**
4. Give 0.05678 to 3 significant figures   **0.0568**
5. Give 0.0097495793 to 3 significant figures   **0.0975**
6. Give 389540 to 3 significant figures   **390000**
7. Give 85947395925 to 5 significant figures   **85947000000**
8. Give 465906375 to 6 significant figures   **465906000**
9. Give 0.056788947585 to 7 significant figures   **0.05678895**
10. Give 0.0097495793 to 8 significant figures   **0.0097495793**

Standard form

Write each of these in standard form

1. 893000000 8.93×10^{8}
2. 70900000 7.09×10^{7}
3. 38940000000 3.89×10^{10}
4. 72010000000000000 7.20×10^{16}
5. 642310000 6.42×10^{8}
6. 0.025 2.5×10^{-2}
7. 0.000789 7.89×10^{-4}

8. 0.000183 1.83×10^{-4}

9. 0.00000956 9.56×10^{-6}

10. 0.001002 1.00×10^{-3}

Write each of these in long form

1. 6.38×10^{5} 638000
2. 7.29×10^{9} 7290000000
3. 6.09×10^{3} 6090
4. 9.078×10^{7} 90780000
5. 8.112×10^{6} 8112000
6. 8.92×10^{-3} 0.0892
7. 7.25×10^{-6} 0.00000725
8. 2.965×10^{-11} 0.00000000002965
9. 9.385×10^{-5} 0.00009385
10. 8.42×10^{-14} 0.0000000000000842

Fractions and Decimals

1. 2/3   0.67
2. 6/10   0.6
3. 7/11   0.64
4. 9/12   0.75
5. 19/36   0.53
6. 1/3   0.33
7. 18/25   0.72
8. 956/1094   0.87
9. 74/97   0.76
10. 47/97   0.48

Assessment

For all answers to gain marks units must be given.

1. Interval 0.5M range 0.5M → 2M
2. 23.75 minutes
3. Interval 5 minutes, range 5 minutes → 20 minutes. Average 2.3 worms
4. 1.97×10^{2} s

Biology crossword 1

Across

3) lump of cells that are not invading the body [BENIGNTUMOR]

5) carries oxygen around the body, has no nucleus [REDBLOODCELL]

7) small fragments of blood cells that help clotting [PLATELETS]

9) Thinned walled blood vessels that allow diffusion of gases and nutrients [CAPILLARY]

14) Enzyme that breaks carbohydrates into sugars [AMYLASE]

18) Small structural unit that contains a nucleus and cytoplasm [CELL]

19) fluid part of the blood [PLASMA]

20) one copy of each chromosome [HAPLOID]

23) organ system that absorbs nutrients from food [DIGESTIVESYSTEM]

26) Major blood vessel that carries deoxygenated blood back to the heart [VENACAVA]

28) state of mental and physical wellbeing [HEALTH]

29) Type of cell division that ends in two identical daughter cells [MITOSIS]

30) uncontrolled cell division within the body [CANCER]

31) Blood vessel that carries deoxygenated blood from the heart to the lungs [PULMONARYARTERY]

Down

1) Major blood vessel that carries oxygenated blood away from the heart [AORTA]

2) carries water around a plant [XYLEM]

4) organ system that moves oxygen around the body [RESPIRATORYSYSTEM]

6) Produced by the liver, neutralizes stomach acid and emulsifies fats [BILE]

8) the study of organism within and environment [ECOLOGY]

10) long stretch of DNA [CHROMOSOME]

11) Enzyme that breaks proteins into amino acids [PROTEASE]

12) jelly like substance within a cell [CYTOPLASM]

13) a type of cell that can differentiate into any other type of cell [STEMCELL]

15) two copies of each chromosome [DIPLOID]

16) control centre of the cell, that holds the DNA [NUCLEUS]

17) Biological catalyst [ENZYME]

21) movement of ions or gasses from a high concentration to a low concentration [DIFFUSION]

22) Enzyme that breaks fats into fatty acids and glycerol [LIPASE]

24) plant tissue found at growing tips [MERISTEM]

25) carries ions around a plant [PHLOEM]

27) Blood vessels that have values and carries deoxygenated blood back to the heart [VEIN]

Biology Crossword 2

Across

5) medication that contain inactive or dead virus to help develop immunity [VACCINES]

8) large gland in the neck which releases hormone [THYROID]

10) braches of the trachea [BRONCHI]

11) in women, these stores the eggs [OVARIES]

13) can be combined with glycerol to make lipids [FATTYACIDS]

14) DNA within a protein coat that divides by invading cells, the resulting cell death causes illness in the host [VIRUS]

17) parasite transmitted by mosquitoes [MALARIA]

21) system that controls hormones and responses [ENDOCRINESYSTEM]

23) inability of the bod to control blood glucose levels [DIABETES]

24) long chains of amino acids, that carry out the majority of functions within the body [PROTEINS]

27) drugs that kill bacteria [ANTIBIOTICS]

28) green part of a plant [CHLOROPHYLL]

29) in men, these are responsible for the production of sperm [TESTIS]

30) chemical process that occur to maintain life [METABOLISM]

31) arises after anaerobic respiration, needs oxygen to repay [OXYGENDEBT]

32) viral infection causing fever and rash, most common in children [MEASLES]

Down

1) causes illness [PATHOGEN]

2) large gland behind the stomach which produces digestive enzymes [PANCREAS]

3) respiration with oxygen [AEROBIC]

4) bacteria that cause a sexual transmitted disease causing smelly discharge from the penis or vagina [GONORRHEA]

6) stores of energy that can be broken down to form fatty acids and glycerol [LIPIDS]

7) long tube taking air down into the lungs [TRACHEA]

9) virus that interfere with your body's ability to fight disease [HIV]

12) painkiller developed from willow bark [ASPIRIN]

13) group that includes mushrooms and moulds, they live of decomposing material [FUNGI]

15) can be combined with fatty acid to make lipids [GLYCEROL]

16) process where plant absorb and lose water [TRANSPIRATION]

18) nerve pathway including a sensory nerve a synapse and a motor nerve [REFLEXARC]

19) large gland near the kidneys that releases hormone [ADRENALGLAND]

20) virus affecting plants causing a mosaic pattern on leaves [TMV]

22) tiny single celled organism that can cause illness [PROTIST]

25) heart drug that comes from Foxglove plants [DIGITALIS]

26) transport of water across a partially permeable membrane [OSMOSIS]

Biology crossword 3

Across

1) breading of animals or plants for a particular characteristic [SELECTIVEBREADING]

5) change in a spices to suit the environment [ADAPTATION]

9) sex cells [GAMETES]

10) different copies of gene [HETEROZYGOUS]

11) no breading pair of a species exist [EXTINCTION]

13) male sex cell [SPERM]

14) what genes are present [GENOTYPE]

17) eat plants and animals [OMNIVORE]

18) different version of gene [ALLELE]

22) two identical copies of the gene are needed to be expressed [RECESSIVE]

23) the range of different organism that live in an environment [BIODIVERSITY]

24) only one copy of the gene is needed to be expressed [DOMINANT]

25) section of DNA, that controls a characteristic [GENE]

Down

2) non-living factors that affect organism [ABIOTIC]

3) the movement of carbon through the environment [CARBONCYCLE]

4) mechanism to prevent pregnancy [CONTRACEPTION]

5) reproduction with only one parent, resulting in identical offspring [ASEXUALREPRODUCTION]

6) hormone found predominantly in men [TESTOSTERONE]

7) female sex cell [EGG]

8) identical copies of gene [HOMOZYGOUS]

11) the organism and the habitat they live in [ECOSYSTEM]

12) the organism that live in a particular environment [COMMUNITY]

15) harmful substance in an environment [POLLUTION]

16) the movement of water through eh environment [WATERCYCLE]

19) hard parts of long dead organism [FOSSILS]

20) all of the genes in an organism [GENOME]

21) something that gets eaten [PREY]

Chemistry Crossword 1

Across

6) a way of sorting out the elements [PERIODICTABLE]

10) group of (or single) atoms that all have the same chemical characteristics, can be found on the periodic table [ELEMENT]

12) group of metal that are in the middle of the periodic table, form colour compounds and can be used as catalysts [TRANSITIONMETAL]

14) found in the nucleus of atoms, has no charge and a mass of one [NEUTRON]

16) small part of matter, made up from a mixture of protons, neutrons and electrons [ATOM]

17) the number of protons and neutrons in an atom [MASSNUMBER]

21) transfer of electrons between a metal and a non-metal [IONICBONDING]

22) atoms that has lost or gained electrons [ION]

23) giant covalent compound where each carbons atom makes three bonds [GRAPHITE]

26) a way of determining how many of the reactant atoms made it into the desired product [ATOMECONOMY]

27) a state of matter, where the atoms can move and flow but they cannot be compressed [LIQUID]

28) the number of protons in an atom [ATOMICNUMBER]

29) a state of matter where the atoms move atom in a fast and random matter, can be compressed and flow [GAS]

Down

1) in the centre of atoms, contains the protons and the neutrons [NUCLEUS]

2) on the left-hand side of the periodic table, form positive ions [METAL]

3) method for determining concentration of solution [TITRATION]

4) highly reactive metals found on the left-hand side of the periodic table [ALKALIMETAL]

5) found in the shells around the nucleus, has a charge of minus one and no mass [ELECTRON]

7) a type of reaction where one element replaces another in a compound [DISPLACEMENT]

8) found in the nucleus of atoms, has a charge of plus one and a mass of one [PROTON]

9) sharing of electron between two non-metals [COVALENTBONDING]

11) on the right-hand side of the periodic table, form negative ions [NONMETAL]

13) lots of different elements that may or may not be chemically bonded together [MIXTURE]

15) giant covalent compound where each carbons atom makes four bonds [DIAMOND]

18) two or more elements chemically bonded together [COMPOUND]

19) unreactive gases found on the right of the periodic table [NOBELGAS]

20) mixture of atoms that lead to distorted layers that cannot slide [ALLOY]

24) a state of matter, where the atoms vibrate around a fixed position [SOLID]

25) the molecular mass in grams [MOLE]

Chemistry crossword 2

Across

1) burning of a compound in oxygen [COMBUSTION]

2) gain of electrons [REDUCTION]

5) breaking a long hydrocarbon chain to short hydrocarbon chains [CRACKING]

7) water that is safe to drink [PORTABLEWATER]

14) hydrocarbon containing double bonds [ALKENES]

15) point at which a solid turn into a liquid [MELTINGPOINT]

16) orange liquid that can be used to test for double bonds [BROMINEWATER]

18) mixing of an acid and an alkali to give a pH of 7 [NEUTRALIZATION]

20) how acid or alkali a solution is [PH]

21) loss of electrons [OXIDATION]

22) something that speeds up a react of reaction without being use dup [CATALYST]

23) how easily pourable something is [VISCOSITY]

Down

1) a mixture of different length hydrocarbon chains made from decomposing dead plant and animals [CRUDEOIL]

3) a reaction that releases energy [EXOTHERMIC]

4) a reaction that takes in energy [ENDOTHERMIC]

6) hydrocarbon containing only single bonds [ALKANES]

8) separating compounds using electricity [ELECTROLYSIS]

9) the energy needed to start reaction [ACTIVATIONENERGY]

10) gas that traps infra-red radiation [GREENHOUSEGAS]

11) a compound that only has carbon and hydrogen in it [HYDROCARBON]

12) method of separating out mixtures [CHROMATOGRAPHY]

13) mining low yield ores using plants [PHYTOMINING]

17) a solution that has a low pH due to the hydrogen ions [ACID]

19) a solution that has a high pH due to hydroxide ions [ALKALI]

Maths the chemistry bits for science students

The periodic table

Element	Period	Group
Calcium	4	2
Beryllium	2	2
Nitrogen	2	5
Aluminium	3	3
Sulfur	3	6

Mass number and atomic number

Element	Mass number	Atomic number

B 5 Boron 11	11	5	
Mg 12 Magnesium 24	24	12	
Cr 24 Chromium 52	52	24	
Na 11 Sodium 23	23	11	
Si 14 Silicon 28	28	14	
Oxygen	16	8	
Helium	4	2	
Scandium	45	21	
Phosphorous	31	15	
Copper	64	29	

The number of protons, neutrons and electrons

Element	Number of protons	Number of electrons	Number of neutrons
Cl 17 Chlorine 35.5	17	17	18.5
Br 35 Bromine 80	35	35	45
Ni 28 Nickel 59	28	28	31
O 8 Oxygen 16	8	8	8

	53	53	74
53 I Iodine 127	53	53	74
Argon	18	18	22
Boron	5	5	6
Barium	56	56	81
Cobalt	27	27	32
Sulfur	16	16	16

Isotopes

Element	Number of protons	Number of electrons	Number of neutrons
Carbon-13	6	6	7
Oxygen-18	8	8	10
Nitrogen -16	7	7	9
Iron-55	26	26	29
Magnesium-26	12	12	14
Argon-41	18	18	23
Sulfur-34	16	16	18
Fluorine-17	9	9	8
Hydrogen-3	1	1	2
Calcium-38	20	20	18

Ions

Element	Atom		Ion		
	Number of protons	Number of electrons	Number of protons	Number of electrons	Charge
Sodium	11	11	11	10	Na^+
Magnesium	12	12	12	10	Mg^{2+}
Oxygen	8	8	8	10	O^{2-}
Fluorine	9	9	9	10	F^-
Chlorine	17	17	17	18	Cl^-
Lithium	3	3	3	2	Li^+
Calcium	20	20	20	18	Ca^{2+}
Potassium	19	19	19	18	K^+
Lithium	3	3	3	4	Li^-
Iodine	53	53	53	54	I^-

Elements and atoms

Compound	Number of elements	Number of atoms
H_2O	2	3
O_2	1	2

CaCO$_3$	3	5
NH$_3$	2	4
CH$_4$	2	5
H$_2$SO$_4$	3	7
HCl	2	2
HNO$_3$	3	5
CuO	2	2
SO$_2$	2	3

Brackets

Compound	Number of elements	Number of atoms
Ca(OH)$_2$	3	5
Cu(NO$_3$)$_2$	3	9
Cr$_2$(SO$_4$)$_3$	3	17
Fe$_2$(SO$_4$)$_3$	3	17

Conservation of mass

Magnesium	+	Oxygen	→	Magnesium oxide		
5g	+	0.1g	→	5.1g		

Sodium	+	Water	→	Sodium hydroxide	+	Hydrogen
2.1g	+	0.5g	→	2.3g	+	0.3g

Silver sulfate	+	Magnesium	→	Magnesium sulfate	+	Silver
14.65g	+	7.56g	→	13.98g	+	8.23g

Calcium	+	Hydrochloric acid	→	Calcium chloride	+	Hydrogen
17.0g	+	3.1g	→	19.2g	+	0.9g

Iron oxide	+	Carbon	→	Iron	+	Carbon dioxide
45.8g	+	7.7g	→	52.3g	+	1.2g

Balancing Equations-easy!

1. $2H_2 + O_2 \rightarrow 2H_2O$
2. $H_2 + Cl_2 \rightarrow 2HCl$
3. $2Mg + O_2 \rightarrow 2MgO$
4. $N_2 + 3H_2 \rightarrow 2NH_3$
5. $2Zn + O_2 \rightarrow 2ZnO$
6. $N_2 + O_2 \rightarrow 2NO$
7. $2K + S \rightarrow K_2S$
8. $Mg + 2HCl \rightarrow MgCl_2 + H_2$
9. $2Na + 2H_2O \rightarrow 2NaOH + H_2$
10. $2Ca + O_2 \rightarrow 2CaO$
11. $Ca + 2HCl \rightarrow CaCl_2 + H_2$
12. $2Na + Cl_2 \rightarrow 2NaCl$
13. $2SO_2 + O_2 \rightarrow 2SO_3$
14. $2KOH + MgSO_4 \rightarrow Mg(OH)_2 + K_2SO_4$
15. $K_2O_2 + 2H_2O \rightarrow H_2O_2 + 2KOH$
16. $2Na + 2H_2O \rightarrow 2NaOH + H_2$
17. $3NaOH + H_3PO_4 \rightarrow Na_3PO_4 + 3H_2O$
18. $2K + 2H_2O \rightarrow 2KOH + H_2$
19. $Ag_2SO_4 + Mg \rightarrow MgSO_4 + 2Ag$
20. $4Al + 3O_2 \rightarrow 2Al_2O_3$

Balancing Equations-Medium!

1. $Fe_2O_3 + 2Al \rightarrow 2Fe + Al_2O_3$
2. $N_2 + 3Cl_2 \rightarrow 2NCl_3$
3. $C + 2Cl_2 \rightarrow CCl_4$
4. $CaCl_2 + 2KOH \rightarrow Ca(OH)_2 + 2KCl$
5. $P_4 + 6Cl_2 \rightarrow 4PCl_3$
6. $C_2H_4 + 3O_2 \rightarrow 2CO_2 + 2H_2O$
7. $2Mg + CO_2 \rightarrow 2MgO + C$
8. $2H_2O_2 \rightarrow 2H_2O + O_2$
9. $2C_2H_6 + 7O_2 \rightarrow 4CO_2 + 6H_2O$
10. $Fe_2O_3 + 3C \rightarrow 2Fe + 3CO$
11. $TiCl_4 + 2Mg \rightarrow 2MgCl_2 + Ti$
12. $2PH_3 + 3O_2 \rightarrow P_2O_3 + 3H_2O$
13. $2PH_5 + 5O_2 \rightarrow P_2O_5 + 5H_2O$
14. $CuCl_2 + 2NaOH \rightarrow Cu(OH)_2 + 2NaCl$
15. $2KI + Pb(NO_3)_2 \rightarrow 2KNO_3 + PbI_2$
16. $PCl_3 + 3H_2O \rightarrow P(OH)_3 + 3HCl$
17. $C_3H_8 + 5O_2 \rightarrow 5CO_2 + 4H_2O$
18. $2Pb(NO_3)_2 \rightarrow 2PbO + 4NO_2 + O_2$
19. $C_6H_{12}O_6 + 6O_2 \rightarrow 6H_2O + 6CO_2$
20. $4NH_3 + 5O_2 \rightarrow 4NO + 6H_2O$

Balancing Equations- Hard!

1. $2Mg + 2HIO_3 \rightarrow 2Mg(IO_3) + H_2$
2. $BaCl_2 + Na_2SO_4 \rightarrow 2NaCl + BaSO_4$
3. $NaI + 3HOCl \rightarrow NaIO_3 + 3HCl$
4. $4Al + 3MnO_2 \rightarrow 2Al_2O_3 + 3Mn$
5. $Ba(OH)_2 + H_2SO_4 \rightarrow BaSO_4 + 2H_2O$
6. $K_2CO_3 + 2AgNO_3 \rightarrow 2KNO_3 + Ag_2CO_3$
7. $Sr(ClO_4)_2 + K_2SO_4 \rightarrow SrSO_4 + 2KClO_4$
8. $2Al + 3H_2SO_4 \rightarrow Al_2(SO_4)_3 + 3H_2$
9. $2HNO_3 + 3H_2S \rightarrow 2NO + 3S + 4H_2O$
10. $Pb(NO_3)_2 + 2KCl \rightarrow PbCl_2 + 2KNO_3$
11. $MgCO_3 + 2HNO_3 \rightarrow Mg(NO_3)_2 + H_2O + CO_2$
12. $H_2SO_4 + 2NaOH \rightarrow Na_2SO_4 + 2H_2O$
13. $SO_2 + 2HNO_2 \rightarrow H_2SO_4 + 2NO$
14. $8HI + H_2SO_4 \rightarrow 4H_2O + H_2S + 4I_2$
15. $3HCl + Al(OH)_3 \rightarrow 3H_2O + AlCl_3$
16. $2NaOH + CuSO_4 \rightarrow Na_2SO_4 + Cu(OH)_2$
17. $2HF + Ba(NO_3)_2 \rightarrow 2HNO_3 + BaF_2$
18. $2NO_2 + 7H_2 \rightarrow 2NH_3 + 4H_2O$
19. $4NH_3 + 5O_2 \rightarrow 4NO + 6H_2O$
20. $2HCl + 2FeCl_2 + H_2O_2 \rightarrow 2FeCl_3 + 2H_2O$

Relative atomic mass

Compound	Relative mass
H_2O	(2x1) + (1x16) = 18
O_2	(2x16) = 32
$CaCO_3$	(1x40) + (1x12) + (3x16) = 100
NH_3	(1x14) + (3x1) = 17
CH_4	(1x12) + (4x1) = 16
H_2SO_4	(2x1) + (1x32) + (4x16) = 98
HCl	(1x1) + (1x35.5) = 36.5
HNO_3	(1x1) + (1x14) + (3x16) = 63
CuO	(1x63.5) + (1x16) = 79.5
$Ca(OH)_2$	(1x40) + (2x16) + (2x1) = 74
$Cu(NO_3)_2$	(1x63.5) + (2x14) + (6x16) = 187.5
$Cr_2(SO_4)_3$	(2x52) + (3x32) + (12x16) = 392
$Fe_2(SO_4)_3$	(2x56) + (3x32) + (12x16) = 400

Calculating relative atomic mass

1. 35.50
2. 80.00
3. 55.85
4. 40.02
5. 40% 191, 60% 193

Moles

Compound	Relative mass	Mass in grams	Moles
N_2	28	28	1
CO_2	44	22	0.5
CaO	56	112	2
Fe_2O_3	160	40	0.25
PCl_3	137.5	27.5	0.2
$Mg(OH)_2$	58	116	2
$KHSO_4$	136	102	0.75
Na_2SO_4	142	326.6	2.3
H_3AsO_4	142	95.14	0.67
$Cu(NO_3)_2$	188	292.5	1.56

1. 0.1 moles
2. 174g
3. 129.5g
4. 14g
5. 0.15 moles

Percentage yield

1. 75%
2. 62%
3. 66%
4. 83%
5. 80%
6. 86%
7. 85%
8. 90%

Atom economy

1. 56%
2. 48%
3. 56%
4. 56%
5. Hydration 100%, fermentation 51%

Half equations

Reaction	Oxidation or Reduction	Anode or Cathode
$Cu^{2+} + 2e^- \rightarrow Cu$	Reduction	Cathode
$2F^- - 2e^- \rightarrow F_2$	Oxidation	Anode
$Na^+ + e^- \rightarrow Na$	Reduction	Cathode
$2O^{2-} \rightarrow O_2 + 4e^-$	Oxidation	Anode
$Al^{3+} + 3e^- \rightarrow Al$	Reduction	Cathode
$Li^+ + e^- \rightarrow Li$	Reduction	Cathode
$2Cl^- \rightarrow Cl_2 + 2e^-$	Oxidation	Anode
$2H^+ + 2e^- \rightarrow H_2$	Reduction	Cathode
$S^{2-} - 2e^- \rightarrow S$	Oxidation	Anode
$Mg^{2+} + 2e^- \rightarrow Mg$	Reduction	Cathode

Reacting masses

1. 49.8g
2. 36.1g
3. 48.9g
4. 264.9g
5. 136g
6. 26.3g
7. 57g
8. 52.8g
9. 12.7g
10. 11g

Avogadro and gas volumes

Compound	M_r	Mass in grams	Number of moles	Number of particles	Gas volume (dm^3)
KOH	56	56	1	6.02×10^{23}	24
CO_2	44	22	0.5	3.01×10^{23}	12
NaOH	40	80	2	1.02×10^{24}	48
$CaCO_3$	100	50	0.5	3.01×10^{23}	12
PCl_3	137.5	34.375	0.25	1.51×10^{23}	6
SF_6	146	14.6	0.1	6.02×10^{22}	2.4
MgO	40	40	1	6.02×10^{23}	24
C_2H_6	28	28	1	6.02×10^{23}	24
NH_3	17	4.25	0.25	1.51×10^{23}	6
$P(OH)_3$	82	6.83	0.083	5.02×10^{22}	2

Endothermic and exothermic reactions

1. $-486 kJ/mol^{-1}$

2. +103 kJ/mol^{-1}
3. -184 kJ/mol^{-1}
4. -730 kJ/mol^{-1}
5. -81 kJ/mol^{-1}

Titration calculations

1. 4.8mol
2. 0.6mol
3. 0.005mol
4. 1.5 mol/dm^3
5. 33.3 mol/dm^3 not reoccurring-this does not exist in science!!
6. 0.22dm^3

1. 24g
2. 588g
3. 0.3g
4. 63g

1. 0.12 mol/dm^3
2. 0.278 mol/dm^3
3. 0.045 mol/dm^3
4. 0.342 mol/dm^3
5. 4.08 g/dm^3
6. 4.8 g/dm^3
7. 1.035 mol/dm^3

Physics units

Across

7) the units for force [NEWTONS]

9) the units for charge [COULOMBS]

10) the units for mass [KILOGRAMS]

11) the units for current [AMPS]

12) the units for time period [SECONDS]

13) the units for power [WATT]

14) the units for frequency [HERTZ]

16) the units for pressure [PASCALS]

18) the units for initial velocity [METERSPERSECOND]

20) the units for volume [METERSCUBED]

21) the units for specific latent heat [JOULESPERKILOGRAM]

22) the units for density [KILOGRAMSPERMETERCUBED]

Down

1) the units for the spring constant [NEWTONSPERMETER]

2) the units for potential difference [VOLTS]

3) the units for acceleration [METERSPERSECONDSQUARED]

4) the units for work done [JOULES]

5) the units for gravitational field strength [NEWTONSPERKILOGRAM]

6) the units for moment [NEWTONMETERS]

8) the units for area [METERSSQUARED]

15) the units for resistance [OHMS]

17) the units for length [METERS]

19) the units for magnetic flux density [TESLA]

Maths (the physics bits)

$E = m \times c \times \theta$

Make m the subject of the formula

m = $\underline{\ \ E\ \ }$ $c \times \theta$

$E = m \times c \times \theta$

Make c the subject of the formula

c = $\underline{\ \ E\ \ }$ $m \times \theta$

$E = m \times c \times \theta$

Make θ the subject of the formula

$\theta = \underline{\ \ E\ \ }$ $c \times m$

Efficiency = <u>useful energy out</u>   total
energy in

Make useful energy out the subject of the formula

Useful energy out = efficiency x total energy in

Efficiency = <u>useful energy out</u>   total
energy in

Make total energy in the subject of the formula

Total energy in = <u>useful energy out</u>
efficiency

Efficiency = <u>useful power out</u>   total
power in

Make useful power out the subject of the formula

Useful power out = efficiency x total power in

Efficiency = <u>useful power out</u>   total
power in

Make total power in the subject of the formula

Total power in = <u>useful power out</u>
efficiency

$E = P \times t$

Make P the subject of the formula

P = <u>E</u>   t

$E = P \times t$

Make t the subject of the formula

t = <u>E</u>   P

$V = f \times \lambda$

Make f the subject of the formula

f = <u>V</u> λ

$V = f \times \lambda$

Make λ the subject of the formula

λ = <u>V</u>   f

Converting standard units

Number in question	Is this the correct unit?	Converted
5m	Yes	
Electrical energy 19J	No	19kWh
17˚C	Yes	

21J	Yes	
Electrical time 30 minutes	No	0.5 h
10cm	No	0.1m
Electrical energy 7J	No	7kWh
45 minutes (not electrical)	No	2,700s
175g	No	0.175kg
3Km	No	3,000m
93 °C	Yes	
Electrical energy 17kJ	No	17kWh
56 KJ	No	56,000J
Electrical time 3 hours	Yes	
95cm	No	0.95m

Blah Questions

Easy

1. 0.6
2. 12,000kWh
3. 0.9
4. 2,550,000J
5. 114,000J

Medium

1. 0.001kg
2. 12,000,000Hz
3. 0.2m
4. 24,000,000Hz

Specific Heat Capacity

Easy

Energy (J)	mass (kg)	Specific heat capacity (J/Kg °C)	Temperature change (°C)
15,000	2	1500	5
210,600	4	1950	27
270,375	7	2575	15
2,328,336	19	5328	23
15,070,172	26	9502	61

1. 7875J
2. 209,050J
3. 84556.8J

4. **27,261J**
5. **194777.5J**

Medium

Energy (J)	mass (kg)	Specific heat capacity (J/Kg °C)	Temperature change (˚C)
4589	**0.54**	567	15
184	56	**0.053**	62
873956	2	205	**2131.6**
693	**0.025**	826	34
828	68	**0.94**	13

1. **0.00045Kg**
2. **45 J/Kg °C**
3. **0.000599Kg**
4. **0.044 ˚C**
5. **25.0092 ˚C**

Hard

Energy	mass	Specific heat capacity (J/Kg ˚C)	Start temperature (˚C)	End temperature (˚C)	Temperature change (˚C)
155J	123g	**252**	24	29	**5**
1.25KJ	**0.44**	567	37	42	**5**
3.9KJ	0.65Kg	5924	19	**20.01**	**1.01**
345J	**0.0044**	6011	78	91	**13**
0.4KJ	12.5Kg	**10.7**	36	39	**3**

1. **29.2 ˚C**
2. **0.059Kg**
3. **0.049Kg**
4. **Gold**
5. **Iron**

Efficiency

Easy

Useful Energy Out/ Useful Power Out	Total Energy In/ Total Power In	Efficiency
15J	45J	**0.333**
25W	95W	**0.263**
19J	178J	**0.107**
79W	152W	**0.520**
89J	109J	**0.817**

1. **0.536**
2. **0.0960**
3. **0.752**
4. **0.378**
5. **0.621**

Medium

Useful Energy Out/ Useful Power Out	Total Energy In/ Total Power In	Efficiency
127.2J	159J	0.8
23.68W	74W	32%
410.78J	874J	0.47
22.14W	82W	27%
85.5J	90J	0.95

1. **0.525**
2. **0.797**
3. **26.25GW**
4. **TV-B (A=0.442, B= 0.523)**
5. **0.78kW**

Hard

Useful Energy Out/ Useful Power Out	Total Energy In/ Total Power In	Efficiency
34J	**37.0J**	0.92
796W	**1304.9W**	61%
739J	**1040.8J**	0.71
45W	**46.4W**	97%

| 90J | 1000J | 0.09 |

1. **180.6J**
2. **2818.37W**
3. **1275.51W**
4. **294.9J**
5. **Desktop=134.78W, laptop=95.45W**

Energy Calculations

Easy

Energy (J)	Power (W)	Time (s)
230	46	5
63729	873	73
189	63	3
1116	12	93
54	9	6

1. **630J**
2. **206J**
3. **135000J**
4. **40200J**
5. **84000J**

Medium

Energy (J)	Power (W)	Time (s)
345	34	**10.15**
67	**3.94**	17
1.25	12	**0.10**
6783	**127.98**	53
90	37	**2.43**

1. **0.25W**
2. **1.49s**
3. **0.83W**
4. **0.24W**
5. **0.04 minutes**

Hard

Energy	Power	Time

174J	1.3kW	0.13s
5.6kJ	6,.2W	15 minutes
90J	450W	0.2s
3.76kJ	0.52W	2 hours
176J	31.5W	5.6s

1. 0.22W
2. 1.67s
3. 0.57W
4. 237.33s
5. 0.03W

Electrical Energy Calculations

Easy

Energy (kWh)	Power (kW)	Time (h)
135	45	3
268	67	4
162	27	6
96	48	2
837	93	9

Cost of electricity (p)	Number of kilowatt-hours (kWh)	Cost per kilowatt-hour (p)
221	17	13
490	35	14
747	83	9
45	3	15
1575	75	21

1. 315kWh
2. 58.5kWh
3. 35.8kWh
4. 0.6kWh
5. 67.5kWh
6. 630p
7. 82.8p
8. 23.1p
9. 78p
10. 2407p

Medium

Cost of electricity	Number of kilowatt-hours (kWh)	Cost per kilowatt-hour (p)

£3.45	54	**6.39**
97p	**6.93**	14
£1.25	23	**5.43**
£2.94	**42**	7
67p	16	**4.19**

Cost of electricity (p)	Energy (kWh)	Power (kW)	Time (h)	Cost per kilowatt-hour (p)
3024	**252**	36	7	12
1722	**123**	41	3	14
1512	**168**	84	2	9
1120	**140**	35	4	8
600	**48**	12	4	12.5

1. **22.5p**
2. **7.05kWh**
3. **3.6p**
4. **8.26kWh**
5. **2.59p**
6. **402p**
7. **918p**
8. **147.9p**
9. **189p**
10. **2292.5p**

Hard

Cost of electricity	Energy	Power	Time	Cost per kilowatt-hour
£20.25	45 kWh	5000W	**9h**	45p
£9.14	1.2 kWh	4.5 kW	**0.27h**	**761.67p**
£5.88	49 kWh	120 W	**408.33h**	12p
£4.53	26 kWh	20 kW	**1.3h**	**17.42p**
£3.67	14 kWh	900 W	**15.56h**	**26.21p**

1. **1560p**
2. **8.1p**
3. **11.7h**
4. **3.45pm**
5. **900p**

Payback time

Type of energy saving	Cost to install	Reduction in energy bills each year	Payback time
Double glazing	£15,000	£120	125 years
Loft insulation	£4,500	£800	5 years 8 months
Draught excluders	£35	£20	1 year 9 months
Jacket on hot water tank	£20	£60	4 months
Carpet	£450	£75	6 years
Curtains	£575	£45	12 years 9 months
Solar panels	£25,000	£500	50 years

1. Jacket on hot water tank as it is the cheapest and has the fastest payback time
2. Double Glazing, the homeowner is unlikely to be in the house in 125 years' time
3. Sound proofing, water proofing, ascetics
4. Because they like the look or style of new carpets or curtains
5. Impact on the environment of reducing their carbon footprint

Waves

Easy

Wave speed (m/s)	Frequency (Hz)	Wavelength (m)
52.5	35	1.5
5360	268	20
142500	2500	57
24244	836	29
2067	39	53

1. **1000 m/s**
2. **292.5 m/s**
3. **27000 m/s**
4. **67500 m/s**
5. **2.5 m/s**

Medium

Wave speed (m/s)	Frequency (Hz)	Wavelength (m)
3890	28	**138.93**
87328	**23.04**	3790
38	204	**0.19**
39	**0.83**	47

4925	486	**10.13**

1. **4000Hz**
2. **1600m**
3. **16.67Hz**
4. **6.67x10³Hz**
5. **7.69x10⁷m**

Hard

Wave speed (m/s)	Frequency	Wavelength
373	**373Hz**	100cm
900	450cHz	**200m**
271	**0.11Hz**	2.5km
42,800	5kHz	**8.56m**
602,000	**111895.91**	538cm

1. **9.83x10⁸m/s**
2. **171428.57Hz**
3. **1.71x10²m**
4. **19.12Hz**
5. **7.75x10³Hz**

End of book assessment

Easy

1. **6750J**
2. **180m/s**
3. **0.36**
4. **720J**
5. **£37.50**
6. **3649.05m/s**
7. **62776J**
8. **0.084**
9. **5974650J**
10. **315kWh**

Medium

1. **120m**
2. **360W**
3. **60W**

4. 2.46J/kg °C
5. 8.71W
6. 335.2J
7. 18.77Hz
8. 2.71W
9. 1.34kWh
10. 0.039kg

Hard

1. 9.3s
2. 7539.7W
3. 84.66J/kg °C
4. 69.23J
5. 2.5hours
6. 1829268Hz
7. 2p
8. 326.8
9. A 23.5° B 22.7°
10. A

Kinetic energy

Kinetic energy (J)	½	Mass (kg)	Velocity (m/s)
0.5625	0.5	2	0.75
56	0.5	7	4
97.5	0.5	7.8	5
141.204	0.5	4.2	8.2
1.22	0.5	9.75	0.5

1. 2.4J
2. 0.18J
3. 3.35J

4. 202.5J
5. 32J

Medium

Kinetic energy (J)	Mass (kg)	Velocity (m/s)
128	79	**1.8**
594	**49.5**	4.9
56	8	**3.7**
29	**9.28**	2.5
78	7.5	**4.6**

1. 0.083J
2. 7.91m/s
3. 29.44kg
4. 1.03kg
5. 67.6kg

Hard

Kinetic energy	Mass	Velocity
1.2kJ	5kg	**0.69m/s**
450J	95g	**97.33m/s**
0.98kJ	**29.15kg**	8.2m/s
3.78kJ	**1344000kg**	0.27km/h
58J	**1160kg**	1.2Km/h

1. 6
2. 5.01kg
3. 1.73m/s
4. 3.89x10^{-4}J
5. 39.74m/s

Super hard

1. 0.06m/s
2. 47401.9J
3. 3638.88J
4. 7.35m/s
5. 7.21 m/s

Waves and ultrasound

Easy

Wave speed (m/s)	Distance (m)	Time (s)
0.3	4.5	15
0.003	0.2	73
0.04	1.8	48
0.1	3.2	26
2.95	5.9	2

1. 0.5m/s
2. 0.07 m/s
3. 0.3 m/s
4. 0.1 m/s
5. 0.2 m/s

Medium

Wave speed (m/s)	Distance (m)	Time (s)
45	5	**0.1**
8	**47.2**	5.9
9.8	6.2	**0.6**
18	**113.4**	6.3
42	5	**0.1**

1. **448m**
2. **2.7s**
3. **27000m**
4. **147km**
5. **39.6km**

Hard

Wave speed	Distance	Time
450m/s	45m	**0.1s**
728m/s	**3494.4km**	1 hour 20 minutes
23m/s	15km	**652.2s**
4543m/s	**12266100m**	45 minutes
3m/s	250cm	**0.08s**

1. **775.5m**
2. **0.000003s**
3. **90.9s**
4. **165m**
5. **83.8m**

PIV

Answers

Easy

Power (W)	Current (A)	Potential difference (V)
35	5	7
24	8	3
104	13	8
148.5	9.9	15
37.8	42	0.9

1. **85W**
2. **7.7W**
3. **46.9W**

4. **41.4W**
5. **274.4W**

Medium

Power (W)	Current (A)	Potential difference (V)
4.6	1.9	**2.4**
9.8	**3.2**	3.1
45	5.9	**7.6**
73	**9.1**	8
109	59	**1.8**

1. **12.9A**
2. **2.3V**
3. **3.8V**
4. **3.5A**
5. **5.2A**

Hard

Power	Current	Potential difference
1.3kW	950mA	**1368.4V**
0.8kW	**4A**	0.2kV
56W	8A	**7V**
0.045kW	**1.8A**	25V
1.45 x 10^{9}W	9.37 x 10^{2}A	**1.55 x 10^{6}V**

1. **26.7V**
2. **1.5A**
3. **4V**
4. **100A**

Pressure

1. Hydraulics are force multipliers.

2. 58.3Pa
3. 0.28N/cm^2
4. 1.6N/cm^2
5. 5N/cm^2
6. 10869cm^2
7. 274.2N
8. 30,000Pa and 36N
9. 104N
10. 84N
11. 22500Pa

Transformers

Answers to maths questions

5. 44V
6. 242.5
7. 30V
8. 10
9. 1380
10. 1200V
11. 21A
12. 15.5V
13. 0.2A
14. 0.03A

Printed in Great Britain
by Amazon

CAFÉ LOGOS

A COMPREHENSIVE AND EXCITING NEW RESOURCE FOR 11-16 YEAR OLDS

PETE TOWNSEND

Kevin
Mayhew

GW01250360

This edition published in 1999 by
KEVIN MAYHEW LTD
Buxhall
Stowmarket
Suffolk IP14 3BW

0 1 2 3 4 5 6 7 8 9

ISBN 1 84003 394 0
Catalogue No. 1500289

Cover design by Jaquetta Sergeant
Edited by Helen Elliot
Typesetting by Louise Selfe
Printed and bound in Great Britain

CONTENTS

ACKNOWLEDGEMENTS

It is easy to think that putting a book together simply involves one person staring at a blank page and waiting for inspiration to flow. The reality is, nothing could be achieved without a lovely crowd of people who encourage, support, guide and whose lives provide inspiration.

Firstly, thanks to Jonathan and Helen for providing the faith and encouragement for this project. Secondly, thanks to Graham and Avril for their support and acceptance of an oddbod into their family. Thanks to Dave for starting the ball rolling. A special thank-you to Dale, Nathan, Esme and Laurie who always beat me in the race to the biscuit tin.

And to Ruth, in the words of Little Willie John: 'I need your love so bad.'

INTRODUCTION

Welcome to Café Logos. Take a seat and peruse the menu. You will find a feast of ideas to entertain, challenge and tickle your sense buds.

The menu is based on the Common Worship Lectionary Year B. The inspiration for the Café is found in Psalm 34, 'taste and see that the Lord is good' and in 1 Peter 2:1-12, 'a living stone'. The idea is to identify with Jesus as the Living Stone by discussion ('taste and see') and to explore a faith in Jesus through the use of the 'Logos' (God's living message).

Each week is identified as a 'unit'. Units 1-24 are based on the Gospels and explore the life of Jesus. Units 25-42 look at the Epistles and examine the Christian life, while Units 43-48 relate to the Psalms and take a closer look at how being a Christian can affect our daily lives.

All of the main Church calendar events are covered with lots of extra material for you to insert between 'events'. Unit 1 correlates to the beginning of the Lectionary year. However, if you want to start using *Café Logos* before then, simply use some of the later units (namely 33-43). You can identify which units to use by checking with the index of themes.

The menu is divided into six sections, with icons for easy recognition.

Today's special: theme and Bible reading for the day.

Nibbles: activities which focus the group on the day's theme.

Tasty bit: an introduction and link to the teaching, using suggestions for music to listen to, worship songs, drama and other material.

Chewy bit: the main teaching section with ideas and guidelines for sharing.

Munchy bit: discussion, thought and focus.

Afters: prayer, reflection and ideas for sharing.

The references to album tracks and worship songs are only suggestions. You can substitute other material on a similar theme if you prefer. You can either use the worship songs as part of group worship or use the lyrics in discussion. All of the worship suggestions can be found in *The source* (Kevin Mayhew 1998).

The drama material is intentionally kept simple, needing only basic props and two actors. This requires little preparation time and the script can be attached to clipboards so that you can ad lib to your heart's content.

Have fun, enjoy the menu and taste and see that the Lord is good!

TODAY'S SPECIAL

Is this the beginning of the end?

Mark 13:24-37: Jesus tells his followers to be prepared for his return.

Equipment:
a large (A3) piece of paper shaped like a gravestone
one glass jar
small amount of flour
sticky label
pen and paper for each member of the group
music and lyrics or drama sketch

Once all the group have arrived, pick up the glass jar and begin to examine it very carefully. Unscrew the lid and shake the jar so that some flour is thrown into the air. Look at the underside of the lid and read the sticky label: 'Danger! Highly infectious bacteria. Do not breathe dust. Contamination is fatal!' Look at the group and offer a mumbled apology: 'Sorry, looks like we're all going to die in a few minutes. This may be the last chance we have to write a message to someone.'

Distribute pens and paper. Ask the group to think about what they would write as their very last message. For example:

- Would it be a letter to say sorry?
- Would it be a letter to someone they loved?
- Would it be a letter to put something right with someone?
- Would it be a letter to tell someone exactly how they felt about an issue?
- Would it be a letter to an influential person, politician or world figure?

(Allow 10 minutes for this activity.)

Thinking about things ending is never easy and something we put off and ignore if we can. But it can often help us to consider what we would do if today were the last day of our lives.

Have a listen to 'End of the world' by The Electrics from the album *Big silent world*, or take a look at 'Great is the darkness' by Noel Richards and Gerald Coates (*The source*, 136). Have a copy of the lyrics available. Alternatively, you might like to use the drama sketch *De'ath meets . . . Dr Putitov* (see page 12).
(Allow approximately 5 minutes.)

Discuss the piece of music. What did the group feel about the lyrics? What were the lyrics trying to say?

Now ask the group if anyone would like to share the message that they wrote earlier. What kind of messages did the group write? What did the group consider to be important enough to write as their 'last' message? Chat about some of the group's responses. Be sensitive to the content of individual messages. Once you have chatted about the messages, fold each one in half (so that the written part can't be seen) and stick the messages onto the 'gravestone'-shaped piece of paper (this can be placed on a wall or display board).

Read Mark 13:24-37
How would we feel if Jesus were to return now? Discuss some of the group's feelings. Are the messages that they have written still relevant?

Jesus was sitting on the Mount of Olives talking to the disciples about things to come. Some of the disciples were concerned about the things Jesus was saying regarding his death and his return. They wanted to know how they would recognise the things he was talking about (see verses 24-27). Jesus told them to 'learn a lesson from the fig tree'. In Palestine the fig tree loses its leaves in winter. When the leaves begin to reappear, it is a sign that summer is on its way. At the time that Jesus spoke (the Passover time), the leaves of the fig trees were just beginning to sprout. Jesus was encouraging his disciples to keep their eyes open and be ready for anything at anytime!

The challenge that Jesus was giving to his disciples, and all of his followers, was not to sit and wait for things to happen or constantly to be guessing when he would return, but to live in the 'here and now'. As followers of Jesus, the idea of his return should encourage us to live as he would have us live, a life actively involved with the people around us, and try to avoid the 'if only I'd . . .' or 'I wish I had . . .' or even 'If only I hadn't . . .'.

Allow each member of the group to collect their message from the 'gravestone'. Ask them quietly to re-read their message.

Either underneath the message, or on the back of the paper, suggest that they might like to write some positive steps they could take so that the message becomes 'history'.
(Allow 5 minutes for this task.)

Once the group have completed writing some positive action points, ask them to fold the paper and place it in their hand.

Suggest that they might like to think about what they have written while you read this prayer.

Where there is wrong, help me to pardon;
  where there is doubt, let me show faith;
  where there is despair, let me have hope;
  where there is darkness, light;
  where there is sadness, joy.
O Divine Master, grant that I may not so much seek
  to be consoled, as to console;
  to be understood, as to understand;
  to be loved, as to love.
For it is in giving that we receive.
It is in pardoning that we are pardoned.
And it is in dying that we are born to eternal life. Amen.

St Francis of Assisi.
(Allow approximately 5 minutes.)

DE'ATH MEETS . . . DR PUTITOV

Characters	De'ath, chat show host and Dr Putitov.
Scene	De'ath is dressed in suit with very loud tie. Dr Putitov is wearing a baggy jumper, ragged trousers and has a number of pencils sticking in his hair.
Props	small coffee table water jug and two drinking glasses two comfy chairs

De'ath Hello, and good evening. Welcome to my humble accommodation. I trust that you've eaten and that I won't be disturbed by strange gurgling sounds emanating from the back row!

Now, to the purpose of our little gathering. As you may, or may not know, I like to keep up to date with things, such as the cost of coffee, beer consumption and the number of estate agents going broke. However, more importantly, I like to keep on eye on what I call my little 'protégés'. I like to make sure that they are on the right track, as it were, and to offer any help or guidance to encourage them on their way.

Some people might call me an interfering old fool. Still – I like to think of myself as someone who cares enough to make sure that his little 'protégés' fulfil their potential, that they avoid the pitfalls that might keep them on the straight and narrow!

Now, you've heard enough of me. Let me introduce you to my guest for the evening. Throughout his career, my guest has led the way in the study of tomorrow. He has been hailed as a pioneer of idleness, a champion of couch potatoes and is the distinguished author of the best selling book *Maybe*. Ladies and gentlemen, I give you Dr Putitov!

Putitov Thank you, thank you, you're too kind. Such flattery is almost embarrassing, almost but not quite!

De'ath Dr Putitov, you have become a leading expert on the subject of 'tomorrow'. It could be said that you have made 'leave it until tomorrow' an art-form! What is your philosophy?

Putitov   Well, many people have wondered what the secret of life is. How do we live to a grand old age? How do we keep our own teeth? What's the price of parsnips? Well, it's relatively simple! You have to learn to avoid doing anything today which could be left until tomorrow, or even the day after.

De'ath   Ah, yes. This concept of tomorrow. Now, correct me if I'm wrong, but are we not told that tomorrow never comes?

Putitov   Exactly! This is a myth told to us by parents who want the bedroom tidied today when it could be done just as easily tomorrow – maybe.

De'ath   So what you're saying is, tomorrow is a concept that has been threatened with extinction, like the dinosaur?

Putitov   Precisely. It's under threat from people who want something done today which could just as easily be done tomorrow.

De'ath   Have you an example?

Putitov   *(sits back and rubs eyes)* Example? Er, let me see. Could we discuss this some other time? Maybe tomorrow?

De'ath   *(leans forward and replies with anger)* Well, it would be nice if you could give us one or two examples now . . . Oh! I see, that was an example. Very good. You had me going for a moment. What do you put your success down to?

Putitov   You only have to take a look around you to see how useless you all are!

De'ath   *(again leans forward with anger)* How dare you imply that I'm useless. What on earth do you mean? After all that I've done for you!

Putitov   Again I rest my case. Just look at yourself, all flustered and hot under your neatly washed and ironed collar. What a

	waste of effort. Why didn't you wait until tomorrow to become angry?
De'ath	Well, you wouldn't have been here and I would have looked rather daft getting angry at an empty chair! People would talk!
Putitov	Exactly what I'm trying to get at. Deal with things later, leave them until tomorrow. That way nobody gets flustered and nothing gets done!
De'ath	But nothing gets sorted out either!
Putitov	Who wants to get things sorted out?
De'ath	Surely we can't put everything off until tomorrow. It would become a very busy day.
Putitov	Then you put into practice my principle of 'maybe'.
De'ath	Which is?
Putitov	'Maybe' it will be done tomorrow or 'maybe' it won't!
De'ath	So what you're saying is 'leave everything until tomorrow' or 'maybe' leave it!
Putitov	Maybe!
De'ath	Ha, ha, very good. But aren't you a little concerned that using your 'maybe' principle, people will think of you as someone who doesn't get anything done or someone who doesn't sort things out?
Putitov	Saves a lot of energy that way!
De'ath	But what about all those situations which need a decision or need dealing with before they turn into major hassles or mega problems? What do you say to the beautiful woman who asks you out for a date? Maybe?
Putitov	What's with the decisions all of a sudden? Leave it, put it

	off until tomorrow. Tell people 'maybe'! Always leave people wanting more.
De'ath	More what? More blood? Because that's certainly what they'd want if you put everybody off until tomorrow!
Putitov	That's their problem, not mine. Why should I go out of my way to sort out other people's hang-ups? I'm okay. Let them sort out their own lives.
De'ath	Good, good. That's nice and selfish, isn't it?
Putitov	I certainly hope so. I didn't get where I am today by wearing myself out dealing with other people's problems!
De'ath	So your advice is 'maybe put it off' or 'leave it until tomorrow'?
Putitov	Couldn't have put it better myself. You learn quickly. Just one final thing.
De'ath	And what might that be?
Putitov	When do I get paid for this interview?
De'ath	Tomorrow . . . maybe!

TODAY'S SPECIAL

The good news of Jesus.
Mark 1:1-8: John prepares the way for Jesus.

Equipment:
cards, or sheets of paper with parts of headlines written in large letters
paper and pens
candle

Distribute the cards to each member of the group. (Some members may have more than one card.) Divide the group into twos or threes. Ask each group to try and make 'headlines' using the words on their cards. Can anyone make up a story to match the headline?

Headline words:

One man	Purple shoes	for	the
Toffee ice-cream	Mild explosion	and	an
Escaped budgie	in	today	
Last night	Runs around	with	
Toothless monkey	yesterday	next	
Hours	Rubber bucket	of	
Attempts to fly	in	a	

(Allow 10 minutes for this activity.)

Ask the group to think quickly of one or two current TV adverts. Can they remember the catch line or 'hook' for the adverts? It is important to market a product or service as effectively as possible. Unfortunately some companies didn't get it quite right:

• Scandinavian vacuum manufacturer Electrolux used the following advert in America: 'Nothing sucks like an Electrolux!'

• In Taiwan, the translation of the Pepsi slogan 'Come alive with Pepsi' came out as 'Pepsi will bring your ancestors back from the dead!'

• In China, the Kentucky Fried Chicken slogan: 'finger-lickin' good' was translated as 'eat your fingers off!'

• In Italy, a campaign for Schweppes Tonic Water translated the name into 'Schweppes Toilet Water!'

Getting the right message across is important.
(Allow 5 minutes for this activity.)

Read Mark 1:1-8.

The Gospel of Mark is written in a journalistic style giving us short 'news' stories relating to Jesus. John the Baptist began to declare the coming of the 'Good News' against a background of political and civil unrest. The Romans had been in control of Judea since approximately 63 BC. Roman rule was often directed through local kings as a way of trying to put an acceptable 'face' on the Roman occupation. The most famous of these local rulers was Herod the Great, who was king when Jesus was born.

Under Roman rule trade prospered within a single market that stretched from France to Egypt and North Africa. Within this trade area there was relative peace, enforced by harsh penalties for those who 'broke' Roman law. For most Jews there was another negative aspect of the Roman occupation, that of taxation. It is thought that the Jewish public paid out almost half of their income in taxes. Every Jewish male had to pay a tax for the maintenance of the Temple and to keep the priests in food and clothes. To make matters worse, the Romans imposed taxes which included a poll tax, a land tax and a sales tax. It wasn't surprising that several groups who opposed Roman domination were waiting for an opportunity to get rid of the Romans.

In the reading from Mark, we are introduced to John the Baptist who, quoting from the Old Testament, declared 'Clear a path in the desert! Make a straight road for the Lord our God' (Isaiah 40:3). John the Baptist was the 'advertising campaign' for Jesus. He was calling people back to God and everywhere John went crowds gathered to hear what he had to say. The heart of John's message was about Jesus. His, John's, role was to prepare the way and get the attention of the people, to prepare them heart and mind for the 'Good News'.

(Allow 10 minutes.)

Some advertising campaigns use catchy slogans while others use visual images to 'get the message across'. John the Baptist was an extremely effective 'advert' for Jesus: in his actions and in what he said. Ask the group to separate into twos or threes and write a one-sentence headline which John the Baptist might have used to announce the coming of the 'Good News'.

(Allow 5 minutes for this activity.)

2

Place a candle in the centre of the room. As you light the candle read:

> Once again Jesus spoke to the people. This time he said, 'I am the light of the world! Follow me, and you won't be walking in the dark. You will have the light that gives you life.' (John 8:12)

Ask the group to look at the candle and consider what the words of Jesus mean to them. What kind of 'advert' in words or actions are they for Jesus? How can they be an 'advert' for Jesus? As the group consider these questions and look at the candle, read:

> Then Jesus said to all the people: 'If any of you want to be my followers, you must forget about yourself. You must take up your cross each day and follow me. If you want to save your life, you will destroy it. But if you give up your life for me, you will save it. What will you gain, if you own the whole world but destroy yourself or waste your life?' (Luke 9:23-27)

(Allow 5 minutes.)

TODAY'S SPECIAL   **A light in the darkness**

John 1:6-8, 19-28: Jesus, the light of the world.

Equipment:
pens and paper for the whole group
music and lyrics

Ask the group to 'pair up'. Give each person a pen and paper. Ask each pair to interview each other. What they *don't* need to find out are name, age, address or any other personal details. What they *do* need to find out are favourite foods, colours, music, hobbies, books, TV programmes and holiday destinations. Once this has been completed, collect the interview papers and redistribute them around the group. Ask each group member to read out the 'profile' they have been given. Can the rest of the group guess who the 'profile' belongs to?
(Allow 10 minutes for this activity.)

Getting to know someone is often difficult but can be really exciting as well. How well do we know each other? Can we tell if someone is having a 'bad day'?

Try having a listen to 'Alien' by Third Day, from the album *Conspiracy No. 5*. You might also like to have a look at 'Like a candle flame', by Graham Kendrick (*The source*, 322). If possible have a copy of the lyrics available.
(Allow approximately 5 minutes.)

Discuss the piece of music. What did the group understand from the lyrics? Do the lyrics have any relevance to the idea of Jesus as the 'light of the world'?

Read John 1:6-8 (19-28 come later). Announce to the group that, like John the Baptist, you are going to tell them the truth about the 'light'. Read the following to the group:

> Light, or electromagnetic radiation, is the agency by which objects are rendered visible. Newton, in 1666, was the first to discover that sunlight is composed of a mixture of light of all different colours in certain proportions and that it could be separated into its components by dispersion. The speed of light in a vacuum is approximately 300 million metres per second or 186,000 miles per second.

Ask the group if that has made things a little clearer! The reaction may not be too positive! Ask the group for their definition of 'light'. What is it? How does it work?

The writer of the Gospel, John, was anxious that everyone should 'find their way' to Christ (John 20:30-31). So, by referring to Christ as the light of the world he was declaring that this 'true' light would illuminate the way for 'all people' to be reunited with God. This 'true' or 'genuine' light was not a flicker of light in the darkness which would eventually fade and disappear, but a light which would remain constant, the only light which would show everyone the way to God.

Again the writer of the Gospel wanted to make it clear that the light would show the way to God for *all* people regardless of race, wealth, colour or class. Christ was the true light with no shadows (race, wealth, colour or class).

Now read John 1:19-28. John the Baptist was quizzed by the priests who wanted to know who he was. They knew that John's father had been a priest and, as being a priest was hereditary, John was also a priest. But they didn't know who John was claiming to be. John the Baptist made it very clear that he wasn't the Christ or the prophet Elijah. (It was a Jewish belief that the prophet Elijah would return to prepare the way for the arrival of the Messiah.) John the Baptist told the priests that he was nothing more than a voice encouraging people to prepare themselves for the arrival of the Lord. The idea behind John's reply was that most of the roads in that part of the world were little more than dirt tracks. When a king was about to visit an area, all the roads would be smoothed and straightened out in preparation for the arrival of the king. John the Baptist wanted the people to understand that although he wasn't the light he was a pointer to the light.

Ask the group to look at the 'profiles' that they compiled earlier. Suggest that they could now write a 'profile' about their relationship with God. For instance:

- Are there lots of dark areas or shadows to which God has not been allowed to bring light?
- Are there areas that reflect God's light?
- Are there any dark areas where God's light can shine?

Encourage the group to jot down some thoughts to think about as we pray. **(Allow 5 minutes for this activity.)**

Suggest to the group that they might like to be quiet and think about their latest 'profiles'. As they do this, read this prayer:

Lord, it is easy to think that it gets dark too quickly,
    that clouds obscure the sun.
When it's night someone, somewhere else is enjoying the light.
Our darkness can often seem to last longer than everyone else's.
Help us to see.
Help us to open up the dark areas for your light to shine.
Help us to trust you when dark clouds gather on the horizon.
Be with us as the shadows give way to the brightness of your Son.
Amen.

TODAY'S SPECIAL   **A startling piece of news!**
Luke 1:26-38: An angel tells about the birth of Jesus.

Equipment:
a piece of card for each member of the group
a pen for every group member

On each card write a job title. Use a variety of job titles, combining the sensible with the totally wacky! For example, doctor, teacher, politician, dustman, window cleaner, waiter, toilet attendant, couch potato, tea taster, deck chair attendant, pig farmer.

Give a card to each member of the group. Ask them to look at the card and, if they are happy with the job title, keep the card. If they would rather exchange it for another card, they can try and persuade someone else to exchange cards but neither person should know what is on the other's card!

When all the 'bartering' has finished ask the group how they felt about receiving the original card and, if they exchanged it, were they any happier with the new card?
(Allow 10 minutes for this activity.)

Read the following news stories. After each one ask the group if they think it is true or false. Don't tell them if they are right or wrong. When you have read the last story tell them that every story was in fact true!

1. A policeman responded to a report of a robbery at a local school. When he arrived three teenagers started to run away. The policeman, knowing he couldn't catch them, shouted, 'Stop or I'll set my dog on to you' (even though he didn't have a dog). The teenagers kept on running. So, the policeman took the idea one stage further and began barking. Immediately the three teenagers stopped running and gave themselves up!

2. A man in New Mexico got drunk and started to shoot at giant cacti. One fell on him!

3. A man walked into a newsagent's shop and put a twenty pound note on the counter and asked for it to be changed. When the newsagent opened the cash register the man pulled out a gun and demanded the contents of the cash register. He took the cash and ran out of the shop, leaving the twenty pound note on the counter. He escaped with fifteen pounds!
(Allow approximately 5 minutes.)

The group may have guessed that the stories were all true. They may even know of stranger stories! We are used to hearing all sorts of weird and wonderful stories. It's quite possible that Mary had heard a few wacky stories as well. But nothing could have prepared her for the visit of the Angel Gabriel.

Read Luke 1:26-38.

The Angel Gabriel greets Mary and says, 'You are truly blessed! The Lord is with you.' There are two things to note here. First, meeting with an angel was not an everyday occurrence! So this would have put Mary in a bit of a spin. Second, the Angel Gabriel told Mary that the Lord had blessed her! She somehow had found favour with God! She was confused and must have wondered what on earth was going on. The angel notes that Mary is a bit confused and tells her not to worry: 'Don't be afraid'. This is not a gentle pat on the hand or 'Shall we have a cup of tea and talk this over?' No! The Angel Gabriel launches straight in with, 'The Lord is pleased with you and you're going to have a baby. He will be called the Son of God the Most High!' Well, of course this happens to every young woman! Doesn't it? At this point Mary is really feeling the heat. First, she is greeted by an angel. Second, she is told that she is blessed by God and then told she's going to have a baby who will rule the people of Israel! And this is before she is even married!

Mary was engaged to Joseph. The normal engagement lasted about a year and was as legally binding as being married. The engagement could only be broken off through a divorce. Mary listened to the Angel Gabriel's message and answered, 'I am the Lord's servant! Let it happen as you have said'. Mary didn't want to argue with God. She recognised that God had chosen her to do something special for him. She didn't know the full story or have a complete picture of what was going to happen. She didn't know how Joseph would react to the news. She didn't even know why God had chosen her for this task. Mary placed her trust in God.

Ask the group to think of something they would like to achieve in the future or a job they would like to do, and to write it down on the back of the 'job cards'. Can each member of the group trust God to sort out the future for them?
(Allow 5 minutes for this task.)

Suggest the group might like to consider their future and God's role in that during the reading of Psalm 25:1-5.

I offer you my heart, Lord God, and I trust you.
Don't make me ashamed or let enemies defeat me.
Don't disappoint any of your worshippers, but disappoint all deceitful liars.
Show me your paths and teach me to follow;
    guide me by your truth and instruct me.
You keep me safe, and I always trust you.
Amen.

TODAY'S SPECIAL

A different kind of lamb!

Luke 2:15-21: The shepherds hear about Jesus.

Equipment:
large cards or A4 sheets
music and lyrics or drama sketch

Take ten cards and write the following headlines:

'Budgie eats tube of Smarties!'

'Sales of coloured tissues drop'

'Two injured in ice-cream fight!'

'Forty witnesses to chocolate bar theft'

'Lorry carrying paint overturns. Multicoloured motorway'

'Police fear local car thief may strike again'

'Government declare national holiday every Monday'

'Island disappears after volcanic eruption'

'United Nations calls for world-wide nuclear testing ban'

'Local man swallows Guinness book of records!'

Show each headline to the group. For each headline ask the group whether it should be reported in the local newspaper or national newspaper; on local radio or national radio; local TV or national TV?
(Allow 10 minutes.)

Have a listen to 'More to this' by Third Day, from the album *Conspiracy No. 5*. Alternatively, look at 'Mighty God' by Mark Johnson, Helen Johnson and Chris Bowater (*The source*, 356). You might like to use another piece of music which reflects the theme of 'news'. Have a copy of the lyrics available. Alternatively, you might like to use the drama sketch *De'ath meets . . . Gemma Gossip* (see page 28).
(Allow approximately 5 minutes.)

News seems to travel fast, particularly when it may be something that we would like kept quiet!

Discuss the lyrics or drama sketch. Why are we interested in knowing what goes on everywhere? Who is the first person we tell our 'news' to? You can chat about some of the news stories which are sold to the highest bidder according to their news 'value', i.e. will it increase sales or audience figures?

Read Luke 2:15-21.

Would you have chosen shepherds to tell this news to? Shepherds didn't enjoy a good press in Biblical times. The shepherds were thought to be amongst the lowest form of worker around. The nature of the job meant that the shepherds spent more time with sheep than they did with people! Their job was demanding and didn't allow them to observe all the rituals and traditions of religious worship. It's interesting that the news about the birth of Jesus should be told to people who were not seen as the best representatives of the Jewish faith!

It is quite likely that these shepherds were 'Temple' shepherds. These were shepherds who looked after the Temple's private sheep flocks. The flocks mentioned in the reading were kept in pastures close to Bethlehem. The shepherds' duty was to look after the lambs and present a flawless lamb for morning and evening sacrifice.

The angels came to tell the news to the shepherds who were amongst the first to hear of the birth; not the kind of people who would automatically be the first to be told other 'important' news. Another interesting point to make is that these shepherds, who were responsible for providing the sacrificial lambs, were introduced to the Lamb of God, the ultimate sacrifice (see John 1:29).

The angels didn't just come to tell the shepherds about the birth. It was custom that when a baby boy was born the local musicians would go to the house and welcome the new-born boy by singing simple songs. As Jesus was born in a stable, away from his parents' home, this custom could not have ordinarily been carried out. It seems that God arranged for some extra-ordinary singers and musicians to welcome the birth of Jesus!

Ask the group to consider a possible 'headline' which gives a good insight into the Bible reading. Try to brainstorm some ideas quickly and agree upon a headline which everyone feels sums up the reading. **(Allow 5 minutes for this task.)**

Suggest to the group that they might like to close their eyes and picture the scene where the angels are singing praise to God while the shepherds watch in amazement. While the group are quiet, read Psalm 136.

Praise the Lord! He is good.
God's love never fails.
Praise the God of all gods.
God's love never fails.
Praise the Lord of lords.
God's love never fails.
Only God works great miracles.
God's love never fails.

DE'ATH MEETS . . . GEMMA GOSSIP

Characters	De'ath, famous chat show host, and Gemma Gossip.
Scene	De'ath is dressed in casual jacket with loud scarf wrapped around neck and partly thrown over one shoulder. Gemma Gossip arrives a little flustered, carrying a large shopping bag from which she takes out a clipboard. Gemma is dressed in dull grey clothing.
Props	small coffee table water jug and two drinking glasses two comfy chairs

De'ath   Hello and welcome once again to my ever-so-humble show. Our guest tonight is someone you might think you know but you're never quite sure! You may have met her at some long-forgotten party but, there again, you might not even have noticed she was there. I'm proud to say that she is one of my most industrious students. She has kept herself extremely busy and has worked very hard to become one of the leading gossips in the country. Ladies and gentlemen, I present to you, Gemma Gossip!

Gemma   Thank you, you are almost too kind. But before we go any further, you'll never guess who I bumped into on the way here!

De'ath   Gemma, as always it is a pleasure to meet such a dedicated gossip as yourself. I'm sure we would rather hear about you than some nobody you met on the way here.

Gemma   Never mind me and my little contribution to the art of communication. You really should listen to what I've got to tell you.

De'ath   Okay Gemma, what little snippet of information have you got to tell us?

Gemma   Well, I was just minding my own business, as I always do.

De'ath	Of course, Gemma, of course. We couldn't imagine you any other way.
Gemma	Ooh, you flatter me. Still, as I was saying. I was keeping my nose to myself and who should I bump into but him from down Grass-your-neighbour Close, you know, him from number twenty.
De'ath`	It's been a long time since I was in that neck of the woods, but do tell us what's been going on there.
Gemma	Well, you see, there's been so much happening I don't know where to begin.
De'ath	Why not start with who you bumped into while you were so busy minding your own business!
Gemma	Why yes, that is a good idea. As I was saying, I was busy thinking about that little incident that's going to happen between Rodney Crumb and Emily Bull. Wouldn't do for them to get married at all! She would have a double-barrelled surname, Crumb-Bull, you know as in 'apple crumb-bull'. They could have lots of mini crumb-bulls, and . . .
De'ath	Gemma, I'm sorry to interrupt, but what 'incident that's about to happen'?
Gemma	(*checks her clipboard*) Didn't I say? Sorry, that's most unbecoming for someone in my position! Well, Rodney has been seeing this most awful girl called Emily Bull. If you could just see her, I ask you! Miss Prim-and-proper and no mistake. Try as I might, I just cannot find anything 'interesting' about her. You know, those little bits of juicy almost-facts that make life so, so . . .
De'ath	Entertaining?
Gemma	Yes. That's right. Entertaining! You see, hardly anyone has anything 'interesting' to say about Emily. So, I thought we couldn't have our Rodney being saddled with Miss Prim-and-proper. Dear me no! No fun at all! And that's where Lisa comes

in. She's such an 'interesting' girl, such a rich history of little indiscretions. Makes for the most entertaining chat at our weekly coffee mornings.

De'ath   I think I'm beginning to see where you're coming from. But how are you going to replace Emily with Lisa?

Gemma   Now! That's the clever bit, you see. I don't know how it started . . .

De'ath   Really?

Gemma   No need to look at me like that! I can't imagine for a minute that you'd think I would have any involvement with anything that wasn't above board and 'factual'.

De'ath   'Factual'?

Gemma   Yes. 'Factual', particularly the facts as I see them! *(looks at clipboard)* Now, I don't know how it all started but somehow Emily heard that Rodney was planning to take Lisa to the cinema at the weekend.

De'ath   And was he?

Gemma   He was after I'd told him that Emily was planning to go to see the exhibition of eighteenth-century spoons with Eric Bickerstaff.

De'ath   And was she?

Gemma   Not until she'd heard that Rodney was taking Lisa to the cinema!

De'ath   Quite the little matchmaker, aren't we?

Gemma   I like to think I do my bit for the sake of true love.

De'ath   'True' love?

Gemma   Well, as near as you can get with a little extra added spice!

De'ath	You were telling us about someone you knew who you saw on your way here.
Gemma	Oh, yes. I was, wasn't I. Now, as I said, I was busy with my creative thoughts when who should I see but the man from number twenty. Well, you'd never guess who he was with, would you?
De'ath	Let's not start that all over again. I hate these guessing games. Couldn't you just tell us. Please?
Gemma	You do take the fun out of things. It's so much more fun to let you guess. If you're right there's no harm done. But, if you're not quite right, what a lot of fun we all have while you put two and two together and make seven!
De'ath	Gemma, you're a marvel! Now please tell us who him at number twenty was with.
Gemma	Okay, okay. Now, it wasn't his wife and by the look of her she could have done with a little bit of cosmetic help. You know, a tuck here and a fold there and a diet of figs would do wonders for her figure. She looked old enough to be his mother!
De'ath	Perhaps it was his mother!
Gemma	Oh! I hadn't thought of that. How boring!
De'ath	Never mind, Gemma. You're not one to let something like the truth stand in the way of a good bit of gossip, are you?
Gemma	You do flatter a girl. Thank you so much.
De'ath	Gemma. Thank you for being with us tonight and allowing us into your world of gossip. Thank you.

TODAY'S SPECIAL

The Word, the whole Word and nothing but the Word!

John 1:1-18: Christ comes to the world.

Equipment:
A4 paper for each group
pens
music and lyrics
candle

You need groups of seven to ten, each with a piece of paper. The first person in the group writes down a word at the top of the page and passes it to the person next to them. The second person should write a word just below the first which relates to the first word, and then fold the paper so that the first word cannot be seen. This process is repeated with each member of the group, writing a word and then folding the paper so that only their word can be seen. When the last person has written their word, unfold the paper and the last person reads the group's 'poem'! The 'poems' can then be displayed on the wall for everyone to admire! **(Allow 10 minutes for this activity.)**

Have a listen to 'Let everything that has breath' by Matt Redman, from the album *Intimacy*. You might also like to look at 'Say the word' by Stuart Townsend (*The source*, 445). Have a copy of the lyrics available if possible. **(Allow approximately 5 minutes.)**

Ask the group what they thought the music and lyrics were trying to say. Could they imagine the angels singing something like this?

Words are very powerful. They can make someone feel happy or sad. Words can be used to give someone confidence or to make them feel inferior and insecure. Words can create and they can destroy.

Read John 1:1-18.
John writes that in the beginning was the 'Word'. The term 'in the beginning' is to remind the reader of Genesis, the first book of the Old Testament. It is a reminder of the creation, the beginning of the world.

John is saying, particularly to those readers with a Jewish background, that Jesus was God's spoken Word which brought about creation. The 'Word', Jesus, gave life and light (vv. 3-4) to the world when it was dark and without form. In other words, Jesus is the life-force by which everything exists. John then tells us that this light (v. 5), which lit up creation, can never be put out; it cannot be extinguished!

Now God's Word, Jesus, who had brought light and life to creation, was coming into the world to bring light where there was darkness (sin) and life where there was death (evil). John says that the Word became a human being (v. 14) and lived 'here with us'. That is to say, Jesus knows the problems we have and he wants to bring us light and life. Jesus doesn't want our problems to fester in the darkness or cause us pain. He would rather 'live with us' and help us overcome those problems. This is what the angels were rejoicing about. This is why they were so happy to see the 'Word' of God coming into the world to be light and life for us.

Remind the group that the random words which formed their 'poems' earlier were words which they used without being given any focus or direction. The 'poems' haven't really got any form and they were written 'blind'.

Now, split the group into two. Give each group a piece of paper. Tell one group to write the word 'Light' on their paper and the other group to write 'Life'. Ask each group to brainstorm words which they would link to the main word, for example, Light: bright, shines, no darkness, sun, stars; or Life: breath, heart, blood, birth, human. Look at the results and display them next to the 'poems'.
(Allow 5 minutes for this activity.)

Place a candle in the centre of the room. Ask one of the group to light the candle and suggest that the group focus on the candle while you read the following prayer:

You, Lord, are the light which keeps me safe.
You are the light which drives out shadows.
You protect me from the darkness which causes me to stumble.
In you I will place my trust.

You keep me safe in times of trouble.
You listen when I call your name.
You take care of me when others ignore me.
In you I will place my trust.

You show me the path to follow.
You light each step of the way.
You bring life to my every day.
In you will I place my trust. Amen.

TODAY'S SPECIAL

Follow that star!
Matthew 2:1-12: The wise men.

Equipment:
sticky labels
pen and paper for each person
plate or bag

Before the group arrive write the following words onto the sticky labels:

Pebble	Boulder	Tree	Raspberry
Bush	Twig	Lemon	Banana
Carrot	Potato	Lettuce	Onion
Jam	Butter	Honey	Salt

You can add more items to suit the number of the group. As the group arrive stick one of the labels on their backs, but don't tell them what it is. Tell everyone to move around and ask other members of the group, 'What is my item?' The other group members have to mime the item and can only answer yes or no to questions. When someone has guessed correctly what their item is they can sit down and watch the others trying to guess theirs.
(Allow 10 minutes for this activity.)

Give each member of the group a piece of paper and a pen. Ask the group if there was any gift that was missing from their Christmas wish list. Is there something that they would like to make sure goes on this year's list? Suggest that they write on the paper the name of one gift that they would like to receive. It doesn't matter at this stage whether it is extravagant or expensive. When they have finished ask them to place the paper out of sight and forget about it for a few minutes.
(Allow approximately 5 minutes.)

Read Matthew 2:1-12.

The account of the visit to the infant Jesus, by the wise men (or 'Magi') was the fulfilment of a promise that had been made by the prophet Micah, who lived near a village called Gath, about twenty-five miles from Bethlehem. Micah had written, over 800 years before the birth of Jesus, that a Messiah would be born in Bethlehem (Matthew 2:5-6 and Micah 5:2).

The wise men had travelled a great distance over a long time to find the 'king of the Jews'. To this baby they brought gifts of gold, frankincense and myrrh. Each of the gifts has a significant meaning for Jesus.

- Gold is a symbol of something of genuine worth, of great value. It is a gift which was used in the Old Testament to decorate the Temple and was also used as a sign of royalty.

- Frankincense has a sweet odour and was used by the priests in the Temple. One of the main duties of the priest was to make an offering to God of an animal which was sacrificed in place of the people. The Latin word for priest is *pontifex*, which literally means a bridge-builder.

- Myrrh was a perfume used to anoint the bodies of the dead.

These gifts pointed to the mission of Jesus. He was the Messiah, a holy king who is the 'bridge-builder' between us and God. To bridge the gap Jesus was to suffer and die as the ultimate sacrifice. He paid the price. The gifts of the wise men were symbols relating to the greatest gift of all, the gift of Jesus who makes it possible for us to have a relationship with God.

Ask the group to look at the gift ideas they wrote on their piece of paper. Turn the idea around. Suggest that the group might like to think about what gifts they could give to somebody. Encourage them to think of people they know and what those people need. What would improve the quality of their lives? Write the ideas down on the piece of paper, fold it up and place the paper on a plate or in a bag which will be placed in the centre of the room.

(Allow 5 minutes for this task.)

Ask the group to be quiet and consider the gifts which they have written down on the paper. While they are reflecting on the gifts, read the following:

Lord, I may not have much to offer,
    I'm not always sure what I have to give.
There are times when all I can think about is me,
    what I want and what would make me feel good.
Lord, it isn't always easy to think what other people need,
    especially when there are so many things I want.
But you have promised to watch out for me,
    I'm never out of your sight or out of your thinking.
You want the best for me and you gave your best for me,
    nothing I can give can match that!
Thank you for your gift of life,
    the greatest gift of all. Amen.

TODAY'S SPECIAL

A change of heart.

Mark 1:4-11: Jesus is baptised.

Equipment:
a large plastic bowl
4-6 jam jars each filled with coloured water (use food colouring)
music and lyrics
sheets of A3 paper and pens
stoneware bowl of water
sticky labels

On each of the jars place a sticky label which has a snappy title such as 'licky lemon', 'gungy green', 'bluebottle blue', 'risky red'. Have the jars displayed as the group arrive. Don't mention anything about the jars until everyone has arrived and they are wondering what the jars contain. Announce to the group, with enthusiasm, that you have discovered a way of recycling mouthwash! The colours are, in fact, flavours which help disguise the previous flavour! Ask the group if anyone would like to try your recycled mouthwash. If anyone dares, the plastic bowl is there to empty the contents of their mouths into!

Explain to the group that the jars only contain coloured water but you are working on a way to recycle toothpaste and you will let them be the first to test!

Ask the group if they know what products use water? (Mouthwash! shampoo, fizzy drinks, soups.) What do we use water for? (Washing, cleaning the car, drinking, making tea and coffee.) Write some of the ideas down on a sheet of A3 paper.

(Allow 10 minutes for this activity.)

Water has many uses and is an essential component of our bodies. It gives us life and refreshes us. Have a listen to 'Deeper' by Delirious? from the album *King of Fools*, or take a look at 'River, wash over me' by Dougie Brown (*The source*, 441).

Try and have a copy of the lyrics available.

(Allow approximately 5 minutes.)

Have a chat about the lyrics from the song. Do the words tell us anything about the idea of baptism?

Read Mark 1: 4-11.
The use of water in the Bible for washing was not just for getting clean! In the Old Testament book of Leviticus, many of the chapters (11-25) discuss the use of water to bathe in after certain circumstances made you 'unclean'. Considering that water wasn't exactly 'on tap' this made for a lot of hard work, getting the water from a well or stream.

In the reading, John the Baptist is introducing a new concept to the Jewish people. Previously, if anyone wanted to become a Jew, one of the ceremonies they needed to go through was to be immersed in water. This was a symbol of being cleansed from all the contamination of a previous life and starting a fresh, new existence. The other two ceremonies were for a male to be circumcised because that was the 'mark' of the Jew. Then a sacrifice had to be made because only blood could answer for sin or doing wrong in God's eyes. Now, John the Baptist was calling for everyone to be immersed (baptised), Jews and non-Jews alike. It wasn't enough to rely on observing religious traditions and rituals, a fresh start with God was needed.

John was calling everyone to change the direction in which they had been going, to turn around and live their lives according to the way God wanted them to. The message was simple – to turn away from the life which polluted their relationship with God. The baptism became a public statement of turning back to God and having the past 'wiped clean'.

Ask the group to divide into threes and fours. Give each small group a sheet of A3 paper and pen. Ask each group to 'brainstorm' ideas for the use of water.

• What is water for?

• Why do we use water?

Encourage the groups to think of different ways in which water is used and try to come up with one word for each idea. Display the completed ideas on the wall.
(Allow 5 minutes for this task.)

Suggest to the group that they should take a little time to be quiet and reflect on the 'water words' which are on display. Perhaps they can think about the images that the words create. Place a stoneware bowl of water in front of the group while you read the following extract from Psalm 51.

You are kind, God! Please have pity on me.
You are always merciful! Please wipe away my sins.
Wash me clean from all my sin and guilt.
I know about my sins,
    and I cannot forget my terrible guilt.
You are the one I have sinned against;
I have disobeyed you and have done wrong.

Help me to speak, and I will praise you, Lord.
Offerings and sacrifices are not what you want.
The way to please you
    is to feel sorrow deep in our hearts.
This is the kind of sacrifice you won't refuse. Amen.

TODAY'S SPECIAL

Walk this way!

John 1:43-51: The first followers of Jesus.

Equipment:
empty can of dog food, complete with label!
small cutlery fork
two Mars bars cut into small chunks
one small cup which will fit into the can of 'dog food'
a flipchart
music and lyrics or drama sketch
paper and pens
metal tray or heat-resistant plate
matches

When the group has arrived and you are ready to begin, start to complain that you have been really busy today and haven't had time to eat since you woke up. On the way to the session you popped into a shop to buy something to eat. Unfortunately the only thing they had was a can of dog food. Well, the label said how nutritious the food was and that it kept dogs healthy, so what's good for a dog is good enough for you! Begin to eat from the can, using the fork. Chew away with a huge smile on your face, exclaiming how good the food tastes!

Ask if any of the group are hungry and would they like to try some of your food? Really encourage one or two of the group to try the 'food' and get them to agree that the food tastes good without them saying what they think the 'food' is. When you (or the group!) have had enough of the 'dog food', let everyone know that the 'food' was in fact a Mars bar.

Ask the group what thoughts went through their head as they watched you eat the 'dog food'. Why didn't some of the group accept your offer of sampling the 'food'? What made some of the group want to sample the 'food'? Why did they trust you? Write some of the responses down on the flipchart.
(Allow 10 minutes for this activity.)

Trusting in someone or something takes a lot of courage. Have a listen to 'Blind Faith' by Three Crosses, from the album *Jefferson Street*. Also take a look at 'His love is higher' by David Ruis (*The source*, 171). Try to have a copy of the lyrics available. Alternatively, you might like to use the drama sketch *De'ath meets . . . Terry Trustless* (see page 44).
(Allow approximately 5 minutes.)

Discuss the chosen piece of music (or the drama sketch.) What did the group think about the lyrics? Did the lyrics have anything to say about trust and faith? What does 'faith' mean? Can the group suggest any possible meanings? Write the responses on a flipchart or A3 sheet of paper. It isn't important to find an acceptable definition of 'faith' at this moment.

Read John 1:43-51.

Jesus travelled to Galilee where he met Philip. Philip was from Bethsaida, the same town as Andrew and Peter who had travelled to Galilee with Jesus. It is quite probable that Philip knew both Andrew and Peter, who were fishermen. Jesus tells Philip, 'Come with me'. Quite a simple statement but one which Philip responds to with enthusiasm. The important point for Philip is that Jesus had gone out of his way to 'find' him and Philip puts his trust in what Jesus said. Philip goes to find Nathanael and tells him that the one Moses and the prophets wrote about is fulfilled here in Jesus of Nazareth. Nathanael's response is, 'Can anything good come out of Nazareth?' – In other words, can anything good come out of a place which was seen as a bit of a joke for a lot of Jews. Nathanael doesn't think that God would have anything to do with a fairly new town which has little heritage and no culture! He can't believe that God would have the Messiah come from somewhere like Nazareth! But when Nathanael actually meets Jesus he discovers that there is nothing outside God's control and nothing or nobody that God will not work with!

Two important points stand out from the reading:

• Firstly, it doesn't matter to God who we are or what other people think of us. God isn't interested in status or our credibility. When Jesus said, 'Come with me' he knew exactly the type of people he wanted to work with! He just wants us to trust him.

• Secondly, even though we find it difficult to believe that God would want to work with people others call 'ordinary', this doesn't limit God. We need faith in a risk-taking God!

How will we respond when Jesus goes out of his way to find us and says, 'Come with me'? How do we deal with our reactions – 'Why me?' 'I can't do that!' 'Don't you mean somebody else?' 'I haven't got the right background!' 'I would, but . . .'

Ask the group to reconsider the concepts of faith and trust.

- Can they think of other definitions?
- What do the responses of Philip and Nathanael tell us about trust and faith?

Jot some of the discussion ideas down on the flipchart.
(Allow 5 minutes for this task.)

Distribute a small piece of paper and a pen to each member of the group. Suggest that they consider their own responses to the question of faith. What obstacles stop them having faith in God? What difficulties do they have in trusting God? Ask the group to write their obstacles and difficulties on the piece of paper and fold the paper when they have finished. Collect the folded papers and place them on a metal tray or heat-resistant plate. Set light to the papers and read the following prayer as the papers go up in flames. (Alternatively, place the papers in a rubbish basket or refuse bag.)

God, it's not easy.
There seem so many things that get in the way.
It's difficult to understand,
    why you want to work with me.
I can't imagine what you have in mind
    when you say, 'Come with me'.
But you know me better than anyone,
    although there are some things I would rather you didn't know!
Even knowing all my doubts and fears,
    you still look my way.
I place all my obstacles and difficulties before you.
Deal with them.
Though they appear huge to me,
    together we can work through them.
Thank you for trusting me.
Help me to trust you. Amen.

DE'ATH MEETS . . . TERRY TRUSTLESS

Characters	De'ath, the ever-charming chat show host, and Terry Trustless
Scene	De'ath is dressed in casual clothes. Terry Trustless is dressed in hat, scarf and winter coat.
Props	small coffee table water jug and two drinking glasses two comfy chairs

De'ath   Ladies and Gentlemen. It is a privilege to welcome our next guest tonight. I have known him for more years than I care to remember. He first came to my attention when I met him standing outside a shop trying to stop the flow of blood from his nose. When I enquired what had happened he informed me that he had gone into the shop to purchase a fridge. He hadn't believed the salesman's story that the fridge light would go out automatically when the fridge door was shut. Trying to prove the salesman wrong by opening and closing the fridge door quickly, our guest hadn't been quite quick enough to remove his head from the inside of the fridge. His nose formed a wedge between the fridge door and the fridge! Welcome, Terry Trustless!

Terry   Thank you for such an inspiring introduction.

De'ath   It's a pleasure to have you here, Terry.

Terry   I wasn't sure I'd get here.

De'ath   Why's that?

Terry   You know you can't trust public transport!

De'ath   I know what you mean. They're never on time, are they!

Terry   Time isn't the problem.

De'ath	So what is?
Terry	It's just the fact that you can never trust the driver not to make some totally unnecessary mistake and cause a gigantic accident!
De'ath	Surely that's a bit extreme?
Terry	Not at all! It might not be the driver's fault. There might be some mechanical problem that nobody knows about until it's too late. Or even worse, there might be a maniac riding a motorbike delivering pizza who darts out of a side street causing the bus to swerve into the side of a building which in turn starts to crumble causing the whole building to collapse and fall into the street, showering passing cars with debris and . . .
De'ath	Terry, it's okay. I think we get the idea!
Terry	You can never be too careful, you know. Anyway, it's all the bank's fault.
De'ath	The bank? How do you make that out?
Terry	It's simple really. You just can't trust them, that's what. They take your mind off the task in hand. Which, as you know, can cause accidents. For a start, what do they do with all that money that they get every day? Answer me that!
De'ath	Well . . .
Terry	I'll tell you what they do. They spend it, that's what they do!
De'ath	Well, aren't banks supposed to lend money to people and charge interest and make money that way?
Terry	That's spending!
De'ath	You can still go to the bank at any time and get your money back.
Terry	Oh no you don't. You don't know what goes on behind those counters and when the doors are shut!

De'ath	Surely you have to trust that the bank are acting in your interest?
Terry	Interest! I'll give you interest! They take my money and spend it on what they are interested in!
De'ath	You are taking things a bit too far, aren't you?
Terry	Not at all. You don't get your money back because they are spending it!
De'ath	I think you'll find you do get your money back.
Terry	Oh no you don't! I wrote my name on a ten pound note and gave it to the bank. When I asked for it the next day they couldn't find my ten pound note!
De'ath	But you still got a ten pound note.
Terry	But not *my* ten pound note. They'd spent it!
De'ath	I think somehow you've lost the plot.
Terry	Not at all. I'll tell you another thing; you can't trust them doctors either!
De'ath	But surely the doctors are there to help you, to make you well?
Terry	That's what they want you to believe! How do you know they're qualified to find out what's wrong with you and give you the right treatment?
De'ath	They have certificates and the initials GP after their name, haven't they?
Terry	Don't give me certificates! They're printed by the handful in China. You can get them down the market if you know where to look! And as for GP! What does GP stand for? I'll tell you, Generally Pathetic, that's what!
De'ath	Just a bit touchy, aren't you, about doctors?

Terry	You can't trust them! I went to my local doctor with a pain in my teeth and he sent me to a dentist!
De'ath	Surely that's where you should go if you've got toothache?
Terry	Not when you've got a toothpick wedged between your molars! Anyway, the dentist was no better. How can you trust them when you can' t see what they're doing? I ask you, you've got no control over your mouth after the injection, the dentist is up to his elbows in your mouth and then asks you where you went for your summer holidays! And then, if that isn't enough, they ask you to rinse your mouth with funny coloured water and spit into the sink. Into the sink! They're lucky if I can hit the wall! No wonder the dental nurse keeps an umbrella!
De'ath	So you don't trust anybody?
Terry	S'right! They're all in it together, these bankers, doctors and dentists. They ask you to trust them, they mutter some unpronounceable economic or medical terminology and get you to discuss your private matters behind closed doors.
De'ath	Isn't that just for privacy?
Terry	Not at all. That's so that nobody else can hear or see what they are doing!
De'ath	Aren't you being just a bit too critical?
Terry	No! I'm just being careful. Now, if you'll excuse me, I want to catch the number 54 bus before too many people get on and the weight proves too much for the bus.
De'ath	Terry Trustless, thank you for being with us tonight. I trust we'll meet again soon. My secretary will send you a cheque for tonight's appearance. The cheque shouldn't bounce but you never know, you can't trust anyone these days!

TODAY'S SPECIAL

Come to the celebration!

John 2:1-11: The wedding at Cana.

Equipment:
sheet of A4 paper for each member of the group
pens
music and lyrics

Ask each member of the group to print their name vertically on the left-hand side of the A4 paper. Pass the paper to the person on the left of the writer. Ask that person to write a compliment about the person whose name is on the paper. The compliment must begin with one of the letters in the person's name. Pass the paper to the left again and repeat the process until each letter of the name has been used for a compliment. After the papers have been completed, pass the sheet of compliments to the 'named' person. This exercise works best if the group has got to know each other during the past few weeks.
(Allow 10 minutes for this activity.)

Have a listen to 'All I need' by Kevin Prosch, from the album *Reckless mercy*. Alternatively, take a look at 'He is the Lord' also by Kevin Prosch (*The source*, 159). Try and have a copy of the lyrics available.
(Allow approximately 5 minutes.)

Discuss the piece of music. What were the lyrics attempting to say? Did the lyrics have anything to say about change or things becoming different?

Read John 2:1-11.
Cana was a little village not far from Nazareth. It was here that Mary, the mother of Jesus, was helping with the arrangements for the wedding. She was worried when she discovered that the wine was running out. The lack of wine was not a result of the wedding guests over-indulging in the falling-over juice! To be drunk would have brought disgrace to everyone concerned.

Weddings were special events which were regarded as great celebrations. Jewish tradition held that the wedding ceremony should take place in the evening with the centre of attention being the bridegroom rather than the bride! The bridegroom was expected to pay for the entire celebration which would often last for several days. After the wedding ceremony the newly married couple would be escorted through the streets with burning torches lighting their way to their new home. The couple would not go on a honeymoon but keep their house open for the entire week for people to come along and celebrate the special occasion. The celebrations and showing hospitality to their guests was a sacred duty for the married couple. It was important for the couple to provide a wedding celebration which would not disappoint their friends and neighbours. To run out of wine would have been really embarrassing and spoilt the celebrations entirely.

When Mary told Jesus about the lack of wine, he realised that the bridegroom hadn't been able to afford enough wine to last the week. Jesus performed his first miracle to save the newly married couple from the embarrassment of running out of wine and the problems involved in borrowing money for more wine at the start of their married life. Jesus asked for the six water pots to be filled to the top with water. These pots were kept for the Jewish traditions of washing dirty feet before entering the house and for washing hands before and during meals. Each pot would have held approximately twenty-five gallons of water (one hundred and fifty gallons all together) which, when turned into wine, would have provided a total of about seven hundred bottles of wine! This was far more than the bridegroom needed!

The story is an example of all that Jesus can do in our lives. Jesus wants to take the ordinary (water) and do extraordinary (wine) things with it. The question is, are we willing to put our trust in a God who wants to do extraordinary things?

Suggest to the group that they look again at their sheet of 'compliments'. These are the qualities that other members of the group have identified in us. But we have other things which we want to do or ambitions which are part of our dreams. Ask the group to fold the paper in half and on one side write down some of their dreams, some of the things that they would like to do with their lives.

• Have they particular ambitions or goals?

• Have they a job or career which they would like to follow?

Ask if any of the group would like to share some of the things which they have written down. Invite the rest of the group to write down the dreams and ambitions of other members of the group.
(Allow 5 minutes for this task.)

Ask the group to be quiet and reflect on their dreams and ambitions for a couple of minutes. After this, think about the dreams and ambitions of other group members. If the group feel comfortable with the idea, suggest that they pray for each other and the dreams and ambitions which they each have. After an appropriate time, close with the following psalm as a prayer.

Psalm 146:1-5.
Shout praises to the Lord!
With all that I am, I will shout his praises.
I will sing and praise the Lord God for as long as I live.
You can't depend on anyone, not even a great leader.
Once they die and are buried,
    that will be the end of all their plans.
The Lord God of Jacob blesses everyone
    who trusts him and depends on him. Amen.

TODAY'S SPECIAL

Come out of there!

Mark 1:21-28: A man with an evil spirit.

Equipment:
plastic beaker
pen
egg
cloth large enough to cover beaker
music and lyrics
a cross

Announce to the group that you are going to perform a magic trick! Place the egg under the beaker and then cover the beaker with the piece of cloth. Tell the group that you are now going to use your magic to turn the egg into a chicken! Take the pen and wave it over the beaker. Say, in a theatrical voice, 'Eye of toad, nose of rhino with dark blue eyes, turn this egg into a chicken surprise!' Tap the beaker three times and then remove the cloth. Lift the beaker to reveal the egg. 'What, no chicken?'

Apologise to the group and tell them that your powers of magic seem to have left you. Ask the group if they have any idea why the egg didn't turn into a chicken. Once they have offered several ideas for your lack of success, explain to the group that you obviously have no authority over creation and nature. Perhaps we need to investigate someone who does! **(Allow 10 minutes for this activity.)**

Ask the group to have a listen to 'Much Afraid' by Jars of Clay, from the album *Much Afraid*. You might also like to look at 'You are mighty' by Craig Musseau (*The source*, 594) or you might prefer to use a different piece of music which reflects the theme of authority. Try and have a copy of the lyrics available.
(Allow approximately 5 minutes.)

Discuss the piece of music. What were the lyrics attempting to say? Did the group agree with the lyrics?

Read Mark 1:21-28.
Jesus had been sharing a few thoughts with some Jews in the synagogue. Suddenly he was interrupted by a man who was recognised as having an evil spirit.

The idea of someone having an evil spirit does not just mean they have a bad temper or always seem to be behaving in an anti-social way, but that their personality and character is 'controlled' by an occupying force! The Jewish term for evil spirits, or demons, is *mazzikin*, which means 'one who does harm'. Jesus openly opposed the activities of these demons who were intent on damaging God's creation. The demons recognised Jesus and the authority that he had. Mark writes that those who were under the control of an evil spirit called out to Jesus, using such phrases as: 'You are God's Holy One' (Mark 1:24), 'You are the Son of God' (Mark 3:11) and 'Jesus, Son of God' (Mark 5:7). The evil spirits recognised who Jesus was and that his authority came from God.

The Gospel writers didn't believe that just because someone was ill meant that they were under the control of an evil spirit. Matthew writes that Jesus healed people who were sick, mad or had 'demons in them' (Matthew 4:24).

Jesus opposed anything which corrupted God's creation. The ministry of Jesus was to overcome evil and make it possible to have a relationship with God through the sacrifice of Jesus and his defeat of death. The resurrection of Jesus spelt defeat for the evil which is intent on doing harm to God's creation.

There are lots of superstitions about evil spirits, with spells to keep evil away, good luck charms and certain types of behaviour – touch wood, fingers crossed, doing things in a particular way, like not looking at the new moon through glass, not walking under ladders. Jesus didn't use any of these or perform special rituals. Whenever Jesus was opposed by an evil spirit he used his authority and ordered the evil spirit to 'shut up and get out!'

Ask the group to think about some of the things they do for 'good luck' or to make sure that a particular situation will work out okay. Isn't it better to put our trust and faith in someone who has authority over creation and who has defeated evil for good?
(Allow 5 minutes for this task.)

Place a cross in the centre of the room. Ask the group to focus on the cross and consider what the death and resurrection of Jesus represents. After a short time, read the following prayer:

Lord, thank you.
Although thank you doesn't really seem enough,
    considering that you didn't trust your lucky rabbit's paw,
    or keep your fingers crossed, just in case.
When you touched wood it wasn't for luck,
    or even to make sure that everything would work out alright.
You touched wood,
    the wood of the cross,
    to turn harm into good;
    to bring life where there was death;
    to give hope where there was doubt.
Lord, thank you. Amen.

TODAY'S SPECIAL

Amazing scenes!

Mark 1:29-39: Jesus heals many people.

Equipment:
sheet of paper and pen for each member of the group
music and lyrics

Ask the group to write their responses to the following situations. Encourage them to be as honest as they can as no one will be reading their completed sheets. Read each of the situations below, allowing approximately one minute for each group member to write their response.

1. You open your Christmas present to find it is an awful pair of socks with pictures of cuddly bunnies on them.

2. A letter arrives telling you that you have just won a year's supply of chocolate.

3. You receive a telephone call telling you that you were unsuccessful in your application for the part-time job you applied for at the local music store.

4. On your way to the group meeting you slipped over and your jeans are covered in mud.

5. A well-known magazine publisher has written to you saying how impressed they were with the article you wrote for a major youth magazine. The publisher wants to know if you would consider writing a regular feature article on youth issues.

6. All your favourite clothes are still waiting to be washed and you have had to come to the group wearing a large plastic coat to hide your old clothes.

When the group have finished writing their responses, ask each member to fold their piece of paper and put it in their pocket or under the chair. **(Allow 10 minutes for this activity.)**

Try having a listen to 'Refine me' by Jennifer Knapp, from the album *Kansas*, or have a look at 'This love' by Geoff Bullock (*The source*, 521). You might prefer to use another piece of music with a similar theme. Try and have a copy of the lyrics available.

Ask the group to discuss the lyrics for the chosen song. What did the group think about the lyrics? Did the lyrics have any particular point to make?

Read Mark 1: 29-39.
Jesus has had a really busy time during the last few days. Apart from a spot of teaching, he'd had crowds of people coming to him to be healed. Jesus healed people in the Synagogue (the Jewish meeting place), in homes (Simon's mother-in-law's) and in the streets (vv. 33-34). News of the healings and teaching spread all over Galilee, and turned Jesus into a local celebrity. Expectations were high and Jesus was surrounded with people who wanted to see a demonstration of his 'healing touch'. The people were used to seeing elaborate demonstrations of healing. Simon's mother-in-law had a fever (quite probably malaria, which was common in Galilee). The 'cure' for this type of fever was to take an iron knife and tie it to a thorn bush with a piece of hair from the sick person. Then, during the next three days, some verses from the Old Testament were read, with a special 'quote' said on the fourth day and the healing was supposedly complete!

Jesus didn't go in for any of this healing ritual or use elaborate methods for driving demons out of people. He simply spoke with authority and power and people were made well and free from 'occupying forces'! The popularity of Jesus was enough to make him a person of status and power. The response of Jesus to all this was not what his disciples expected. Jesus knew that healing people was not the most important part of his ministry. He knew that the most important stage was yet to come: his suffering, death and resurrection. His response was to find a quiet place and pray to his Father. Would our response have been the same?

Ask the group to look again at their 'response' papers. Suggest that they think about some issues or situations which they have faced recently.

• How did they respond?

• Did the idea of praying, either to say thank you or ask what was going on, have any part in their response?

(Allow 5 minutes for this task.)

Ask the group to remain quiet and continue to think about how they respond to issues and situations. While they are quiet read the following as a prayer.

Proverbs 3:1-7.
My child, remember my teachings and instructions
    and obey them completely.
They will help you live a long and prosperous life.
Let love and loyalty always show like a necklace,
    and write them in your mind.
God and people will like you and consider you a success.

With all your heart you must trust in the Lord
    and not in your own judgement.
Always let him lead you,
    and he will clear the road for you to follow.
Don't ever think you are wise enough,
    but respect the Lord and stay away from evil. Amen.

TODAY'S SPECIAL   **News travels fast!**

Mark 1:40-45: Jesus heals a man.

Equipment:
tube of 'Smarties' or similar sweets
paper and pens
small candle for each member

As the group arrive, select two or three members to sit alone in a corner of the room, well away from the other members of the group. Ask the remaining group members to ignore the two or three members sitting on their own. Sit close to the rest of the group and ask them what kind of week they have had, and what interesting things have happened to them. While you are talking, begin to share the sweets with these group members. (Keep some sweets for the two or three 'outsiders', but don't make this known.)

After a few minutes gather all the group together and ask the 'outsiders' what they were thinking while the rest of the group were talking and eating sweets together. Ask the rest of the group how they felt about the group members who were 'left out' of things? Did the 'outsiders' feel rejected? Feel amused? Did they feel they had done something wrong? **(Allow 10 minutes for this activity.)**

Feeling alone is something we all go through at times. One of the hardest times must be when sitting an examination. You are on your own. You cannot talk to anyone, check facts in a reference book or even sing to yourself to keep awake! At these times strange things happen with our brains and the results are often really funny . . . for other people! The following is a collection of student answers to exam questions, proving that sometimes some things are best left unsaid or unwritten.

Biblical studies?
'The inhabitants of ancient Egypt were called mummies. They lived in the Sarah Dessert and travelled by Camelot. The climate in the Sarah is such that the inhabitants have to live elsewhere, so certain areas of the dessert are cultivated by irritation. The Egyptians built the pyramids in the shape of a huge triangular cube. They are a range of mountains between France and Spain.'

'The Bible is full of interesting caricatures. In the first book of the Bible, Guinesses, Adam and Eve were created from an apple tree. One of the children, Cain, once asked 'Am I my brother's son?' God asked Abraham to sacrifice Isaac on Mount Montezuma. Jacob, son of Isaac, stole his brother's birthmark. Jacob was a patriarch who brought up his sons to be patriarchs, but they did not take to it. One of Jacob's sons, Joseph, gave refuse to the Israelites.'

'Pharaoh forced the Hebrew slaves to make bread without straw. Moses led them to the Red Sea where they made unleavened bread, which is bread made without any ingredients. Afterwards, Moses went up on Mount Cyanide to get the ten commandments. David was a Hebrew king skilled at playing the liar. He fought with the philatelists, a race of people who lived in biblical times. Solomon, one of David's sons, had 500 wives and 500 porcupines.'

Makes you think!
(Allow approximately 5 minutes.)

Read Mark 1:40-45.
While Jesus was in Galilee a man with leprosy came to him, asking to be healed. The man recognised that Jesus had the power to heal him.

Leprosy was a term used for a variety of skin diseases. Under the Jewish law anyone with 'leprosy' was considered 'unclean'. The person with the skin disease was expected to keep apart from other people and wear ragged clothes, keep their hair long and unwashed, cover the lower part of their face and call out 'unclean' whenever they were near other people!

As if that wasn't enough, the leper was also expected to live alone and away from the nearest settlement. An unexpected meeting with a leper meant that the other person was also considered unclean. Even worse, if the meeting with a leper took place in a house, both the other person and the house were then considered unclean!

The disease of leprosy was thought to be the result of being involved with some form of evil action. The leper was considered an outcast and an offence to society.

The leper in the Bible reading went against every convention and law relating to lepers. He went into a settlement where he shouldn't have been and made contact with a Jewish teacher, Jesus. Rather than have the leper 'run out of town', Jesus reached out and touched the leper. Jesus broke the laws and conventions which kept the leper isolated from society. With a simple act of love Jesus healed the leper. Jesus was not made unclean by being in contact with the leper but made the leper clean. He also asked the man to conform to the Jewish ritual of telling the priest of the healing and to do as Moses had commanded, which was to take a gift offering to the Temple. An act of compassion brought the former leper out of isolation and into the open: from darkness into the light!

Ask the group to think about friends or people they know who are not always accepted by other people, who feel nervous in a group or who don't have many friends. Perhaps they might like to write some names down on a piece of paper.
(Allow 5 minutes for this task.)

You will need the small candles for this section. Suggest to the group that they might like to light a candle to represent the people whose names they have written on their piece of paper. Ask each group member to consider ways in which they can help make people feel wanted and accepted. Place the candles close together and read the following:

> Once again Jesus spoke to the people. This time he said, 'I am the light of the world! Follow me, and you won't be walking in the dark. You will have the light that gives life.' (John 8:12)

TODAY'S SPECIAL

Faith through the roof!

Mark 2:1-12: Jesus heals a crippled man.

Equipment:
sufficient paper and pens for each pair
a wooden cross
small stones or pebbles
music and lyrics

Ask the group to divide into pairs and read them the following problem: The disciples have walked for hours and have reached the banks of the River Jordan. Unfortunately they need to get to the other side without walking any further. There is no bridge in sight and the river is far too deep and wide to walk or swim across. Simon Peter looks across the river and sees two small boys playing on the other bank. Near the boys is a small rowing boat. The rowing boat can hold two boys or one disciple. After a while all the disciples succeed in crossing the river in the boat. How?

Answer: The disciples are on the east side of the river and the two boys are on the west. One of the boys rows the boat from the west side to the east side, gets out and one disciple rows back to the west side. The disciple gets out at the west side and the second boy rows back to the east side of the river. Both boys now row back to the west side. Repeat these four steps for every disciple carried from east to west.
(Allow 10 minutes for this activity.)

Ask the group to listen to 'When I needed a saviour' by Matt Redman, from the album *Intimacy*. Also, take a look at 'We serve a God of miracles' by Mark Altrogge (*The source*, 555). Use an alternative piece of music if you wish. Try and have a copy of the lyrics available if possible.
(Allow approximately 5 minutes.)

Discuss the piece of music with the group. What do they think the lyrics were attempting to say?

Read Mark 2:1-12.
Jesus was in Capernaum taking a quick break 'at home' (thought to be the home of Simon Peter). Word soon got around that Jesus was 'in town' and before long a crowd had gatecrashed the house! The tradition at that time was to leave the door to the house open, allowing anyone to enter and be made welcome. So, as soon as word spread about the location of Jesus, the house overflowed with visitors wanting to hear what Jesus had to say.

News about the activities of Jesus would have reached the ears of everyone. Expectations about what Jesus would say and do were high. It was for this reason that four men carried their crippled friend on a stretcher to meet Jesus and hopefully be healed.

The crowd around the house proved impossible to get through for four men with a stretcher. A little bit of ingenuity was needed! The house in Capernaum was typical of the majority of houses in Palestine. It had a flat roof which was often used as a place of rest and quiet, and could be reached by an outside staircase. The roof itself was constructed of beams laid from wall to wall. The space in between the beams was filled with brushwood or straw and fixed into place with clay. It was the easiest thing literally to 'dig' through the roof and lower the man down on the stretcher. The hole would have been easily repaired and caused no permanent damage.

You can imagine the scene below. Jesus would be teaching while the people stood, tightly packed, unable to move very far. From the ceiling bits of dried clay and straw would begin to fall onto the listeners. It's doubtful that the people below would have had any idea as to what was going on above them! Suddenly daylight would have shone through the hole, only to disappear again as something began to descend.

When everyone understood what was happening there would have been quite a bit of laughter, apart from the house owner who must have wondered when he would find time to repair the roof! You can imagine that Jesus would have had a laugh about the situation too. But, as soon as the crippled man was completely lowered, Jesus appreciated how much effort it had been for the man's friends to get the stretcher and the man safely into the house. Jesus responded to this effort and to the men's belief in his power to heal. He told the crippled man 'My friend, your sins are forgiven.'

At the time of Jesus it was a common belief that illness was a result of 'sin' or doing wrong in God's eyes. Jesus rewarded the faith of the men by forgiving the 'wrong-doing' and healing the crippled man.

Suggest to the group that they think about some of their friends and what they could do to help their friends meet Jesus. This can be discussed or just allow them a few minutes to consider it. You might like to help with a few suggestions, such as:

- invite a friend to supper
- offer to help with some task or project
- loan a book or CD which has something relevant to say about Jesus
- simply be a good listener!

(Allow 5 minutes for this task.)

You will need the small wooden cross and small stones or pebbles. Ask each member of the group to think about one particular friend who they think would appreciate getting to know Jesus. While the group are considering this, distribute the stones or pebbles to each member. When each has thought of someone, invite them to place their stone or pebble at the bottom of the cross to represent their friend. Once this has been done read the following prayer:

Lord, these stones represent our friends.
At the moment the stones appear cold and hard.
Let your love bring life and warmth,
   let your love bring light and strength.
Let each one of us be a friend who is willing to help,
    to go the extra mile,
    to go out of our way
    to break down barriers,
    so that we can encourage our friends,
    we can listen to our friends,
    we can be a real friend even when the going gets tough.
Lord, help each one of us to help our friends. Amen.

TODAY'S SPECIAL

That will do very nicely!
John 1:1-14: The Word of life.

Equipment:
large sheet of paper and marker pen
music and lyrics or drama sketch
flipchart

Tell the group that although you know the topic for today's session you thought that it would make a change if they had to work out the topic by playing hangman. Allow each member of the group three guesses. (Either allow each member three guesses only or deduct one guess every time a wrong guess is made.) Once they have run out of guesses they cannot take any further part in the game. The topic is 'Acceptance'.
(Allow 10 minutes for this activity.)

Have a listen to 'Hold me now' by Jennifer Knapp, from the album *Kansas*. You might also like to look at 'I am so thankful' by Loren Bieg (*The source*, 192).

Have a copy of the lyrics available. Alternatively, you might like to use the drama sketch *De'ath meets . . . Emily Whatsername* (see page 65).
(Allow approximately 5 minutes.)

Discuss the lyrics for the chosen piece of music. Did the group agree with the lyrics? Did the lyrics make sense?

Read John 1:1-14.
The Gospel writer is laying out the credentials of Jesus. The first ten verses are a great build-up and then, in verse 11, we are told that he wasn't made welcome. What a let down!

But not everything was a let down. Some people accepted Jesus and put their faith in him. So, he gave them the right to become part of God's family.

Even after being rejected the gift was still available!

Firstly, God *gave* the gift. That is, it wasn't paid for or given in return for some service or help. The gift was a means of escape or saving from the effects of evil and being separated from God. The traditional word for this gift is 'salvation' which literally means 'being rescued'!

The next bit is quite awesome. He gave us the *right* to be part of

God's family. That's like a royal seal of approval but even better! This *right* is given by the only one capable and with the authority to do so – Jesus. This *right* cannot be taken from us and it certainly doesn't have a time limit!

By accepting the gift and becoming part of God's family *by right*, we are part of a unique family. We are accepted totally. We are special. We are no longer subject to another authority (evil). And, as we are accepted, we should also encourage and accept other people in God's family without putting terms and conditions on them!

Acceptance is quite an awesome concept. Ask the group to think about what it means to 'accept' someone. Write some of their responses on a flipchart. It may be a good idea to get some of the responses typed up and enlarged to display on the walls for future reference.
(Allow 5 minutes for this task.)

Ask the group to consider some of the responses which are displayed on the flipchart. Take a few moments to be quiet and reflect on the meaning of 'acceptance'.

Suggest to the group that while they are quiet they might also like to think about people they know who don't feel accepted or who feel rejected for whatever reason. Consider ways in which each group member can help someone they know to feel accepted. While everyone is quiet read the following:

Ephesians 3:14-21.
I kneel in prayer to the Father. All beings in heaven and on earth receive their life from him. God is wonderful and glorious. I pray that his Spirit will make you become strong followers and that Christ will live in your hearts because of your faith. Stand firm and be deeply rooted in his love. I pray that you and all God's people will understand what is called wide or long or high or deep. I want you to know all about Christ's love, although it is too wonderful to be measured. Then your lives will be filled with all that God is.

I pray that Christ Jesus and the church will for ever bring praise to God. His power at work in us can do far more than we dare ask or imagine. Amen.

DE'ATH MEETS . . . EMILY WHATSERNAME

Characters	De'ath and Emily Whatsername.
Scene	De'ath is dressed in his usual smart, sophisticated suit and tie. Emily is dressed in clashing colours and styles.
Props	small coffee table water jug and two drinking glasses two comfy chairs

De'ath Welcome, welcome to my most humble show. As always, it is a great pleasure to be here and to introduce you to a few of my acquaintances. Some of my guests are well known to most of you and some, like my next guest, not so well known – but her influence is felt by many people. Ladies and gentlemen, may I introduce to you Emily Whatsername!

Emily Er, thank you, most kind, possibly.

De'ath Emily, it's a pleasure to meet you again. How are you?

Emily Well, no, I mean, not well, erm, sort of okay, but, erm, what do you think?

De'ath Emily, my dear, you look as charming as you ever did!

Emily Are you sure you're not just saying that? I mean, that is to say, how do I know you're not just trying to make me feel sort of, erm, okay, when you really mean, erm, alright if I had a paper bag over my head?

De'ath Emily, you know me better than that, surely?

Emily That's the point. I do know you!

De'ath Tut, tut. There's no need to be like that.

Emily What do you suggest I should be like? I'm not sure what people expect at times.

De'ath	Do they expect anything at all?
Emily	Of course they do!
De'ath	How do you mean, Emily?
Emily	You know. People have all sorts of expectations when they meet someone. Don't they?
De'ath	I certainly hope so. Sorry, I mean, do they?
Emily	You know they do!
De'ath	Well, I can't be expected to know everything, can I?
Emily	You give a pretty good impression of it then!
De'ath	Now, now, Emily. Let's not forget who you're talking to and why. Where were we? Oh yes, I remember, you were going to tell me how you were feeling.
Emily	Was I?
De'ath	Whether you were or not, it's as good a starting place as any. Now, how are you?
Emily	As well as can be expected under the circumstances.
De'ath	And what circumstances might they be?
Emily	Under the circumstances that, er, well, you know, under the circumstances.
De'ath	My dear Emily, I'm sure the audience would love to know under what circumstances.
Emily	You know, those circumstances!
De'ath	I'm sure there must be someone else we can interview who's a lot more interesting than this one. Anyone know of a lump of concrete that's not doing anything for a few minutes?

Emily	There! See what I mean? Those circumstances.
De'ath	I fail to see what you and a lump of concrete have got in common, apart from density, that is!
Emily	That reminds me of a joke . . .
De'ath	I think we've got the joke.
Emily	Well, really. There's no need to be like that!
De'ath	I'm sorry, but a little bit of a decent response would be most helpful.
Emily	That's all I want, a decent response from people. Not a quick 'how are you', as if you're asking a plank of wood!
De'ath	Concrete actually. But never mind. Could you be a bit more specific about what you mean?
Emily	I must say, you are quite rude to your guests. Is this the way you normally behave?
De'ath	Not all of the time. I save most of my charm for special guests such as yourself!
Emily	It's like I said. Under these circumstances how does anyone expect me to feel okay? People walk past me as if I wasn't there. Even when I stand in front of them so that they have to notice me they ask me questions and don't wait for an answer. How am I expected to feel?
De'ath	I'm sure no one means any harm. It's just that we're so busy, so much to do and so little time to do it. Nothing personal, you understand.
Emily	I understand alright. Nothing personal! Don't get *personal* in case you have to get involved in a conversation or listen to someone say what's bothering them. It's like living in a parallel dimension. You can see what's going on but you can't make contact. Or, to put it more precisely, other people

don't want to make contact. Sometimes it makes my blood boil just to go through the day being ignored or tolerated and . . .

De'ath   I'm sure that everybody here is listening to what you're saying and is most interested.

Emily   And so they should. I'm a real person with real feelings. Not just a plank of wood.

De'ath   Concrete.

Emily   You're doing it again. Why can't you accept me for what I am and not what you would like me to be?

De'ath   My dear, I couldn't possibly say what I would like you to be. This is a public interview, after all. Although I can't get this picture of a donkey out of my head. Still, never mind! Thank you so much for being with us, Emily er, ah, erm – what's her name?

Emily   That's right!

De'ath   Ah, good. I look forward to seeing you later – a lot later.

TODAY'S SPECIAL

Nice here, ain't it!

Mark 9:2-9: The true glory of Jesus.

Equipment:
pen and two small pieces of card for each member of the group
music and lyrics
a cross

Give every member of the group a pen and piece of card. Ask them to think of some situations or phenomena which they find interesting or intriguing, such as: Why is the earth round? Why do we burp? Why don't cows fly? Why can't you eat loads of ice-cream without feeling sick? Ask each group member to write one question on their card which begins with the word 'why?'

Collect all the question cards and give out another card. On the second card the group should write an answer to their question. Each answer should begin with the word 'because'. Collect all the cards.

Shuffle and distribute all the 'why' cards and all the 'because' cards and ask each member to read their 'why' and 'because' cards, creating nonsense such as: 'Why do we burp? Because we'd explode!'
(Allow 10 minutes for this activity.)

We are all fascinated by strange facts and things that seem weird, wacky or totally unbelievable. Have a listen to 'You never cease to amaze me' by Three Crosses, from the album *Three Crosses*, or take a look at 'How can I not love you?' by Wes Sutton (*The source*, 184).
Have a copy of the lyrics available for discussion.
(Allow approximately 5 minutes.)

Discuss the piece of music. What did the group think of the lyrics? Could they understand what the lyrics were trying to say?

Read Mark 9:2-9.
After a hectic time Jesus decided to take some time out. He invited Peter, James and John to go with him on a ramble up a mountain. The disciples

must have been looking forward to a bit of peace and quiet, a bit of sunbathing and generally relaxing.

The disciples had seen many amazing scenes during the last few weeks, things that were beyond their experience and imagination. Just when they thought they had seen pretty much everything, another amazing experience was about to happen.

Without a word of warning Jesus was changed beyond recognition. The disciples must have struggled to describe the scene later. Firstly they struggled to find words which described the brightness and intensity of the light. Secondly, they had to explain the two other figures who were later identified (presumably by Jesus) as Moses and Elijah. Moses represented God's law while Elijah represented the prophets. Together the Law and the Prophets formed the old contract (or covenant) with humankind (see Luke 16:16). This meeting was God's stamp on a new contract (see Romans 3:21-26).

Peter, James and John were totally astonished at what was happening in front of their eyes. Peter immediately asked if they could build 'shelters' (other translations say 'tents' or 'tabernacles') for Jesus, Moses and Elijah. The idea of setting up shelters was an old tradition of the Jews. In the Old Testament shelters, or tabernacles, were built to live in. A special tabernacle was built as a place where priests and the people could 'meet with God'.

What Peter wanted to do was build special tabernacles to remind them of where they had a spiritual experience or 'met with God'.

Just as they were trying to understand one amazing event, they were given another totally unexpected experience. Suddenly they were covered with a cloud from which a voice said: 'This is my Son, and I love him. Listen to what he says!'

The disciples thought they had experienced an all-time high. But for Jesus this was only the beginning. The disciples were not really aware of 'why' Jesus was to die, or 'because' it was the only way to establish a new contract between God and humankind.

Discuss with the group the idea of the 'why' and 'because' of the crucifixion of Jesus. What on earth was it all about?
(Allow 5 minutes for this task.)

Place a cross in the centre of the room. Ask the group to focus on the cross and think about what they have discussed. After a short time read the following:

Colossians 1:21-22.
You used to be far from God. Your thoughts made you his enemies, and you did evil things. But his Son became a human and died. So God made peace with you, and now he lets you stand in his presence as people who are holy and faultless and innocent.

TODAY'S SPECIAL

Getting wet

Mark 1:9-15: The baptism of Jesus.

Equipment:
large plastic bowl filled with warm water
bar of soap
plastic bag filled with wet mud (or you could use cocoa powder mixed to a paste)

Display the bowl of water on a table at the front of the room. Put your hands into the bag containing mud/cocoa and enthusiastically cover your hands in the mixture. Tell the group that someone told you that covering your hands with this mixture would improve the look of the skin. Once you have covered your hands (keeping the mixture on your hands) go to one of the group and ask them to shake your hand and tell you if your hand feels softer! Ask why they won't touch your hand.

Ask the group if any of them would like the mixture put on their face. Now wash the mixture off! Will anyone shake your hand now?

Ask the group what the problem was with having 'dirty' hands. Why did they feel uncomfortable about touching the mixture? Why did washing your hands make a difference?

(Allow 10 minutes for this activity.)

Suggest to the group that they might like to listen to 'Peace' by Third Day, from the album *Conspiracy No. 5*. Alternatively, look at 'For all that you've done' by Dennis Jernigan (*the source*, 108).

You might like to use a similar piece of music which reflects the same theme. Have a copy of the lyrics available.

(Allow approximately 5 minutes.)

What did the group think the lyrics had to say? Did they make any sense?

Read Mark 1:9-15.
Jesus was around 30 years old at the time of his visit to John the Baptist. Jesus had waited for the right moment to begin what he had been sent to do.

* Firstly, Jesus recognised that the time was right, that the moment had come for him to make that decision to leave the comfort of Nazareth and start his ministry.
* Secondly, Jesus wanted to identify with the message of John the Baptist John was reluctant to baptise Jesus, knowing that Jesus was without sin. But it was important for Jesus to identify with the need for forgiveness of sin. It was also a symbolic act. Jesus was to take on the sins of the world (see John 1:29) which would lead to his death on the cross.
* Thirdly, as soon as Jesus came out of the water, the Holy Spirit came down like a dove. The Holy Spirit was to guide and encourage Jesus for the journey ahead.
* Finally, a voice from heaven said, 'You are my own son.' This was a recognition of Jesus and what he had decided to do. It was a fatherly nod to say, 'Yes, you are mine and I'm really happy with you.' This wasn't a 'pat on the head'. Both God and Jesus knew the way ahead was going to be far from easy but at least Jesus knew that he wouldn't be alone, he had his Father's blessing.

The baptism of Jesus was a 'decision' to go the way that God wanted him to go; it was submitting to his father, accepting the Holy Spirit as encourager and guide for the way ahead and by following this step Jesus was given his Father's blessing.

Baptism is a way of deciding to start a new journey, of turning away from the actions that separate us from God, receiving God's blessing on our lives and having the Holy Spirit as our encourager.

The mud/mixture that was used in the 'Nibbles' section is a way of showing how our past actions (sin) separate us from God. By washing (baptism) we have decided to turn our backs on the actions which got us 'muddy' in the first place and to start all over again (see Romans 6:3-11).

74

Place the bowl of water on the table in front of the group. Invite anyone who would like to come and wash their hands in the water. This is a symbolic way of turning our backs on any actions which we feel put 'distance' between ourselves and God.

While some of the group wash their hands (don't expect all of the group to want to take part in this) read the following prayer:

Father God,
    this water is great
    when we're thirsty, we're hot, we're dirty,
    and when we're showing you
    that we don't want to hang on to anything
    which keeps us away from you.
Not our actions or our inactivity
    nor by giving in to thoughts that suggest
    we look away from you and your love for us.
We wash our hands
    as a symbol of our decision to follow you;
    as a symbol of love for your ways;
    as a symbol of thanks for your Son. Amen.

TODAY'S SPECIAL

This will hurt me more than it hurts you!
Mark 8:31-38: Jesus speaks about his suffering and death.

Equipment:
pen and paper for each member of the group
music and lyrics
small cross

Ask the group to close their eyes for a few moments. While they have their eyes closed describe the following scene. Suggest to the group that it would be good if they can visualise the scene as you speak.

> It's a really cold miserable day. Dark grey clouds cover the sky and a fine mist is swirling around. As you look ahead there is a large bridge across a deep river. A man is standing on the bridge, staring at the sky. Suddenly the man climbs onto the bridge railings. He is having trouble keeping his balance but this doesn't seem to bother him. He seems in danger of falling off the bridge and into the river far below.
>
> Running over to him, not wanting to frighten him in case he falls, you ask him if he needs any help. Before you can say any more he shouts at you to keep away, threatening to jump if you come any closer.

Now ask the group to write on their pieces of paper what they would say to persuade the man to climb down from the bridge to safety. Discuss some of the responses.
(Allow 10 minutes for this activity.)

Sometimes it is difficult to appreciate what other people have done for us. Have a listen to 'Love song' by Third Day, from the album *Third Day*. You might also like to look at 'I know a place' by Randy and Terry Butler (*The source*, 209).
(Allow approximately 5 minutes.)

18

Discuss the lyrics with the group. Were they able to appreciate what the lyrics were trying to say?

Read Mark 8:31-38.
Jesus begins to tell the disciples about suffering, rejection and finally death. But it was only a temporary situation. Jesus explained that three days later he would be alive again.

The disciples had experienced some incredible times and seen Jesus doing amazing things. And then he ruins it by saying it's all coming to an end! What will happen after three days? What will happen to the disciples?

Peter was obviously not impressed. He took Jesus to one side and suggested it wasn't a good idea to talk like that in front of the other disciples. The reason that Jesus got so angry with Peter was that Jesus was being tempted to go in a different direction to the one he knew he should take. Jesus knew that he had to fulfil God's purpose and that a sacrificial death was the only way for humankind to be reconciled with God. Jesus didn't want to be 'talked out' of the way he was meant to take.

The disciples had seen Jesus do some awesome things but even they didn't know the full extent of what Jesus could do. As the Son of God, Jesus could have defeated anything the Romans or religious groups could throw at him.

Jesus was facing similar temptations to those he overcame in the desert. Did he really want to suffer? Did he really want to waste his life? Did he really want to disappoint all those people? Jesus knew that the only way ahead was for him to pay the ultimate price: his death on the cross.

Ask the group to look again at their responses to the man on the bridge.

What emotions would the group have felt about what the man was attempting to do?

- Was it a waste of life?
- Surely things couldn't be that bad?
- What about the people who cared for him?
- What about the future?

These were all emotions that Peter and the disciples would have felt. Were some of the group's responses similar to what Peter might have said? Can the group begin to understand how Peter would have felt and why he wanted Jesus to stop talking like that?

Although we should value life and not 'throw it away', Jesus knew that our eternal lives depended on him being the final sacrifice so that we could become part of God's family once and for all.

Place a small cross in the centre of the room. Suggest to the group that they might like to focus on the cross and think about how Jesus may have felt after Peter had spoken to him. Peter was speaking out of genuine concern for Jesus. Jesus knew this but didn't want to be tempted to ignore what God had asked him to do.

Think about the friendship Jesus had with the disciples and how the news of his suffering and death would hurt the disciples. This knowledge must have made Jesus feel sad. But there was no going back or altering course. The way forward for all of humankind was through the cross.

Allow the group time to reflect and consider. After a short time, close by reading the following:

Colossians 1:19-20.
God himself was pleased to live fully in his Son. And God was pleased for him to make peace by sacrificing his blood on the cross, so that all beings in heaven and on earth would be brought back to God. Amen.

TODAY'S SPECIAL

Causing a bit of a stir!

John 2:13-22: Jesus in the temple.

Equipment:
pen and paper for each group member
large sheet of paper and marker
music and lyrics or drama sketch
wastepaper basket

Ask the group to think about all the things that make them angry – really angry. For instance, someone leaving their dirty socks on the table, or borrowing your toothbrush without asking.

Suggest to the group that they choose one of the things which makes them angry and write it on their piece of paper. Chat about the 'angry-making things', write some of them on the large sheet of paper and display it where everyone can see it. The group should keep their sheet of paper for later.

(Allow 10 minutes for this activity.)

Ask the group to have a listen to 'God's House' by Three Crosses, from the album *Three Crosses*. Alternatively, have a look at 'Our God is an awesome God' by Noel and Tricia Richards (*The source*, 418). Try and have a copy of the lyrics available. Alternatively, use the drama sketch *De'ath meets . . . Arthur Angry* (see page 81).

(Allow approximately 5 minutes.)

Discuss the chosen piece of music. What did the lyrics have to say? What was their meaning?

Read John 2:13-22.

The Passover was an extremely important feast for the Jews. The law stated that every adult male who lived within fifteen miles of Jerusalem must attend the feast.

When the male Jews arrived in Jerusalem and visited the Temple, they were asked to pay a temple tax equal to an average day's wage. This tax was to ensure that the temple rituals were carried out each day. But the tax had to be paid in special Jewish currency. Any other coins were considered 'unclean' and not acceptable. To help the pilgrims offer the 'correct' coins, a group of money changers was available in the temple precincts. The money changers charged the equivalent of one day's wage to exchange the pilgrims' coins; that's the wages for two days paid out already and the feast hasn't even started!

The next stage was to offer a sacrifice at the Temple. This sacrifice was an offering of thanks for a safe journey or some other event in the life of the pilgrim. A pilgrim could take their own animal into the Temple for sacrifice or buy an animal from one of the traders outside the Temple. A small animal would cost the equivalent of one day's wages. But the temple rules stated that a sacrificial animal must be perfect. So, any animal that was brought into the Temple was inspected for a small fee – about a quarter of a day's wages.

It was almost certain that any animal bought outside the Temple would be declared 'impure'. This meant the pilgrim would have to buy one of the 'pure' animals from the stall holders inside the Temple. A small animal which cost a quarter of a day's wages outside the Temple would cost the same as twenty days' wages from a stall holder inside the Temple! So, for a quick trip to the Temple, it has cost approximately twenty-two days' wages. Some feast!

If you were rich, the cost of visiting the Temple was not a major problem. If you were poor it was a *major* problem. No wonder Jesus was so angry about this social injustice. More importantly, most people would see no more of God's house than the market where they got ripped off. What did this say about God? It certainly gave the impression that God could be bought and that having faith in God was like a market place, the best deals on offer to those who could afford it!

Jesus found some rope and made a whip. He then created a real stir by chasing everyone out of the Temple while shouting, 'Don't make my Father's house a market place'.

Jesus was angry because the impression that people got of God was so wrong. The injustice and trading that took place created an unnatural distance between God and his people. It also gave the impression that God and his priests were in the faith business for profit. Jesus knew that before long the greatest sacrifice in history would be made. A sacrifice which was totally 'pure' was to be made at no cost to God's people. He alone was going to bear the cost. Jesus had every right to be angry!

Look at those 'angry' statements which were written and displayed earlier.

- What can the group do to stop the 'angry-making' things getting at them?
- Can they suggest ways which would reduce the possibility of getting angry?
- Are some things just too much trouble?

Ask the group to take the piece of paper on which they have written their 'angry' statement. Without looking at it again, screw the piece of paper up into a ball. Keep hold of the 'ball' for a moment.
(Allow 5 minutes for this task.)

Place a wastepaper basket in the centre of the room. Ask the group to place their paper into the basket. Once this has been done, pray the following prayer:

Lord, if I think too much
    there are so many things
    which make me really, really angry.
So angry that they make my head feel
    crowded, heavy, too full to think.
I can't help looking at everything else
    through angry eyes.
I don't want to feel like this,
    as if my life is one long angry statement.
Lord, take this anger from me,
    help me to do what is right in your eyes.
Help me to look beyond the anger
    and see someone who you love,
    even though they can really get under my skin at times! Amen.

DE'ATH MEETS . . . ARTHUR ANGRY

Characters	De'ath and Arthur Angry
Scene	De'ath, in his smart gear, meets Arthur Angry, who is casually dressed and carrying a large paper bag.
Props	small coffee table water jug and two drinking glasses two comfy chairs large paper bag

De'ath   Delighted to be here once again with all you lovely people. It gives me such a thrill to see you all come here to meet me and my guest. Now, our guest today is someone you may have met at times, some of you may have met him on a very regular basis! It gives me great pleasure – it might not give you the same amount of pleasure though – ladies and gentlemen, Arthur Angry!

Arthur   Hrrumph!

De'ath   Welcome, Arthur. And how are you?

Arthur   Yes!

De'ath   Excuse me – yes?

Arthur   S'right.

De'ath   How are you? Did you have difficulty finding your way here? How's the family?

Arthur   Yes!

De'ath   Is that all you're going to say?

Arthur   Yes!

De'ath	I think we wanted a bit more than a 'yes' to every question. Perhaps you could expand on that a little?
Arthur	No!
De'ath	I see, different word but still just the one?
Arthur	Yes!
De'ath	Come on now. Our audience is eager to hear more about you and what you've been getting up to recently.
Arthur	Yes?
De'ath	For goodness sake! Can't you say more than that?
Arthur	Yes.
De'ath	Then why don't you? Got a problem with your vocal chords, or don't you know more than two or three words?
Arthur	Yes!
De'ath	Well, use them then!
Arthur	Okay.
De'ath	Okay what?
Arthur	Okay.
De'ath	Now look here . . .
Arthur	No! You look here. See this bag? Right! That's my breakfast, that is. How do you think I felt, travelling here on an empty stomach, to be greeted by a sleeping doorman who can't find my name on the guest list and tries to block the doorway to stop me getting in.
De'ath	You're here now.
Arthur	No thanks to your doorman. By the way, he's gone visiting.

De'ath	Visiting? Where?
Arthur	The hospital!
De'ath	You didn't . . . ?
Arthur	I did!
De'ath	Was that necessary?
Arthur	No!
De'ath	Don't start that again!
Arthur	I'll start something in a minute. Just let me get me coat off and I'll show you 'start that again'!
De'ath	I'm so glad you haven't forgotten everything I taught you.
Arthur	You what?
De'ath	It's good to see that you haven't lost the knack of rising to the occasion!
Arthur	You mean you wanted to get me all aggravated?
De'ath	Just my little way of checking to see that you haven't gone soft in your old age.
Arthur	What do you mean, 'old age'? I'll give you 'old age'. Just let me . . .
De'ath	Arthur, Arthur. Calm down. Just for a few minutes anyway. Just kidding, okay?
Arthur	Got me going there you did, good and proper.
De'ath	How is everything these days? Keeping up the traditions, are we?
Arthur	You know me, can't let an opportunity go by without raising the blood pressure.

De'ath	Glad to hear it. Can you see any old friends in the audience?
Arthur	One or two. I'd like to get to know a few more if I can. Anyone like to let their nose greet my fist?
De'ath	Some other time perhaps. Now, any little bits of advice you can share with us?
Arthur	Yes.
De'ath	Oh, not again!
Arthur	Got you!
De'ath	So you did.
Arthur	To answer your question, and using more than three words! I get around quite a lot. You know, making sure that those little insignificant things don't remain that way! Why have a mole hill when, with a bit of effort, you can have a whopping great mountain! Doesn't make sense to me, to waste so little energy on small things when you might as well go all the way and make it worth your while. People don't forget you then.
De'ath	I'm sure they don't. Thank you very much, Arthur Angry. I hope you've enjoyed yourself.
Arthur	Yes!

TODAY'S SPECIAL

God's gift.

John 3:14-21: The love of God.

Equipment:
flipchart or large sheet of paper and marker pen
sheet of paper and pen for every member of the group
music and lyrics

Ask for a volunteer to draw on the flipchart. Ask for another volunteer who is to describe an object for the first volunteer to draw. The object should be something which has curves and straight lines, such as a car, train, telephone.

Ask the first volunteer to stand in front of the flipchart with their back to the rest of the group. The second volunteer should describe the object slowly and give instructions to the first volunteer who will attempt to recreate the object from the verbal directions. The second volunteer must not use any descriptive words which might give the first volunteer a clue as to the object's identity. Instructions must be 'draw a line twenty centimetres long', or 'draw a circle about the size of a dinner plate'. The fun will be seeing the completed object resulting from the instructions. Attempt this activity as many times as you want with different volunteers.

Ask the volunteers what it felt like to place their trust in what they were being told or placing their trust in someone else to carry out their instructions.
(Allow 10 minutes for this activity.)

We have to trust many people in our everyday life. Some people inspire confidence while others make you feel uncomfortable.

Have a listen to 'Here I am' by Paul Oakley, from the album *When deep calls to deep*. Or take a look at 'What a friend I've found' by Martin Smith (*The source*, 565). Try and have a copy of the lyrics available.
(Allow approximately 5 minutes.)

What did the group think about the piece of music? Discuss some of the lyrics. What images did the lyrics portray?

Read John 3:14-21.
Within this reading there is one of the most powerful statements in the whole Bible. The verse in John 3:16 is one of the most quoted and also one of the most well known. The verse contains everything we need to know about God's love for us.

- Firstly, we have the amazing statement that God loved the *world*. This tells us that the character of God is love. He doesn't hold grudges or keep a diary of every dodgy event in our lives. God's love isn't just for a race of people, a nation or even a continent; it's for the whole world.
- Secondly, this love was so desperate to build a relationship with the world that he, God, gave the world a gift. The gift, of God's Son, was the only way this relationship between ourselves and God could happen. God gave that which he loved most, his Son, so that he could restore our relationship with him. Prior to the crucifixion of Jesus, a relationship with God was through priests, sacrifice and rituals. With the death and resurrection of Jesus, access to God is forever available to anyone, anytime, anywhere.
- Finally, this gift doesn't depend on buying a certain number of 'products', as in a supermarket, or taking out a subscription to a magazine, or even joining a club. This gift, and a relationship with the creator, is available to all those who have faith in Jesus Christ.

The word 'faith' is often difficult to understand. The dictionary states that faith is having trust or confidence. God is asking that we place our trust and confidence in Jesus. The Bible gives us plenty of detail about God keeping his word and doing what he promised. If we see an advert for a car giving us details of the model, engine specification, colour and price, when we go to the garage to see the advertised car we expect to see what was promised. God has a far better reputation than any car dealer! We place our trust and confidence in many things in the hope that we will get what was promised. Having faith in Jesus is not just hoping for what is promised, it's guaranteed. (And that's more than you can say for most car dealers!)

Invite the group to think of examples to describe 'faith'. For example, press a switch and the light comes on – or does it? Pick up the telephone, dial a number and we speak to the person we wanted to speak to – or do we? Write all of the ideas onto a flipchart or something similar. Ask the group to give each example a 'confidence rating' from 1-10, 1 being the lowest. Ask the group why it's difficult putting our trust and confidence in things we can't see or completely understand.
(Allow 5 minutes for this task.)

Make sure that the group's examples of faith are displayed where everyone can see them. Usually when we pray or spend some time in reflection we close our eyes. But, for this session, having our eyes open is a symbolic act. The Gospels 'open our eyes' to the good news of God's love. Ask the group to look at the written examples of faith while you read the following:

Romans 1:16-17.
I am proud of the good news! It is God's powerful way of saving all people who have faith, whether they are Jews or Gentiles. The good news tells how God accepts everyone who has faith, but only those who have faith. It is as the scriptures say, 'The people God accepts because of their faith will live'. Amen.

TODAY'S SPECIAL

To die is to live

John 12:20-33: Jesus predicts his death.

Equipment:
sliced loaf
butter and jam
knife and small plate
music and lyrics
penlight torch

Have the loaf, butter and jam on display as the group arrive. Announce to the group that you have recently discovered the delights of eating bread and jam; you can't think of anything better to eat for breakfast, lunch, tea and supper. In fact, so obsessed are you with bread and jam that you have given up all other forms of food. But you have decided that this obsession is possibly a bit too silly. After all, jam every day? You need the group to help you out. Can they suggest some different toppings for the bread?

Make a list of their suggestions. Now tell the group that a thought has just struck you. Given the additives that are put into some bread and the different types of bread (white, wholemeal, granary and so on), you think it might be safer to buy the wheat grain before the farmer has sown it! Can you still serve the grain with the toppings the group suggested?

The group should tell you that the wheat grain has to be planted, has to germinate, grow and be harvested, ground into flour and then baked. Ask them why all this has to take place.
(Allow 10 minutes for this activity.)

Ask the group to listen to 'Satisfied' by Miss Angie, from the album *100 Million eyeballs*. Alternatively, have a look at 'Over the mountains and the sea' by Martin Smith (*The source*, 421). You might like to use a different piece of music with a similar theme. Have a copy of the lyrics available if possible.
(Allow approximately 5 minutes.)

Discuss the piece of music with the group. Did the lyrics help the group think about life and how we can make the most of it?

Read John 12:20-33.

Jesus is speaking in Jerusalem at the time of the Passover (a special Jewish festival). A large crowd had gathered to welcome Jesus into Jerusalem. The crowd had shouted, 'God bless the King of Israel!' Expectations were running high. Miracles had been witnessed, people healed, demons sent packing and the dead raised! Now Jesus declares, 'The time has come for the Son of Man to be given his glory.'

His followers must have given the thumbs up to this statement. About time! Just what we need! We'll show those Romans and those religious snobs in the Temple. You can imagine the scene.

But then, before any of this can really sink in, Jesus tells one of his odd stories. 'I tell you for certain that a grain of wheat that falls on the ground will never be more than one grain unless it dies. But if it dies, it will produce lots of wheat' (John 12:24).

What is this bloke on about? Can you imagine the followers' faces now?

One moment Jesus is talking about being glorified and the next about grains of wheat dying! Jesus was telling his disciples that his mission was to die! He was to die to bring glory to the Father and be the sacrifice for humankind. Through his death would come life for everyone.

But Jesus asks his disciples to follow his example: to die to their old lifestyle and allow a totally new life to emerge. His followers must have thought that this was an impossible concept to grasp. To live you must first die? The grain of wheat was simply a grain of wheat until it was 'buried' in the ground. Only when the grain of wheat had 'died' did it develop its potential to grow and become much more than it was before. Only when this process has taken place does the wheat bring life to other people (by being made into flour and then into bread).

If Jesus had been selfish and refused to suffer and die then we could never have a real relationship with God. Jesus gave his life so that everyone could live to have this relationship with God.

We have a choice, whether to hold on to our lives as they are, or give our lives to God. We have the opportunity to become what God has intended for us or to remain inward looking and keep our eyes on the ground. Just as Jesus was lifted up to die, so we can lift up our eyes to see that through his death we can have life.

We have a choice . . .

Discuss with the group what Jesus means about life and death.

• What makes it difficult for us to give our lives to God?

• What fears do we have?

• How do we know that God wants the best for us?

(Allow 5 minutes for this task.)

If it is possible, make the room dark. Shine a small penlight torch directly on the ceiling above the group. Ask the group to lift their eyes to look at the light. While they do this, read the following prayer:

Jesus, at times it's really difficult,
    really difficult to understand what you mean.
It's even more difficult to do what you say,
    even when we understand.
It's not easy.
I know it's about faith, it's about trust.
Easy to say, but not easy to put into practice.
As I lift my eyes
    allow me to see what you meant
    by dying to live;
    by giving to receive.
Thank you for my choice.
Help me to use my choice,
    rather than ignore it.
You died for me to live.
What more can I say? Amen.

PALM SUNDAY

TODAY'S SPECIAL

Jesus finds a donkey

John 12:12-16: Jesus enters Jerusalem.

Equipment:
flipchart and marker pen
music and lyrics
palm cross
paper and pens

Announce to the group that you are going to a party during the week and you are a bit unsure what to wear. Can the group make any suggestions? Ask the group what they would wear if they were going to a really smart party. Make a list of the types of outfits and accessories. What kind of vehicle would each member of the group like to arrive in at the party? Would they invite the press and photographers to record the event of the year? Which magazines or newspapers would they like to see themselves in?
(Allow 10 minutes for this activity.)

A lot of people make up their minds about who and what we are from the way we look. But things are not always what they seem.

Have a listen to 'The Almighty' by Chris Lizotte, from the album *Big heavy world*. And take a look at 'The happy song' by Martin Smith (*The source*, 200). You can use a different piece of music with a similar theme. Try and have a copy of the lyrics available.
(Allow approximately 5 minutes.)

Discuss the piece of music with the group. What did the lyrics have to say about Jesus and/or God?

Read John 12:12-16.
The Passover Feast was an important part of Jewish culture. At least once in their life each male Jew would try and attend the Feast in Jerusalem. There would have been several hundred thousand people gathered in Jerusalem. The atmosphere would have been one of great expectancy and excitement.

Jesus rode into Jerusalem to be met by a huge crowd of people all shouting and waving palm branches. It must have been an amazing sight!

Immediately before arriving in Jerusalem, Jesus had performed yet another miracle by raising Lazarus from the dead. The chief priests were already plotting how to get rid of Jesus. They were also trying to figure out how to kill Lazarus!

Two main features of the entry into Jerusalem stand out:

Firstly, Jesus rode into Jerusalem as a wanted man. Not wanted as a liberator or saviour by the priests but wanted by them as a criminal. Even the disciples were taken up with the idea that Jesus had at last come to claim his place as King of the Jews. The people greeted Jesus with a cry of 'Hosanna' or 'hooray', which roughly translates as 'please save us'. This was a shout of praise to God but it would have made the chief priests even angrier than before, as it was also a shout acknowledging that Jesus was in some way connected with God; worse, that he was a 'saviour'!

Secondly, Jesus rode into Jerusalem on a donkey! This act fulfils the prophecy from the Old Testament book Zechariah (9:9-10). Zechariah writes that everyone in Jerusalem should celebrate and shout 'your King has won a victory and he is coming to you . . . riding on a donkey' (verse 9). We may not think that riding a donkey gives the impression of a king! In Old Testament times, if a king were going to war, he would ride a horse. But if the king rode a donkey it meant he came in peace. Jesus made a significant statement. He rode into Jerusalem as a king of peace; not to liberate the world by force but by peace.

Even though Jesus knew that he was considered a threat to the chief priests (see verse 19) and that he would die a criminal's death, he rode a donkey to make the most profound statement.

God didn't send his Son into the world to condemn its people but to save them (see John 3:17). The Prince of Peace rode a donkey knowing that he would die a violent death at the hands of soldiers for a crime he didn't commit.

Ask the group to consider the entry of Jesus into Jerusalem. Picture the scene with the excited crowds all waving palm branches and shouting.

- What do they think the disciples and followers of Jesus thought?
- Did they think a major change was about to take place?
- Did they think that Jesus was going to cause a revolt against the Romans?

(Allow 5 minutes for this task.)

Place a palm cross in the centre of the room. Give each member of the group a piece of paper and a pen. Ask them to write on the piece of paper an issue or situation that is causing trouble or giving them concern. The issue or situation may or may not involve the group member directly. When each member has written an issue or situation which they are concerned about, ask them to fold the paper and place it by the palm cross. When everyone has placed their piece of paper by the cross, read the following prayer:

Lord, trouble seems to have a habit of getting under my skin.
It itches and aggravates,
    and the more I scratch it, the more it itches.
How does trouble find me?
I certainly don't go looking for it,
    it seems to find me wherever I am.
It's not always my fault,
    well, sometimes maybe, but not every time!
Please help me to see things your way,
    because my way sometimes misses the point
    or makes the trouble worse!
I need to see things your way,
    because I have the knack
    of sometimes missing the obvious
    or making up my mind
    without knowing all the facts.
You seemed to know what you were doing
    on the way into Jerusalem.
Even though others thought it odd
    that a king should ride a donkey.
But you had other thoughts in mind,
    beyond what could be imagined
    by your closest friends.
Prince of Peace, take my troubles
    and bring your peace instead. Amen.

TODAY'S SPECIAL

Wipe away the tears

John 20:1-18: Jesus is alive.

Equipment:
large sheet of paper
broad-tip felt pen
music and lyrics
small piece of paper and pen for each group member

Write the words 'LOVE IS . . .' on the sheet of paper. Ask the group to think about some definitions of love. For example: love is . . . kind. Write all the group's ideas on the paper. Don't ignore any of the ideas even though they may be a bit flippant.

    Discuss some of the group's definitions. Can the definitions be put into categories, such as boy/girl relationships, brother/sister, parent/son/daughter, friend/friend, stranger/stranger? What does this tell us about our understanding of the word 'love'?
(Allow 10 minutes for this activity.)

We have many ideas about what love is and how we can find love. Love is often seen as a form of giving.

Have a listen to 'The stone was rolled away' by Three Crosses, from the album *Jefferson Street*. You might also like to take a look at 'Because of your love' by Russell Fragar (*The source*, 39). You might like to use a different piece of music with a similar theme. Have a copy of the lyrics available.
(Allow approximately 5 minutes.)

Discuss the piece of music with the group. What did the group think about the lyrics? Did the lyrics offer any other definitions of love?

Read John 20:1-18.
After the reading the first question might be: What's love got to do with it? The popular way to consider this passage from the Bible is to think about the stone being rolled away from the tomb.

    The common way to cover a tomb in those times was to cut a large groove in front of the tomb opening and wheel a large circular stone along the groove to close the tomb entrance. The authorities had taken the further precaution of 'sealing' the large circular stone on Jesus' tomb to try and make sure no one could get in.

None of Jesus' friends could visit the tomb on the Sabbath (our Saturday); to do so would break the Jewish law.

Mary Magdalene gets up as early as she can, before 6am, and goes to the tomb of Jesus. Once there she finds the stone rolled away and the tomb appears empty. Mary immediately runs and tells Peter and John that someone has taken Jesus from the tomb.

A while later, Mary is standing by the tomb alone, weeping. Mary has followed Jesus ever since he set her free from evil spirits. Mary is distraught. Not only have the authorities killed Jesus, either someone has robbed the grave or the authorities have taken his body away to avoid any further problems with the followers of Jesus.

Inside the tomb are two angels who ask Mary why she is crying. Mary's response is extremely personal: 'They have taken *my* Lord (not *our* Lord). And *I* (not *we*) don't know where they have put him.'

Immediately Mary senses someone is behind her and she turns around. Mary is standing by the tomb entrance and looks into what little light there is available at that time of the morning. Through her tears and the dull light she can make out the shape of a man who she assumes is the gardener. It isn't until Jesus speaks her name that the light of recognition dawns. The person who she thought lost is now in front of her! She is overwhelmed. But Jesus comforts her and reassures her that he isn't going anywhere straight away so there is no need to 'hold on' to him; he isn't going to the Father straight away.

Mary, although very sad, was able to recognise the voice of the Lord she loved so much. Even though all the evidence seemed to underline her grief, her love enabled her to hear Jesus speak. Mary was able to 'see' through her tears, her grief, her fear and hear the voice of Jesus speaking her name with love.

Is our relationship with Jesus one which allows us to 'see' through all the garbage and hear what he has to say to us?

Ask the group to look again at their definitions of love.
• Can they now add any new definitions?
• How can we, or do we, express our love?

Discuss with the group ways in which we express our feelings.
(Allow 5 minutes for this task.)

Place the sheet of paper with the definitions of love onto the floor by the group. Give each member of the group a small piece of paper and a pen. Ask the group to be quiet and reflect on some of the definitions and also to consider Mary Magdalene and her expression of love.

Suggest that the each member of the group might like to write on the piece of paper something which is a problem to them in their relationship with Jesus.

Perhaps it is

• fear of the future

• feeling insecure

• does God exist?

Invite those who have written something on the paper to fold it up and place it onto the large sheet of paper on the words 'Love is . . .'.

While the group is quiet, read Psalm 16:1, 2, 5-8.

Protect me, Lord God!
I run to you for safety, and I have said,
'Only you are my Lord!
Every good thing I have is a gift from you.'
You, Lord, are all I want!
You are my choice, and you keep me safe.
You make my life pleasant, and my future is bright.
I praise you, Lord, for being my guide.
Even in the darkest night
    your teachings fill my mind.
I will always look to you,
    as you stand beside me and protect me from fear.

THE SECOND SUNDAY OF EASTER

TODAY'S SPECIAL

How did you get here?
John 20:19-31: Jesus appears to his disciples.

Equipment:
sheet of paper and a pen for each member of the group
music and lyrics or drama sketch

Ask each group member to write three statements about themselves on the piece of paper. Suggest that they make one statement true, one statement totally over the top and one statement believable, but not absolutely true (not necessarily in that order).

Ask each member of the group to read their 'statements'. Can the rest of the group decide which is true, which over the top and which is almost true?

If the group guess the 'almost true' statement, what made them doubt the truth of the statement? Was it a lucky guess or did something make them question the statement?
(Allow 10 minutes for this activity.)

Try having a listen to 'Something must be happening' by Fono, from the album *Goes around comes around*. Or take a look at 'I sing a simple song of love' by Craig Musseau (*The source*, 239). You might like to use a different piece of music with a similar theme. Have a copy of the lyrics available if possible. Alternatively, you might like to use the drama sketch *De'ath meets . . . Doug Doubt* (see page 100).
(Allow approximately 5 minutes.)

Discuss the piece of music. What did the lyrics have to say about truth and doubt? Or, if you have used the drama sketch, what was Doug Doubt all about?

Read John 20:19-31.
Thomas the Twin is often referred to as 'Doubting Thomas'. The term is more often than not used more as an insult than a compliment. But Thomas had already shown a willingness to follow his faith in Jesus by his actions (see John 11:16). Thomas was willing to give everything for

his belief in Jesus. So his 'doubt' was not so much to do with unbelief as with his inability to understand what had happened.

Thomas wasn't with the other disciples when Jesus appeared. All that Thomas knew was that Jesus had been crucified, the body of Jesus had 'disappeared' (had the authorities taken it?) and the disciples were afraid of what the Jewish leaders might do to them! It isn't clear why Thomas was not with the other disciples. He may have been on an errand or maybe he just wanted to be on his own for a while after all the events of the previous days. Thomas may have questioned in his own mind those events and how they affected what he believed. Knowing that the person you had seen raise people from the dead was now dead himself would cause doubts in anybody's faith!

The news that Jesus had appeared to the disciples was not enough for Thomas. He may have thought that they had all drunk too much wine or it was the result of a bit of wishful thinking. His doubts needed more than a second-hand account of something that might have happened.

A whole week went by during which Thomas must have thought 'I told you so!' But Jesus has a way of getting to the point and he made sure Thomas was around when he next dropped in on the disciples. This time Thomas need not rely on a second-hand story or gossip. He could have said, 'Nice stunt, Peter! Who's the actor?' But the facts were there before his eyes. His doubts vanished when he saw the risen Jesus. He could have then mumbled an apology and crept to the back of the room. His response was incredible: 'You are my Lord and my God.' No one else is recorded in the Gospel as acknowledging Jesus in this way. Thomas was honest about his doubts. He didn't pretend or keep his thoughts to himself. Instead he chose to face his questions and doubts. When he was faced with the truth he went all the way and left no one in any doubt about who he thought Jesus was.

Can we be as honest as Thomas about our doubts? Are we able to stand out from the crowd and admit we are not sure about something?

Give each member of the group a piece of paper and pen. Ask them to write on the paper any doubts they may have about Jesus. Collect all the pieces of paper and read some of the 'doubts' out to the whole group.

- Does anyone else have similar doubts?

- Has anyone had a similar doubt but had an experience which cleared the doubt?

- Are there any doubts which no one has an answer or experience for?

(Allow 5 minutes for this task.)

Place all the 'paper doubts' on a Bible. Suggest that the group may like to be quiet and think about a personal doubt or some doubts that have been discussed. While everyone is quiet read the following prayer:

Lord, I don't understand philosophy,
    I can't get my head around psychology,
    and theology leaves me cold.
I'm not trying to make trouble,
    or cause anyone a problem.
I just want to be honest,
    well, as honest as I can be.
Don't get me wrong,
    I'm not saying I know it all,
    I'm glad I don't,
    know it all, I mean.
I want my faith to be real,
    not based on some second-hand account,
    or a set of rules which make me choke.
If I'm going to believe in you,
    properly, not some Sunday saint,
    or weekday wonder,
    but real, like a proper relationship
    between two hearts,
    then help me see the truth
    of who you are,
    and what you mean to me. Amen.

DE'ATH MEETS . . . DOUG DOUBT

Characters	De'ath and Doug Doubt
Scene	De'ath, dressed smartly and confidently, and Doug, with belt, braces and a piece of string to hold his trousers up, seated at a coffee table.
Props	coffee table
	two easy chairs
	jug of water and two glasses

De'ath   Hello and welcome to yet another of my chat shows where we get to know some of our friends a little better. I take great delight in reminding you of these friends who go to extreme lengths to make sure that your life is, how should I say, a bit interesting? And now, without any further delay, would you please welcome Doug Doubt!

Doug   Thank you, I appreciate your show of appreciation.

De'ath   Now Doug, your name doesn't leave us in any doubt (ha ha) as to what you're all about!

Doug   I'm glad to see you haven't lost your knack of making a pun out of anything. You're such a laugh, you kill me!

De'ath   Give me time, give me time!

Doug   Stop it, you'll give yourself a bad reputation.

De'ath   Flattery will get you everywhere, Doug!

Doug   Are you sure?

De'ath   Now, that brings me very nicely to the point of our little chat. Do you live up to your name?

Doug   It's not a case of living up to it. More of a case of *being* it, if you see what I mean.

De'ath	Explain yourself.
Doug	Well, I do like to put things into perspective.
De'ath	How do you mean?
Doug	Well, you shouldn't really take everything for granted.
De'ath	Like what, for instance?
Doug	Life!
De'ath	Life? How do you mean?
Doug	It's all very well getting up in the morning, but is everything as it should be?
De'ath	You mean two of everything on the outside and one of everything down the middle?
Doug	Steady, this is a family show don't forget!
De'ath	How could I forget? I just like to add a little bit of interest, stretch the limits, push the boundaries.
Doug	As I was saying, is everything as it should be? It's not what's on the outside but what's on the inside that counts.
De'ath	Now you go steady! You're beginning to sound like someone I'd rather not mention. This is a family show don't forget!
Doug	Are you referring to . . .
De'ath	Don't you dare mention that name!
Doug	Surely you're not frightened of a little bit of competition?
De'ath	You call that fair competition?
Doug	I'm sure that the Big G isn't worried.
De'ath	Can we move on before the audience think they've come to the wrong show?

Doug	What I'm trying to say is that we shouldn't expect things to remain the same.
De'ath	Surely nothing really changes?
Doug	Oh but it should. That's my point.
De'ath	I'm sorry, but I think that something has got lost in the translation.
Doug	Let me put it simply.
De'ath	I wish you would.
Doug	Imagine a world where everything is the same. Everybody knows where they are going and why.
De'ath	Sounds an awful place!
Doug	Precisely. Now, if everything was so predictable and unexciting, we'd soon get bored.
De'ath	There would be no challenge.
Doug	That's where you're wrong. You see, if we got up every morning confident that everything was the same as the day before and everything was okay, would it be worth getting up at all?
De'ath	It all depends . . .
Doug	You've got it! It all depends on what's going to happen or not.
De'ath	Or not what?
Doug	Well, how do you know that something hasn't begun to go seriously wrong with your insides during the night?
De'ath	I have that feeling on a regular basis. Especially after a Tandoori goat with fried squid.
Doug	Serves you right! But my point is, how can you expect things

to be okay? How do you know that you can rely on your body to function properly? How do you know that you can rely on your friends to do what they've promised? How do you know your trousers won't fall down in public? *(indicates belt, braces and string)*

De'ath   Yes, how?

Doug   You can't. That's the whole point!

De'ath   What, that you can't rely on anything?

Doug   Nothing!

De'ath   Sounds a bit frightening.

Doug   That's what's so exciting. That's what adds a bit of spice to life.

De'ath   I think last night's snake Balti had a bit too much spice. Would you excuse me while I go for a repeat performance of last night . . . ?
(De'ath rushes to the door, clutching his stomach.)

TODAY'S SPECIAL

A funny thing happened on the way to the Temple!

Acts 3:12-19: Peter speaks in the Temple.

Equipment:
pen and paper for each group member
music and lyrics

Tell the group it's now time for them to use a little bit of their imagination. (If they haven't got any, tell them to go home immediately and get it from under the bed or to try the delicatessen counter at the local supermarket!)

Ask the group to write on the piece of paper one thing that they would like to achieve in the next twenty years. (Any comments about still breathing or avoiding becoming a fossil should be ignored, or better still, display an 'Old is Beautiful' banner!)

Ask the group if they can think of anyone who has had a major achievement during the last couple of years. They might refer to a sports personality or musician, or someone they know who has achieved a long term ambition.

(Allow 10 minutes for this activity.)

We may have great ambitions or ideas for the future, but to help us achieve anything we need the support and love of people really close to us.

Have a listen to 'All I really need is you' by Late, Late Service, from the album *Dry bones dancing*. Alternatively, take a look at 'Don't let my love grow cold' by Brian Doerksen (*The source*, 81). You might like to use a different piece of music with a similar theme. Try and have a copy of the lyrics available.

(Allow approximately 5 minutes.)

Discuss the song with the group. Did the lyrics have anything to say about faith?

Read Acts 3:12-19.
A large crowd had gathered in Solomon's Porch as a result of the crippled man being healed. The crippled man, who would have had to be carried to his begging place, had chosen a spot to beg where people on their way to pray could hardly ignore him. The cripple would have considered

a good day to be one where he took home a pocketfull of money. This day was different. In his wildest dreams he couldn't have imagined that the best tip he would get was to be told to get up and walk!

The people at the Temple knew the beggar and were familiar with seeing him begging at the 'Beautiful Gate'. It's no wonder that a crowd gathered to see what had happened to the crippled man . . . Peter's first words were, 'Why are you surprised . . . ?' Who wouldn't be surprised to see a well-known cripple suddenly walking and leaping around like a young child! Immediately Peter made sure that the crowd understood that the power to heal the cripple was not from the disciples but from the person whom they had rejected and had killed (see verses 14-15). Peter wasn't exactly the best person to start accusing others of rejection, was he? But Peter knew the love and forgiveness of Jesus. He also knew that faith in Jesus made dreams come true. Peter knew that no matter how useless he felt, how guilty or weak, Jesus was greater than all of these things. The crowd were told that no matter what had gone before all they had to do was turn to God and ask him to forgive them.

The crippled man was healed because he put his faith in Jesus. What had he got to lose apart from a generous tip? Whatever our dreams or ambitions, the most important thing is that we have placed our trust in Jesus; he is the fulfilment of our dreams. Providing that we put our relationship with Jesus as our number one priority, then we can forget all the fears and doubts and get on with life.

Ask the group to look again at what they put down as the one thing they wanted to achieve.

- What do they think they need to achieve this ambition?
- What qualities or skills will they need to learn before they can realise their ambition?
- Do they need to have faith in their own abilities?
- Do they need to be determined to succeed?

Suggest to the group that faith in our own abilities is essential if we want to succeed at something. Although problems, doubts or fears can weaken our faith in ourselves, we should be confident of our faith in Jesus who likes to do the most extraordinary things with ordinary people.

Ask the group to fold their piece of paper and to place it in their hands. Ask them to put their hands out in front of them, if they would like to, while you read the following Bible verse:

Psalm 145:13-16.
Our Lord, you keep your word
    and do everything you say.
When someone stumbles or falls,
    you give a helping hand.
Everyone depends on you, and when the time is right,
    you provide them with food.
By your own hand
    you satisfy the desires of all who live. Amen.

THE FOURTH SUNDAY OF EASTER

26

TODAY'S SPECIAL

By whose authority?

Acts 4:5-12: Peter and John are brought in front of the council.

Equipment:
pack of playing cards
perhaps some 'task' cards (see under Nibbles)
music and lyrics
large sheet of paper and pen

Deal one card, face down, to each member of the group. Ask them to look at their card. The person with the highest card (ace equals high) is asked to think of a task or errand which they would like to see carried out. The task or errand can be as wacky as they want it to be. Then the person with the lowest card is told that they have to carry out the task or errand at the end of the session. Alternatively, you could have some tasks already written on pieces of card. The tasks can be quite simple and carried out straight away, such as:

- do twenty press-ups with your nose

- sing a nursery rhyme backwards

- divide 1,000,000 by 14

The person with the lowest card simply takes, at random, one of the task cards. You can repeat this game as often as you want.

Ask the group what they thought about being asked to do wacky tasks. Did any of the group do them? If so, why? Have a brief discussion about the idea of authority. Who said the tasks had to be done? What would have happened if someone had refused to do a task?
(Allow 10 minutes for this activity.)

Are we confident in everything we do? Is confidence simply knowing how to do something or is it not letting on to anyone that we don't know how to do something?

Have a listen to 'Emotional' by Kosmos Express from the album *Simulcast*. You might also like to look at 'I need you more' by Lindell Cooley and Bruce Haynes (*The source*, 226). You might like to use a different piece of music which reflects the same theme. Try and have a copy of the lyrics available.
(Allow approximately 5 minutes.)

Have a chat about the piece of music. What did the lyrics have to say?

Read Acts 4:5-12.

Peter and John had just spent the night in prison. Room service was well below normal high standards and, feeling in need of at least a quick wash and brush-up, Peter and John were brought before the Jewish leaders. Rather than ask the two men if they'd had a good night and did they enjoy breakfast, the leaders immediately wanted to know: 'By what power and in whose name have you done this?' The leaders were referring to the cripple who had been healed the day before. They were basically asking, 'Who gave you the authority to do this?'

In the Jewish religion there was no higher power on earth than that of the high priest, Annas, who was present at the questioning. The Jewish leaders were well aware of who Peter and John were and with whom they had been associating for the past few years (Jesus). The leaders had, or so they thought, successfully dealt with one threat to their authority (by the crucifixion), but were now facing another threat.

Peter did not respond by putting the Jewish leaders down and asking by whose authority they had arrested and questioned himself and John; instead he told them that they were referring to a 'kind deed'. The leaders may have thought that everything was going quite smoothly, and there didn't appear to be any threat to them, when Peter quickly made his next point. He reminded the Jewish leaders that the cripple had been healed because of the power of Jesus Christ of Nazareth. (Now for the crucial point): 'You put Jesus to death on a cross but God over-ruled you and brought Jesus back to life!'

By this time a few faces would have been getting a bit red and angry. Peter didn't leave it there: he went on to tell the leaders that the person they thought so unimportant was, in fact, the most important person they were ever likely to meet! And not only that, 'Only Jesus has the power to save!' Peter was making the point that religion is nothing more than a set of beliefs and rules and can't save anyone from illness, decay or evil. This was a direct reference to authority. Peter was underlining the point that the healing of the cripple was not the result of an earthly power but was done by the authority of God!

Peter and John were not well educated or practised speakers. They were two humans who had placed their trust in Jesus. They were confident of God's love and his power to heal. That was all the authority they wanted. Have we the same kind of confidence?

Ask the group to think of a definition for authority.

- What is authority?
- How do we get it?
- Do we need it?
- Is authority a positive thing to have or negative?

It might be a good idea to write some of the group's ideas on a large sheet of paper headed 'Authority'. Display the paper on the wall.
(Allow 5 minutes for this task.)

Make sure the whole group can see the word 'Authority' and their definitions. Suggest to the group that they should consider authority and what it means while you read the following Psalm:

Psalm 100.
Shout praises to the Lord, everyone on this earth.
Be joyful and sing as you come to worship the Lord!
You know the Lord is God!
He created us, and we belong to him;
    we are his people, the sheep of his pasture.
Be thankful and praise the Lord
    as you enter his temple.
The Lord is good!
His love and faithfulness will last forever.

THE FIFTH SUNDAY OF EASTER 27

TODAY'S SPECIAL

How can I understand?
Acts 8:26-40: Philip and an Ethiopian official.

Equipment:
pen and paper for each member of the group
a selection of chocolate bar wrappers
large piece of paper with Spanish words on

Have the chocolate bars on display in front of the group. Select one of the bars and hold it up to the group. Ask them to write down all the ingredients that are in the bar. The person with the list of ingredients which most closely matches those written on the wrapper can have the bar to eat. Repeat this for each bar that you have.

When you have finished, ask the group what they found difficult about listing the ingredients. Ask them how many of the bars they eat each day/week/month. If they eat the chocolate bars on a regular basis, why don't they know all of the ingredients?
(Allow 10 minutes for this activity.)

You will need a large piece of paper on which you have previously written the following: *Si senor, dar diego, tirty lores inaro. Fulof geesan duckanhens.*

Ask if any of the group can understand Spanish or Portuguese. Show them the piece of paper with the writing. Can any of the group help you translate the writing?

Let the group have a couple of minutes attempting to translate the writing. Ask them what is difficult in translating the writing. Look at the group in disbelief and tell them that you are surprised that they cannot understand the writing, it's simple! Then read out aloud to them: 'See senor, there they go, thirty lorries in a row. Full of geese and ducks and hens!'
(Allow approximately 5 minutes for this activity.)

Read Acts 8:26-40.

Why did the Ethiopian official have difficulty in understanding the reading from Isaiah? Was it because he wasn't a Jew? Was it because he was Ethiopian?

The Ethiopian official had travelled from a remote region (quite possibly from an area that we now know as Sudan). He had gone to Jerusalem to worship and was on his way back home. To help pass the time, he was reading aloud from the book of Isaiah. It was very common at that time to read aloud, whether you were with a group of people or on your own. The official was reading but did not understand to whom or what the words were referring. It is important to note that the official was firstly a very important person in his own country. Secondly, his desire to go to Jerusalem gives an indication that he was sincere about his belief in God and was familiar with parts of the scriptures and had read and heard them many times.

Philip caught up with the Ethiopian and asked him whether he understood what he was reading. Philip could not consider himself an equal to this important Ethiopian but this did not stop him from explaining that the reading in Isaiah (chapter 53:7-8) was all about Jesus. Philip was able to tell the official about the teaching, miracles and finally the crucifixion of Jesus. For the first time the official understood the scripture and what it meant to him personally. As soon as they reached a suitable place with enough water to be baptised in, the Ethiopian followed the teaching of Jesus and accepted him as his Lord.

The Ethiopian, important as he was in his own country, was not too proud to ask a question. It didn't matter that Philip was not his social equal. Philip was able to explain what the Ethiopian hadn't been able to understand. What would have happened if the Ethiopian had not asked Philip to explain the scripture? What would have happened if Philip had not obeyed God?

Give each member of the group a piece of paper and a pen. Ask them to think for a short while and then write on the paper any questions that they might have about God, Jesus, the Bible or any other issue that concerns them.

If the group feels comfortable about having the questions read aloud then read some of the questions, at random, to the group. Can any of the group respond to the question? It doesn't matter if they haven't got an answer, they may even have another question based upon the first!

Between the group and yourself, you might be able to give some response to the questions.

If you cannot help straightaway, it doesn't matter. Suggest to the group that they could try and find a response during the next week or so; or they might like to talk to someone on a one-to-one basis.
(Allow 5 minutes for this task.)

Place all of the questions on a table in the middle of the room. Ask the group to be quiet while you read the following prayer:

Lord, I have a question for you,
    in fact I've got more questions than a quiz book!
But with a quiz book, the answers are in the back.
I've looked in the Bible but I can't find the answers at the back!
Have you got any ideas?
Better still, have you got any answers?
Lord, I don't want to be afraid to ask,
    you know, all those awkward questions,
    the ones that you know everybody else wants to ask,
    and everybody is waiting for someone else to ask them.
Don't let anyone put me down,
    just because I've got more questions than answers.
Don't let anyone put me down,
    just because I've dared to open my mouth.
Don't let anyone put me down,
    just because I've asked something they've wanted to know
    for ages but didn't dare ask.
Lord, I know you love me for who I am,
    and not for what I know.
I may not know the answer to everything,
    but I've put my trust
    in someone who not only has the answers,
    but someone who created the questions too! Amen.

TODAY'S SPECIAL

What's going on here?
Acts 10:44-48: The Holy Spirit.

Equipment:
approximately twenty balloons of assorted colours
music and lyrics

Take four to six of the balloons and blow them up. Do not explain to the group what you are doing; they will think you've finally lost it!

When you have finished blowing up the balloons, place them safely in a corner of the room. Do not refer to the balloons again until later.

Ask the group what they think about situations where people have been discriminated against because of their social class, income, dress, religion, education, speech, beliefs or race.

- Why do the group think that some people discriminate against others?

- Do those who discriminate have a reason for their behaviour?

- Are they justified in doing what they do?

(Allow 10 minutes for this activity.)

There are many things which we don't understand or have answers for. Thankfully, we are not alone when situations prove too difficult for us to get our head around.

Listen to 'Holy Spirit' by Third Day, from the album *Third Day*, or have a look at 'Holy Spirit, come' by Geoff Bullock (*The source*, 180). Try and have a copy of the lyrics available.
(Allow approximately 5 minutes.)

What did the group think about the piece of music? Did the lyrics make a point or touch on anything in particular?

Read Acts 10:44-48.
Ask the group what they think the verses mean. Suggest to them that they look particularly at verse 45.

During his teaching and healing Jesus never discriminated against anybody. He didn't make all those who wanted to be healed form an orderly queue while he chose those he wanted to heal and those he didn't want to heal! Jesus spent time with people who were often discriminated against and whom the rest of society had rejected. He didn't turn his back or walk on the other side of the road to avoid 'undesirable' people. He often spent time talking to people whom most religious leaders and followers ignored. The Jewish followers were astonished when God ignored religious rules and regulations. By giving the Gentiles the gift of the Holy Spirit, God made it impossible for the Jewish leaders to refuse the Gentiles baptism (see Acts 11:18).

If God, the Creator, refuses to be selective in his dealings with people, what excuses can we have? Throughout his time on earth Jesus didn't seem at all bothered by class, wealth, social position or status. Considering who he was, he was very unselective when it came to choosing friends! What arguments can we give for being selective about who we talk to, who we spend time with or help?

Jesus was concerned that all people should understand that their relationship with God was the most important thing (see John 16:4-15). We also need to be aware of our relationship with God and must always be aware of how much God cares for other people.

Collect the balloons which you blew up earlier. Explain that the balloons represent different people. Each 'balloon' is filled with air, which represents the Holy Spirit. Everybody has the potential to be filled with the Holy Spirit. Jesus made it clear that the Holy Spirit would help us appreciate the truth; that being right with God comes only through accepting Jesus as the Son of God, and that the Holy Spirit would speak to us what Jesus wants us to hear. Take some of the 'empty' balloons and breathe 'life' into them.
(Allow 5 minutes for this task.)

Ask the group to think about ways that they may have been 'selective' in their behaviour towards other people. While they are thinking read the following prayer:

Lord, sorry!
I don't have to list all the things I'm sorry for,
   do I?
I'm just sorry, okay?
I'm not proud of my behaviour,
   or the way I speak, or don't speak!
It's not easy, you know,
   going out of my way to pass the time of day
   with people I'd rather not know;
   or stopping to help people who wouldn't stop for me.
How can I spend time with people
   who don't like the same things as me?
Who don't watch the same TV programmes?
Who don't dress as they should?
Who don't listen to the music that's good for their ears?
What's that you're saying?
Sorry, I can't quite hear you,
   I think I've got selective hearing.
Speak up, Lord,
   what's that . . . you love me?
Thanks, I really appreciate that.
Pardon? Could you repeat that?
Love who?
Oh! Sorry! Amen.

TODAY'S SPECIAL   **Eeny, meeny, miny, mo!**
Acts 1:15-17, 21-26: Someone to take the place of Judas.

Equipment:
10-12 postcards
music and lyrics or drama sketch

Take two of the postcards and on one write 'NO' and on the other write 'YES'. On the remaining postcards write the following questions, or create your own.

1. Should I paint my toe nails bright green?

2. Should I give all my money to charity?

3. Should I shave my head?

4. Should I wear purple lipstick?

5. Should I have my belly button pierced?

6. Should I wash my face with baked beans?

7. Should I wear a pair of blue fluffy slippers?

8. Should I wear a dress next week?

Take the question cards and place them face down in front of you. Shuffle them around and then invite one of the group to choose a card. Take the two other cards with 'No' and 'Yes' written on them. Place them both face down in front of the volunteer. Ask the volunteer to close their eyes while you shuffle the two cards around. When you are ready, ask the volunteer to pick one of the cards using the 'eeny, meeny, miny, mo' method. Ask the volunteer to turn over the card they have chosen to see what their answer will be!

   Repeat the process until all your question cards are used up. The results should be good for a laugh!
(Allow 10 minutes for this activity.)

Ask the group to have a listen to 'Feel like I could fly' by Paul Oakley, from the album *Deep calls to deep*. Alternatively, have a look at 'There's a wind a-blowing' by David Ruis (*The source*, 501). You might like to use another piece of music with a similar theme. Try and have a copy of the lyrics available. If preferred, use the drama sketch *De'ath meets . . . Charlie Chance* (see page 119).
(Allow approximately 5 minutes.)

Discuss the piece of music with the group. What did they think of the lyrics? What were the lyrics trying to say?

If you used the drama sketch, what did the group think about what Charlie Chance had to say?

Read Acts 1:15-17, 21-26.

The number of followers meeting together (about 120) is quite important in Jewish terms. This is the smallest number of people required for a 'council' to be formed. The traditional role of a council was to comment on problems and offer solutions for a 'population' of people. The council was made up of one councillor for every ten members of the 'population', so for 120 followers, a council of twelve would be formed. With the death of Judas another council member was needed to make up the twelve required councillors.

The followers, having carefully considered the qualities needed by someone who was to help tell others about Jesus, selected two men: Justus and Matthias. Then everyone prayed and asked God to show them which of the two men should be chosen. The followers then drew names to see who would be chosen. The use of drawing names was not a new idea amongst the Jewish people who regarded it as a way of making decisions which were always subject to God (see Proverbs 16:33).

The selection process between the two men happened just before God gave all the followers the gift of the Holy Spirit, who Jesus had said would show them what is true (John 16:13). The followers had used a three-stage process to choose who should be the twelfth person. Firstly, they considered carefully the qualities needed by such a person. Secondly, they prayed and submitted the whole thing to God and then they chose one of the two men by taking a name 'out of the hat'.

- Do we carefully consider all the issues and points before we make a decision?
- Do we then pray and give the whole thing over to God?
- Do we then wait for the Holy Spirit to show us the truth about the situation, or about the decision that we want to make?

Ask the group to talk about the kind of decisions that they have to make. Suggest to everyone that they might like to make a list of some of the decisions that they have made or want to make.

- Are some decisions too insignificant to ask God about?
- Do we only consult God when we can't make up our own minds?
- Is God interested in what we want to do and how we think?

(Allow 5 minutes for this task.)

Ask the group to look at the list of decisions that they have made or want to make. Suggest to the group that they might like to chat to God about some of these decisions while everyone is quiet. After a short time, read Psalm 23.

> You, Lord, are my shepherd.
> I will never be in need.
> You let me rest in fields of green grass.
> You lead me to streams of peaceful water,
>   and you refresh my life.
> You are true to your name,
>   and you lead me along the right paths.
> I may walk through the valleys as dark as death,
>   but I won't be afraid.
> You are with me,
>   and your shepherd's rod makes me feel safe.
> You treat me to a feast, while my enemies watch.
> You honour me as your guest,
>   and you fill my cup until it overflows.
> Your kindness and love will always be with me each day of my life,
>   and I will live for ever in your house, Lord.

DE'ATH MEETS . . . CHARLIE CHANCE

Characters	De'ath and Charlie Chance
Scene	De'ath, dressed in his finest flat cap, winter jacket and scarf. Charlie Chance, dressed in loud suit, cravat and wellingtons.
Props	coffee table jug of water and two glasses pair of binoculars sports pages from a daily newspaper on the table two comfy chairs

De'ath Welcome again to another opportunity to listen and learn from the master of the unspoken, your ever-youthful host, Mr Modesty himself. Ladies and gentlemen, I give you myself. And (as a special treat, but not as special as time spent with me) I would like to introduce a good friend of mine. He is the best bookie in the business. He has relieved many people of the burden of carrying around far too much money. At great cost to himself he has even been known to part with a little money at times. May I introduce Charlie Chance.

Charlie Thank you very much. But not so much about the parting with money bit, alright?

De'ath I do apologise, Charlie. It's comforting to know that we all have our little weaknesses.

Charlie You're looking very flash today.

De'ath Thank you. I've just returned from the greyhound track.

Charlie Felt lucky, did we?

De'ath Not as lucky as some of your colleagues, Charlie!

Charlie Well, you win some and you lose some.

De'ath	But not in equal proportions!
Charlie	You wouldn't want to see me a poor man, would you?
De'ath	Oh, I wouldn't like to see one of my favourite characters suffer. Just remember who gave you a start in life.
Charlie	How could I forget such an excellent teacher as yourself? If it wasn't for you there would be far too many people with more money than they know what to do with!
De'ath	How would you describe yourself to somebody who hadn't met you before?
Charlie	As a social worker!
De'ath	I'm not sure many of those who already know you would describe you as a social worker!
Charlie	I'm an unsung hero really! It doesn't do to tell everyone about my acts of human kindness.
De'ath	Modesty has always been your strong point!
Charlie	If everyone knew about my activities they might think of me in the wrong way.
De'ath	What way would that be exactly?
Charlie	Just your everyday Mr Do-Good. Things would get out of hand and people would begin to think of me as a charity. Can't have that.
De'ath	But I thought you saw yourself as a social worker?
Charlie	A social worker, yes, but not a poncy charity!
De'ath	A bit touchy on that point, aren't you?
Charlie	It wouldn't do for people to get the impression that I should stack all the odds in their favour!

De'ath	But aren't the odds stacked in your favour?
Charlie	Well, perhaps just a little. But you need to consider my overheads. There's the upkeep of my residence in London, my little holiday home in Skegness and my part shares in the donkeys on Blackpool's beach. And then you have to consider how expensive it is to keep up appearances – dry cleaning bills alone cost me a small fortune!
De'ath	I'm sure we appreciate you have some running costs. But how do you justify the kind of profits that you make?
Charlie	*Profits!* What profits? After I've finished paying for all that lot I'm out of pocket!
De'ath	Let's get back to the kind of person that you would like people to think of you as. Now you say that you see yourself as a social worker?
Charlie	That's right. I go out of my way to make sure that people enjoy themselves and help them not to think too much about the next day.
De'ath	The next day?
Charlie	It's no fun if you can't keep your mind on the gambling. You need to think straight.
De'ath	Straight from their pocket and into yours?
Charlie	To put it bluntly, yes. It's a kind of redistribution of wealth.
De'ath	But who benefits?
Charlie	Everyone. I'm able to squeeze out an existence from the modest profits while I stop people from worrying about what to do with the money in their pockets.
De'ath	How do you help them to stop worrying?
Charlie	By getting them to think of what they could do with all that money.

De'ath	That's if they win?
Charlie	Of course. But just suppose that you could lay your hands on loads of money. Think what you could do with it all!
De'ath	Chance would be a fine thing!
Charlie	Exactly, that's me. Don't think of the short term. Everybody wants money from you. Invest some of your money in racing. Back anything with odds of say, 100-1!
De'ath	And buy all those things I've wanted for ages?
Charlie	Not quite. You could reinvest the money in another race and get the chance to win even more and buy more things than you could dream of.
De'ath	So, just think, it could be my lucky day!
Charlie	And hopefully mine!
De'ath	Any tips for the greyhound race next Thursday?
Charlie	For a friend, of course. Bet on the rabbit, it always wins!
De'ath	With friends like you, who needs a bank balance? Thank you, Charlie Chance.

DAY OF PENTECOST: WHIT SUNDAY **30**

TODAY'S SPECIAL

Power to live
Acts 2:1-21: The coming of the Holy Spirit.

Equipment:
postcard for each member of the group
music and lyrics
candle
sticky tape

On each postcard write *one* letter from the alphabet. Either allow each group member to take a card at random (have the cards face down), or tape a card under each seat. If the group is fairly small, simply ask them to get their cards and try and make as many words as they can using some or all of the cards. If the group is large enough, give each member of the group a number. Call out a sequence of random numbers and those members must try and form a word from their letters.

When you have finished ask the group what was difficult about the game.
(Allow 10 minutes for this activity.)

Ask the group to have a listen to 'Psalm 102' by Kevin Prosch, from the album *Reckless mercy*. You might also like to look at 'I've found a friend' by Russell Fragar (*The source*, 251). You might like to use a piece of music with a similar theme. Have a copy of the lyrics available.
(Allow approximately 5 minutes.)

What did the group think about the lyrics? Did the lyrics have anything particular to say?

Read Acts 2:1-21.
It wasn't only the followers of Jesus who were gathered in Jerusalem. Pentecost was an important Jewish festival, celebrating the wheat harvest. Jerusalem would have been filled with Jews gathering together to celebrate Pentecost (see verse 5).

The Lord's followers had gathered together in one place, most likely to join in the celebrations of the festival. Then came the unexpected!

Although Jesus had made it clear that, after he had gone, he would send a 'comforter' or 'counsellor', his followers were not sure how this would happen. All the followers knew was that Jesus had told them to wait in Jerusalem until the Father gave them the Holy Spirit (see Acts 1:4). Suddenly, a sound of a mighty wind filled the house where the Lord's followers were gathered. The word for 'wind' and 'spirit' are the same in Greek, the language in which most of the New Testament was written. To the amazement of the Jews who had travelled from most of the known countries, the Lord's followers began speaking their languages (see verses 8-11).

The Holy Spirit was given to speak about the wonderful things that God had done, to give the Lord's followers encouragement that they were not alone and to give them the power to live a Christian life.

The Lord's followers had met together in Jerusalem unsure of what the future held for them. They didn't know how they could fulfil what Jesus had asked them to do when he told them 'go to the people of all nations and make them my disciples, baptise them in the name of the Father, the Son and the Holy Spirit' (see Matthew 28:19).

Now, on the day of Pentecost, they had been given the gift of the Holy Spirit. The Jews from many countries had heard the Lord's followers declare what God had done and now the followers knew that God was with them wherever they went. They now knew that God keeps his promises. He wasn't going to leave them alone and without the help that they needed to do the things that Jesus had asked them to do.

How does this relate to us? God has promised us the gift of his Holy Spirit to help us live our lives as Jesus wants us to. The Holy Spirit also allows us to listen to God and hear the truth about Jesus. We have access to a source of power which allows us to face questions like:

• Why do I exist?

• What does God want?

• Where is my life going?

This same source of power also gives us the strength we need to work through those questions.

Ask the group to think about the experience of the Lord's followers when they were gathered together in Jerusalem.

• What do the group think the followers were expecting? Anything?

• When they heard the sound of a mighty wind, do you think the followers would have been just a touch frightened, scared, shocked?

• How do they think the Jews would have felt when they heard so many languages being spoken by the followers?

The day of Pentecost didn't work out the way anyone was expecting but it made an impact on everyone who was there!

- Do we sometimes feel the same as some of the followers about what God is doing?
- Do we have questions which never seem to get answered?

Ask the group to write down some of their fears about allowing God to have a say in their life. Collect the written notes together.

Place a candle in the centre of the room. Light the candle and place all the notes around the base of the candle. Ask the group to be quiet while you read the following prayer:

Lord, I hope you're there.
I'd feel really stupid if I was talking to myself!
It would be like being in a football ground
    when the team was playing away.
Or at a cinema when the film had finished two hours ago.
It might be like singing a song which had no tune,
    or trying to read a book in the dark.
All a bit pointless really!
So, God what is the point?
Why am I here?
Why do I feel so alone at times?
Why don't I hear you speak?
Why does everything feel such a mess?
Why?

I need to hear your voice.
I need to feel you near.
I need to know your love.
I need you.
But I don't know how any of that can happen.
I don't know what you want from me.
Still, here I am,
I'm listening – are you? Amen.

TODAY'S SPECIAL   ## Under the influence!
Romans 8:12-17: Living by the power of God's Spirit.

Equipment:
two large sheets of paper (A3) or overhead projector and acetates
music and lyrics
small pieces of paper and pens
oil burner and fragrant oil

Draw the outline of a male on one sheet of paper or acetate and a female on the other. Discuss with the group what makes a good 'image', in other words, what do we need to look good to other people?

With an appropriate pen, draw on the person outlines the ideas of the group, for example hair-style, shoes, clothes, jewellery and accessories.

Ask the group what is important about the way we look.
• Does it matter how we look?
• Why should we follow any particular style or fashion?
(Allow 10 minutes for this activity.)

Have a listen to 'When deep calls to deep' by Paul Oakley, from the album *When deep calls to deep*. Alternatively, have a look at 'When the music fades' by Matt Redman (*The source*, 576). You might like to use a different piece of music which has a similar theme. Try and have a copy of the lyrics available.
(Allow approximately 5 minutes.)

Have a chat about the piece of music. What did the group think about the lyrics? Did the lyrics have anything particular to say?

Read Romans 8:12-17.
Refer to the earlier activity in 'Nibbles'. Was the group able to come up with any ideas as to why we may follow a particular style or fashion? Adopting a particular style or fashion helps to give us an identity or helps us to feel accepted by our peer group. We are all influenced by advertising, fashion, and peer pressure in various ways.

In his letter to the church in Rome, Paul says ' . . . we must not live to satisfy our own desires. If you do, you will die!' Strong words, but what was he getting at? We each have a desire to be accepted, to be appreciated and to be acknowledged as individuals. We can try various ways to gain acceptance, appreciation and acknowledgement by the way we act or the way we dress. Sometimes our feeling of acceptance means liking the type of music that our peer group likes or adopting the same style of dress or 'look'.

To a certain extent there is nothing wrong with all this; it's a part of life. The problems occur when we go to desperate lengths to be accepted, appreciated and acknowledged. We can sometimes spend most of our time trying too hard to be somebody that everybody will like. It can become our main driving force. It can consume every moment we have. That is when we start to die inwardly.

Paul was saying that if we put all our effort into trying to be accepted by other people and follow whatever desires we have, then we lose sight of who we really are.

One of the Old Testament kings, Solomon, wanted to search for what would make him happy. He said, 'I wanted to find out what was best for us during the short time we have on earth' (Ecclesiastes 2:3).

Money was not a problem and so he bought the best wines available and created a huge royal cellar. He set out to drink as much as he could and more.

Then he decided to be a bit more creative and built houses, planted vineyards, created gardens and orchards and accumulated vast wealth, became famous and got whatever he asked for.

Not satisfied with that, he decided to check out his sexuality. He eventually acquired so many wives that to see a different wife each day would have taken two years!

After all that Solomon sat back and had a think. 'Then I thought about everything I had done . . . and it was simply chasing the wind. Nothing on earth is worth the trouble' (Ecclesiastes 2:11).

We don't have to go to such extreme lengths to find acceptance, appreciation and acknowledgement. Nothing can fill the God-shaped hole in the middle of our being. We can try filling it with possessions, exotic substances or try and ignore it all together. The Holy Spirit will always make us aware of God's love for us. He accepts us for who we are. God isn't bothered with what we may think of as imperfections. He loves us as a father, and we become his children (Romans 8:15-16). If we accept that God loves us anyway, then our desires can be influenced by the Holy Spirit. We don't have to fit the moulds that other people might want us to fit. The important thing is that God loves us as we are; no matter what.

Give each member of the group a small piece of paper and a pen. Suggest to the group that they might like to write down some of the things that make them feel unacceptable to others, unappreciated and unacknowledged. Ask them to fold the pieces of paper in half and then tear them up into small pieces.
(Allow 5 minutes for this task.)

Place an oil burner in the centre of the room. Light the burner and use a light fragrant oil. Ask each member of the group to put their torn pieces of paper in a pile next to the burner. As they remain quiet, read the following prayer:

Lord, allow your Holy Spirit to fill this room.
Lord, allow your Holy Spirit to be in my life.
Lord, allow your Holy Spirit to show me your love.
Take my worries and doubts,
   take my insecurities and fear,
   take my hurt and pain.
Heal me, love me and keep me. Amen.

UNIT 32

TODAY'S SPECIAL

Never give up

2 Corinthians 4:5-12: Treasure in clay jars.

Equipment:
three large sheets of paper and a marker pen
postcard or similar for each person

Ask the group to think about items that are fragile, such as glass, paper, ice, skin. Write all their ideas down one side of the large sheet of paper. Once you have a fairly long list, ask the group to list things that would break or damage the fragile items that have already been listed. Write these items against the fragile items. (You can use the same item against as many fragile items as you want.)

Some of the suggestions may include thermonuclear devices which deal with the whole list! Or include stones, metal, cars and so on.

Discuss with the group how some of the fragile items get broken or damaged.

• Is it accidental or intentional.

• Can we do anything to avoid accidental or intentional damage?

(Allow 10 minutes for this activity.)

You will need another large sheet of paper. Ask the group to name some of their all-time favourite films and write all the responses down on the sheet of paper:

• What was it about the film that they liked so much?

• Can they remember any dialogue from the film?

• What types of film seem to be the most popular?

• Why?

• Do some of the films give us a dodgy view of life? For example, thrillers, action films, horror films?

• Do some of the films make life appear cheap?

• Does the action depend upon dozens of people getting killed or maimed?

• Why is this used so much in films?

• Is it a fair reflection of reality?

(Allow approximately 5 minutes.)

Read 2 Corinthians 4:5-12.

I don't know about you, but being likened to a clay jar is not quite the image I want to shout about! The point that Paul is making is that we are fragile and can be easily damaged! When you think of it, there are so many things which can hurt us.

Hurts range from one extreme to the other, that is, we can be hurt by someone ignoring us or by them saying something hurtful, or, at the other extreme, our bodies very rarely win an argument with an articulated truck!

Paul describes the treasure we have inside us as God's light shining in our hearts. In other words we have the truth about the Good News of Jesus Christ.

In fact, Jesus made a similar point when he said rather than store up treasures on earth, store up your treasures in heaven, because your heart will always be where your treasure is (Matthew 6:19-21). Paul and Jesus were both saying if we put all our hopes and security in ourselves and what possessions we can acquire, then we are going to be very disappointed if anything happens to them. It is much better to place our hope and trust in Jesus Christ and have God's love flowing through our hearts. If we can place our hope and trust in Jesus then no matter what happens nothing can destroy that 'treasure' within us.

There are so many things which can 'destroy' our hopes and security. We can feel rejected if people seem to ignore us. We can feel hurt if a relationship doesn't work out the way we wanted it to. If we get turned down for a job that we were hoping to get, we can feel that we are not good enough. If one of our friends passes on something which we told them in private, we can feel humiliated.

It is so easy to feel like giving up when everything seems to be going against us. But if we are confident of having God on our side then, as Paul wrote to the Corinthian Church, 'Even when we don't know what to do, we never give up. In times of trouble, God is with us, and when we are knocked down, we get up again.' (2 Corinthians 4:8-9.)

Give each member of the group a postcard or similar-sized piece of paper. Ask the group to think for a few moments about the things which they feel might have hurt them or made them feel useless. Suggest that they try and think of one word which describes the way they feel or felt at the time. Ask them to write the word, whatever the word is, onto the piece of paper. Collect all the pieces of paper and shuffle them. Take each piece of paper and stick it onto a larger sheet of paper which has the title 'What can we say about all this? If God is on our side, can anyone be against us?' (Romans 8:31.)

(Allow 5 minutes for this task.)

Ask the group to spend a little time thinking about the word they have written on the piece of paper and the issue which caused them to feel the way they did. Suggest that they remain quiet while you read the following prayer:

Lord,
    life feels like a game of skittles –
    you've guessed it! I'm not the ball.
Even when I try to keep my eyes open
    to avoid taking a knock.
Bang! Out of nowhere the ball comes flying,
    and I'm left staring at the sky.
Sometimes things seem to be going wrong all the time.
Is it really me or something I said?
I try so hard to do the right thing,
    but I don't think that other people think the way I do.
Or do some people enjoy knocking me down?
It certainly seems that way.
You must know the feeling:
    'can't do right for doing wrong.'
Sometimes I think that my face doesn't fit,
    and it hurts like hell,
    trying to squeeze into a mould
    that's just not my shape.

Still, it's a good thing
    that you don't turn your back
    or pretend to be deaf
    when my mouth opens and the verbal begins.
Lord, thank you
    that no matter what,
    you are for me,
    and you want the best for me.
Thanks for being there, or rather, here. Amen.

TODAY'S SPECIAL

Stepping out

2 Corinthians 4:13-5:1: Faith in the Lord.

Equipment:
small candle
box of matches
clear glass jam jar
large sheet of paper and marker pen
music and lyrics

As you enter the room, or when all the group have arrived, walk over to the light switch and flick the switch on and off a few times, looking at the light bulb each time. After a short pause stroke your chin and mutter 'hmmm'. Say nothing more before you light the small candle with the matches and gaze at the flame. After a short time place the jam jar over the candle and wait for the flame to go out (which should happen very quickly). Look at the group and then at the candle and mutter 'hmmm' again. Ask the group why the candle went out. Someone should be able to tell you that the flame went out because of a lack of oxygen.

Pick up the jam jar (be careful as it may be hot), look into the jar and say, 'Where's the oxygen?' Hopefully, someone will explain that it's all around us, which is useful or else we would have a slight technical problem with breathing!

Ask the group how they know that the oxygen is all around us. What evidence do we have? For example, the ability to breathe!

Walk over to the light switch again and begin to switch it on and off. Ask the group how it works. (By electricity.) What evidence do we have that electricity exists? (Power to lights, heaters, TV, video, electric cookers and electricity bills!)

Now, ask the group what other things exist even though we can't see them. Make a list of the group's responses, such as smells, thoughts, sounds, the wind.
(Allow 10 minutes for this activity.)

Having faith can mean putting our trust in something when we are not sure what will happen.

Have a listen to 'Faithful to me' by Jennifer Knapp, from the album *Trinity*. You might also like to take a look at 'I walk by faith' by Chris Falson (*The source*, 253). You may prefer to use a different piece of music which reflects the same theme. Try and have a copy of the lyrics available. **(Allow approximately 5 minutes.)**

Discuss the piece of music. Did the lyrics have anything to say about a particular theme? Ask the group if they felt the lyrics helped them understand something about God and our relationship with him.

Read 2 Corinthians 4:13-5:1.
• Why is it difficult to be confident in what we cannot see?

• Is something less real because we cannot see it?

How do we know that the planet Jupiter exists? We have confidence in and trust the people who have seen the planet through a telescope. We believe their account of what they have seen. Do we say to people that China doesn't exist, purely because we haven't been there? There are plenty of people who have been there and we can listen to their experience and make up our minds about China and the Chinese people based on their accounts.

We may not know how oxygen allows us to breathe or how oxygen is produced but we know it exists. We trust that when we go to sleep our lungs will continue working to keep us alive! So we have a kind of faith because of our experience and the experiences of other people.

In his letter to the Corinthian Church, Paul was making the point that if we only believed what we could see with our own eyes then life would be pretty desperate! Paul made a very depressing comment about our bodies gradually dying: what a positive thought to wake up to every morning!

We are able to see the changes in our appearance since we were very young by looking at pictures of ourselves. Hopefully, we don't look at the pictures and then spend the rest of the day worrying how much longer we have left on Planet Earth!

Paul was encouraging the Corinthian Church to place their trust in things that last forever. God is with us in every detail of our lives. He wants to be involved in everything we do, especially the things that begin to worry us. If we put our confidence in God, the things that concern us from day to day will appear temporary; though God is really keen to help us enjoy each day and get through difficult times with his support. As time goes by we can look back, as we can with our pictures, to each event where God has been with us in difficult times. Our faith grows as we experience God in our daily lives.

Ask the group to list ways in which they can say that God exists even though we cannot see him.

• Is it helpful to listen to other people talk about their experiences of God?

• How can listening to other people talk about God affect our own faith?

(Allow 5 minutes for this task.)

Faith is a difficult topic to discuss and even more difficult to put into words. Perhaps words are sometimes unnecessary? Ask the group to be quiet for a few moments. Encourage them to think about situations where they think God has done something in their lives that made a difference to a particular situation. Are there new circumstances or situations where a bit of help from God would be useful? Suggest to the group that they might like to think about these situations during this quiet time.

After a short time read this extract from Psalm 25:1-5.

I offer you my heart, Lord God, and I trust you.
Don't make me ashamed or let enemies defeat me.
Don't disappoint any of your worshippers,
    but disappoint all deceitful liars.
Show me your paths and teach me to follow;
    guide me by your truth and instruct me.
You keep me safe, and I always trust you. Amen.

TODAY'S SPECIAL

It's not what you say

2 Corinthians 5:6-10, 14-17: Following God.

Equipment:
postcard and pen for each member of the group

Supply each group member with a postcard and a pen. Ask the group to put their name at the top of the postcard and then pass the card to the person on their right. Once this has been done, ask the person holding the card to write down one thing that they appreciate about the person whose name appears at the top of the postcard. Then pass the card on to the person on the right and repeat the process until the person whose name is at the top of the postcard receives their own card.

Ask the card owners to read the comments that have been written about them.

• What did they think about the comments?

• Is it difficult to accept positive comments?

Ask the group if they found it difficult to write what they appreciate about another person.

• Why is it difficult?

• Would it be more difficult or easier to speak to the person directly?

(Allow 10 minutes for this activity.)

Being honest isn't always easy. Here are a few things that people say when they really mean something else:

'What a great idea!' – *It'll never work and I need a good laugh.*

'You don't understand me.' – *I've run out of excuses.*

'It would take too long to explain.' – *I've got no idea how it works.*

'That's very interesting.' – *Get a life!*

'You're looking fit.' – *What's up, did the batteries run out in your TV remote control?*

'I've bought you a present.' – *It was free with my comic.*

'I broke up with him/her.' – *They dumped me.*

'Great colour eye shadow!' – *Especially on a clown.*

'Did you make that yourself?' – *Nobody else would own up to it!*

'It's only a small cut.' – *I think I've just cut my arm off!*

(Allow approximately 5 minutes.)

Is it sometimes easier to say something that sounds okay rather than say what we really think? Why?

Read 2 Corinthians 5:6-10,14-17.

We have all possibly heard the rhyme 'sticks and stones may break my bones but names will never hurt me'; but is it true? You could argue that we don't have to be physically violent to hurt somebody; the words we use can do just as much damage, if not more.

It takes courage to say what we think. But sometimes it is extremely difficult to say what we think or feel without hurting someone's feelings. It always seems easier to think and say negative things; either because we are angry with a person or it's a way of trying to 'put them down'.

We can be cruel even when we make a joke about something. We can use laughter to disguise quite brutal comments. The target of our comments will join in with our laughter because they don't want people to see how much the comments hurt. Only later, in private, will the target of our comments feel the full effect of the verbal arrows.

In his letter to the Corinthian Church, Paul suggests that our aim should be to please God by what we say and do. At some time we will meet God face to face and he will ask us what we meant by our comments and actions. Paul is encouraging the Corinthian Church to follow God as best they know how (see verse 9).

We do not have to behave in a way that damages or destroys someone's confidence or feelings. The encouragement is to live a life influenced by Christ's love for us and other people. By developing a relationship with God, we don't need to be controlled by the driving forces of a competitive society. We do not need to put someone down so that we might look or sound better. We do not have to make other people appear inferior so that we might appear superior.

Christ's love is free to all for all time. It isn't something we earn or deserve more than someone else. Rather than become known as someone who finds it easier to say something negative about another person, we should become known as encouragers and people who are influenced by Christ's love and not selfish ambition. (You might like to take a brief look at Barnabas, the 'son of encouragement'. See Acts 4:36-37, 11:23-24 and chapters 13, 14 and 15.)

Ask the group to look again at their 'appreciation' postcards. Can they select one comment that they think makes them feel positive about themselves? Now suggest that on the reverse of their postcard they write a short, one-line thank you prayer. Underneath that prayer, ask them to write another one-line prayer about someone they feel needs to know that they are appreciated.

(Allow 5 minutes for this task.)

Suggest to the group that they remain quiet for a few moments and think about the person who would benefit from knowing that they are appreciated. After a short while, pray the following prayer:

Lord,
    being without friends
    is like being alone, in a desert
    with only the sand and wind to keep me company.

Lord,
    being without friends
    is like a song
    without a voice to sing.

Lord,
    being without friends
    is like a book
    which has no words.

Help me to be your voice
    to those who need to hear
    a whisper of hope,
    a whisper of love,
    a whisper of joy.

Help me to be strong
    in the face of doubt
    in the dark of night.

Help me to be strong
    when others are weak.
Help me to show your love
    wherever I can. Amen.

TODAY'S SPECIAL

What can I do?

2 Corinthians 6:1-13: Serving God.

Equipment:
postcard or similar sized piece of paper for each person
music and lyrics
paper, envelope and pen for each person

On each card write one of the following titles:

Car Park Attendant	Lion Tamer	Farmer	Opera Singer
Computer Programmer	Painter	Writer	Tea Taster
Actor/Actress	Guitarist	Decorator	Chat Show Host
Gardener	Jelly Taster	Traveller	Window Cleaner
Elastic Band Maker	Zoo Keeper	Baker	Lorry Driver

Stick or pin one card to the back of each group member. Make sure that the group member does not see the title on their card. The object is for each group member to try and find out what title is written on their card by asking questions of other group members. Each person can only respond with a 'yes' or 'no' to any question asked. Once a person has guessed their title correctly, they can sit out of the game; making it more difficult for those left playing!

When the game has finished (or when everybody is totally fed up!) ask the group how it felt not knowing what their 'title' was.

• Was it difficult to find out their 'title'?

• Were they satisfied or unhappy with the 'title' they were given?

(Allow 10 minutes for this activity.)

We each have something to offer, no matter what we think of ourselves.

Have a listen to 'Livin' for Jesus' by Third Day, from the album *Third day* or have a look at 'Let your love come down' by Noel and Tricia Richards (*The source* 319). You might like to use another piece of music with a similar theme. Try and have a copy of the lyrics available.
(Allow approximately 5 minutes.)

What did the group think of the lyrics? Did the lyrics help in trying to understand something about serving God?

Read 2 Corinthians 6:1-13.
What do you think the word 'servant' means? The dictionary might include definitions such as: 'someone hired to perform a service', or 'a slave'. But it can also mean someone who gives their time and abilities freely to someone. This is the way that Paul intends the word 'servant' to be used. It is the idea that we freely follow Jesus and want his love to influence all that we do. God gives us the power to do things through the Holy Spirit. It is up to us to use the abilities and gifts that God has given us to share with other people the love of Christ.

But what does serving mean to each of us? What abilities do we have? It is always easier to look at someone else and think that they have better abilities than we do; that they can do things better than we can. Is this an excuse?

God has given each one of us at least one unique ability. We can allow God to develop that ability or gift, or we can ignore it or even ignore God!

If we believe that God loves us and that he has given us an ability to do a particular thing, then doesn't it make sense that he will help us develop that gift or ability fully?

It isn't always obvious, at first, what sort of gifts or abilities God has given us. Some gifts and abilities are easily recognisable, for instance, being musical, good at acting or talking, artistic, a leader or sports person. Some gifts and abilities are not instantly obvious, for instance, being a good listener, being able to offer advice, being an encourager, a writer, a good organiser or someone who is willing to lend a 'pair of hands' for whatever job.

All of the gifts and abilities are as important as each other. Developing our gifts and abilities means being aware of where they can be used most effectively. More importantly, using our gifts and abilities doesn't always mean doing things that we hate. Some things are easier to do than others, and we should all be willing to help someone if the need arises. But it doesn't help matters if someone needs to talk about a problem and all you want to do is talk!

God loves us. He loves us to use our gifts and abilities to share Christ's love and for us to feel fulfilled, worthwhile and willing to serve.

Give every member of the group a pen, paper and an envelope. Ask them to think for a few moments about what they consider to be their 'strong points'. What do other people think are their 'strong points'? Write down their findings on the piece of paper and seal it in the envelope. Get them to write their name on the front of the envelope, write the date of sealing and then the date of opening (at least a year later). At the end of the session, either collect the envelopes and store them away or ask each member of the group to store their own away safely.
(Allow 5 minutes for this task.)

Ask the group to hold their envelope in their hands.
Read the following prayer:

Lord, we give you these thoughts and ideas.
You gave them to us,
    and now we offer them to you.
Use our gifts and abilities,
    use our lives,
    to share your love and your life. Amen.

UNIT 36

TODAY'S SPECIAL

How much?
2 Corinthians 8:7-15: Generous giving.

Equipment:
large sheet of paper and a marker pen
music and lyrics or drama sketch

When the group have arrived, appear to be in an extreme state of excitement. Announce to the whole group that you didn't give any money to the Church last week. Instead you spent the money on some lottery tickets and . . . guess what . . . you didn't win!

Explain that you nearly won. In fact, you would have won if you'd guessed the right numbers!

Write the figure £1,000,000 on the large sheet of paper. Ask the group to list some of the things that they would buy if they won that amount of money. Once you've got quite a long list, look it over and circle all those items that are for personal use only, such as: car, house, jewellery.

- Were there any listed items left which would be bought for other people?
- Why do we think about what we want to buy for ourselves first?
- Is it easy to think about giving some of the money away? Why?

(Allow 10 minutes for this activity.)

Giving, in any shape or form, is never easy.

Have a listen to 'Mama' by Third Day, from the album *Third day* or take a look at 'Where there once was only hurt' by Tommy Walker (*The source*, 577). You may prefer to use a piece of music with a similar theme. Try and have a copy of the lyrics available. Alternatively, you might like to use the drama sketch *De'ath meets . . . Wally Wingepacket* (see page 144).
(Allow 5 minutes.)

Have a chat about the lyrics of the chosen piece of music or drama. What do they say about possessions? Do the lyrics say anything else?

Read 2 Corinthians 8:7-15.
If there is one thing that will cause an argument, this is it. Money has a value to us which we measure in more than just financial terms. When

you meet someone or you go to a party, people tend to ask you what job you do or what you earn. Some people will think more highly of you if you say you are a business consultant or a director of a business. Your earning power gives you status and the salary that you are paid enables you to buy the things that show you have a well-paid job.

In his letter to the Corinthian Church, Paul is saying that having money and status is no bad thing, it's what you do with it that counts. Often, because we associate our wealth with security, giving money away is difficult. There is a part of us which says, 'I've had to earn that. I'm able to earn that money because of my abilities'. Giving money away is like giving part of yourself away.

Our gifts and abilities are God-given. He is really pleased when we feel satisfied and fulfilled. As God has freely given to us, is it okay to walk past someone who hasn't been able to use their gifts or abilities because of certain circumstances?

We all feel sympathy for starving children when their images appear on the TV or when we see the destruction caused by a natural disaster. But what about those people around us?

Sometimes people feel too proud to tell anyone that they or their family are having money difficulties. It's embarrassing because a lack of money is seen as a failure in our society.

Paul is saying that we have a responsibility to those people who have less than we do. Not that we should give everything away so that we then become poor, even though that is exactly what Jesus did. Paul is urging the Church to put love into action. Care for those who have needs which they can't sort out themselves. If you can't do anything directly, give the money to a group or organisation which has been set up to deal with particular issues.

If you are happy to help when it's needed then, if the time comes when you need help, others will help you.

Make a list, with the group, of as many organisations as you can think of which help and support people in need, for example: Oxfam, Red Cross, Red Nose Day, Prince's Trust, Christian Aid, Amnesty International.

Ask members of the group to take one organisation each and find out everything they can about that organisation. Share the findings with the group the next time you meet.
(Allow 5 minutes for this task.)

Ask the group to spend a few moments being quiet, and to think about those people who struggle to live a normal life. In particular think about those people who suffer because of natural disasters. After a short time read the following extract from Proverbs 31:8-9.

But you must defend those who are helpless and have no hope.
Be fair and give justice to the poor and homeless.

DE'ATH MEETS . . . WALLY WINGEPACKET

Characters	De'ath and Wally Wingepacket
Scene	De'ath and Wally are seated on comfy chairs around a coffee table. Wally has a large wallet which he regularly opens to count his money.
Props	the ever-present comfy chairs coffee table jug of water and two glasses large wallet and money for Wally

De'ath   Ladies and gentlemen, it is a continual delight to greet you again and again. I do hope that you are learning something from our little searches into the realms of our guests' minds. Makes you shudder at times though! Now, tonight I have a special treat for you. Until recently this person was a complete and total nobody. You wouldn't have given him the time of day, much less look at him when you passed him in the street. That was yesterday. Now, after a small wager on the lottery, he is someone we all want to meet. Ladies and gentlemen, I give you Wally Wingepacket.

Wally   Thank you for such a warm welcome. Is it too soon to ask about my appearance fee?

De'ath   Just a bit premature. Could you wait until later, say the next millennium?

Wally   What! Do you mean to say I've come all this way for nothing? Do you know what it costs nowadays to travel? Have you any idea how much wear and tear my clothes get?

De'ath   Just my little joke. No need to get upset. It's funny, that, a lot of my guests seem to get upset. I wonder why? Anyway, let's discuss you your money.

Wally   Do we have to? You never know who's listening. As soon as someone gets to know you've got enough for two cups of coffee, they get out the pen and paper and, before you can say 'two sugars', there's a begging letter through your door.

De'ath   Disgraceful! How do you put up with it?

Wally   It's not easy, you know. There's a lot of responsibility goes with having a bit of money. It's a good job there's not more people like me.

De'ath   I think we all agree with you on that one, Wally!

Wally   I'm glad you think that way.

De'ath   Tell me, Wally, has money changed you in any way?

Wally   Well, it's made me take my responsibilities seriously. You know, before it didn't matter about money. There wasn't that much to get concerned about. But now there's so much to think about. Interest rates, share prices, mergers and monopolies, taxation and fraud.

De'ath   You understand all that?

Wally   Not really. My accountant helps me with the fraud bit!

De'ath   I see. Life isn't quite so easy then?

Wally   No way! Sometimes I just can't sleep at night, worrying about money.

De'ath   Didn't it worry you before, having no money?

Wally   Not really. I was too busy thinking about how to get more of it to worry about not having it.

De'ath   Didn't it bother you, not being able to pay the rent or gas bills?

Wally   Never!

De'ath   Really?

Wally	No, I never paid them anyway!
De'ath	So, having all this money is a pressure you're not used to?
Wally	It's a very nice pressure. It really is so nice to feel that you've dug yourself out of poverty and made something of yourself.
De'ath	Bit of luck though, wasn't it?
Wally	It wasn't luck. It's a skill being able to pick the right numbers with your eyes closed!
De'ath	I'm sure it is. Do you still 'skilfully' choose your winning numbers?
Wally	I certainly do. I can't sit back and think it's all easy street from now on. You never know what might happen next.
De'ath	I'm sure there's lots of people would agree with you there, but they haven't got the luxury of a decent financial cushion.
Wally	Well, they should follow my example. Get out and do something about it. It's no good feeling sorry for yourself. You need to be positive.
De'ath	But they are not all as fortunate as you, are they? We don't all have your skill with shaping our destiny, do we?
Wally	That's no excuse for people standing around on street corners or cluttering up the pavements looking as if they haven't eaten for days.
De'ath	Perhaps they haven't.
Wally	All the more reason to do something about it.
De'ath	Isn't that what they're doing?
Wally	What? Do you call clutching a piece of cardboard and holding out a dirty old cap doing something?

De'ath	It's better than nothing.
Wally	It's a disgrace. Shouldn't be allowed.
De'ath	You don't agree with it then? You're not tempted to give them a bit of help by putting some loose change in their cap?
Wally	Certainly not! If you do it for one they'll all want some. Anyway, how would I show that on my tax forms? It would cause my accountant a headache. Can't have that.
De'ath	So you're not in favour of self-help then?
Wally	God helps those who help themselves. So my accountant says.
De'ath	But aren't these people trying to help themselves?
Wally	What, my accountant?
De'ath	No! We all know they do. I mean those less fortunate than yourself.
Wally	They need to stand on their own two feet, like what I am.
De'ath	You're sitting very comfortably, if I may say so. Wally Wingepacket, thank you for gracing us with your presence.

TODAY'S SPECIAL

'Erm, well, it's like this . . .'
Ephesians 1:3-14: Blessings in Christ.

Equipment:
postcards and pen
music and lyrics

On each of a series of postcards write one of the following:

Snails	Teddy bears
Making paper planes	Ice-cream
Jelly babies	Apples
Flowers	Toffees
Solar power	Parachuting
Plastic spoons	Light bulbs
Lawn mowers	Dogs
Worms	

Give each member of the group a number, up to the number of postcards used. Choose a number and give the corresponding group member one of the cards. The group member has ten seconds to look at the card and must then speak for thirty seconds about the topic on the card. They are not allowed to use any delaying tactics or pause during their thirty seconds. If someone pauses or runs out of words then that person is out of the game. Continue playing until all the cards are used up or there is a clear winner.

Consider the following:

- Was it easy?
- How difficult did the group find talking about an unusual topic?
- What were the problems?

(Allow 10 minutes for this activity.)

Have a listen to 'You know my name' by Chris Lizotte, from the album *Big heavy world*. You might also like to look at 'Father, I want you to hold me' by Brian Doerksen (*The source*, 98). You may prefer to use an alternative piece of music with a similar theme. Try and have a copy of the lyrics available.
(Allow approximately 5 minutes.)

Discuss the piece of music with the group. Did the lyrics suggest a particular theme or topic?

Read Ephesians 1:3-14.

Usually, when we write a letter, we start the first sentence by asking, 'How are you?' But in his letter to the Church at Ephesus, Paul starts by reminding the Church immediately of all that God has done for them!

The first statement is that God has given us everything. As a father he gave his only Son to bring back what we have lost, a relationship with God which is made possible by the ultimate sacrifice, the death of Jesus. It no longer matters what we have done because Jesus became our forgiveness through his death and resurrection.

Paul goes on to state that God gives everything freely, we don't owe a thing! God has given each of us the chance to relate to him as our Father. And, as he is our Father, we have access to everything that a child would expect from a father. He loves us, wants the best for us and looks out for us in every situation. We don't have to worry about the future because God is our future! He is in control and nothing can separate us from his love (see Romans 8:35).

However, although Paul emphasises that our future is secure, that through our belief in Jesus Christ, God has blessed us for today and all the next 'todays', this does not mean that we can ignore 'why' Jesus lived his life or 'how'. The 'why' of Jesus' life was to become the final sacrifice for us and restore our relationship with God. The 'how' Jesus lived his life is the 'how' we should live our lives today and all our 'todays'.

Jesus gave us an example of how to live our life in the here and now. He added two commandments (and gave loads of other examples of the 'how'): love God with all your heart and treat other people as you want to be treated. Quite a tall order!

God cares for us in every detail. He gives his love freely and encourages us to share his concern for other people. But it isn't always easy to put everything into words and it is sometimes really difficult to put God's love into action. No real problem, as long as we are honest with God and honest with other people, even when we think we've got things wrong.

Ask the group to make a list of all the people they come into contact with on a regular basis.

• How many hours a week do they spend talking to each of those people?

• Does God ever come into the conversation?

• What makes it difficult to chat about God and our faith?

(Allow 5 minutes for this task.)

While the group think about the different people on their list, read the following prayer:

Lord, be fair –
    it isn't easy you know,
    and it's really difficult
    with a hot sausage roll in your mouth!
I can't help it,
    it's just . . . well, you know,
    not easy.
It's not that I don't care
    or that I can't be bothered;
    that's just not true,
    even though it may seem like it.
I want to chat about you
    and what you mean to me,
    but it's just not very easy.
And it's really difficult
    when the jokes get out of hand;
    and it's really difficult
    when I can't take my eyes
    off the spot on her chin.
But I'm not giving up,
    I'll give it a go.
But promise me one thing –
you'll back up everything I say! Amen.

TODAY'S SPECIAL

Break down the walls
Ephesians 2:11-22: United in Christ.

Equipment:
sheet of paper and a pen for each member of the group
music and lyrics or drama sketch
candle for each member of group

To introduce this activity, ask the group to think of things that would stop people shopping at a particular supermarket; for example, high prices, bad-tasting food, abusive shop assistants or locked doors! Now ask the group to think how they can stop people talking to each other and begin to consider each other as enemies; for example, spread rumours, gossip about people or insult them. Get the group to write all their ideas down on the left-hand side of the piece of paper. Make sure that you leave space on the right-hand side of the paper for other comments (which will be dealt with later on.)
(Allow 10 minutes for this activity.)

Have a listen to 'Only Natural' by Steve Curtis Chapman, from the album *Signs of life*. Alternatively, have a look at 'Behold his love' by Geoff Bullock (*The source*, 43). You might like to use a different piece of music which reflects the same theme. Have a copy of the lyrics available. Alternatively, you might like to use the drama sketch *De'ath meets . . . Tracy Touchbucket* (see page 154).
(Allow approximately 5 minutes.)

What did the group think of the lyrics? Did the lyrics make any particular point?

Read Ephesians 2:11-22.
The titles 'Jew' and 'Gentile' had an important meaning for the early Christians. Originally, the term 'Jew' would have referred to an inhabitant of Judah, but was later used to describe any citizen of Israel, while the term 'Gentile' was used as a general term for anyone who was not an Israelite.

During Old Testament times, God called for his people, Israel, to have nothing to do with those nations who worshipped statues and idols.

God asked the Israelites to worship him alone and not get involved in rituals and behaviour which would turn the Israelites away from him. So, the terms 'Jew' and 'Gentile' became associated with the concept that the Jews were those who belonged to God, and the Gentiles were those who worshipped and behaved in a manner which was hostile to God.

Jesus made it quite clear that he was not impressed with social and political divisions. He would talk and spend time with anyone. Jesus went out of his way to break down the social barriers which kept people apart. This made him extremely unpopular with the religious leaders and the Jewish politicians. But Jesus knew the hurt and damage that these social barriers caused.

In *Romeo and Juliet* (one from Shakespeare's best-seller list), we find Romeo passionately in love with Juliet and Juliet head-over-heels in love with Romeo. All they wanted to do was watch the sunset together, kiss and cuddle. But, as always, there was a problem. Romeo belonged to the Montague family and Juliet to the Capulet family, and the families hated each other, although the reasons were lost in distant time and space. The end result was both the star-crossed lovers committing suicide.

Jesus broke down the walls which separated the Jews from the non-Jews. He broke down all the hatred and hurt which had caused the two factions to remain apart. Until the moment that Jesus' death healed the rift and provided a way of peace, every action was driven by hostility which ultimately brought about the death of peace, friendship, love and life. Jesus came to break down the barriers and heal the rift between ourselves and God and between ourselves and other people. It is only through God's love that hurts are healed and peace replaces anger.

Go back to the pieces of paper that were used earlier. Look again at the list and for each negative idea write a positive one on the right-hand side of the paper. For example, to cause a breakdown in communication: stop talking to someone (negative). To turn it into a positive, go out of your way to make someone feel part of things, talk to them. Rather than gossip about someone, refuse to gossip. Eventually, each member of the group will have a list of negatives and, opposite, a list of positive responses.

Discuss ways in which the group can put some of the positive ideas into practice.
(Allow 5 minutes for this task.)

Have a candle available for every member of the group. Ask each member to think about situations where there may be 'walls' or 'barriers' between themselves and someone else. If there is a situation where a group member wants God to help sort things out, ask them to light a candle and place it in the centre of the room. After a short time read the following prayer:

Lord,
    help me to bring your peace
    to everyone I meet.

Help me to be positive
    when all around seems negative.

Help me to break down barriers
    through the power of your love.

Help me to ignore the silence
    and communicate your heart.

Help me to live the life
    that you intended.

Help me to be the person
    that you created.

Help me to have confidence
    when things start to get tough.

Help me to help others,
    but I would appreciate it
    if you started . . . with me. Amen.

DE'ATH MEETS . . . TRACY TOUCHBUCKET

Characters	De'ath and Tracy Touchbucket
Scene	De'ath sitting as usual in a comfy chair, but his appearance is slightly less formal than we have come to expect. Tracy is dressed very neatly, almost too fussily, and appears nervous and preoccupied. She holds a handbag which she fiddles with continuously.
Props	comfy chairs coffee table jug of water with two glasses handbag for Tracy

De'ath   Good evening and welcome to another rip-roaring (or is that tip-snoring?) edition of my ever-so-popular chat show. Thank you for giving up something much less important to come and hear my honeyed voice. You are such a lucky audience. But still, we must move on and start the show. Tonight's guest has something we all recognise in ourselves from time to time. She has a quality which I admire in others. Well, never mind the quality, let's see the quantity that is Tracy Touchbucket.

Tracy   It's not Touchbucket! It's Touchbouquet, as in flowers, you know.

De'ath   I'm so sorry, Tracy. But Bucket is what's written down here and I can only repeat the information that I have in front of me, can't I?

Tracy   Well, it's not the way I expected to be greeted. I've put myself out to come here and from the start you go out of your way to insult me. It's terrible.

De'ath   My dear Tracy, why would I want to insult you? We've known each other for such a long time. I've known you since you were a snotty little kid running around in soggy nappies.

Tracy	There you go again! Making me feel inferior and small in front of your guests.
De'ath	My dear, don't upset yourself. It's nothing to be getting in a state about.
Tracy	Nothing. You call embarrassing me in front of all these people 'nothing to get upset about'? Wars have been started for less. Let me tell you, I don't put up with being insulted in front of strangers!
De'ath	So it's okay in front of people you know, then?
Tracy	No! And you know it's not. You've got a real cheek.
De'ath	I know. It's something I pride myself on. Would you like to hear some more?
Tracy	No, I would not. And let me tell you, I'm far from impressed with the way you've dressed. You could at least have put some decent clothes on. Call yourself a host!
De'ath	My dear Tracy, I wouldn't comment on my appearance if I were you. Not with your sense of, shall we say, 'style'?
Tracy	You absolute horror! How dare you speak to me like that. I've a good mind to ignore you for the rest of the show.
De'ath	Go on, make my evening!
Tracy	That does it! You've gone too far this time.
De'ath	Aren't you getting a little touchy for someone like yourself?
Tracy	What do you mean, 'touchy'? I'm a perfectly polite and sociable person.
De'ath	No doubt. But you must admit that you get, how shall we put it? – You tend to make a mountain out of a dung heap!
Tracy	I certainly do not!

De'ath	So you admit to being happy in a dung heap?
Tracy	How do you get away with speaking to your guests in such a rude manner? I don't normally let anyone talk to me the way you have. I usually ignore them. Walk past them in the street and let everyone know what total donkeys they are.
De'ath	Little tough on donkeys, wouldn't you say?
Tracy	Well, you know what I mean. People have such a silly tendency to say and do the most stupid things. You just wouldn't believe the problems they cause. Just because they won't appreciate that they are totally wrong and wouldn't know if the sky fell down and hit them.
De'ath	How would you know if the sky had fallen down, as a matter of interest?
Tracy	Don't be so picky. It's just a figure of speech.
De'ath	So the sky doesn't fall down, or you wouldn't know if it had fallen down or not?
Tracy	You're just impossible. How does anyone put up with you?
De'ath	Well, you know . . . charm and sophistication win every time.
Tracy	Not with me they don't! I can't stand people who have high opinions of themselves. They need to be brought down a peg or two. Made to see the error of their ways.
De'ath	I see you're all for compromise then.
Tracy	Don't be so provocative. You know that's not what I'm about.
De'ath	You don't say!
Tracy	Are you always so charming or is this especially for me?
De'ath	Tracy, for you I would put the sun in the sky, I would make the clouds float.

Tracy	Doesn't that happen anyway?
De'ath	Precisely.
Tracy	Just you wait until I tell my friends about you.
De'ath	Well, that's ten seconds used up. What will you do with the rest of your day?
Tracy	I'll have you know I've got plenty of friends, thank you.
De'ath	Do they know that?
Tracy	Of course they do. They know they can rely on me.
De'ath	Been friends a long time, have they?
Tracy	Not yet, but give them time.
De'ath	Time for what?
Tracy	Time to come around to my way of thinking. Either that or they can join the rest of the ignorant crowd.
De'ath	Time for our little friendship to end. Tracy Touchbucket, thank you for leaving.

TODAY'S SPECIAL

No limit!
Ephesians 3:14-21: Christ's love for us.

Equipment:
small sheet of paper and a pen for each member of the group
music and lyrics
small piece of card for each person

Explain to the group that you feel a bit like a cardboard box . . . dull on the outside and empty inside. Or that you feel like a rusty car . . . showing signs of wear and your upholstery needs repairing. Before the group begins to think that you've totally lost your chewing gum, tell them that sometimes it's easier to say how you feel by using a word picture.

Ask the group to think of some of their own word pictures which explain how they feel and write them down. When they have thought of a word picture, collect the sheets of paper and mix them up. At random, take one of the sheets and read the word picture. Can anyone guess who wrote it? Ask the group if they felt it easier to describe how they felt using the word pictures. Why is that?
(Allow 10 minutes for this activity.)

Being honest is difficult. When you know that the other person listening to you loves you no matter what you say, that's simply amazing.

Have a listen to 'What a friend I've found' by Delirious?, from the album *King of fools*. Or you might like to look at 'Thank you for saving me' by Martin Smith (*The source*, 472). Try and have a copy of the lyrics available. You might like to use a different piece of music which has a similar theme.
(Allow approximately 5 minutes.)

Did the lyrics help the group to understand anything about God's love? Was there any part of the lyrics which was difficult to understand?

Read Ephesians 3:14-21.
Sometimes things are far too awesome for us to understand. No, we're not thinking about the next story line in an Australian soap opera! It has

been referred to as the greatest love story of all time, or even the ultimate act of compassion. And it doesn't involve sharing your last piece of chocolate with the one you love! We are talking of the total expression of God's love for each one of us. Trying to understand this love is as frustrating as trying to count every grain of sand on a beach (although more interesting and mentally stimulating than watching an Australian soap opera!)

Have you ever tried gazing into the night sky and contemplating the sheer size of the universe? Science can go some way to explaining what keeps the stars in space and even what is happening to the different galaxies, but that doesn't help us appreciate the complexity of the universe. There are many theories about the origins of the universe, but just as one theory is put forward, another discovery puts a different angle on our theories. Just when we thought we had a grasp of the universe something happens to blow our theories away. God's love is something like that. Just when we thought we had got God all worked out, he throws us another line which simply blows us away.

In the Bible reading, Paul prays that we will understand how wide, how long and how high God's love is. The answer to that is quite simple, there is no limit! God's love has no boundaries. It is greater than we can ever know, but the most important thing is that we can experience that love no matter what! No matter what we feel or think, God's love is constant. He loves us without limits, without judgement and without cost. Everything has been done to allow us to experience God's love. So, even though we may feel like a cardboard box at times, it doesn't make any difference to God – he loves us.

Give each member of the group a small piece of card. Ask them to write 'God loves me even when I feel like . . .'. The rest of the sentence should contain the word picture they wrote earlier. Suggest to the group that they might like to put the card where they will see it every day to remind them of God's love for each of them.
(Allow 5 minutes for this task.)

While the group look at their completed cards, ask them to remain quiet for a few moments while you read the following prayer from Psalm 36:5-7:

Lord, your love reaches to the heavens,
 your loyalty to the skies.
Your goodness is as high as the mountains.
Your justice is as deep as the great oceans.
Lord, you protect both people and animals.
God, your love is so precious!'

TODAY'S SPECIAL

Stand firm

Ephesians 4:1-16: Unity with Christ.

Equipment:
postcards (sufficient for most members of the group to take part in the game)
music and lyrics
cross

Each of the cards should have a word on but with a variety of definitions. This is a type of biblical *Call my Bluff*. For example:

BAMAH

Definition 1. During Old Testament times people who were unfortunate enough to find themselves homeless could go to a small community where they would be looked after and provided with basic accommodation. The word *Bamah* refers to a kind of supervisor or manager of the community who would be in charge of all the people who cared for the temporary residents.

Definition 2. In the Hebrew language there are some words which have a very general meaning. The word *Bamah* simply means a high place. So, rather than say 'on top of a tall building', or 'a mountain peak', the word *Bamah* is used.
(Correct definition.)

SACKBUT

Definition 1. A *sackbut* is, in fact, a type of musical instrument. It's a kind of early trombone which was used during Old Testament times.
(Correct definition.)

Definition 2. A *sackbut* was an early form of washing basket. It wasn't used for domestic clothes but for storing the sacks that grain and herbs were kept in. After you had emptied a sack of grain or herbs, you would place the dirty sack in the *sackbut* to be washed, ready for re-use.

You can write more cards and make up definitions by using a Bible dictionary and a little zany imagination. Divide the group into teams and give each team a selection of words. Each player reads out a definition and the other team have to decide which is the correct definition.
(Allow 10 minutes for this activity.)

Ask the group to listen to 'Collide' by Fono, from the album *Goesaround-comesaround*. You might also like to take a look at 'I believe in Jesus' by Marc Nelson (*The source*, 195). You may prefer to use a different piece of music which has a similar theme. Try and have a copy of the lyrics available. **(Allow approximately 5 minutes.)**

Chat about the lyrics with the group. What did the group make of the lyrics? Was there a particular theme?

Read Ephesians 4:1-16.
If you have ever tried using the Internet to search for ideas or material for a project, you will have been amazed at the number of sites wanting to give you information and links to other sites with even more information. How on earth are you supposed to know what is okay and what is a load of garbage? The same goes for politics, philosophy and religion. There are so many theories and ideas that it can leave you wishing you hadn't asked a question in the first place.

From the Bible reading, it seems that the problem isn't a new one. Paul is encouraging the Ephesian Church to avoid getting into arguments or listening to people who want their opinions and beliefs to be accepted. He reminds the Church that there is one Lord, one faith and one baptism. And that above all there is one God who is the Father of all people.

Jesus made a point of telling his followers that there would be loads of people who would shout about new ways of living, claiming to have a hotline to God and asking people to follow them (see Mark 13:5-6 and Hebrews 13:9). But even though lots of different voices call out, the important point is to follow the way of Jesus and keep up the relationship with God (see John 14:6). It is good to be with other people who will encourage you and care for you (see also Hebrews 10:25). Paul emphasises the need for everyone to be patient with each other and care for each other. And, if we hear anyone shouting about a different spiritual way or thinking they know better than God, being with people who love God will help us to avoid feeling threatened or feeling as if someone is trying to drive a wedge between ourselves and God.

Ask the group if they found it difficult to guess the correct definition for the words used in the 'Nibbles' section.

- Why is it possible to be 'misled' about the meaning of something?
- Can the group think of any instances where people have been misled or given wrong information?
- How can we avoid being misled or being given dodgy information?

(Allow 5 minutes for this task.)

Place a cross in the centre of the room. Ask the group to look at the cross while you pray the following:

Lord,
    at times there seem so many voices,
    so many people
    shouting, calling, pointing,
I can't hear myself think.
What am I expected to do?
Whose voice should I listen to?
Where can I look?

Then, in the middle of the noise,
    the confusion, the chaos,
    I think I can just hear
    a small, persistent voice
    whispering, calling, comforting.
It's a voice I recognise,
    a voice that I've come to appreciate;
    always there, always speaking
    with a love that's awesome;
    a love that's there for me.
Everything else becomes distant,
    as I turn my ear towards the voice,
    and hear you speak my name.
You're here for me, I'm listening. Amen.

TODAY'S SPECIAL

Let love be your guide
Ephesians 4:25-5:2: The new life.

Equipment:
small piece of paper and a pen for each member of the group
large sheet of red paper and pins or sticky tape
drama sketch if required
candle

Introduce the unit by telling the group about the things which really irritate you. For instance, the top left off the toothpaste tube, an empty biscuit tin, somebody crunching a sweet in the cinema, dogs barking late at night or programming the video to tape your favourite film and then finding it has taped a documentary about slugs.

Ask the group about the things which irritate them. Get them to write these things down on their pieces of paper. Consider questions such as:

- Do these things always irritate me?
- Do I get more irritable when I'm tired?
- Do certain people make me irritable?
- Do I get irritable with other people when things haven't gone my way?

Now ask the group to pin or stick their pieces of paper to the large sheet of red paper.
(Allow 10 minutes for this activity.)

Do the group know of any instances where someone has been really angry and then done something really daft?

Some true life examples:
A motorist was stopped for speeding in a residential area. As the policeman walked towards the now stationary car, the driver began to wreck the inside of his car. First he ripped off the interior mirror, then he pulled the head-rests off; he then kicked the passenger door, thumped the steering wheel, opened the glove compartment and threw the contents into the car; finally he opened the window and threw his wallet across the street.

An office worker, having just received a telephone call from an angry customer, slammed the phone down, ran across the room and began kicking a filing cabinet. After several minutes the worker returned to his desk saying how much better he felt and he would repair his filing cabinet later. His colleague then pointed out that he had just trashed her filing cabinet and not his own!

A salesman, angry at having just received a telephone call cancelling a large order, banged his fist on the desk and then pushed everything off the desk. Papers were all over the floor, the telephone was in the waste bin, pictures of family and friends were smashed on the floor, and a briefcase lay empty and upside down on the other side of the room. The salesman then realised that he was sitting at his boss's desk!

Alternatively, you might like to use the drama sketch *De'ath meets . . . Ingatius the Irritable* (see page 167).

Read Ephesians 4:25-5:2.
Unfortunately we all get angry at one time or another. Things or people can irritate us to such an extent that we lose control of our emotions and say or do things which, at a later date, we wish we had never said or done. It isn't easy to stay calm when someone says or does something which really annoys you. And, sometimes, other people have extremely annoying habits which can drive you insane, such as chewing their finger nails and spitting the bits across the room, or sounding like a drain when they have a drink or even the way they lick their mouth with their tongue after they have eaten a sticky bun.

Dealing with our anger is difficult. Paul's advice to the Ephesian Church is to avoid letting anger be the cause of something which they will later regret, and, more importantly, to deal with the situation quickly and not to let the problem go on too long.
    The longer you wait to sort the situation out, the more likely it is that the problem will get worse. If you have said something to someone as a result of your becoming angry, then it's likely that what you said has caused the other person to get angry as well. The longer you leave it, the more time you allow the devil to twist and turn everything that was said until the whole situation is like an exploding volcano.

We don't have to react in a negative way. God will help us to deal with situations in such a way that we can encourage people rather than get angry with them. It's always easier to see the negative things about people than the positive. But with God's help we can get past the things we find difficult and respond to situations in a way which doesn't allow the devil to get us into a real mess.

Light a candle and place it in the centre of the room. Ask the group to collect their pieces of paper from the display. On the back of the paper ask the group to write down some ideas about ways in which they can deal positively with situations which make them irritable.
Allow 5 minutes for this task.)

Once the group have written down some ideas, get them to place their pieces of paper around the bottom of the candle. Suggest to the group that they might like to think about the situations and their ideas for dealing with them while you read the following prayer:

Lord,
    come on, it's not easy you know,
    trying to ignore those things
    which get on your nerves and generally drive you mad.
How can some people be so irritating?
(Do they use some kind of anti-social deodorant?)
How can some people live with themselves?
(Have they got rhinoceros skin or what?)
How can other people put up with them?
(Or are all their mates the same?)
Can you imagine having breakfast with them?
(Weetabix, pickled onions and marmite!)
Can you imagine having to spend time with them?
(It would be like watching stones grow.)

You can?
How do you do it?
What do you mean, 'love'?
Do you mean ignoring the irritations
    and all those really awful habits that people have?
Do you mean looking for the best in someone
    even though it could take some time?
You mean it, don't you,
    that idea about love?
Being kind and watching out for each other
    sounds okay, but I'll need some help.
How are you fixed? Amen.

DE'ATH MEETS . . . IGNATIUS THE IRRITABLE

Characters   De'ath and Ignatius the Irritable

Scene   De'ath and Ignatius are seated on comfy chairs, with a coffee table in front of them over which a collection of magazines is scattered. De'ath wears a brightly coloured shirt and contrasting tie, also patterned socks. Ignatius is dressed in sober style.

Props   two comfy chairs
coffee table
collection of assorted magazines

De'ath   Welcome, welcome to my chart-busting show: the show that gets under your skin and irritates like a ferret in your trousers. The show that has done as much for the director's salary as it has found the cure for haemorrhoids. And you, the audience, what can I say? As a friend once said, 'where there's a bunch of clowns, there's a circus'. Now, for tonight's show, I want to introduce to you a close friend of mine. Here's a man whose motto is 'I should have done it myself'. Ladies and gentlemen, may I introduce to you Ignatius the Irritable.

Ignatius   Thank you. Okay, that's enough clapping. It'll give me a headache, all that noise. It's a bit warm in here. Have you got the heating set a little too high?

De'ath   Ignatius, welcome. I hope you found the dressing room to your satisfaction.

Ignatius   I wouldn't know. I couldn't find the dressing room. Couldn't you have put some signs up or at least sent me some directions. It's like a rabbit warren out there. A bloke could get lost tying his shoe lace.

De'ath   I'm so sorry you couldn't find a place to rest for a few moments before our little chat.

Ignatius	A rest would have been most welcome. I hardly had chance to draw breath before some pimple-faced urchin pushed me along a corridor and before I knew what was happening, here I was.
De'ath	And I'm glad you managed to get here. Now, there are several things I'd like to talk to you about. But first, could I ask you to tell us a bit about your background, as I gather you come from a really unusual family?
Ignatius	Not that unusual a family. Just the normal run-of-the-mill mother, father and fifteen kids.
De'ath	Fifteen kids! You call that normal?
Ignatius	It's as normal as you'd get around our way. Anybody with less than ten kids was considered weird.
De'ath	But surely fifteen kids was a bit out-of-the-ordinary?
Ignatius	It's what you get used to, I suppose. Anyway, what's your interest in my family? Can't you ask me some normal questions?
De'ath	I think we'd have a difference of opinion as to what's considered normal. I don't think you'd know what normal was if it crawled into your left ear and came out of your right one!
Ignatius	What are you referring to my ears for? What's wrong with them?
De'ath	Nothing – that is, if you watch a lot of *Star Trek* and have an interest in alien life forms.
Ignatius	I'll pretend I didn't hear that.
De'ath	That's a wonder with those ears.
Ignatius	Call yourself a host! First I can't find my way around the building and then I'm pushed around until I find myself sitting here being insulted. And just look at the mess on the table. Couldn't you have tidied up a little before I arrived?

De'ath	It's only a few magazines. I like to glance at an article or two when my guests give a boring response to one of my questions.
Ignatius	Your tone of voice is getting on my nerves. Haven't you had any training in how to project your voice in a confident and reassuring manner?
De'ath	My dear Ignatius, I could charm the birds out of the trees and worms out of the ground if I so wished. But I prefer to talk to people like yourself. It's so much easier on the vocal chords.
Ignatius	Do you have to do that with your hands?
De'ath	What? *(De'ath twiddles his thumbs.)*
Ignatius	That!
De'ath	You certainly live up to your name.
Ignatius	What's wrong with my name?
De'ath	Nothing at all. It's a perfectly good name for a gerbil.
Ignatius	A what!
De'ath	Sorry, are your ears playing up?
Ignatius	I just didn't catch what you said, that's all. I can't stand people who mumble. You can't understand a thing they say.
De'ath	That's just as well. Now, we were talking about your name. Is it a name passed down through the family as a kind of tradition?
Ignatius	It's a very famous name. I'm named after the famous Bishop of Antioch from the first century. He was thrown to the lions, you know.
De'ath	Does the family follow the tradition?
Ignatius	I don't go anywhere near furry animals. They irritate my nose and make me sneeze an awful lot.

De'ath	Just as well for the lions then, really.
Ignatius	How do people put up with you? You're rude, ignorant and annoying.
De'ath	I think you'll find that most of my guests consider my chats interesting and informative. Which is more than I can say for some of my guests.
Ignatius	See what I mean? And could I just point out that you really shouldn't wear those colours together? They make my eyes go funny and, before you make any insulting remarks about my eyes, let me tell you another thing. Never wear that type of sock with those kind of shoes. It shows a lack of thought and co-ordination and . . .
De'ath	Before you carry on, take a breath and deprive some other poor unfortunate of oxygen. Now, could we get back to our original discussion about the number of brothers and sisters you had.
Ignatius	Twelve brothers and two sisters.
De'ath	Wasn't life a bit cramped?
Ignatius	Oh, you got used to it. We shared everything. Well, almost everything. It used to drive me loopy to find someone had used my toothbrush. I was fifteen before I realised that toothpaste tubes came with tops on them!
De'ath	That's all we've got time for, I'm afraid.
Ignatius	You're infuriating. I've just got started and you cut me short.
De'ath	Yes. I've always said my timing was perfect. Thank you very much, Ignatius the Irritable.

UNIT 42

TODAY'S SPECIAL

What do I do now?

Ephesians 5:15-20: Living in the light.

Equipment:
handout and pens, or overhead projector
paper and pens
music and lyrics
large envelope

Give each group member a copy of the following hand-out (or use an overhead projector):

1. My friends think I'm . . .
    A. about as bright as a lump of coal
    B. quite clever
    C. a real genius
    D. out of this world
    E. could do with some ego deflating

2. I think I'm . . .
    A. a few slices short of a loaf
    B. a whole loaf short of a loaf
    C. a bakery
    D. loaf, butter and jam in one
    E. could do with some ego inflating

3. I can be persuaded by . . .
    A. flattery
    B. bribery
    C. raspberry jam
    D. common sense
    E. nothing if I don't want to be

4. I sometimes . . .
    A. act the fool to get attention
    B. get embarrassed in groups
    C. talk too much
    D. don't talk enough
    E. pretend to be something I'm not

5. If somebody doesn't agree with me I . . .
   A. make them look stupid
   B. pull a face
   C. agree to disagree
   D. try to convince them they are wrong
   E. listen to their opinion

Ask the group to tick the response which they feel is most like them or to add their own response. If you are using an overhead projector, they will need pen and paper to jot down their answers.

Consider some of the difficulties of trying to live life as Jesus would want us to.

• Why do we find it hard to accept ourselves for who we are?

• Do we find it easy to be persuaded to do things that we regret later?

• Do our lives reflect anything about Jesus?

Have a listen to 'Your love endures' by Third Day, from the album *Conspiracy No5*. Alternatively, look at 'I know it' by Darlene Zschech (*The source*, 80). Have the lyrics available if possible.

Read Ephesians 5:15-20.
What do the group think about Paul's comment in verse 17: 'Don't be stupid'? What do they think Paul meant?

It is really difficult to be honest with yourself and with others at times. It certainly isn't easy admitting to someone that you don't know something or you'd rather not go to see a dodgy film. We all want to be accepted by our friends and peer group. It doesn't matter what age we are, we all want to feel part of a group. But does being accepted mean doing things or acting in ways which make us feel uncomfortable or go against what we believe? We can feel pressured to do something or behave in ways that we know are not going to be any good for us. It's difficult to say no in front of our friends and peers.

How do we know what we should do or what is best for us? How do we find out what 'the Lord wants us to do'? The most important way is spending time with God and chatting about things. Just getting to know someone takes time. It's a bit difficult trying to build a relationship with someone if you never speak! So, chatting about whatever concerns you is a good place to start. Just as chatting to God helps us develop a relationship with him, time spent with other people who have a relationship with God is 'good time'. You will also find that meeting together and hearing other people share their faith and experience of God is a useful way of getting to know what God wants you to do in certain situations. One really good thing about meeting together with other Christians is the encouragement that you can give to one another. And you can have a good time, too!

Ask the group to look at some of their responses to the questions on the hand-out or overhead projector used earlier.
• Are there areas of their lives that they find difficult to accept?
• Do they think they are too easily influenced by other people?
• Do they find it difficult to chat to God?
Ask the group to write what they find difficult on the back of the hand-out, or on their paper.
(Allow 5 minutes for this task.)

Have a large envelope ready. Ask the group to place their hand-outs or papers into the envelope. Write on the front of the envelope, in large letters, 'TO GOD'. Place the envelope on the floor in front of the group. Read Psalm 28:1-2:

Only you, Lord, are a mighty rock!
Don't refuse to help me when I pray.
If you don't answer me, I will soon be dead.
Please listen to my prayer and my cry for help,
    as I lift my hands towards your holy temple.

Ask the group to be quiet for a few moments and chat to God about some of the things they find difficult in their lives. After a short time read the following, Psalm 28:6-9:

I praise you, Lord, for answering my prayers.
You are my strong shield, and I trust you completely.
You have helped me,
    and I will celebrate and thank you in song.
You give strength to your people, Lord,
    and you save and protect your chosen ones.
Come, save us and bless us.
Be our shepherd and always carry us in your arms.

TODAY'S SPECIAL

So what's this all about?
Psalm 84: The joy of worship.

Equipment:
large sheet of paper with 'POWRISH' written in large letters
paper and pen for each person
music and lyrics

Split the group into pairs and give each pair a piece of paper and a pen. Challenge them to make as many words as they can from the letters on the sheet. The winning pair can be awarded a clean paper tissue each.

Did any of the pairs manage to make the word 'worship' out of the letters? If not, rewrite the letters on the sheet to read 'WORSHIP'. Now ask the group to suggest definitions for the word 'worship'. What do they think it means? Try to agree a short sentence which the whole group are happy with as a definition of worship.
(Allow 10 minutes for this activity.)

The concept of worship is not always an easy one to appreciate.
- Why do we worship?
- Who do we worship?
- Where do we worship?

There are many questions and a range of responses from different people which may not give us a clear understanding.

Consider listening to 'Now to live the life' by Matt Redman from the album *Intimacy*. Have a copy of the lyrics available, if possible. Alternatively look at 'Though I feel afraid' by Ian White (*The source*, 522).
(Allow approximately 5 minutes.)

Read Psalm 84.
What do the group make of the Psalm? Do they think the writer was under the influence of some exotic substance when he wrote it?

The Psalmist was definitely under an influence and its impact on his life was reflected in everything he did. When we think of worship, it often conjures up images of a building full of wrinklies playing bingo, at least that's the media image. But, when we dig a bit further, worship doesn't necessarily mean candles, hymn books and mint humbugs.

Worship, as depicted by the Psalmist, is a unique expression of our heart attitude. This does not mean that we can label 'worship' as only a happy-clappy-singsong-hop-skip-and-jump time. Obviously, there are times when the real expression of our hearts is to feel an overwhelming sense of joy. If you've ever seen a group of football supporters celebrating their team scoring a goal, then you have some idea of the feeling. At other times the real expression of our hearts is far from a feeling of joy. There are times when you feel as if you've just swallowed a beach at low tide. Not a particularly good feeling. But expressing how we feel to God in the low times is just as much an expression of worship as in the happy times.

God is really interested in how we feel all of the time. He can see through the masks we put on, such as the times when we are asked, 'How are you?' and we respond with a polite 'Okay, thanks', when inside we feel about as happy as a pig in an abattoir. Worship is not a state of mind but an expression of the heart. Worship is an intimate part of our existence. A quick browse through the Psalms will show that the writers (not all of the Psalms were written by David) were not afraid to tell God exactly how they felt. And God just loves it that way. At the very least it means you're on speaking terms with him, and that's a really good start.

Give each member of the group a piece of paper and a pen. Ask them to write down a few examples of situations where they felt really good and other times when they felt really low.

On the reverse of the paper get the group to suggest some characteristics and attributes of God. For instance:

- he loves me
- he protects me
- he never leaves me
- he is on my side
- he thinks I'm great
- he died for me
- he fights my battles

(Allow 5 minutes for this task.)

Once the group has finished writing some of their ideas about the characteristics and attributes of God, ask them to fold their pieces of paper and hold them in their hand. Ask them to consider some of the feelings, good or bad, which they have experienced during the last few weeks. While they are quiet, read the following prayer:

Lord,
    sometimes trying to express my feelings
    makes me feel
    vulnerable,
    hurt,
    sensitive,
    stupid,
    useless.

But at other times I feel
    glad,
    happy,
    gobsmacked,
    astonished,
    and, not very often,
    totally speechless.

Thanks for being there.
Thanks for being you.
Thanks for standing by me
    even when you have every right to walk away.
I may not always be honest with you,
    and I definitely can't be honest with some people.
But you know that grin I have
    hides a thousand hurts.

I like being real with you,
    because you are real to me
    even when I can't get a handle on you.
Thanks,
    thanks for being who you are.
Thanks from me, to you. Amen.

ALL SAINTS' DAY

TODAY'S SPECIAL   **Following God**
                             Psalm 24:1-6: The earth belongs to the Lord.

                             Equipment:
                             postcards
                             music and lyrics
                             candles – one for each member of the group

Write one of the descriptions below on each postcard.

1. Bananas are, in fact, an alien life-form. Their leaders are so angry at so many of their people being eaten that they threaten to invade the earth tomorrow.

2. All plants can communicate with each other. To understand their language you need to be able to hear a certain audio frequency.

3. Computers have a personality and can get extremely upset when you get annoyed with them and may refuse to work.

4. If you stare at traffic lights long enough, you can make them change colour.

5. Some humans are evolved from a race of super moles. That is why some humans like to spend so much of their time crawling around in caves deep underground.

6. Dentists have been instructed by the Government to place a miniature micro-processor into one of our back teeth whenever we need to have a tooth filled. The micro-processor enables a Government department to locate us at any time.

Give the cards to group members who can talk freely without getting flustered. The idea is for one group member at a time to persuade the rest of their group that the statement written on their card is true.
(Allow 10 minutes for this activity.)

We are exposed to so many different ideas and read or see so many adverts, that it is difficult to know who or what to believe at times. How can we know what is the truth, what is marketing hype or what is myth?

Have a listen to 'Sanctify' by Delirious? from the album *King of fools*. Try and have a copy of the lyrics available. Alternatively look at 'In every circumstance of life' by Dave Fellingham (*The source*, 227).

Read Psalm 24:1-6.
You will have been aware, through the media, that around this time the festival we know as 'Halloween' is often celebrated. The origin of 'Halloween' is in the Celtic festival of Samhain, which celebrated the first day of winter on 1 November. It was thought that supernatural creatures, the spirits of the dead, witches and hobgoblins were most active at this time, which made it a convenient time to tell fortunes. During this time, it was common for people to burn peat on bonfires to 'scare away the witches'. Later the Roman worship of Pomona, a goddess of the harvest, was celebrated around the same time. From these two festivals came the tradition of using fire (a candle) and a pumpkin, which is still practised today.

Throughout the Bible you can read accounts of people worshipping idols or celebrating a festival in honour of some mystical being (see 1 Kings 18:1-40 or Acts 17:16-24). In Psalm 24, David is reminding us about the one and only true God. David is declaring God's credentials (much as Paul does in the rest of Acts 17).

The number of beliefs and superstitions to which we are exposed not only divert our attention away from a relationship with God, but also attempt to persuade us that he is just one of a number of supernatural beings who can be worshipped. This is precisely what the devil would like us all to think, that you can 'pick and mix' who or what you believe in. We constantly need to remind ourselves and each other that God is Lord of all. It is only through a faith and trust in Jesus Christ that we can have a relationship with God. There is no other way to God and there is no set of superstitions or rituals which can allow us to have a relationship with God. There are plenty of things which want to take our focus off God. But God has given us the Holy Spirit to guide us and give us encouragement in every situation. Our decision to follow God is never easy and there are plenty of distractions. The Psalmist sets us a great example of focusing on God and putting our trust in him as we try to follow his ways.

Encourage the group to try and find a few Bible verses that contain the word 'light'. You might like to have a few examples ready or bring a list of references for the group to find. Ask the group why we need light – to help us see what we're doing, to help us to walk without falling down. Do the ideas or definitions of the group give a clearer understanding of the importance of focusing on God and following him?

Place the candles in the centre of the room. Ask each member of the group to light one of the candles and then sit quietly for a few moments. After a short time read the following extract from the Bible:

John 1:1-4.
In the beginning was the one who is called the Word. The Word was with God and was truly God. From the very beginning the Word was with God. And with this Word, God created all things. Nothing was made without the Word. Everything that was created received its life from him, and this life gave light to everyone. The light keeps shining in the dark, and the darkness has never put it out.

FOURTH SUNDAY BEFORE ADVENT

TODAY'S SPECIAL

Go my own way?

Psalm 119:1-8: In praise of the law of the Lord.

Equipment:
postcards
music and lyrics
blindfolds
chairs and objects

Write one of the following instructions on each postcard.

Turn left one step
Turn right one step
Go forward one step
Go backwards one step
Go forward two steps
Go backwards two steps

Have several copies of each instruction. Invite one member of the group to be blindfolded. Stand them in the centre of the room. Place a number of chairs or objects around the room. Shuffle the cards and ask another member of the group to take one card and read it aloud. The blindfolded member of the group must do exactly what the card tells them to do. Invite a second member of the group to read the next card and again the blindfolded member must do what the card tells them to do.

Repeat the process until all of the cards are used up or the blindfolded member cannot go any further. If the group member reaches a wall or chair, take another card until one gives them an opportunity to move away from the obstacle.

To make the game even more fun/difficult, have two or three people blindfolded and start them at different points of the room, each responding to the same card.

(Allow 10 minutes for this activity.)

Ask the blindfolded group members what it felt like to receive instructions and not be able to see where they were going. Ask other members of the group how it felt for them to see the obstacles and not be able to give any other instructions apart from those on the cards.

Have a listen to 'I am yours' by Matt Redman from the album *Intimacy*. Try to have a copy of the lyrics available. Alternatively, take a look at 'We want to see Jesus lifted high' by Doug Horley (*The source*, 559).
(Allow approximately 5 minutes.)

Read Psalm 119:1-8.

Why does the Psalmist seem to spend so much time writing about 'doing what God wants'? Don't we spend half our lives trying to make decisions for ourselves? Why do we have so much hassle from people wanting us to do things their way? Most of our memories are of being told to do this or do that. From early childhood we are told how to do things and how not to annoy people. Isn't all this just a bit irritating?

The Psalmist doesn't have a problem with saying 'I don't ever want to stray from your laws' (verse 5). So what's his secret? The secret is . . . there isn't one. The Psalmist learned from experience that listening to God and doing as he asked was the best way to live. It wasn't, and it isn't, a case of 'you can't do this and you can't do that'. The Psalmist knew that God loved him and wanted the best for him at all times. He knew that, even through the rough times, God wanted the best for him. The Psalmist didn't follow God's way just because he had been told to. He followed God's way because he knew that ignoring God eventually led to more hassle than he, the Psalmist, knew how to cope with.

Even though the Psalmist had followed his own ideas, and ignored God at times, he had also learnt a valuable lesson, that God doesn't show us how to live just because he's on a power trip, but because he loves us, continues to love us and always will love us. And he wants the best for us all the time. It isn't easy to accept that someone else knows what's best for us. It takes a lot of courage to admit that we haven't got all the answers or don't always know the best way to do something. Jesus often reminded the disciples that he hadn't come to replace one set of religious rules with another set, but he came '. . . so that everyone would have life, and have it fully' (John 10:10).

Jesus didn't impose a set of hard-to-follow rules. In fact, when he was asked which were the greatest commandments, he didn't give a list as long as a toilet roll, he said the most important were to love God with all your heart and to love others as you love yourself (Mark 12:30-31). No enormous list that is impossible to follow. But these two commandments provide us with the essential guide to living life and following God's way. If we use these two commandments as our starting point then our hearts and minds have a perfect focus.

Although we try to keep the two commandments of Jesus in mind, it still isn't always easy to know what is best or what God would want us to do in certain situations. One of the best ways of developing our relationship with God and learning a lot more about his thoughts and ways, is to meditate on the Bible. This doesn't mean using the Bible as a pillow – bit hard for that unless you have a soft-cover version! It simply means reading the Bible and giving it some thought. Sometimes a good way is to read a short piece from the Bible and then find a quiet place to think about what you read and ask God what on earth it means and how it relates to us. Refer to the game the group played earlier. Sometimes we cannot see where we are going and we need help to guide us. The Bible is an important guide for us every day. As the Psalmist wrote, 'Your word is a lamp that gives light wherever I walk' (Psalm 119:105).

Ask the group to look at Mark 12:30-31. Give the group a few moments to think about the reading. After a short time ask the question:

What does it mean to you?

(Allow 5 minutes for this task.)

Again, keeping the Bible reading as a focal point, ask the group to be quiet for a few moments and consider the implications of these two commandments for their lives. After a short time, read the following prayer:

Lord,
    at times I would rather chew sand
    than do what you want.
I'm not being a pain,
    just trying to find my way about.
The trouble is,
    although I'm not trying to be a pain,
    I'm in pain
    because I have a tendency to walk into things,
    to trip over the obvious,
    to attempt a backward somersault
    with a bag over my head.
I think I'm learning
    that your love for me
    is so great
    that following your ways
    makes a lot of sense. Amen.

TODAY'S SPECIAL

Who's worrying?
Psalm 62:5-12: Trust in God.

Equipment:
small sheets of paper and a pen for each member of the group
large sheet of paper in the shape of a heart, placed on the wall
music and lyrics
dictionary
tacks or pins

Give each member of the group a piece of paper and a pen. Ask the group to agree on a definition for 'worry'.

*   Is it being a wimp?

*   Is it being stupid?

*   Is it being too sensitive?

*   Is it being realistic about your situation?

*   Is it being frightened?

You might like to have a dictionary definition to give to the group after they have agreed on their definition.

Ask the group to write the agreed definition for 'worry' on the top of their piece of paper. Now ask them to write about one issue or concern that is 'worrying' them at the moment. When they have done this, ask them to fold the piece of paper and pin it to the heart-shaped piece of paper. **(Allow 10 minutes for this activity.)**

What may worry one person may not be a problem for someone else. We each have different concerns and different things worry different people. Just because it doesn't concern anyone else, doesn't make somebody's 'worry' any less important.

Have a listen to 'In the name' by Jennifer Knapp from the album *Kansas*. Try to have a copy of the lyrics available. Or take a look at 'They that wait on the Lord' by Kevin Prosch (*The source*, 509).
(Allow approximately 5 minutes.)

Read Psalm 62:5-12.

Either the Psalmist was talking a load of garbage or he had found, through experience, that only God could give him an inward peace. Why write that he could depend on God if he hadn't a clue what he was talking about?

A brief look at the life of David (have a look at *David* by Sir Fred Catherwood*) will show that here was a man whose life could rival the best and worst soap operas. He rose to fame as a young boy, became a popular musician who played for royalty and then was hunted and threatened with death. Eventually he became a king and won major victories against his enemies. And, at the height of his power and influence, he took a liking for another man's wife, had the husband killed and then married the widow. Although he later made his peace with God, the result was a family that fought amongst itself continually, even after David died. That's some storyline.

To say that David wasn't worried about some of the things that happened to him doesn't reflect the man who wrote 'I feel like a shaky fence or a sagging wall . . .' (Psalm 62:3). The Psalms are full of sentences showing that the Psalmist often felt like the inside of a sewer. But his experience told him that, whatever the problem, there was only one place to go, to God. This couldn't have been easy, particularly when he knew he'd screwed up, big time. David had everything he needed to try and sort out any mess he made. As king, people would obey him or he could bribe anyone to do the dirty if he needed them to. At times he did just that, but he only made matters worse. Having everything didn't sort out the hassle or give him peace. At times the stress was enough to give him the sort of indigestion that a city full of chemists couldn't deal with. The one route, going to God, was the only alternative left to David. He had come to understand that, rather than try and sort out the hassle himself, the best thing to do was to go straight to God and trust him to sort things out, even though he had no idea how God would do it.

God is really interested in us. He gets concerned when we are worried and would rather we trusted him to help us than dug the pit deeper. But trusting someone isn't easy and we can't always be sure that things will turn out exactly how we want them to. Giving God our worries and trusting him takes a lot of bottle. But David found that it was much better to trust in a powerful and kind God than listen to a bunch of monkeys talking bananas.

David, by Sir Fred Catherwood, published Intervarsity Press 1993

Ask each member of the group to take their piece of paper from the heart-shaped sheet. Take a look at Psalm 62:8. Suggest to the group that they rewrite verse 8, putting their own name before the verse and making the verse personal to them. For example: 'David, trust God, my friend, and always tell him each one of your concerns. God is your place of safety.'
(Allow 5 minutes for this task.)

Ask the group to hold their piece of paper in their cupped hands while you read the following prayer:

Lord,
　　you know I get worried about things.
They might seem really daft to some people,
　　but to me they are worse than
　　a face full of spots.
I don't go out of my way to worry,
　　it sort of stomps around my head,
　　making itself known,
　　just in case I try to ignore it.
Hiding my face in my hands doesn't seem to change things,
　　I can't blink and make things go away.
I can't turn my back and hope they'll go away.
It never seems long
　　before the finger of despair
　　taps me on the shoulder
　　and I'm faced with the reality
　　of sinking under the ocean of my worry.

Help me, shield me,
　　so that I can feel secure
　　in your love.
I don't want to go it alone,
　　or drown in anxiety.
I want to put my trust in you,
　　I want to feel at peace
　　with you. Amen.

TODAY'S SPECIAL   ### All I could ever wish for
Psalm 16: The best choice.

Equipment:
small jigsaw puzzle for each group (you could make these by cutting up old birthday or Christmas cards)
music and lyrics

Divide the large group into several smaller groups, each containing about three to four people. Give each group one of the jigsaws and ask them to put the jigsaw together with the picture face down. They are not allowed to look at the cover of the jigsaw box or look at the picture on the jigsaw pieces. Try not to have jigsaws with too many pieces – it could take forever!

Once the groups have finished, ask them what it felt like to have nothing to refer to when trying to complete the jigsaw. If you have time, get the groups to swop jigsaws and put them together using the picture.

• Did the group find this easier?

• Why was that?

(Allow 10 minutes for this activity.)

Has any of the group ever been in a maze? Ask them to describe the maze and how they found their way out of it.

• Did they have a map?

• How did they feel when they were in the centre of the maze?

Have a listen to 'All the way' by Delirious? from their album *King of fools*. Have a copy of the lyrics available if possible. Alternatively, take a look at 'I have come to love you' by Matt Redman (*The source*, 204).
(Allow approximately 5 minutes.)

Read Psalm 16.
It's difficult to guess what prompted David to write this Psalm. It gives the impression that he had recently been ill or in danger and was really thankful to be alive. Some of the advice he may have been given was to worship or make a sacrifice to idols. David found that placing his trust in God was all he needed. In verse 5 David says to God, 'You, Lord, are all

I want'. He was obviously feeling better and safer by this time but wanted God to know that, whatever happened, he recognised that there was no other way but to trust and follow God (see verses 5-6).

It's really easy when we feel alone, frightened, angry or just plain confused, to look for an easy way out. None of us like pain and we want to get rid of the hurting as quickly as possible. If we hurt ourselves when we were young, our first reaction would have been to run to one of our parents who could make us feel better just by hugging us. Even though the pain may not have stopped, just the knowledge that we were not alone helped make us feel better.

Feeling alone in a situation is like being in the middle of a maze with no map. It's possible to get out of the 'maze' without a map but that is usually only achieved after going down several dead ends, going around in circles and with loads of frustration. Much easier if you have a map and someone to help you find your way. The Psalmist had discovered that there was no better guide than God and that whatever the situation, no matter how dark and bleak it looked, God could help him feel secure and loved (see verse 7).

There is no guarantee that we will not end up in the middle of a maze, alone and afraid. We may not like to admit it or show it, but pain hurts. We all like to maintain an image of being in control and pretend that very little can get under our skin. We are no different from David. He had found a 'guide' to show him the way out of the 'maze'; someone he could trust and someone he knew loved him. The Psalmist had found the best answer. God was all he could ever wish for. He knew that whatever the circumstances he wasn't alone. He had been shown the 'path to life' (verse 11), and that made him feel really good.

Ask the group think about being lost in a desert. All around are sand dunes. The blazing hot sun beats down. Everywhere looks the same and there seems no way of escape. Suddenly a figure appears on the horizon. Gradually the figure gets closer and closer. Before long, a man is standing in front of you holding out a bottle of clear, cool water for you to drink. After draining the bottle, the man beckons you to follow him. Before long you arrive safely at an oasis surrounded by tents offering shade from the sun.

Ask the group to imagine how they would feel towards the man who rescued them.
(Allow 5 minutes for this task.)

Suggest to the group that they might like to close their eyes and picture the scene of the man coming to their rescue. Imagine the cool water flowing down their throats. After a few moments, read the following:

Luke 15:4-7.
If any of you has a hundred sheep, and one of them gets lost, what will you do? Won't you leave the ninety-nine in the field and go and look for the lost sheep until you find it? And when you find it, you will be so glad that you will put it on your shoulder and carry it home. Then you will call in your friends and neighbours and say, 'Let's celebrate! I've found my lost sheep'.

Jesus said, 'In the same way there is more happiness in heaven because of one sinner who turns to God, than over ninety-nine good people who don't need to.'

TODAY'S SPECIAL   **You are the business!**
Psalm 93: The Lord is King.

Equipment:
paper and pen for each member of the group
music and lyrics
large sheet of paper

Ask the group to think of a situation or issue which has been in the news recently and which has made them feel angry, annoyed or sad. Get them to write it down on a piece of paper. Is any member of the group willing to talk about what they have written?

• Why is it important to them?

• What do the rest of the group think?

• How would they go about changing the situation?

After you have listened to all the ideas, get the group to vote for the idea they consider to be the most important.
(Allow 10 minutes for this activity.)

It would be really great if we could change things for the better; to be able to find a cure for disease or get rid of poverty. Whichever way we look at it, the problems appear to be far greater than we can cope with, or even understand completely. Why do these situations exist in the first place?

Have a listen to 'What kind of love' by Three Crosses from the album *Jefferson Street*. If possible, have a copy of the lyrics available. Alternatively, have a look at 'With all my heart' by Steve McGregor (*The source*, 581).
(Allow approximately 5 minutes.)

Read Psalm 93.
It would be really interesting to be able to play 'God' for a time – or would it? What would be our first priorities? Would we have any priorities or would we just sit back and admire ourselves? If we really stop to consider it, the idea of being 'God' isn't such an appealing one! Just think, whenever something goes wrong, who gets the blame? When a tragedy happens, who should have prevented it? When someone we love is ill, or even dies, who do we think should have done something about

it? How often have we heard someone say that if God really cared for us he wouldn't have allowed 'that' to happen. Is it fair and justified to feel like this or should we look a bit closer to home?

A lot of 'natural' disasters could have been avoided. Often the problem is that someone somewhere has ignored scientific warnings or turned a blind eye to technical defects in order to make an economic or political 'killing'. For instance, earthquakes can be detected well in advance of their happening. But the deaths that occur as a result are frequently due to the inferior construction quality of the buildings, or to constructors building in known problem areas. Some of the avalanches, mudslips and landslides that have killed hundreds of people would never have happened if the buildings hadn't been put up in dangerous areas. It's no good pinning the blame on God when an innocent pedestrian gets killed by a joyrider or a drunken driver. Neither is it worth ranting at God when a child is abused or murdered. Unfortunately the blame lies with us. God put the world in its place and put the human race on board. Rather than make us boring and docile, he gave us free will and choice. How we exercise that choice and free will is up to us. God can, and does, get involved to alter things but, if he did that all the time, what kind of creatures would we be? We have to learn how to use our free will and choices to create the best situations for ourselves and for others.

Although we cannot be held personally responsible for the death toll on the roads, or for violent crimes, we are responsible when we choose to turn away and ignore something which we know shouldn't be happening. We can improve some situations by giving some of our time or money to a charity or organisation that helps people in difficult circumstances.

The attitude of our heart and minds is crucial to the way in which we behave in any given situation. It is the first thing that needs to change, before the situation can be altered. This change is only really possible when we turn to God and agree 'Our Lord, you are King' (verse 1). By accepting his love and becoming part of his family, we choose to follow his ways. God is Lord of all that we see and all that we have. Our actions can make the situation change from a negative to a positive. It is God's love for us that influences the way we behave; and it is by our behaviour that we can affect a situation and reflect God's love.

Give each member of the group another piece of paper. Ask them to write a letter to God expressing how they feel about the situation or issue which they discussed earlier. Encourage them to be as honest as they can with themselves and with God.

CHRIST THE KING

Place a large sheet of paper on the wall with the heading 'Our Lord, you are King'. Ask each group member to place their letter on the sheet of paper. They may want to fold the letter to keep it private.
(Allow 5 minutes for this task.)

Ask the group to be quiet for a few moments and consider their letters to God. As they are quiet, read the following prayer:

Lord,
    although the desert sands may freeze,
    and the oceans dry up,
    your love remains.
Although the mountains may crumble,
    and the sky turn black,
    your love remains.
My Lord, you are King.

Even though I see death and destruction
    and rivers of tears,
My Lord, you are King.
Even though I see hatred and violence
    and broken hearts,
My Lord, you are King.

Let me remember you
    when the clouds gather
    and the rain falls.
Let me remember you
    when the thunder sounds
    and my feet tremble.
My Lord, you are King.

You keep me secure
    in your warm embrace.
Your love is as high as the heavens
    and as deep as the oceans.
My Lord, you are King. Amen.

BIBLE READING AND TOPIC INDEX

YEAR B

ADVENT

Unit 1	First Sunday of Advent	Mark 13:24-37	Live the life
Unit 2	Second Sunday of Advent	Mark 1:1-8	Good News
Unit 3	Third Sunday of Advent	John 1:6-8, 19-28	Light of the world
Unit 4	Fourth Sunday of Advent	Luke 1:26-38	Birth of Jesus

CHRISTMAS

| Unit 5 | First Sunday of Christmas | Luke 2: 15-21 | The shepherds |
| Unit 6 | Second Sunday of Christmas | John 1:1-18 | The Word |

EPIPHANY

Unit 7	The Epiphany	Matthew 2:1-12	The wise men
Unit 8	First Sunday of Epiphany	Mark 1:4-11	Baptism
Unit 9	Second Sunday of Epiphany	John 1:43-51	Faith
Unit 10	Third Sunday of Epiphany	John 2:1-11	Miracles
Unit 11	Fourth Sunday of Epiphany	Mark 1:21-28	Authority

ORDINARY TIME

Unit 12	Proper 1	Mark 1:29-39	Healing
Unit 13	Proper 2	Mark 1:40-45	Loneliness
Unit 14	Proper 3	Mark 2:1-12	Forgiving

LENT

Unit 15	Second Sunday before Lent	John 1:1-14	Acceptance
Unit 16	Sunday next before Lent	Mark 9:2-9	Going on
Unit 17	First Sunday of Lent	Mark 1:9-15	Baptism
Unit 18	Second Sunday of Lent	Mark 8:31-38	Death
Unit 19	Third Sunday of Lent	John 2:13-22	Anger
Unit 20	Fourth Sunday of Lent	John 3:14-21	God's love
Unit 21	Fifth Sunday of Lent	John 12:20-33	Unselfishness
Unit 22	Palm Sunday	John 12:12-16	Peace

EASTER

Unit 23	Easter Sunday	John 20:1-18	Love
Unit 24	Second Sunday of Easter	John 20:19-31	Doubt
Unit 25	Third Sunday of Easter	Acts 3:12-19	Faith
Unit 26	Fourth Sunday of Easter	Acts 4:5-12	Authority
Unit 27	Fifth Sunday of Easter	Acts 8:26-40	The Bible
Unit 28	Sixth Sunday of Easter	Acts 10:44-48	The Holy Spirit
Unit 29	Seventh Sunday of Easter	Acts 1:15-17, 21-26	Decisions
Unit 30	Pentecost: Whit Sunday	Acts 2:1-21	The Holy Spirit
Unit 31	Trinity Sunday	Romans 8:12-17	Desires

ORDINARY TIME

| Unit 32 | | 2 Corinthians 4:5-12 | Persevering |

SCRIPTURAL INDEX

THEMATIC INDEX

SIDE ORDERS

The Internet provides ideas and information on any and every topic under the sun. Finding your way around can sometimes be similar to walking around a maze at 2am in the morning, blindfolded and listening to a Walkman playing a selection of whale music.

To help you get a start and access useful information from the start, I have listed a selection of web sites which will provide you with information and resources to accompany most of the units contained in this book.

Please note that although these web-sites were current at the time of writing, this does not mean that they will remain current or active. If you cannot locate a web-site, use one of the many search engines to find a similar site.

BIBLE STUDIES
www.ccel.wheaton.edu/wwsb/
www.castyournet.com
www.biblestudytools.net/
www.cutcom.net/biblenotes/
www.psiaz.com/backdoorbible/

GAMES
www.prysm.net/~elliot/youth.html

GENERAL
www.expage.com/page/christianteenzlinx (Loads of teen site links)
www.gospelcom.net/ys/ (Wide range of resources)
www.geocities.com/athens/5355/index.html (EGAD: ideas for youth leaders)
www.anglican.org/online/youth (Anglican youth ideas)
www.members.xoom.com/mntx/ (Features and resources)

HUMOUR
www.graceland.gentle.org/humor.html (Bag o laughs. Jokes and cartoons)
www.biblenet.net (Chat and jokes)

ISSUES
www.christiandailynews.org (Daily news for Christians)
www.creativeye.com/goodnews/bible.htm (Various issues discussed)
www.cincyvineyard.com (A range of issues dealt with)

MAGAZINES
www.7ball.com/ (Music and chat)
www.realmagazine.com/ (Articles and assorted info)
www.word.net/zino/ (Zinograffiti with variety of topics)

SIDE ORDERS

MUSIC AND WORSHIP
www.1christianity.net (Chat, reviews and music)
www.afri.org/~mrblue/ccm/ccm.html (Links to Christian artists)
www.delirious.net (Delirious?)
www.geocities.com/thetopics/3729/matt.html (Matt Redman)

NEWS
wwwchurchnet.org.uk (Christian affairs in the UK)

ORGANISATIONS
www.fyt.org.uk (Frontier Youth for Christ)
www.ywam.co.uk/ywamhome.htm (YWAM)
www.ravello.co.uk/soul-survivor/welcome.htm (Soul Survivor)
www.yfc.co.uk (Youth for Christ)
www.geocities.com/paris/parc/4919/ (Teens4Christ)

PRAYER
www.conline.net (Christians online)
www.churchnet.org.uk (Request and items)
www.members.aol.com/startlinge/nailcros.htm (The Christian surf shop)

SEARCH
www.members.aol.com/clinksgold/omnet.htm (Directory of Christian sites)
www.saltshaker.co.uk/webway (UK Christian links)